The Ford Century in Minnesota

The Ford Century in Minnesota

BRIAN McMAHON

University of Minnesota Press
Minneapolis · London

This publication was made possible in part by the people of Minnesota through a grant funded by an appropriation to the Minnesota Historical Society from the Minnesota Arts and Cultural Heritage Fund. Any views, findings, opinions, conclusions, or recommendations expressed in this publication are those of the author and do not necessarily represent those of the State of Minnesota, the Minnesota Historical Society, or the Minnesota Historic Resources Advisory Committee.

MINNESOTA HISTORICAL
& CULTURAL GRANTS

Published by the University of Minnesota Press
111 Third Avenue South, Suite 290
Minneapolis, MN 55401-2520
http://www.upress.umn.edu

ISBN 978-0-8166-3729-5 (hc)
A Cataloging-in-Publication record for this book is available from the Library of Congress.

Printed in the United States of America on acid-free paper

The University of Minnesota is an equal-opportunity educator and employer.

22 21 20 19 18 17 16   10 9 8 7 6 5 4 3 2 1

Contents

Introduction

The Ford Century

The Ford Motor Company closed the Twin Cities Assembly Plant in 2011, ending a century of manufacturing in Minnesota. During that time more than eight million cars, trucks, tractors, armored cars, and other products were made in the state at four different locations. Henry Ford felt a personal connection to the "Viking farmers" who shared his values of rugged individualism, hard work, sobriety, and pacifism, and he chose this state to experiment with issues that were of special interest. His activities in Minnesota demonstrated his evolving attitudes on such critical issues as industrial decentralization, navigation, vertical integration, hydroelectric power, environmental sustainability, the car dealership system, aviation, labor relations, and the global economy. Ford's involvement was welcomed, but because he worked intuitively, by trial and error, his experiments and abrupt policy changes often made things difficult for employees, dealers, suppliers, and the local communities.

Hundreds of books have been written about Henry Ford, and he himself wrote several with help from coauthors. His colorful personality, as much as his remarkable achievements, contributed to the public's fascination. Many books have focused on his manufacturing and marketing innovations, and others addressed his pacifism, anti-Semitism, and other personal interests and activities. Some offered a harsh assessment, including Upton Sinclair's *The Flivver King* and Aldous Huxley's dystopian novel *Brave New World*. This book looks at Henry Ford and his company through the lens of one place, Minnesota, over what has become known as the "Ford Century." It portrays the interactions between the Ford Motor Company and the communities in the state, and links events on the international stage to the Main Streets of Minnesota. It is the story of people who worked at all levels of this iconic company, whether in the front office, on the assembly line, in the sand mines, the glass plant, the dealerships, or the service centers.

The Ford Motor Company has had an enormous local economic impact, employing tens of thousands of workers, with payrolls sometimes exceeding $130 million annually. The company purchased materials, parts, and services from many local suppliers. Economists estimated that each job in the plant created approximately another five to ten jobs locally. Ford's engineers and production staff interacted with many local companies, including 3M, Control Data, and Graco, bringing technological expertise and manufacturing sophistication to the region.

While Minnesota benefited from the special attention of Henry Ford, it can also be said that several Minnesotans played large roles in his success. Harry G. Ukkelberg, an agricultural chemist who graduated from the University of Minnesota, led Ford's large agricultural research department, which discovered plants that could be converted to raw materials used in making a car. William Stout, a prolific inventor from St. Paul, formed an airplane manufacturing company that Ford acquired, one of the very few corporate acquisitions the company made. Stout, and L. H. Brittin, a St Paul economic development official, secured startup funding from Ford and several of his executives to establish Northwest Airlines, headquartered in St. Paul. Many plant engineers and managers from Minnesota traveled frequently to Detroit and worked with top company officials. A number of Minnesota manufacturers also played a prominent role in developing accessories and attachments for the new "aftermarket" that Ford created with the long runs of the Model T and Fordson tractors.

The importance of Ford's activities in Minnesota was underscored in a company publication, *Ford at Fifty*: "The making of a car begins in Minnesota when miners gouge out a scoopful of iron ore from the red earth of the Mesabi Range." The maiden voyage of the freighter *Henry Ford II* delivered coal from Henry Ford's mines to a large dock in Duluth that the company leased, and returned loaded with Minnesota iron ore. Ford also mined silica one hundred feet beneath the floor of Twin Cities Assembly Plant and made glass in the plant.

Henry Ford was perhaps the most transformative figure of the twentieth century, making it challenging to shift attention away from him to the people who toiled in his shadow. This book aims to showcase the remarkable stories and contributions of Ford's supporting cast in Minnesota. Chapter 1 sets the stage by highlighting Henry Ford's special connection to the state. Even before the Ford Motor Company was incorporated in 1903, Ford established a car dealership in St. Cloud with Stephen Tenvoorde. Four generations later, it continues to be run by his family, and is now the oldest Ford dealership in the world. Prosperous farmers and doctors in the state were a huge market for the Model T car. In 1909, Ford shipped forty-one railcars to Minneapolis, each loaded with three automobiles—the largest shipment of cars in history up to that time. To meet the enormous local demand, Ford built a ten-story assembly plant in Minneapolis in 1914, which was the tallest structure ever built for automobile manufacturing. The Minneapolis plant, and a three-story subassembly branch plant in St. Paul, were part of Ford's first "decentralization" phase, instituted mainly because of rail congestion in Detroit and to reduce the expense of shipping fully assembled cars. In one decade, Ford built more than thirty plants around the world, mostly in urban areas with good rail access. Chapter 1 also describes Ford's ambitious experiments to create a new marketing and distribution system that was needed to sell all the cars being mass-produced.

As the Minneapolis plant was being constructed, Ford developed the movable assembly line in Detroit, which made the Minneapolis factory functionally obsolete before it even opened. Multistory buildings were no longer viable for mass production and Ford started exploring options for a new site in the Twin Cities. Chapter 2 examines Ford's second decentralization phase, as he built sprawling single-story structures on large sites in rural areas with ample room for assembly lines, expansion, and parking. The sites also had to be on waterways with potential for hydroelectric power and navigation, which he deemed essential to offset the monopolistic power of railroads. Henry Ford was drawn to a bluff in St. Paul overlooking the newly built High Dam on the Mississippi River. The prospect of the company's move from Minneapolis to St. Paul reignited the long-standing rivalry between the Twin Cities, and raised a host of federal policy issues relating to navigation and hydroelectric power. Henry Ford's promise to create jobs at a time of high unemployment won him the hydroelectric permit—in spite of considerable opposition to the precedent of transferring a public asset to a private company.

Henry Ford rarely visited a branch assembly plant site, before or after construction, but in 1923 he insisted on walking around the High Dam site before construction. He was making it clear that he intended to build a model project in St. Paul. Ford and his entourage even crossed the Mississippi River to view the 167-acre parcel from Fort Snelling. From that perspective, he decided to change the building orientation so that the front facade, designed by prominent architect Albert Kahn, would face the "Father of All Rivers." Chapter 3 documents the plant's construction. When it opened, the Twin Cities Assembly Plant was Ford's largest branch plant. It had the company's largest hydroelectric plant, and it had a wharf for navigation. This project was arguably the most complete realization of Henry Ford's unified vision for decentralization, navigation, hydroelectric power, efficient manufacturing, and environmentally sustainable practices.

The new Twin Cities Assembly Plant opened by producing the same Model T car it had been making in Minneapolis, even though it was widely seen as unfashionable and obsolete. By the time Ford finally accepted the need for developing a new car to compete with the Chevrolet, the process of converting his plants to the Model A resulted in massive worker layoffs, civic unrest, and even disruptions to the national economy.

The promise of job creation, which won him the permit, would be sorely tested by this disruption and the later effects of the Great Depression, during which Ford discharged tens of thousands of workers onto the streets with little safety net. If government had a role in creating jobs, it would quickly learn that it had a responsibility to protect those workers when they lost their jobs.

The convergence of industry and government greatly accelerated during the Depression and wartime. During the First and Second World Wars, "essential" industries were basically nationalized as the government dictated which companies would receive raw materials, which products would be manufactured, and how much profit could be earned. Chapter 4 examines how the Twin Cities Assembly Plant fared during those tumultuous years of Depression and World War II, making M-8 armored vehicles and airplane engine parts. Because labor unrest and strikes were deemed to be detrimental to the war effort, the federal government stepped in to assume the role of labor mediator. President Franklin Delano Roosevelt, who supported the expansion of organized labor, threatened to take over the Ford Motor Company to complete military contracts if Ford did not accept the United Auto Workers (UAW) union, an outcome that he fought his entire life. Ford had finally met his match as a negotiator. He could not have envisioned the extent to which his early collaboration with the public sector would open the door for such government intrusion. Convergence was probably inevitable, but wartime controls, government purse strings, and regulatory authority greatly accelerated other forces that were at work. Industry and government were now partners, and the balance of power between them would ebb and flow over time due to economic and political forces. The process of making cars had become a very different enterprise during Henry Ford's lifetime.

Chapter 5 documents the difficult transition to postwar prosperity. Many women workers who were indispensable during the war were forced out of the workplace by the returning soldiers. The United Auto Workers pressed for generous contracts that provided unprecedented financial security to workers and their families. By the 1950s, the union had essentially created the new middle class that transformed America. This chapter examines the production process within the plant, detailing how the popular cars from that era were made. However, the good times were not sustainable. The "shared monopoly" of the Big Three automakers (General Motors, Ford, and Chrysler) lulled them into a complacency that obscured many looming threats. With a sharp decline in quality, safety, and gas mileage, consumers turned away from American cars and flocked to imported brands. To maintain profits as market share plummeted, automobile manufacturers responded by weakening the power of labor unions through automation and robotics, the outsourcing of parts' manufacturing to nonunion companies, and most effectively by shifting production to countries with low labor costs and few environmental regulations. The process of "offshoring" was greatly facilitated by foreign trade agreements and other federal policies. Foreign automakers, facing angry public sentiment and increased tariffs, eventually were pressured to build plants in the United States. This was initially welcomed by the UAW, but later deeply regretted because foreign companies rebuffed all union organizing efforts, which further accelerated the decline of labor.

Chapter 6 chronicles how the shrinking of the American car industry impacted workers. Automakers were unable—and some would say, unwilling—to compete in the modern global economy, and the national leadership of the UAW could not come up with a strategy to counteract globalization or protect workers. However, officials at UAW Local 879 in St. Paul had a plan. They bucked their national union to directly support the organizing campaigns of workers in Mexico and other foreign countries. Officials at Local 879, and other progressive organizations in Minnesota, became national leaders in the fight for fair trade and international human rights. Despite their strenuous efforts, they could not reverse the effects of the new global economy. The social compact that was constructed after the war with the Big Three car companies and the UAW unraveled.

Chapter 7 explains how global economic factors contributed to the decision to close the Twin Cities Assembly Plant in spite of its consistently high rankings for quality and productivity. This chapter also traces the efforts of local governments to save the plant, and the effects its eventual closing had on its workers and local communities.

At the beginning of the Ford century, it was Henry Ford standing alone as a rugged individualist, but by the end it was the Ford Motor Company, the UAW, and multiple levels of government propping up each other to compete in the global marketplace. Worker benefits that took decades to win disappeared overnight. The leadership of the UAW accepted contracts that not only reduced wages and benefits, but also for the first time allowed for several "tiers" of workers. By the time the Twin Cities Assembly Plant closed in 2011, autoworkers were driven back to the heralded "five dollars a day," when adjusted for inflation. The sacred forty-hour workweek disappeared as the company instituted mandatory overtime schedules requiring fifty or fifty-eight hours a week. Workers gave up fighting for "another nickel"—now it was only about resisting "givebacks." With the hard times, fault lines opened within the ranks of organized labor. It became less of a fight between the International UAW and the Ford Motor Company, and now more of a fight between the International UAW leadership and the dissidents and rebellious leaders of local unions.

In the complex world of automobile manufacturing many activities outside of the state and many seemingly unrelated events had enormous impact on Minnesota. Two giants of the twentieth century, Henry Ford and Walter Reuther of the UAW, left their imprint even though their actual time in the state was limited. The legacy of the Ford

Motor Company is far richer than the few remaining brick-and-mortar artifacts and the much-beloved antique cars. It has shaped the state's economy, politics, culture, and, indeed, the way it operates in the world today. But even as Ford impacted Minnesota, there can be no doubt that people and events in the state helped shape Henry Ford and his company.

1

Model T for the Northwest Territories

Ford Arrives in Minnesota

Stephen Tenvoorde was among the crowd swarming around the horseless carriage that drove into St. Cloud, Minnesota, on a fall day in 1900. Everyone in the small town had undoubtedly heard of these strange machines, but this was likely the first any had seen. As a blacksmith tending to horses, and as a partner in a bicycle store, Tenvoorde had particular reason to be curious about the new contraption. Not long afterward, he placed an order for a $950 Milwaukee Steamer car, which was delivered to town by rail—unassembled. With the help the best mechanics in town, Tenvoorde put the Steamer together and "exercised" it about the city, creating quite a stir.

After enjoying the Steamer for a while, Tenvoorde was eager to try a different model. He drove the Steamer to Minneapolis, where he parked it on the curb with a "For Sale" sign. After selling it for $325, he bought a new Oldsmobile and drove back to St. Cloud. By 1903, the ads for Tenvoorde's bicycle shop included motorcycles and automobiles. He advertised the $125 Marsh Motorcycle as "The Best Motor Cycle Made," and three cars, including the Knox, priced at $1,299, the Oldsmobile at $650, and the Hoffman at $950. All three vehicles had been displayed at the Automobile Show in Chicago several months earlier. Tenvoorde likely attended the Chicago show, one of the largest in the country, as it was readily accessible by an overnight train ride. It offered a complete introduction to all the latest automotive developments. He could closely examine the 325 vehicles displayed by more than eighty manufacturers, talk with the inventors, and even test-drive the vehicles.

It was a natural progression for Tenvoorde to move from bicycles to automobiles as the two industries had much in common. The leading bike brands were mass-produced in large factories and were distributed by independent dealers. Bicycle shops made repairs and sold used bikes, tires, and accessory items—much like later car dealerships. Bicycle enthusiasts established associations and organized shows, touring events, and racing competitions. They also worked to overcome early resistance in rural areas. A St. Cloud newspaper reported in 1900 that farmers were taking delight in "tearing up cycle paths with their teams." One farmer was charged with intentionally ramming several riders with his wagon, causing serious injuries. Many early automobile dealers had backgrounds in blacksmithing and bicycles.

Henry Ford was finalizing the design of his new car in 1903 and getting ready to launch the Ford Motor Company, his third car company, when he likely traveled from Detroit to attend the Chicago Automobile Show. He went to most trade shows in those early years, including the National Bicycle Show in Chicago the previous year. Ford did not have a car on display in Chicago but he was probably known to many attending the show because of his racing accomplishments and his earlier car ventures. Ford had already had two car companies fail by 1903. He had difficulty getting along with partners, a character trait he retained throughout his life, but with his mechanical genius and self-confidence he had little difficulty attracting financing. He committed early to the use of gasoline engines, at

Stephen Tenvoorde in St. Cloud, Minnesota, in the 1890s. He was typical of many early car dealers, who owned bicycle shops before gradually transitioning to automobiles. Courtesy of Tenvoorde family.

Henry Ford's development of the automobile lagged far behind industry leaders, and he turned to building race cars as a way to promote his efforts and raise capital. He is seen here (in goggles) in 1905 next to his Model K racer. Courtesy of the National Automotive History Collection, Detroit Public Library.

a time when steam or electric batteries powered most of the four thousand cars being manufactured. Because he lagged considerably behind the progress of other inventors, he decided his best hope was to develop a race car to raise his visibility and perhaps generate some prize money. In October 1901, Ford debuted his race car in Detroit, at an event that opened with a procession of more than one hundred steam, electric, and gas cars. He won the race, driving his own car and beating the favored Winton automobile. He later broke a speed record for the mile with a thirty-nine-second run on a frozen Lake St. Clair in Michigan.

Stephen Tenvoorde likely met Henry Ford at the 1903 Chicago show. At the age of thirty-eight, Ford was eighteen months older than Tenvoorde. Both had exceptional mechanical skills and enjoyed tinkering with machines. Tenvoorde would later invent several devices for bicycles and a hand jack that could move cars around a shop—a patent that Ford acquired. A month after the Chicago auto show, on March 21, 1903, Tenvoorde signed a preliminary agreement with Henry Ford, representing the Ford & Malcolmson Company, to sell "Fordmobiles." At the time, the Ford Motor Company had not yet been incorporated, had not built a workable car, and apparently did not even have any product literature. The dealership contract was finalized on June 9. Improbably, the Ford Motor Company flourished, and the Tenvoorde dealership is still operating as a family business in St. Cloud and is now the oldest Ford dealership in the world. Several months after signing with Tenvoorde, Ford contracted with the Northwestern Automobile Company to serve as distributor for the state of Minnesota and the firm opened showrooms in Minneapolis and St. Paul. As a distributor, Northwestern was responsible for recruiting individual dealers and overseeing their operations. Dealerships operated as independent franchises, which generally received one-year contracts from Ford spelling out projected sales goals. Dealers initially had specified sales territories, but those that underperformed could have their areas assigned to other dealers. By 1905, Ford also established company-owned branch stores in New York and Philadelphia, and branch agencies in Boston, Chicago, Kansas City, and Cleveland. The distinction between stores and agencies is somewhat unclear. Both were expensive to set up, but direct sales by the company saved Ford the dealer's discount, which could amount to 25 percent.

In its first nine months, the Ford Motor Company sold 658 automobiles, a number that grew to 1,700 within fifteen months. This was an impressive start, but Ford still lagged far behind a number of companies, including industry leader Oldsmobile, which sold four thousand cars during that time. Stephen Tenvoorde sold only one Ford car his first year. Fortunately, he continued to carry other car brands in his newly renamed shop, the Bicycle and Automobile Headquarters.

Henry Ford's 1904 and 1905 model lineup featured a variety of styles and prices, but his ambition was to produce an inexpensive car for the masses. He announced his intention to build ten thousand automobiles a year to be sold for $400—at a time when the company was producing about twenty-five cars a day with prices ranging from $800 to $2,000. He never shied away from bold pronouncements on a variety of topics, but with this audacious statement he expressed the overarching goal of his life. Ford's investors had other ideas, though, preferring to build higher-priced cars that were more profitable. This difference in strategy generated conflict, but the company's fast start eased tensions in the short term. Dividend payments and distributions in the first year returned all of the partners' initial investment, which undoubtedly reinforced Ford's expectation for complete autonomy in running the company.

The tension did not subside, however, and Ford decided he needed to force his resistant partners out of the company. He created a separate manufacturing entity, called the Ford Manufacturing Company, to supply the parts for the cars assembled by the Ford Motor Company. At that time, most cars were typically assembled from parts made by outside suppliers. To raise money for the new venture, he sold stock only to people who supported his vision for a less expensive car. Ford's intention was to shift profits away from the assembling company to the new manufacturing company, which his disgruntled partners immediately recognized and fought. But Ford was determined, and the partners were ultimately forced to sell their shares to him. When the various transactions were completed, Ford had taken majority control of the Ford Motor Company and became its president. He also continued to run the Ford Manufacturing Company, which operated in its own factory separate from the assembly plant of the Ford Motor Company. An advertisement of 1906 described the new venture:

> Henry Ford's idea is to build a high-grade, practical automobile, one that will do any reasonable service, that can be maintained at a reasonable expense, and at nearly $450 as it is possible to make it, thus raising the automobile out of the list of luxuries, and bringing it to the point where the average American citizen may own and enjoy his automobile.

With two plants, Henry Ford became completely immersed in every aspect of building a car. Shuttling between the plants, he worked to improve the design of component parts and the manufacturing process. In 1906 Ford introduced the six-hundred-dollar Model N, which was an instant hit. Ford factories could not keep up with the huge demand for the car, which was the conceptual forerunner of the Model T. At this point, Ford made the historic decision to focus on improving the manufacturing process rather than changing the design of the car. He would stick with one model, which he would simplify and improve over time, and would no longer invest energy and resources into annual model changes. The strong sales of the Model N generated a backlog of six thousand orders, and by 1907 the company was earning the enormous sum of more than a million dollars a year ($24 million in today's dollars). The entire automobile industry was booming; in 1907 there was one car for every eight hundred people, up from one car to 1,500,000 people just five years earlier. Europe, which had been the leader in automobile manufacturing, relinquished its position in 1906 to the United States, which was soon making more cars than the rest of the world combined.

The Birth of the Model T

The introduction of the Model T car in 1908 was the most significant event in the history of the Ford Motor Company—and indeed a major milestone for the country. This "universal car" offered a completely original combination of features, including an improved planetary transmission, compensating gears, a magneto that replaced older batteries, improved oil systems, a greatly improved carburetor, a three-point suspension for the motor, and springs attached to the ends of the axle housings. It had a simple design, overall lightness with its new high-strength metals, and rode high above the early roads, which were often rutted. The Model T also provided considerable power while achieving about twenty miles per gallon. Unlike his earlier cars, Ford put the steering wheel on the left side of the Model T, which soon became the industry norm.

Orders for the new Model T came pouring in, and to meet the demand, Ford added a second shift in his factories. With long waiting lists, Ford was one of the first companies to produce cars year-round without first securing a down payment. Ford believed that the Model T would eventually become his "car for the masses," but initially it sold for the relatively high price of $825. Ford spelled out his philosophy: "I hold that it is better to sell a large number of articles at a small profit than to sell a few at a large profit. This enables a larger number of people to buy and it gives a larger number of men employment at good wages." Minnesota was one of the most important markets for Ford with its large number of prosperous farmers. In 1909 Ford shipped forty-one railcars to Minneapolis, each loaded with three automobiles, reportedly the largest shipment of cars ever made.

That year there were so many orders for the Model T that Ford had to suspend sales to allow production to catch up.

With the extraordinary demand for the Model T, Ford decided to consolidate his manufacturing and assembling operations into one greatly expanded facility. He purchased a sixty-acre tract in Dearborn, a suburb of Detroit, and started construction on the massive Highland Park complex. The four-story building was 865 feet long and 75 feet wide, making it the largest structure in Michigan. With more than fifty thousand square feet of glass, it was dubbed the Crystal Palace. Its architect, Albert Kahn, had designed a number of plants for other car companies in Detroit. Kahn worked closely with Ford's industrial designers, who believed that the plant's architecture should be built around the manufacturing process. A little over a decade later, Kahn would be called on to design another Highland Park plant—this one in St. Paul, Minnesota.

Ford moved into the Highland Park plant in 1910, and over the next several years expanded the complex to increase production of the Model T. Much of the machinery and equipment was specially designed and built by company tool and die craftsmen. To bolster his tooling capabilities, Ford acquired a machine shop in Buffalo, New York, in 1911 that had developed innovative metal-stamping techniques. He intended to keep that plant operating, but those plans were scuttled when a number of workers went on a wildcat strike. When informed by phone, Ford ordered his managers to immediately shut the plant down and ship all the machinery to Highland Park. On more than one occasion in future years, Ford forestalled labor unrest by threatening to shut a plant down—a threat that workers knew was not idly made.

123 FORD AUTOMOBILES
41 CAR LOADS
CONSIGNED TO
NORTHWESTERN AUTOMOBILE CO.
MINNEAPOLIS
"WATCH THE FORDS GO BY"

In 1909, before Ford had a branch assembly plant in Minneapolis, the company shipped forty-one railcars to Minneapolis, each loaded with three automobiles, reportedly the largest shipment of cars up to that point. From the collections of The Henry Ford (64.167.13.31).

Ford car parts are unloaded from a boxcar in Spring Grove, Minnesota. Workers from the Onsgaard and Foss dealership assembled the cars right on the freight platform, which is how rural dealers typically operated. Courtesy of the Houston County Historical Society.

The Model T car was an extraordinary achievement, but the Highland Park plant was equally impressive. It was featured in numerous publications around the world, and toured by visitors from every continent. The general manager of the Benz plant in Germany described the plant "as the most remarkable in the world; it is the best in equipment and method." Ford was very generous in sharing his manufacturing innovations, and he welcomed competition which he felt would continually challenge him and benefit the entire industry. Of course, he also knew that very few competitors could afford the level of capital investment necessary for mass production.

Stephen Tenvoorde had been a car dealer for more than a decade and reportedly had been losing money the entire time. His profitable bicycle business offset the losses and he remained confident that his early entry into the car business would eventually pay off.

The Gerde Auto Company, located at 1112–1114 Lake Street, Minneapolis, was a Ford dealership in the 1910s. Like many dealers of the time, it also sold motorcycles and other products. Author's collection.

There were a number of other early Ford dealerships throughout Minnesota, operating under similar circumstances. Typically, they received cars shipped by rail that were either fully assembled or partially assembled. At the Crowley Motor Company in St. James, Minnesota, disassembled Model Ts would arrive by rail in early January, and the dealers spent the rest of the winter and early spring putting the cars together for the summer season. Only five tools were reportedly needed to assemble a car: a screwdriver, pliers, a punch, a hammer, and a monkey wrench.

1,000 CHASSIS, A DAY'S OUTPUT AT THE FORD MOTOR COMPANY'S PLANT, DETROIT, MICH.

Henry Ford took great pride in documenting company milestones. This postcard shows one day's car production. This vast output contributed to rail congestion in Detroit, prompting Ford to build branch assembly plants closer to buyers. Author's collection.

A System of Branch Assembly Plants

The increased production of cars and the general expansion of industry in Detroit created an enormous logistics problem, as railroads could no longer handle the sheer volume of shipping. Ford alone was transporting a thousand boxcars a day. His solution to the enormous problem of railroad congestion was to decentralize manufacturing operations, placing branch assembly plants closer to customers. Improvements in communications technology, particularly long-distance telephone service, helped make Ford's expansion feasible. A branch assembly plant was built in Kansas City in 1909, followed by Long Island City in New York City in 1910. However, before proceeding with a larger expansion that included plants in Minnesota, Ford needed to remove a major obstacle: a patent dispute that threatened the survival of his company.

In 1899, George Baldwin Selden, a patent lawyer from Rochester, New York, with very little experience in actually inventing anything, received a patent for a vehicle with an internal combustion engine. His patent drawings were so vague as to be meaningless—

a working model that was made years later could only sputter for five yards before dying—nonetheless Selden managed to attract considerable financing from investors eager to get in on the ground floor of this new technology. With his aggressive efforts to defend the patent, Selden intimidated many companies that did not want to be dragged into court. In 1903 an alliance known as the Association of Licensed Automobile Manufacturers (ALAM) was formed to acquire and control the patent rights. ALAM was generally successful in collecting royalty payments but Ford resisted, vowing to fight the legitimacy of the patent. ALAM responded by intimidating Ford's dealers and distributors with a national advertising campaign threatening to hold them liable for the sale of any Ford products.

Ford countered with his own advertising campaign stating that "The Selden Patent . . . does not cover any practicable machine, no practicable machine can be made from it and never was . . . We are the pioneers of the GASOLINE AUTOMOBILE." For the next six years the issue was fought in the courts and, in a stunning blow to Ford, a New York court upheld the Selden patent in 1909, leaving Ford potentially liable for millions in royalty payments. By this time, most other manufacturers, including Cadillac, Buick, and Oldsmobile, had agreed to pay the royalties, with Ford being the last significant holdout. He pledged to continue the fight with ALAM, vowing to take the suit all the way to the Supreme Court. He claimed that the Ford Motor Company had done more to advance the industry than "any dozen other manufacturers" and that the patent was a "freak among alleged inventions . . . worthless as a patent and worthless as a device." Ford had to post a $12 million indemnification bond during the ongoing litigation, which reassured his skittish dealers.

Ford's feisty response and his willingness to tackle the "monopolists" on principle turned into an extraordinary public-relations coup. A *Detroit Free Press* editorial carried the headline "Ford, the Fighter," and proclaimed: "As a human figure he presents a spectacle to win the applause of all men with red blood; for this world dearly loves the fighting man." But Ford's actions were also a gamble as a loss in court would be financially devastating to the company—at a time when Model T sales were exploding. The litigation dragged on for several more years, delaying plans for a national expansion. In 1911 a federal appeals court struck down the Selden patent with language so repudiating that ALAM had no choice but to abandon its claim. Ford won an enormous legal victory, but it was more than a personal victory. Robert Lacey put it best: "thanks almost entirely to Henry Ford, the American car industry was liberated from what soon came to be seen as an audacious and shameless conspiracy to limit its freedom."

With the legal threat removed in 1911, top Ford executives moved quickly with expansion plans. James Couzens, treasurer and secretary of the company, toured the West

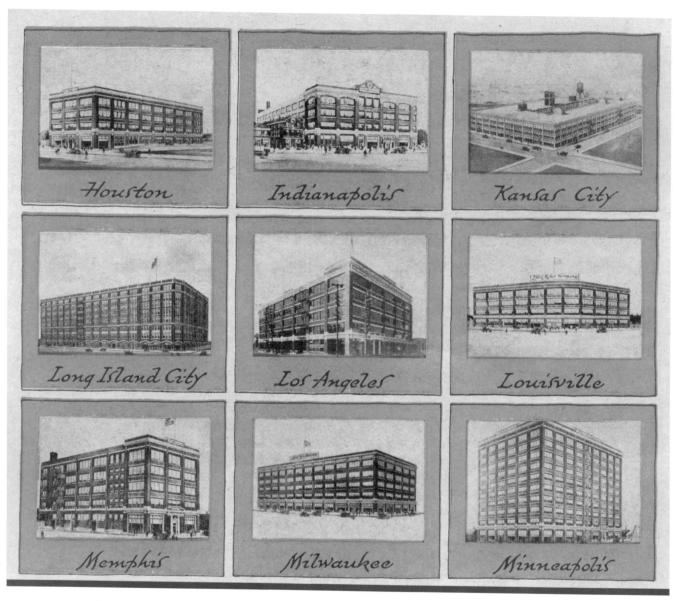

By 1913 the Ford Motor Company embarked on a massive expansion program, building branch assembly plants in cities around the country, including Minneapolis, St. Paul, and Fargo. Most were designed in a similar style by Seattle architect John Graham. Author's collection.

Coast and lined up sites in Los Angeles, San Francisco, Portland, and Seattle. Soon thereafter, locations were selected in Denver, Minneapolis, St. Paul, Fargo, St. Louis, Chicago, Memphis, Boston, and Philadelphia. Locations were largely based on railroad freight rates, as there were significant differences around the country determined by a complex and fickle regulatory system. Moving aggressively, Ford built thirty-five assembly plants by the start of World War I, twenty-two of which also manufactured parts. John Graham, a Seattle architect, designed most of these plants, which were typically multistory buildings near rail lines in downtown locations.

Ford made most of the parts for the Model T in Detroit. They were shipped to assembly plants in tightly packed railcars, an approach that offered considerable savings in transportation costs. A regular boxcar could hold only three or four fully assembled cars, but enough parts for as many as twenty-six unassembled cars. It was also cheaper to ship industrial parts "knocked down," saving the 10 percent surcharge added to finished products. An additional benefit was that railroads billed for a minimum weight of ten thousand pounds per boxcar, no matter how heavy the load. Because three assembled autos weighed only six thousand pounds, Ford was giving up 40 percent of the allowable weight load. These various savings in shipping costs were not passed on to the customer, who continued to pay freight charges set for fully assembled cars. Car bodies were often built locally by other companies and then attached to the chassis in the assembly plant. In addition to providing considerable savings in transportation costs, branch assembly plants generated local goodwill because of the jobs created, and because their service departments carried a plentiful supply of parts.

A 1913 Ford Company newsletter made the case for building assembly plants in the Twin Cities:

> There is something about the hardy life of the farmers, most of them descendants of the Vikings, that led them to appreciate peculiarly the clean-cut strength of the Ford. In a way, the Ford is like one of these farmers . . . As the years passed, the Ford cars rolled out of Minneapolis in numbers increasingly large. Year by year the business of the Ford dealers in that territory grew. Year by year the demand for cars became greater. This increasing demand made it absolutely necessary to establish a Ford branch in Minneapolis this year, with a sub-branch in St. Paul.

Minneapolis had a population of 315,000 and boasted the highest industrial output per capita of any city in the country. It was the principal economic hub for the entire region, which included a rich farm belt that generated more than $1 billion income annually. More than $50 million was projected to be spent in the region on automobiles. In 1912, Ford leased the lower four floors of the Great Northern Implement loft building at 616 South Third Street in Minneapolis to assemble cars. Boxcars with parts for seven cars were shipped to the rented loft, where they were placed on sawhorses and assembled by workers with hand tools in approximately one and a half hours. No conveyer belts were

In 1912, shortly before constructing the new Minneapolis plant, Ford leased four floors of a Minneapolis loft building to assemble Model T cars. Parts were shipped by rail and put together with simple tools before the introduction of the assembly line. Courtesy of Minneapolis Public Library, Special Collections.

utilized. A Ford press release stated: "There were only six major functions to get a Model T to sputter to life . . . assemble the body to the chassis, put on the fenders, tires, wheels, and windshield, fill the tank with gasoline and it was ready for the customer." The parts were painted in Detroit before being shipped, but a paint booth was installed in the loft in early 1913. Of the six Model T car models offered by Ford, only the Touring and Roadster were assembled in Minneapolis. During the winter, work halted as demand fell because customers could not drive the open cars on the frigid, snow-packed streets.

On June 18, 1912, the Ford Motor Company announced plans to build a two hundred thousand–dollar assembly plant in the Minneapolis warehouse district at Fifth Street and Fifth Avenue. The one-acre site was adjacent to the tracks of the Great Northern, Burlington and St. Louis Railway. Ford also planned to build a smaller "sub-branch" in St. Paul at 117 University Avenue near the state capitol. This was widely seen as a consolation prize that would spare Ford from being drawn into the bitter rivalry between the two cities.

Challenge of Building in Minneapolis

Almost immediately after Ford announced the Minneapolis project, forty adjoining property owners signed a petition complaining that that the new plant would block construction of a planned rail spur to their land on the north and diminish their property values. The city held off granting Ford a construction permit pending discussion of the issues. At a contentious city council meeting, property owners and representatives from the North Side Commercial Club and the North Minneapolis Civic Federation opposed the construction permit. Most in attendance wanted to keep Ford in the city—they just wanted a different location. A council member from South Minneapolis offered to find a free site in his ward, and another council member from the city's east side touted desirable locations along University Avenue. Some speakers, however, expressed doubts about Ford's claim that employment levels would reach as high as four hundred workers. After three hours of deliberations, the city council decided that a committee should visit the North Fifth Street site to better understand the issues. One news account of the meeting sounded an ominous note with the headline "City May Lose Big Automobile Plant."

The Ford site was surrounded on three sides by railroad tracks. Fourth and Fifth Streets were raised on viaducts approximately eighteen feet above the tracks, and Fifth Avenue was raised approximately ten feet. The property owners challenging the Ford project were from five adjoining blocks, extending from Fifth Avenue to Tenth Avenue, between Fourth and Fifth Streets. They had counted on a rail spur being built on an alleyway that would connect their undeveloped property to the tracks of the Great Northern Railway. Ford's proposed project would cut off access, making it impossible to build the spur. The owners were looking to the city to do a friendly condemnation of part of their property for a needed alley.

Notwithstanding the controversy, Ford's architect, John Graham, continued to design the Minneapolis plant, in association with the prominent Minneapolis firm of Kees and Colburn. Initially it was designed as a four-story building, but with enough structural capacity to add another four floors. By the time of the next city council committee meeting, Ford had already committed to an eight-story building. Trains would enter the building at the basement level accessing interior loading platforms, and there would also be several hundred feet of exterior platforms.

Trying to head off a major conflict between Ford and the property owners, in August 1912, the Minneapolis city council "invited a friendly suit from the Ford Motor Company by voting to abandon proceedings toward opening a straight alley." If the court ruled that the city did not have the right to open an alley for a rail spur for a private company, then a construction permit would be granted. Ford was not content to wait for the courts to resolve the issue, nor were officials in St. Paul, who were unhappy about receiving the smaller "sub-branch." Their mutual interests led to the possibility of building the larger plant in St. Paul. A representative from the St. Paul Association traveled to Detroit and met with Henry Ford, who said it was very possible that the larger plant might be built in St. Paul. Several weeks later, architect John Graham visited the St. Paul site and disclosed that "the Ford people are now thinking of building the factory in St. Paul . . . and that all matters would be held in abeyance."

Fearing that Ford would move the larger plant to St. Paul, the Minneapolis Civic and Commerce Association secured a five-year option on a property adjoining Ford's site that could be used for an alleyway for the rail spur if necessary. Several months later, the alleyway dispute was again taken up by the Minneapolis city council, where it faced continued opposition from the adjoining property owners. The prospect of losing such an important development prize, especially to its bitter municipal rival, left Minneapolis officials scrambling for a resolution. They turned to the Minneapolis Civic and Commerce Association for mediation. A compromise was reached "to adjust the traction difficulties which for a time threatened to cause the Ford Motor Company to abandon its intention to build a factory in Minneapolis." While discussions were ongoing, the size of the building increased yet again to ten stories in height plus the basement, with each floor measuring 145 feet by 198 feet.

With its construction permit finally approved, Ford broke ground on August 11, 1913. The foundations required an extensive piling system consisting of two thousand fifty-foot Norway pines. The building had twenty-eight-inch steel columns encased in concrete. This reinforced concrete structural system allowed for larger windows that brought considerable light and ventilation to the interiors. The windows were made by United Steel Sash, a subsidiary of the Trussed Concrete Steel Co., a business established by architect Albert Kahn and his brother Julius. The ten-story structure was finished in red pressed brick trimmed with matte glazed cream-colored terra cotta.

A newspaper account attributed the high quality of finish to "the interest of the civic improvements that are now being agitated in the city of Minneapolis," but in actuality John Graham had been using this architectural treatment for assembly plants all over the country. The rail spur that entered the building was a fairly unusual feature at the time that underscored Ford's determination to maximize transportation efficiencies. As the

MPLS. JULY 7TH 1914

The Minneapolis branch assembly plant was being built in 1913 as Ford was perfecting the movable assembly line in Detroit, making the building functionally obsolete even before it opened. The main entrance was originally at street level, but after the bridge was raised, the sidewalk was lifted slightly above the entrance. From the collections of The Henry Ford (THF127063).

When completed, the Minneapolis plant was the tallest structure ever built for the purpose of assembling cars. As with all of Ford's plants from this period, it depended on rail access. Photograph by C. J. Hibbard. Courtesy of the Minnesota Historical Society.

site was being readied for construction, the Minnesota state legislature passed a railroad safety law, known as the Clearance Act, which mandated minimum clearances around and above all railcars. The basement ceiling height, as designed, would not have met those standards. Ford appealed and won an exemption, arguing that if it raised the height of the basement, the main entrance on the first floor would be lifted above the sidewalk. Ironically, several years later the trestle bridge crossing Fifth Street was raised, placing the main entrance below the new sidewalk level. The building, still standing at 420 North Fifth Street, had four elevators, including one that went to the roof, and a high-speed dumbwaiter for smaller parts. A machine shop and foundry were located at the top of the building. The new plant also had a sophisticated painting operation that dipped the parts in paint, throwing the excess off by centrifugal force, and then baking them in

This interior view of the Minneapolis plant shows workers putting together car bodies for the Model T. The reinforced concrete columns were individually numbered, a practice Ford employed on most of his buildings, in part to accommodate the many workers who did not speak English. Courtesy of the Minnesota Historical Society.

The first-floor showroom of the Minneapolis plant displayed a number of Model T cars. It was adorned with mounted animal heads as well as a large fish, reflecting the early popularity of automobiles for recreational use. The decorative plaster column capitals feature the letter F, as was done at all of Ford's branch plants. Author's collection.

gas ovens. An outside shipping platform long enough to accommodate seven railcars extended to Fourth Street. Ford continued to occupy the rented loft space in the Great Northern Implement building until the new Minneapolis assembly plant was completed.

At ten stories in height, with a basement abutting the tracks, the Minneapolis plant was likely the tallest structure in the world ever built for automobile manufacturing. Ford typically incorporated gravity feed systems to move materials through his multistory buildings. Freight elevators hauled smaller parts and materials to the upper floors, where workers assembled them into modules that could be ramped down from floor to floor, each module increasing in size along the way.

Plants in St. Paul and Fargo

St. Paul lost out on the larger plant, but it did receive a three-story "subassembly" plant, just a block west of the Minnesota state capitol at 117 University Avenue. The Saint Paul Building Department records list both John Graham and the local firm of Kees and Colburn as architects for the plant, although evidence suggests that Graham had the more prominent role. The building clearly incorporates the trademark design motifs that Graham used on the Minneapolis plant and dozens of other Ford buildings around the country. In addition, an architectural drawing has been located with only his firm listed. The St. Paul sub-branch was more ornate than the utilitarian Minneapolis plant, perhaps in deference to its prominent location next to the new state capitol building. It featured an elaborate entrance with tall, fluted classical columns, a design element also used in plants in other cities, including Seattle.

Construction of the smaller St. Paul plant went more smoothly than that in Minneapolis. It was a three-story building with a basement measuring 100 by 150 feet, for a total of 60,000 square feet. Freight elevators reportedly could bring cars to the tiled roof of the reinforced concrete building to be tested. The plant was slated to assemble five hundred cars in 1914. The manager of the St. Paul branch was A. J. Sarjeant, the former manager of the Northwestern Automobile Company in St. Paul, the original Ford sales agency. His appointment was greeted favorably in the *Pioneer Press*: "Mr. Sarjeant is one of the most popular men in the automobile game in the Twin City. He is liked both by users of machines and by dealers."

Several years later, Ford built a three-story branch assembly plant in Fargo, North Dakota, at a cost of $150,000. It was located along the Great Northern Railway tracks and had a rail spur that went directly into the building. Showrooms, stockrooms, and a garage were located on the first floor, offices and a shop were on the second floor, and the

A three-story subassembly plant was built as a consolation prize for St. Paul after the larger plant was located in Minneapolis. Note that construction materials were still being delivered by horse-drawn wagons. This design is almost identical to that of a Ford plant in Seattle. Author's collection.

The design of the St. Paul subassembly showroom is more decorative than that of the Minneapolis plant in deference to its location next to the state capitol. Even the column capitals are more ornate, incorporating a plaster shield with a decorative F. Author's collection.

assembly plant was on the third floor. John Graham was the architect of record for the 100 x 200–foot building. For the opening celebration in 1915, the fifty-five-piece "big Ford Band" gave a concert in a downtown park. When fully staffed, there were approximately two hundred employees at the building. Its first manager, W. H. Schmelzel, later moved to the St. Paul plant.

The similar designs and shared motifs of the many plants designed by John Graham represent an early instance of a standardized corporate architecture. Ford probably didn't set out to create a "visual brand" of the sort perfected by later companies but these buildings did establish a unique precedent in commercial architecture. Their uniformity could be attributed in part to Ford's needing to move quickly and on a large scale after the Selden patent case was resolved. In addition to being attractive, the new plants were functional and well suited for the assembly of Model T cars, although innovations in manufacturing techniques soon required a very different form of architecture.

Ford's vast network of assembly and manufacturing plants revolutionized industry in much the same way his assembly line transformed manufacturing. An article in *Ford Times* in 1915 describes the new concept of "just-in-time" manufacturing: "This arrange-

FORD BUILDING, FARGO, N. D.

The Ford building in Fargo, North Dakota, is one of the smaller branch plants, but its design draws from John Graham's architectural pallet. Author's collection.

ment [branch plants] enables the Ford factory to approach the ideal manufacturing basis; that is to maintain a steady production all the year around without being compelled to provide storage at the factory. There is no provision for storing accumulated production at the Ford factory because there is no need for it. The factory is simply a huge machine shop, cleared for action." Ford's transportation systems connecting the company's branch plants and supply chain had become an integral part of the manufacturing process.

Continuing Problems with Minneapolis Plant

While still on the drawing board, the Minneapolis plant increased in size from four to ten stories to allow more Model Ts to be assembled, but this additional production also required more storage space. Ford acquired three adjoining parcels, giving it ownership of the entire block. At this point, Ford apparently backed out of the negotiated agreement not to challenge future efforts to build a rail spur to the adjoining properties. Ford sued to prohibit Minneapolis from condemning the alleyway between Fifth and Tenth Avenues for the rail spur. Ford lost at the district court and appealed to the Minnesota Supreme Court, but while that was pending, Ford filed for a permit to build a tunnel under North Fifth Street to access properties across the street for loading platforms.

This application also required approval by the city council, where it became conflated with the alleyway issue. Having been burned by Ford on the rail spur, a key council member objected: "It was a matter of principle that the council should not grant the company a permit . . . while it was opposed to the city in other litigation." He offered a resolution that would approve the tunnel permit in exchange for Ford's agreement to withdraw its suit on the rail spur. Ford objected—too strongly objected—according to Alderman Kean. He alleged that "the Ford Company had instigated the formation, by its employees, of political organizations in the various wards which had threatened aldermen with political ruin if they dared to withhold the permit." "I was given such a telephone warning last week," he stated. "I refuse to be bludgeoned into action." A Ford representative denied the allegation and said that he merely spoke to employees "of congested shipping conditions and stated that unless the tunnel was constructed I would be obliged to lay off men from time to time during the summer." However, he admitted that "Several employees suggested that they see their respective aldermen and also that they obtain petitions from residents in the section seeking the granting of the permit. I consented, but there was no thought of any political activity." Ford later publicly stated that it would probably need to lay off 150 workers or possibly even move out of the city if the tunnel permit was denied.

Workers assemble Model T cars in Minneapolis before the assembly line. Author's collection.

The city council tried to head off another conflict and again turned to the Civic and Commerce Association for help in the form of binding arbitration. Representatives from the city, Ford, and the association met several times and inspected the proposed tunnel site. The association followed up with a report that supported the tunnel proposal. The city council accepted the recommendation and approved the permit for the tunnel.

While the matter of the tunnel was settled, the litigation relating to the rail spur continued to drag on. On June 10, 1916, the Minnesota Supreme Court emphatically reversed a lower court ruling won by the city. According to a newspaper account, "In a decision which practically questioned the good faith of the city of Minneapolis, the state supreme court upheld the Ford Motor Co. in its contention against the city's condemnation of part of its land for alley purposes." The court ruled that "eminent domain cannot be exercised to take private property for a private purpose." The right-of-way for a rail spur was deemed to be a private use. The city appealed the decision, claiming it had new evidence. The case went back to district court before the same judge who originally ruled in favor of the city, and resulted in the same outcome. The judge declared a second time that Minneapolis had the right to condemn land for the alley. Ford then again brought the case back to the supreme court on appeal.

The "famous Ford alley" case continued for another five years with a total of four appeals before the supreme court. The city eventually won a significant, but partial, victory, allowing for an alley to partly cross the Ford property. However, there was no provision for the railroad switching track in the decision. In 1922, ten years after the litigation started, the city moved to require the construction of a railroad bridge over the alley, assessing the twenty thousand–dollar expense to the adjoining property owners, who were happy to accept their share of costs. At a public hearing, however, a Ford representative called it "outrageous" and disputed the city's assertion that the company had ever agreed to build the rail spur. He added that he even had a letter from company attorneys denying they had ever consented to a rail spur across their property. The city attorney at that point embarrassed the Ford representative by producing a letter "indicating such an agreement had been made."

As the deliberations over the rail bridge continued, Ford claimed it was losing $1 million a month at the downtown Minneapolis plant because of lack of space to assemble cars and threatened to "move its plant or fight the action in court." The large amount of losses claimed by Ford gives some idea of the scale of operations. At its peak in 1923, the Minneapolis plant assembled ninety-three thousand vehicles. Notwithstanding the impressive totals, Ford felt it could build many more cars with a more efficient plant. Although this was undoubtedly true, the company's concerns were probably as much owing to the fact that its vertical assembly plant had become a white elephant because it could not fully accommodate the new assembly line. Ford's discussions with adjoining property owners, city officials, and engineers seemed to inch toward a workable compromise, but the issue became moot when it was revealed in 1922 that Ford was thinking of building a modern plant on a large rural site in St. Paul.

Ford's numerous conflicts in Minneapolis may have contributed to the company's ultimate decision to build on the other side of the Mississippi River, but these experiences also generally highlighted the difficulties of operating in any developed urban area. Another lesson Henry Ford could take from Minneapolis was that he was in a very powerful negotiating position when talking with city officials about the possibility of creating or eliminating hundreds of well-paying jobs. His determination and effective use of power were critical reasons for the success of the company in the short term, but unchallenged and impulsive use of this power would eventually create problems for the company.

The Assembly Line, Mass Production, and a Car for the Masses

Ford plants had always incorporated some elements of mass production, including subdivision of labor, standardization of parts, product simplification, machining with custom tools, and sequencing of workers and materials into a production line, but none had reached the fully integrated system Henry Ford perfected in Detroit in 1913. Every movement in the factory was studied and timed with stopwatches to find ways to increase productivity. Ford and his skilled team created a manufacturing process with synchronized timing and continuous motion, using slides and conveyors alongside and above the assembly line to facilitate the handling of materials. Ford did not invent these improvements—efficiency guru Frederick W. Taylor had been preaching the merits of scientific management all over the country, including in Detroit and Minneapolis. But Ford perfected and implemented the system in the most comprehensive way. His overriding goal was to produce a car for the masses and cost was of secondary concern.

In his book *My Life and Work*, Henry Ford wrote of the movable assembly line: "The idea came in a general way from the overhead trolley that the Chicago packers use in dressing beef." In addition to Ford's account, recollections by several other key participants in the early experiments give a fairly clear understanding of the process. In the summer of 1913, there were 250 assemblers and eighty parts carriers working on the chassis assembly. It took approximately twelve-and-a-half man-hours to produce each chassis. As an experiment, Ford set up a crude assembly line where the chassis was pulled by rope, allowing parts to be installed as it moved. It seemed to speed up production. Ford then installed a motor-driven pulley to create a continuous motion line. This cut the chassis assembly time in half. The trial-and-error process continued over the next few months, and on December 1, 1913, a three hundred–foot long line with 177 assemblers dropped the production time to two hours and thirty-eight minutes. With additional modifications, the time was reduced to one hour and thirty-three minutes, from the original twelve hours and thirty minutes. These gains in productivity were not nominal or incremental—they were astounding. Ford experimented with other parts of the manufacturing process. The magneto coil assembly required skilled workers, who typically produced thirty-five to forty

The movable assembly line was developed in Ford's existing Highland Park plant near Detroit. This photograph from 1913 shows the assembly line being powered by the belt and pulley power system before the widespread use of electrical motors. Courtesy of the Library of Congress.

units a day. With the introduction of the movable assembly line, the work was divided into twenty-nine separate operations performed by twenty-nine unskilled workers. In the old system it took twenty minutes to make a part; under the new system it took thirteen.

What Ford begot, in the words of Keith Sward, was a mechanized process that was "like a river and its tributaries." Walter Flanders, the Ford engineer most responsible for reorganizing the factories for the new mass-production techniques, understood the implications: "There was a process now, a line, and the process was going to demand more and more money and employees." Each small improvement on the line would speed up production and cut the cost of the car. It would also transform the nature of manufacturing. "Henceforth," Flanders told a Detroit reporter, "the history of the industry will be the conflict of giants." The assembly-line improvements brought this revolutionary insight to Ford, "We actually changed from making automobiles to making parts. Then we found that we had made another new discovery, that it was by no means all of the parts had to be made in one factory."

The new manufacturing system opened the floodgate to revamping the entire production process, both inside the walls of Highland Park, and throughout the entire supply chain. With these improvements in efficiency, production of Ford vehicles rose from

78,440 in 1911 to 730,041 in 1916–1917. Ford passed the savings on to consumers in the form of lower prices, and was finally able to deliver on his pledge to build a $400 car. Ford claimed, "Every time I reduce the charge for our car by one dollar, I get a thousand new buyers." In 1910 a Model T cost $780. It dropped to $690 the following year, then to $600, to $550. By 1914, Ford was selling a car every 24 seconds, and announced yet another price drop to $440. On the eve of World War I, the price dropped to $360. Because of high sales volume, Ford's total profits grew even as the profit he made on each car fell from $220 to $99.

Ford was out producing all other manufacturers in the world. In 1914 the Ford Motor Company with 13,000 employees produced 267,000 cars; the other 299 American auto companies with 66,350 employees produced only 286,770 cars. As he lowered his price, his market share surged from 9.4 percent in 1908 to 20.3 percent in 1911, to 39.6 percent in 1913, and with the benefits of his mechanization to 48 percent in 1914. By 1915 Ford had $100 million in annual sales and the Model T became the biggest selling car in history. David Halberstam marveled, "The world had never seen anything like it. The cars simply poured off the line. Ford's dreams in a startlingly brief time had all come true. He had lived his own prophecy."

Ford's business partners wanted these enormous profits to be distributed in the form of dividends, but he had other ideas. He intended to continue lowering the price of his cars, which he characterized as profit sharing for the buyers. He also was committed to reinvesting the profits back into the company, as he had always done. In fact, he was gearing up to build a huge new plant on the Rouge River.

The Assembly Line and Workers

Ford's movable assembly line changed the very nature of work. Assembly-line workers no longer had to think on the job—company managers would assume that responsibility. The assembly line reduced all jobs to a series of simple tasks that could be performed by a person with virtually no skills. New machinery was needed to simplify these manual operations to a single task. Ford hired more than 1,200 machinists just to design and fabricate the new tooling. By 1914, 95 percent of the tools on the line were basically jigs and dies. Ford installed fifteen thousand machines, several thousand more than the number of workers employed at the time. Every movement, every step on the assembly line would be planned, designed, and timed, and the workers had to adapt. They were now just cogs in the machinery. Personnel managers looked for a new "mental attitude" that could tolerate handling repetition and boredom. Scientific management experts and efficiency experts suggested that less intelligent workers were preferable, and one even claimed that "an intelligent gorilla could be trained." Worker morale sagged. A new management position, line foreman, had to be created to enforce worker discipline.

Leaders of organized labor recognized that a "de-skilled" workforce would lose much of its negotiating power. Historically, technical skills were passed down from generation to generation through an apprenticeship system in which skilled workers were both the educators and the gatekeepers for employment. Mass production would undo that system, as a Detroit Metal Trades circular predicted in 1914: "Improvements in machinery and methods, and the specializing of operations are constantly reducing the necessity of skilled labor. It is up to us to change our plan of organization to meet these changed conditions or sink in the mire of degradation and become mere slaves." One line worker said, "If I keep putting on Nut No. 86 for about 86 more days, I will be Nut No. 86." Another wrote: "workers cease to be human beings as soon as they enter the gates of the shop. They become automatons and cease to think . . . Many healthy workers have gone to work for Ford and have come out human wrecks."

Henry Ford denied that his intention was to "de-skill" the workforce and insisted that he had to rely on the efficiencies of the assembly line because there were not enough skilled workers available to make the number of cars needed in the marketplace. He also claimed that the assembly line gave opportunities to many new immigrants who had no basic skills. In 1908, the Ford Motor Company had 450 workers. Six years later, when the new plants were opening in Minneapolis and St. Paul, the company had fourteen thousand workers, three-quarters of whom were immigrants who spoke little or no English.

Whatever the rationale, the transformation of the workplace took a huge toll on the workers. Turnover rates reached 370 percent, meaning that Ford had to hire 52,000 workers every year to maintain his targeted workforce of 14,000. One labor official described the situation as a "continuous unorganized strike." Considerable nonproductive energy went into the hiring process, and the turnover was estimated to cost the company more than $1.2 million annually. Henry Ford realized that additional improvements to the assembly-line process would only bring marginal returns—the gains would be eaten up in the human carnage. He realized he needed a different approach. On January 5, 1914, Ford announced that "the greatest and most successful" automobile company in the world would "inaugurate the greatest revolution in the matter of rewards for its workers ever known to the industrial world." He instituted "the five-dollar day" for eight hours' work, at a time when industrial workers were typically receiving $2.50 for a nine-hour day. James Couzens, Ford's business manager, explained: "It is our belief that social justice begins at home. We want those who have helped us to produce this great institution and are helping to maintain it to share in our prosperity . . . Believing as we do, that a division of our earnings between capital and labor is unequal, we have sought a plan of relief suitable for our business."

The five-dollar-day announcement was front-page news around the country, but there were few details, other than that it applied to male workers over the age of twenty-two. Ford later clarified that the $10 million set aside for the workers was not actually an increase in wages but rather profit sharing—a dividend to *qualified* workers. "This is neither charity nor wages," he said, "but simply profit sharing. In a way it is a piece of efficiency engineering too. We expect to get better work, more efficient work as a result." The search for efficiency no longer was restricted to machinery and process, it also applied to people. It was also an acknowledgment that major increases in labor productivity were needed if he hoped to continue lowering the price of the Model T. Under the terms of the profit-sharing plan, employees over the age of twenty-two were eligible but had to work on a probationary status for six months. Workers under that age could qualify if they were "sober, saving, steady, industrious."

Marv Saline recalled that his father, who washed cars at the Minneapolis plant in 1915, met Ford's criteria:

> He considered himself very fortunate. He was making five dollars a day, when most skilled craftsmen were only making $2.50 a day. I remember my dad saying that he started out with a six-month probationary period and in order for him to get hired at the full wage he had to show the superintendent his bank book and how much he saved . . . The Ford workers had badges, which they were proud to wear, but it did have its drawbacks. One time he went into a neighborhood clothing store to buy a necktie for twenty-five cents. The shop owner saw the Ford badge, and then said, "Anyone who works at Ford should be able to afford a fifty-cent tie."

To help workers become eligible for the profit-sharing plan, Ford established the Sociological Department in 1914, which had a staff of thirty investigators to monitor the company's 12,880 employees, including their home environment. Although the program was extremely paternalistic and resented for its invasion of privacy, it did benefit many workers as home ownership and savings rates rose dramatically. Henry Ford and his top managers had a genuine desire to share the company's prosperity with workers, but there was also recognition that morale and worker engagement would be critical to the bottom line. Increased home ownership and stable family life also increased financial responsibilities, providing additional motivation for workers to keep their jobs. The immediate results affirmed the value of the program. Worker turnover rates dropped from 370 percent to 16 percent. Ford was pleased with the results of the "distinctly utopian" program, describing the $10 million payout to his workers as the company's best cost-saving plan.

Mass Production Needs Mass Consumption: Distributors, Dealers, and Branch Agencies

Henry Ford needed to make sure there were buyers for all the cars streaming off the assembly line. He could not produce an inexpensive car for the masses unless there literally were masses of buyers. In effect, the customer became his partner. With his characteristic flair for public relations, he made that point by promising that if he sold more than three hundred thousand cars in 1915, buyers would receive a forty- to sixty-dollar rebate. The marketing strategy was successful and Ford paid the rebates.

Lower prices, higher wages, and occasional marketing gimmicks like the sales rebate expanded the pool of buyers, but that was still not sufficient. Ford committed to

Stephen Tenvoorde built a one-story brick garage in 1910, which was later expanded. Ford placed the steering wheels on the left side of the Model T, which quickly became the industry norm. Courtesy of the Tenvoorde family.

In 1917, Thomas Owens built an attractive Ford dealership at 713–719 University Avenue, St. Paul. The building was expanded in several stages and still stands. Courtesy of the Minnesota Historical Society.

overhauling the entire process of marketing and distributing cars in the same way he overhauled manufacturing. Employing his customary trial-and-error approach, he created a multi-tiered distribution system of assembly plants, branch stores, branch agencies, dealers, sub-dealers, and authorized service outlets.

Ford consolidated all marketing and distribution efforts for the Northwest territory in the new Minneapolis assembly plant and ended its relationship with its distributor, the Northwestern Automobile Company. A company agency in Minneapolis, Ford reasoned, would allow for better relations with dealers and would also save the distributor's fee. Stephen Tenvoorde traveled to Minneapolis where he met with Ford branch officials and placed an order for fifty cars. With the new branch assembly plant, and the enormous popularity of the Model T, Tenvoorde's dealership seemed to finally be on solid financial ground. By 1915, he dropped other car brands and carried only Fords.

In addition to establishing branch sales agencies, Ford moved to exert more oversight and control of its dealers by establishing rigid requirements over such things as the skill of mechanics, the number of replacement parts to be carried, and the method of

Ford established dealerships in most towns with a population of more than two thousand people. He had a network of forty-five thousand independently owned service centers that carried authorized parts, typified by this garage in Avon, Minnesota, circa 1915. Photograph by Briol Studio. Courtesy of the Minnesota Historical Society.

bookkeeping. It also specified "Absolute cleanliness throughout every department. There must be no unwashed windows, dusty furniture, dirty floors."

The dealer was responsible for knowing the name of every potential automobile buyer in his territory, "including all those who have never given the matter a thought." Every prospect was to be approached, preferably in person, and the "necessary memoranda" kept on all contacts. Ford also warned dealers that if they could not achieve this goal, "they may have too much territory." Early dealers did not have to invest significant capital in inventory as they typically received a deposit before placing an order, but they were required to carry a large number of parts.

Ford had the largest sales force in the country, probably more than all other car companies combined. The network of approximately seven thousand dealerships covered virtually every town with a population of two thousand or more. Most of the early dealers carried several different car companies—as late as 1916, the Woodhead Motor Company in Brainerd, Minnesota, advertised Ford and Overland cars. Ford eventually insisted on exclusivity as a way to exert more control. A regional agency manager provided oversight for all the dealerships within his district, which varied in number from 150 to six hundred. The manager regularly visited dealers offering advice, inspecting operations, and doing annual written evaluations. On a tour of dealerships in South Dakota, Minneapolis branch manager C. C. Hildebrand visited C. P. Anders of White River, a town of about five hundred people. In his performance review, he wrote: "New country, mixed population. Considerable farming. Many Indians." Hildebrand was impressed with Anders: "Business ability and appearance good." Because Anders's dealership was almost thirty miles from the nearest railroad at Murdo, Hildebrand suggested he tack on a mileage charge to the buyer.

Allan Nevins and Frank Ernest Hill described Ford's relationship with the branch agencies: "Control was authoritarian, and designed to preserve the line of relationship from dealer to roadman to branch head to Detroit . . . Branch managers . . . were categorically forbidden to exchange information with each other, or to discuss common problems—unless specifically told to do so. Consultations between branch heads, declared the company, represented neither the proper way nor a healthy condition." Branch managers passed down the strict oversight to their dealers. According to Nevins and Hill, "Indeed the discipline was military . . . Dealers were firmly discouraged from complaining to the company about alleged injustices perpetrated by roadmen or branch managers, although in desperation, many of them did. The branch, severely controlled from Detroit, often controlled its dealers even more severely."

A plentiful supply of replacement parts and readily accessible service stations were essential to Ford's strategy to increase car sales. He complained: "The repair men were

The chaotic appearance of Gerde Auto Company's service area on Lake Street in Minneapolis revealed the challenges Ford faced as he tried to "rationalize" the repair and service business. Stephen L. McIntyre selected this dealership to illustrate "the small, cluttered nature of most repair shops in the 1910s" for an article in a national academic journal. Author's collection.

for a time the largest menace to the automobile industry . . . We would not have our distribution blocked by stupid, greedy men." From the very beginning of the automobile industry, manufacturers, dealers, and customers have been perplexed as to the best way to maintain and repair cars. The Ford Motor Company was especially sensitive to this problem because many of its buyers were on a tight budget and could not afford expensive repairs. To sell more cars, Ford believed he had to create a seamless, inexpensive process for repairing cars that incorporated the efficiencies and cost savings found in his factories. In 1913, even as he was perfecting the assembly line, he was working to

GENERAL REPAIR LINE.

41383

(*left*) The Owens Motor Company in St. Paul had a well-organized repair shop, with cars lined up in a neat row near tools, emulating the order of the factory floor. Courtesy of Rihm Motor Company. (*right*) The neatly organized parts' bins of the Woodhead Motor Company in Brainerd, Minnesota, exemplified the standard that Ford tried to instill among his dealers. Note the wheel with wooden spokes for the Model T; wire spokes on the Model A would not be introduced for a few more years. Courtesy of John Woodhead.

"rationalize" the repair process by identifying the most common problems and developing ways to complete those repairs more efficiently. At company-owned branch plants around the country, he instituted a series of time-and-motion studies that documented—to no one's surprise—the wide variation in costs and completion times for typical repairs. Ford designed new tools specifically for repair projects and created a variety of instructional materials for mechanics, including slide shows, film, and comprehensive manuals.

By 1914, Ford was pushing his independent dealers and distributors to adopt these best practices and to institute a "flat-rate" system for standardized repairs, but he faced considerable opposition from dealers and their mechanics. Service work was a significant part of a dealer's revenue. Mechanics were typically paid on an hourly basis, with all of the costs passed on to the customer. A flat-rate system, recommended by Ford, would introduce considerable uncertainty as to who would bear the risk for overruns. Both the dealers and Ford were already facing stiff competition from independent garages that were attracting over half of the repair business. The company feared that garages would not use authentic Ford parts, which were an important source of revenue. Given the many complexities, Ford backed off from his various experiments to "rationalize" repair services and abandoned his interest in establishing company-owned branch service agencies in major cities.

Aftermarket Accessories and Attachments for Model T

The Ford Motor Company sold more than fifteen million Model T cars between 1908 and 1927. Rather than making significant changes to the design of the car, Ford focused on improving the manufacturing process to continually lower costs. Henry Ford's reluctance to go beyond "natural improvement" opened the door for others. Gordon Schindler noted a paradox with the Model T: "The more successful a product is, the greater the chance of someone trying to improve on it." Thousands of amateur inventors pursued the huge "aftermarket" for customized accessories and attachments for the Model Ts. There were so many devices specifically designed for the Model T that *Horseless Age* magazine published a feature article titled "How to Display Accessories for Fords." Inventors from Minnesota took the lead in creating agricultural attachments for the Model T, building upon the existing cluster of implement manufacturers in the Twin Cities. A number of new companies were formed, including the American Ford-A-Tractor and the Auto-Pull companies in Minneapolis, and the Me-Co and the Convertible Tractor Corporation in St. Paul. The Staude Company on University Avenue in St. Paul manufactured the Mak-a-Tractor, one of the most successful attachments in the country. Staude sold more than thirty thousand tractor kits for the Model T priced at $225, and at its peak had more than two thousand dealers. The company later produced complete tractors built on Ford chassis, which it purchased in lots of 150 from the Twin Cities Assembly Plant.

The Pillsbury Manufacturing Company of Minneapolis made a device that could help pull the car from the mud. Several companies, including the Western Body Company, made attachable auto bodies that turned the Model T into a sports car. Other devices converted the Model T into rail inspection cars, snowmobiles, and even boats and planes. The engine of the Model T, and the later Model A, were used to power an airplane made from a kit designed by inventor Bernard H. Pietenpol. Many saw the Model T as a mobile power plant that opened up almost unlimited applications, including cutting lumber, hoisting materials, and even cutting lake weeds. Several local companies tried to capitalize on Ford's name. In 1917, one in Minneapolis manufactured an attachment for the Ford car under the brand name Handy Hank. The use of the nickname "Hank" may have played into the folksy, approachable image of Henry Ford, but ironically, other than very early career in his career he was always known as "Mr. Ford," even to his closest associates.

One company fraudulently appropriated the Ford name. The Ford Tractor Company, with no connection to Henry Ford or the Ford Motor Company, was formed by a group of disreputable investors who named the company after Paul B. Ford, a day laborer they hired. The Ford Tractor was a three-wheeled vehicle with two drive wheels in front, and a steering wheel in the rear. The tractor was assembled in Minneapolis from a variety

FROM ST. PAUL TO LONDON – ENGLAND'S
FARM PRODUCTIONS WILL BE HELPED BY
500 STAUDE MAK·A·TRACTORS

The nineteen-year run of the Model T car gave rise to a flourishing aftermarket industry for accessories and attachments. One of the largest companies was the Staude Mak-a-Tractor in St. Paul, which provided attachments that converted the Model T to a tractor. Courtesy of the Minnesota Historical Society.

THE FORD TRACTOR

$350

Fully Equipped, including Magneto, Carburetor, Governor and Oiler.
Develops 8-H. P. at draw-bar and 16-H. P. at belt.

Will be with you at Minnesota State Fair, September, 6-11.	*Some choice territory still open to live agents. Write today.*

THE FORD TRACTOR COMPANY
2625 University Ave. S. E.
MINNEAPOLIS, MINN.

Henry Ford did not produce a tractor until 1917, which opened the door for others to capitalize on the Ford name. In 1915, a group of disreputable promoters in Minneapolis introduced the Ford Tractor, which had no connection to the Ford Motor Company. It was an inferior product, and officials of the company were ultimately brought up on criminal charges. From *Farm Implements* magazine, August 31, 1915.

of stock parts. Capital was raised through an aggressive advertising campaign to the general public, with the motto "Do work better and cheaper than horses." The Ford Tractor Company started production in 1915, two years before Henry Ford's tractor. It was launched with extensive marketing and promotions, including an exhibit at the Minnesota State Fair, but it quickly ran into trouble owing to poor design and manufacturing. Some farmers did not receive their promised tractors and could not get their seventy-five-dollar deposits back. Within a year, disgruntled shareholders forced the company into liquidation. Its executives were charged in New York federal court with mail fraud, and one of principals reportedly fled the country. The unpleasant experience caused at least one state to enact regulations that required minimum performance standards for tractors.

Two years after the three-story subassembly plant on University Avenue in St. Paul opened it was converted to sales and service operations. This was part of Ford's ongoing experiments in adjusting the marketing and distribution system. In July 1916, Ford designated the building as a "direct factory branch . . . for distribution in parts of Wisconsin and southern Minnesota," taking that territory away from the Minneapolis branch agency. W. H. Schmelzel was transferred from Fargo to run the new operation. Schmelzel started working for Ford in 1912 as a retail salesman in the Omaha branch agency. Within ten months, he had become its leading salesman and was promoted to assistant manager. In 1915, Ford appointed him manager of the Fargo agency, where he sold more cars than the Minneapolis branch agency at a time when North Dakota did not have a mile of paved roads.

Schmelzel got off to a very fast start in St. Paul, outselling his colleagues in Minneapolis by a wide margin. Henry Ford was so impressed he brought him to Detroit and made him assistant manager of sales for the company. Ford probably decided at that time to close the sales office in St. Paul, and to consolidate operations with the Minneapolis branch agency. Schmelzel preferred selling cars to managing and must have suggested to Ford his desire to return to St. Paul as an independent dealer. In April 1917, he established the W. H. Schmelzel Company and received a contract to operate a dealership as a tenant in the former sub-assembly plant in St. Paul. He was no longer an employee. The standard dealership agreement signed by Schmelzel included a number of responsibilities and restrictions. The dealership entity could not include the name Ford as the company tried to maintain some degree of legal separation. Dealers could not disparage Ford or other dealers in their advertising. Dealers were obligated to use only Ford replacement parts, but in consideration of carrying a large inventory they earned a 40 percent commission on the sale of those parts. Schmelzel was given a specified sales territory, which included St. Paul and much of its surrounding suburbs, but not on an exclusive basis. Schmelzel approached his new venture with enthusiasm, and joined various local trade and civic organizations. By 1920, his agency was selling more than one thousand vehicles a year with six sales staff. Repair and service work brought in considerable additional revenue.

When Ford established a branch sales agency in Minneapolis in 1912, it terminated its agreement with the Northwestern Automobile Company. By 1920, however, Ford reversed course as he concluded that salaried company employees were not as productive as independent distributors or dealers working on commission. Additionally, Ford instituted a major change in his dealership agreements by eliminating the exclusive right to a defined sales territory, which had given some measure of security. Nevins observed "The company felt that the fixed territory plan represented both an abuse and a nuisance: a nuisance because when an energetic dealer made a sale in another's territory, the company had to fix percentages of profit, often in dispute; an abuse because lazy dealers were inclined not to push sales, but to demand their 'take' on a more industrious agent's work." Ford's elimination of the fixed-territory plan quickly became the industry norm. Ford's dealings

Shortly after it opened, the subassembly plant on University Avenue in St. Paul was leased to the W. H. Schmelzel Company, which operated a Ford car dealership. This business was initially successful but failed largely because of Henry Ford's harsh and conflicting policies toward dealers. A series of other dealers attempted to operate in the building after Schmelzel, but all suffered the same fate and closed. Author's collection.

with his dealers turned increasingly harsh. According to Keith Sward, "In place of the earlier two-sided instrument, it substituted franchises which were mere permits to do business. The new relationship had neither temporal guarantees nor any legal status. It could be canceled at a moment's notice, at Ford's discretion."

The system of independent dealerships was indispensable for automobile companies. It would have been prohibitively expensive and unmanageable for car manufacturers to operate sales outlets all over the country. In 1908, more than half the population lived in towns of fewer than five thousand, and these communities had a much higher per-capita automobile usage than larger cities. In Minnesota, more cars were sold to farmers than to any other group. Because so many dealerships were needed in small towns, manufacturers concluded that it was better to "outsource" the sales and servicing function to independent dealers, along with the task of monitoring customer experiences and generally representing the company. To the car buyer, the dealer was the car company, a perception reinforced by the obvious level of control exerted by the manufacturer.

The system enabled car companies to vertically integrate without significant financial cost or liability. Friedrich Kessler observed in his article "Automobile Dealer Franchises: Vertical Integration by Contract": "Through their dominant economic position, the manufacturers have employed the franchise, 'a one sided document which is neither contract, license, or agreement,' to gain maximum control over the management of the dealers' business without corresponding 'legal' responsibility. Under the terms of the franchise, 'the factories give the orders and the dealer takes the losses.'" To protect their interests, dealers formed the National Association of Automobile Dealers in 1917 and the organization frequently challenged franchise agreements in the courts and legislatures.

The Fordson Tractor and Henry Ford & Son, Inc.

Schmelzel's car dealership was initially successful, but his second venture with Ford proved to be disastrous. In 1917 Schmelzel signed a contract to distribute Fordson tractors throughout Minnesota with Henry Ford & Son, Inc., a legally separate entity from the Ford Motor Company, which held his car dealership agreement. Henry Ford's venture into manufacturing tractors was anything but straightforward. In 1915 he announced plans for a new tractor factory, claiming that the tractor was always his primary goal and that automobiles were merely a necessary interlude. "The tractor is and always has been my pet hobby," Ford said. "It is something that will do much toward the betterment of mankind, and that is what I am largely interested in." He believed his tractor would bring about social change, particularly in Europe: "Vast estates will be a thing of the past. They will be supplanted by producing farms. The nobles will be forced to give way to the common people, and then the English people will once more get back to the soil."

The tractor project and its numerous problems originated deep within the psyche of Henry Ford. Anne Jardim, in her book *The First Henry Ford: A Study in Personality and Business Leadership*, observed: "Indeed [Ford's] twenty-five-track mind comes more and more to look like a single track of the narrowest gauge, intercepted by spurs leading nowhere, and laid out in an inexorable line from the farm and the farmer to the farmer's car." Jardim believed that "The Farmer" became "an abstract entity for which [Ford] could admit a compassion that was entirely lacking in his conscious relationship to the elder Ford." Ford was thirteen when his mother died during childbirth, and Jardim argued that this traumatic experience led to Henry's subconscious rejection of his father, a successful farmer who wished that his son would take over the family farm.

Young Henry rejected farming and sought to escape at a very young age. In rationalizing his actions, he maintained that he left because his father did not support his mechanical tinkering, but this is not supported by the recollections of his older sister and is contradicted by the fact that the elder Ford helped his son find work as a mechanic in Detroit. In a revealing interview, Ford said, "I never had any particular love for the farm, it was the mother on the farm I loved . . . You know, farm work is drudgery of the hardest sort. From the time I left that gate as a boy until now my only interest in a farm has been to lighten its labors. To take the load off the backs of men and put it onto metal has been my dream. If I can do that I shall have rendered a real service to humanity—the sort of service she tried to teach me to perform."

Ford started his tractor experiments by 1910 and had created a working model by 1915. He did not involve his partners, principally the Dodge brothers, in this venture. Outraged that company funds were being used to develop the tractor and even build a factory for that purpose, they filed a lawsuit in November 1916 demanding that Ford distribute dividends from the accumulated profits of the car company, which had reached the astounding level of $50 million (more than $1 billion in present value). Ford had other plans—he wanted to build the River Rouge plant, not only for his tractor, but also to consolidate all his operations into a vertically integrated, self-contained manufacturing colossus. M. Todd Henderson summed up the partnership conflict: "Like many entrepreneurs, Ford was stubborn, arrogant, confident in his own abilities, and fiercely independent. Although he needed other people's money to turn his ideas into reality, Ford, like most inventors, didn't want their opinions or their oversight—just the money."

Ford continued work on the Rouge plant, but had to reimburse the Ford Motor Company forty-six thousand dollars for the use of company employees and equipment, and agreed to not use the Ford name for his tractor, calling it the Fordson instead. (The scandal with the Ford Tractor Company in Minneapolis may have had a part in the decision as well.) In late July 1917, Ford formally incorporated Henry Ford & Son, Inc., and put the Fordson tractors on the market in October. The Dodge brothers won an injunction on December 5, 1917, barring Ford from using company funds for the River Rouge complex and directing him to make dividend payments to the corporate shareholders. Ford appealed the decision, even as he was preparing to buy out his partners if necessary. The purpose of Henry Ford & Son, according to the incorporation papers, was "to manufacture tractors, agricultural implements and appliances and self-propelling vehicles and mechanisms of every description," which clearly left the door open for setting up another car company. He had used this tactic previously to pressure different partners in 1905 when he established the Ford Manufacturing Company under very similar circumstances.

The Fordson

ISSUED EACH WEEK BY THE W. H. SCHMELZEL CO., SAINT PAUL, MINN.
In the interest of Fordson Dealers in Minnesota

JUNE 20, 1919

Fordson Tractor

NEW PRICE ON "FORDSON" TRACTORS EFFECTIVE
JUNE 17TH, 1919.

$750.00

F. O. B. DEARBORN

All dealers have been notified by telephone and letter of the change in price as shown above.

If you have placed your order to care for present needs, all well and good; if not, better wire, write or telephone before it's too late and the supply exhausted. We cannot possibly provide you with all the "FORDSONS" you can sell during harvest and fall, therefore, act quick. **Phone Your Shipping Orders Today!**

Nothing but **immediate orders** accepted at this time, which means early July delivery to you.

In addition to operating a car dealership, Schmelzel was the Minnesota distributor for the Fordson tractor. As with the car dealership, this venture got caught up in Henry Ford's evolving policies for marketing and distribution. Schmelzel and his associates ultimately sued Ford to recoup their losses. Author's collection.

Schmelzel, who had worked for Ford in Detroit in 1916, was certainly aware of the conflict between Henry Ford and the Dodge brothers, and knew that Ford would have to use independent distributors to market the Fordson rather than his automobile dealership network. Schmelzel asked to be the distributor in Minnesota. As a condition of receiving a contract, Henry Ford required Schmelzel, and all other Fordson distributors, to sell one thousand tractors in their sales territory during a trial period at cost—without any commission. He also required a letter from the governor of each state pledging their cooperation and assistance in the mass distribution effort. These stipulations further underscored the extent to which he saw his Fordson tractors as a public service and not a normal commercial venture. When finally produced, Ford's tractors did indeed "take the load off the backs of men and put it onto metal," but top company officials feared they were doing so at a financial loss. Ford reluctantly agreed to do an audit. When told the company was losing fifty-five dollars per tractor, Ford responded: "I'm glad of it. If we can give the farmer $55 with every tractor that's just what I want." Ford's sentiment was heightened by the start of World War I, which placed a premium on food production. He believed that the Fordson would become as popular as the Model T, and that distributors would readily recoup their investment of selling one thousand tractors at cost. Schmelzel concurred and moved quickly to distribute his quota.

As a Fordson distributor, Schmelzel became a "middleman," a wholesaler who found independent dealers to sell the tractor directly to farmers. Ford no longer used distributors to sell cars, but because of the lawsuit with the Dodge brothers he reverted back to that system for his tractors. Schmelzel, therefore, had two agreements with Ford, as a dealer for Model T cars and as the Minnesota distributor of Fordson tractors.

Schmelzel established tractor dealerships all over the state, including a number at Ford automobile agencies. He organized tractor demonstrations and a well-attended event at the state fair in June 1918. Later that year he used Fordson tractors for a community service project, clearing a landing field in St. Paul's Desnoyer Park for the nearby aviation training center. For a while, Schmelzel operated his tractor distributorship alongside his car dealership at the Ford Building in St. Paul, but with his business expanding and lingering concern about the ongoing litigation, he decided he needed a separate building for tractors.

At a meeting of Fordson distributors in Detroit in December 1918, Schmelzel told Charles E. Sorensen of his plans to build a two-story structure on University Avenue in the Midway of St. Paul for his tractor business. Sorensen, who was second -in command after Henry Ford and manager of the Fordson project, responded: "That is not what you want. You want acres, not feet. Don't buy space in feet and put up a building in air. That is not the modern way of building. The modern way is to buy acres and spread it out one story high . . . this tractor business is going to be bigger than the automobile business, and if you are going to hold your distribution contract and be prepared for this business and to handle this business, you have got to have the facilities for it." Schmelzel found a ten-acre lot at Rice and Atwater Streets, just north of the state capitol, and retained prominent local architect Clarence Johnston to design a "modern distributing depot."

In February 1919, Fordson distributors met again at a convention in Kansas City, Missouri. Rumors had been circulating that Henry Ford would end the distributor system and transfer the responsibility for selling Fordson tractors to his automobile dealerships. Given the mounting anxiety among distributors who had invested heavily in starting their companies, Charles E. Sorensen addressed the issue head-on. According to Schmelzel and other distributors, he explicitly denied the rumors, and gave assurances that the two systems would never be merged. After the meeting, Schmelzel showed Sorensen his architectural plans for the new warehouse. Henry Ford happened to stop by Sorensen's office and also saw the plans, but he deferred to Sorensen, who approved the plans. Given what he felt were ironclad promises, Schmelzel bought the ten-acre parcel five days later and built the warehouse.

The rumors about merging distribution systems and the conflict with the Dodge brothers continued, however, fueled by a number of pronouncements from Henry and Edsel Ford. In March 1919, Ford suggested to reporters that they would part ways with the Ford Motor Company and set up a new company to build a $250 car. The Dodge brothers recognized that this announcement was intended to pressure them to sell, but Henry Ford claimed he would keep his Ford stock and was merely trying to make a car for the working man that would compete with the streetcar. Another published report speculated that Ford was getting ready to sell to General Motors. The issue was finally resolved in late July 1919 when Henry Ford agreed to buy out the Dodge brothers, leaving him in full control of both companies. An anxious Schmelzel was reassured to receive a sales agreement on September 6, 1919, to distribute five thousand tractors with a fixed commission rate of forty dollars per unit, but his relief was short-lived. Just two weeks later, on September 23, 1919, Charles Sorenson gave notice to all "distributing organizations" that Henry Ford & Son, Inc., would be "dispensed with" and merged with the Ford Motor Company, which would take over all distribution responsibilities. On July 31, 1920, Schmelzel's tractor contract was terminated, only months after his company moved into its new warehouse. In late December 1919, Henry Ford resigned as president of the Ford Motor Company to pursue his many other interests. His son Edsel assumed the presidency, a post he held until his untimely death in 1943.

Relations between Schmelzel and executives at Ford had been strained for some time even before the sales agreement was terminated. The tractor industry was very competitive, with many companies already in operation long before Ford launched the Fordson. Being the eyes and ears of the manufacturer in the field, Schmelzel regularly reported back to officials in Detroit about other tractors being distributed in Minnesota, giving sales figures and customer reactions. He would also give feedback on problems with the Fordson. Initially, there were some performance issues with the Fordson, as with any new

The signage on Schmelzel's trucks lists his office location in the Ford Building, and his Fordson tractor warehouse and showroom at Rice and Atwater Streets, St. Paul, which also carried many attachments and accessory products. Author's collection.

product. Henry Ford may have felt rushed to bring it out sooner than he planned because of the wartime need to increase food production. Although most of the problems were relatively minor, a number of drivers were killed when the tractor flipped over backwards, leading to charges of negligent design.

Minnesota Fordson dealers who worked closely with farmers were impatient with Ford's slow response to address the problems. In late 1918, a group of dealers signed a petition urging Ford's prompt attention, which Schmelzel forwarded to officials in Detroit. They were not pleased that Schmelzel appeared to sanction what they perceived to be an open insurrection. Occasionally, Schmelzel's reports would present customer feedback that compared some features of the Fordson unfavorably to other tractors. Rather than accept the comments as constructive criticism, Ford officials were incensed.

In March 1919, Schmelzel passed along a proposal from a Minnesota farmer to improve the malfunctioning governor, a part that was used to measure and regulate the tractor engine's speed. The farmer had invented a simple adjustment and was willing to bring some drawings to Detroit to share with company officials. Charles Sorensen fired back to Schmelzel:

> Anybody that you cared to send us now, I know will only be in the way, and would only take up a lot of time that we would care to spend on a good many other things which are of more importance at this particular time. I feel that at the present time, there is a great need of orders for tractors. If I were you, I would avoid inventors and governor experts in every way possible and do everything in my power to get more orders, for that is the thing that we need more than anything else in the world right now.

Two years later a Fordson dealer in upstate New York was still having problems with the faulty governor, and he learned of a part that was commercially available that he installed on all his tractors. He said, "We think that if every dealer would install a Superior Governor on the Fordson, half of the hardships on the part of the salesman would be ended." Ford engineers eventually modified the part, which greatly improved the tractor's performance. The Fordson went on to become the industry leader, with widespread sales around the world.

Schmelzel also had strained relations with many of his dealers over the issue of tractor attachments. Tractors require a variety of implements and attachments, which were often sold through the Fordson dealerships. Schmelzel spent considerable time monitoring the performance of attachments designed for the Fordson tractor, including plows, spreaders, bailers, threshers, and drills. Implement manufacturers eagerly sought Ford's approval of their products, and Schmelzel often arranged for field tests and demonstrations. The Fordson was designed to be a "universal" tractor, but it often had to be customized for local planting and climate conditions around the country. The sale of these implements and attachments provided a substantial source of revenue for the Schmelzel company. Some dealers under Schmelzel complained to Ford management that he was pushing them to buy unnecessary equipment as a condition of receiving tractors. Others claimed he practiced favoritism with dealers who sold the most implements. Schmelzel argued that he had to find ways to reward the high-performing dealers. Some dealers believed that Schmelzel was trying to recoup some of the expenses he incurred in selling the first thousand tractors without receiving a commission. One dealer accused Schmelzel of intentionally deceiving Ford by pretending to break up sales territory into a number of smaller companies, when in reality it was one larger company with multiple names.

Ford officials caught wind of the dealer discontent and showed little understanding for Schmelzel's difficult job as a distributor. Schmelzel was caught in the cross fire between his seventy dealers, his customers, and the top management in Detroit, whose only concern was the number of tractors sold. A letter from Ernest Kanzler, a top Ford official, to Schmelzel in June 1919 captured the frosty tone: "You are a gentleman business man who has his large office, makes his many telephone calls and calls in dealers to see him, but you are not the kind who goes out with a big club banging around the territory and overcoming sales resistance wherever it is encountered."

The tension and uncertainty lifted on July 31, 1920, when Ford formally terminated Schmelzel's contract for distributing tractors. However, he retained his car dealership at the Ford Building, which he had renewed just a few weeks earlier. Schmelzel reported on a Dealer's Questionnaire that he had six car salesmen, one tractor salesman, and sixty-five mechanics. The high proportion of mechanics gives some idea of the economic importance of the service and repair business to his dealership. He estimated that his company did sixty repairs a day, but he had the capacity to do seventy-five to one hundred. Schmelzel estimated that he could sell 1,308 cars and twenty tractors (as dealer, not distributor) that year.

Ever the innovator, in 1921 Schmelzel offered a free course for mechanics on servicing and repairing Ford cars and trucks. This incorporated 1,800 feet of "animated film" made by his company "to illustrate the points that will be made by the experts." This was presumably a part of Ford's continuing effort to "rationalize" the repair process. In early 1921, Schmelzel sold his company to his vice president and brother-in-law, J. W. Hutchins, because he was "seeking health in the south." Ford accepted the transfer and J. W. Hutchins assumed the lease for the Ford Building, but this arrangement was short-lived. Just months later, on July 1, 1921, Ford entered into a sales agreement and lease with the M. J. Osborn Company to operate the Ford dealership at 117 University Avenue. Schmelzel and Hutchins lost most of their investment. But for them the matter was far from over. In 1923 the J. W. Hutchins Co. filed a lawsuit against the Ford Motor Company and Henry Ford & Son, Inc. for $627,817. The filing papers for the lawsuit offer a remarkable inside look at those turbulent times as Henry Ford was sorting out the many complex issues relating to car dealerships and the distribution of the Fordson tractors. The lawsuit did not go to trial; it is likely that Ford settled because Schmelzel and Hutchins seemed to have a very strong case. By that time, Ford had turned his interest to planning a new building in St. Paul, and the publicity from the trial would not have helped his public campaign to secure the hydroelectric permit.

New Dealers at the Ford Building Face Problems

As a young man, M. J. Osborn moved to St. Paul from Indianapolis to work for Hamm's Brewery selling a medicinal malt extract called Digesto. He switched fields in 1910 to take a job with the Schurmeier Motor Company, which had partnered with Herbert Bigelow in a truck manufacturing venture. Bigelow was also an owner of the very successful Brown and Bigelow Company, the largest printer of remembrance advertising in the country. Bigelow's truck venture failed, but Osborn stayed in the automobile field. Over the next several decades, he was a dealer for the White Steamer Touring Car, White Motor Trucks, Willys-Overland car, and the Willys-Knight car. Osborn had also been a Ford dealer in Farmington and Hastings, Minnesota, where he had earlier found favor with W. H. Schmelzel for being willing "to take a lot of implements far greater in numbers than the three dealers whose territory he absorbed." Osborn's experience with tractors also included a stint as receiver for the bankrupt Minneapolis-based Nilson Tractor Co. When Osborn opened his dealership, the Ford Motor Company was selling one of every three cars in the United States, and these investments were generally perceived to be safe and lucrative investments. He was clearly qualified to operate the Ford dealership in 1921, but he would soon face a variety of challenges he had not anticipated.

Merritt J. Osborn and other dealers operated at a time when Ford was sorting out his distribution policies, which created a great deal of uncertainty and anxiety. They also had to deal with his arbitrary policy edicts on a variety of issues and other disruptive activities. Henry Ford, who had nominally relinquished his position as president of the company, started a highly publicized anti-Semitic campaign in May 1920 in a weekly newspaper he had acquired, the *Dearborn Independent*. This campaign, discussed in greater detail in chapter 2, alienated many potential customers and caused considerable hardship for dealers, who were particularly incensed because they also had to sell subscriptions to this scurrilous newspaper. The backlash caused at least one dealer in southern Minnesota to lose his lease. In addition, automobile dealers were now required to sell Fordson tractors—even those like Osborn who were located in urban areas. In response to dealer complaints, the company said, "Dealers are supposed to exert themselves . . . and every dealer who has received tractors will sell them as soon as he gets to work. And getting to work on tractors will but keep him in good merchandising condition to keep his sales of cars up."

Even dealers in rural areas had problems selling the Fordson. "Tractor sales have not been exceptionally good," said L. B. Luther, office manager of the Tenvoorde Ford agency. "The farms in central Minnesota are not large and until very recently the price of tractors has not made their use profitable to the small farmer." The policy of marketing tractors

Henry Ford's policies about advertising changed over the years. As he shifted costs entirely to dealers, many resorted to creative marketing techniques. The Owens Motor Company in St. Paul built a replica locomotive that became a popular fixture in community parades. Courtesy of the Rihm Motor Company.

and cars together proved to be difficult and ultimately weakened Ford's brand at a time when competitors were going more upscale. Dealers were also irritated that they were expected to support Ford's numerous other interests and hobbies. They had to sell coal on occasion, and the company's fertilizer, which was produced as a manufacturing by-product, and even support Ford's political and environmental advocacy campaigns.

Ford's advertising policies also hurt his relationship with his dealers. In the early years, Ford advertised heavily throughout the country, but as his fame grew, especially after his "$5 a day" announcement in 1914, he felt he no longer had to advertise. Henry Ford had indeed managed to garner millions of lines of free publicity on the front pages of newspapers around the country. The Associated Advertising Clubs of the World conference voted him the "Best Advertised Man," declaring that there were "two kinds of automobile advertisers—first those who pay for their advertising and second, Henry Ford." Ford discontinued advertising altogether by World War I and shifted that responsibility entirely to local dealers. In 1920, Ford modified its approach by providing advertising copy to dealers, but still without any funding.

On September 15, 1923, Ford announced yet another approach. The company established an advertising department that would prepare copy and split the expense for advertising with the dealers. However, the ads were generic, aimed at a national audience, and did little to promote individual dealers on a local level. Some dealers felt compelled to invest in additional advertising to highlight their local connections. Occasionally, Ford and the dealers would run cooperative ads for a number of dealers within the same city, as occurred in Minneapolis and St. Paul. Some people speculated that Ford's renewed interest in advertising in late 1923 was a transparent effort to raise his national profile as he was preparing to launch a presidential campaign. Keith Sward reported that key staff members had organized Ford for President clubs around the country and were "prepared to flood the Ford dealer organization with free copies of a Ford biography specially prepared for the coming campaign. The mailing list of Ford's 7,000 dealers was made available to the Ford-for-President Club of Dearborn."

Even with all the burdens that dealers faced, none could have imagined the crushing blow they received in 1921 when Ford shipped more than $80 million in unordered inventory. Ford had needed to borrow $60 million to buy out the Dodge brothers to end

The Owens Motor Company sponsored athletic teams to promote its dealership, and a marching band, seen outside its building. Courtesy of the Rihm Motor Company.

the lawsuit, and the bank note was coming due. To avoid giving up control of the company to bankers, he concocted an audacious plan—raise the money from his dealers. He shipped his entire inventory of automobiles and parts valued at more than $80 million from Detroit to showrooms around the country. Dealers received about 10 percent of their yearly quota, without any advance notice, and they had no choice but to pay for the goods or risk losing their franchise.

Many dealers found a way to pay for the unwanted inventory by borrowing from their banks, but M. J. Osborn was apparently one who was unable or unwilling to make the payments. He was forced to sell the dealership he had just opened. The dealers resented Ford's outrageous scheme, but financiers were in awe. One banker told the *New York Times* that Ford "had performed a feat that will probably go down in the annals of financial history as one of the most remarkable achievements of postwar liquidation." And another said, "Mr. Ford is an absolute genius at organization and efficiency." Within one year, Ford had dug out from his debt and was well positioned for the next wave of corporate expansion.

Osborn was forced to sell his agency, but it turned out to be a blessing in disguise. He took his last five thousand dollars and established the Economics Laboratory, Inc., the forerunner of Ecolab, Inc., which is now a $3 billion company with more than fifteen thousand employees headquartered in St. Paul. Many years later, Osborn was still known as an unabashed car buff. He sold his used 1953 Cadillac to a work associate at Ecolab, whose daughter was present at the transaction. She recalled suggesting to Osborn that he was such brilliant salesman that he should go into the car business. "Oh, little girl," said M. J., "I did that more than once and failed, so I started making soap!"

A. C. Hall and H. F. Herschbach, who were described as "Old Auto Men," purchased the Osborn agency in 1922 and moved from Springfield, Illinois, where they had been operating a dealership. They selected St. Paul as their headquarters "because of the unique advantage in being the gateway to a great and growing Northwest." One of their early newspaper ads touted "Good Used Fords, all models, at prices $35 and up." Another advertisement offered cars with the "Ford Weekly Purchase Plan" with a five-dollar down payment. This program was instituted to compete with the financing plans offered by General Motors and other manufacturers. Ford had resisted offering a real financing plan because of his reluctance to deal with bankers. His option was little more than a basic layaway plan. Prospective buyers could make weekly payments for a new car to either a dealer or a participating bank until the purchase price was reached. Under some circumstances, "where good references can be given the car will be delivered when one-third the price has been paid in accordance with the regular deferred payment plan." This proved to be woefully unappealing in contrast to the genuine financing plans of other companies.

Ford acquired the Lincoln Motor Company in a distressed sale in 1922. Dealers were then required to carry the upscale car alongside the Model T and the Fordson tractor. They complained about the challenges of such a varied product line as they were struggling to compete with the popular Chevrolet. This picture, circa 1925, shows the showroom window of the A. M. Smith Company in Minneapolis. Photograph by the *Minneapolis Journal*. Courtesy of the Minnesota Historical Society.

Ford dealers faced other significant problems, including the steep drop in sales of the Model T. Other manufacturers, particularly GM with its Chevrolet brand, were introducing new models every year that were reasonably priced and attractive alternatives to the now old-fashioned Model T car. The expanding used-car market was also beginning to cut into Ford's price advantage. After 1919, more used cars were sold than new cars. Henry Ford refused to believe the problem was his cherished Model T. He blamed the sales decline on his dealers.

In 1922, Ford acquired the Lincoln Motor Company in a distressed sale from his old nemesis Henry Leland, who had helped force him out of his second automobile company in 1902. During the negotiations it was widely assumed that the Lincoln brand would continue to operate as an independent subsidiary, but Ford decided to sell the Lincolns through his Ford dealerships, alongside the Model T and Fordson. Some former Lincoln dealers groused that "buying a Lincoln at a Ford agency was like buying expensive jewelry at a Five-and-Ten store." Clearly, the Ford brand would tend to get muddled with the Model T, Lincoln, and the Fordson tractor side by side in the showrooms. However, the Lincoln brand did help Ford compete with General Motors, which had adopted a strategy of producing a car for every price range.

Morale and profits for Ford dealers plummeted, and several banks withdrew lines of credit. Some of Ford's best dealers switched to the Chevrolet brand, accelerating the company's decline. Henry Ford stubbornly refused to replace the Model T. In Detroit, Edsel Ford and W. A. Ryan, the company's head of marketing, were aware of the rising tensions with dealers, and in 1922 they embarked on a national goodwill tour. They visited Minneapolis, where they were feted with a parade of 150 Ford vehicles. To boost dealer morale, they announced that the company was increasing sales commissions on cars from 17.5 percent to 20 percent, and on tractors to 25 percent. This improved relations in the short term, but the following year Ford intensified the resented "crossroads policy." Not only did Ford eliminate protected sales territories, he greatly increased the number of dealerships around the country. From 1923 to 1926, Ford added 1,300 new dealerships—some just blocks away from older established dealers. More agencies were now competing for a shrinking share of the market. Ford believed this would help keep the price of cars down because dealers would have little choice but to reduce commissions in an effort to stay in business. Hall and Hershbach, at the Ford Building, were now in competition with two other dealerships along University Avenue, Owens Motor Sales and Muessel Motor Company, as well as several others in St. Paul. After getting off to a slow start, Tenvoorde Ford in St. Cloud sold more than one thousand Ford vehicles by 1922. Ford's experiments and misguided policies took a toll on the morale and fortunes of most dealers. By 1926, it was estimated that 70 percent were losing money.

It was a tumultuous and extraordinary decade for Henry Ford. He broke the chokehold of a bogus patent, created the Model T and the Fordson tractor, launched a national plant expansion program, developed the movable assembly line, introduced the five-dollar day, sorted out his sales and marketing strategy, forced unhappy partners out of his company, and, most important, achieved his goal of creating a car for the masses. While the turmoil swirled around Ford and his company, cars continued to be assembled at the ten-story plant in Minneapolis. But Henry Ford concluded that it was time to build a manufacturing facility in the Twin Cities that met all his modern production requirements.

Drawn to the River

Hydroelectric Power, Navigation, and a New Plant in St. Paul

Ford had twenty-eight branch factories in the United States by 1916, but none was designed to accommodate the assembly line and few could be retrofitted. The footprint of multistory buildings was generally too small, and most had centrally located freight elevators, making it difficult to add assembly lines or conveyors. The long Highland Park, Michigan, plant was able to add an assembly line. At the plant in Atlanta the railroad tracks that ran through the center were removed and an assembly line was installed. The Minneapolis plant managed to insert a ninety-foot assembly line, but this was considerably shorter than the one thousand-feet-long lines that Ford wanted. He decided to scrap most of his existing multistory assembly plants by 1919. Very few manufacturers who had just invested millions of dollars in a network of assembly plants would have been willing to underwrite a second major expansion, but Ford was committed to making a car for the masses and he needed a new building type.

A Ford executive described the process: "I insisted that the Layout Department . . . give me a layout so that the column spacing would be correct and so there would be no interference with the assembly lines, drying ovens, and other installations. In other words, we built the buildings around the layouts." Albert Kahn, the prominent industrial architect, worked with the Ford engineers and designed the new structures, which were typically long, single-story structures. These were located on sites large enough to also accommodate parking, railroad sidings, and future expansion. Parking was a new concern, as an estimated 7,500 workers parked their cars at Ford's Dearborn plant, and

The Minneapolis plant was functionally obsolete because of the development of the movable assembly line. Ford did manage to squeeze a small section of an assembly line into the building several years after it was completed. Author's collection.

by 1929, fifty thousand workers were driving to the Rouge plant, which had set aside 122 acres for parking. The size of these new parking lots showed the enormous impact the automobile was having on shaping the built environment.

Architects and engineers developed the conceptual design of the new industrial plants in a straightforward, rational manner. But Henry Ford decided on the location of the plants and how they would relate to the overall business plan—and this thought-process was far less rational. The popularity of the Model T, the financial success of the company, and the incredible acclaim of his five-dollar-a-day program had a liberating effect on Ford, freeing him to pursue a number of personal interests that were sometimes described as "distinctly utopian." Ford's worldview encompassed a wide range of interests and beliefs, including pacifism, environmentalism, square dancing, anti-Semitism, collecting Americana, and an aversion to bankers, unions, monopolies, smoking, milk, and alcohol. Ford's pacifism would especially complicate the ability of his company to operate during the two world wars, and colored his relationships with the military on issues relating to navigation, hydropower, and aviation. Ford would look for ways to incorporate these varied personal interests into his business operations, including selecting the site for the new plant in the Twin Cities.

Ford had a commitment to farmers that could be described as going beyond that of a hardheaded business calculation. Ford not only built a tractor, he wanted to bring "The Farmer" directly into the automobile manufacturing process. His goal was to "grow" all the raw materials needed for a car. Ford spent millions of dollars on soybean research that yielded new plastics for auto bodies and steering wheels. Harry G. Ukkelberg, a Minnesota native and agricultural chemist who graduated from the University of Minnesota, headed up efforts to find new industrial applications from agricultural crops, including exotic plants from around the world. Ford conducted biofuel experiments and made alcohol from cull sweet potatoes that was mixed with gasoline. Henry Ford was confident that biofuels would replace gasoline, but his research was restricted during Prohibition.

Ford's obsession with "The Farmer" even played a role in his most bizarre and troubling foray, the anti-Semitic campaign launched in his weekly newspaper the *Dearborn Independent, Chronicler of the Neglected Truth*. His slurs resulted in several libel suits, including one with a Minnesota connection. Aaron Sapiro was a Chicago lawyer who organized more than sixty farm cooperatives that generated $400 million in annual revenues. Ford wrote in the *Dearborn Independent* that "a band of Jews—bankers, lawyers, money-lenders, advertising agencies,

Henry Ford proclaimed that he would "grow" all the raw materials needed for a car, and he invested heavily in plant research. A Ford agricultural scientist stands next to a full-grown soybean plant. Ford used soybean plastic for a number of parts for the car, and he even built experimental car bodies from soybean plastic. Author's collection.

fruit-packers, produce-buyers—is on the back of the American farmer." One of the articles in the *Independent* described at length the reputed mismanagement of the Minnesota Potato Growers Exchange, operated by an associate of Sapiro. Ford seemingly went after Sapiro with a particular vengeance not just because he advocated for "organizing agriculture like industry," which smacked of trade unionism, or that he was a Jew, but because Sapiro had committed the ultimate offense of affronting Ford's mystical belief in "The Farmer." Another article in the *Dearborn Independent* was titled "How the 'Jewish Question' Touches the Farm." "The Jew," it states, "is not an agriculturalist"; only "land that produces gold from the mine, and land that produces rents" interests him. The article warned "of a new movement" fueled by "Jewish millions" that would take over the independent family farm. The newspaper even offered a one thousand–dollar reward to anybody who could identify a Jewish farmer.

Ford's anti-Semitic campaign was widely criticized. Although the response in Minnesota was not as strong as in other places, Minneapolis rabbi Dr. S. N. Deinard wrote a stinging rebuke in the *Minneapolis Morning Tribune* pointing out the dangers of not standing up to Ford's "dastardly, malevolent campaign." Ford was oblivious to the fact that his bizarre anti-Semitism hurt the profitability of the company and its dealers. Ernest Liebold, the Ford executive who led the anti-Semitic campaign, wrote to a Minnesota dealer who was being threatened with eviction that he should "buy his own building where he would be immune from such pressures."

An editorial in the *Minneapolis Morning Tribune* in 1920 reflected on Ford's strange odyssey:

> Mr. Ford is a successful manufacturer of automobiles. In his mechanical field, he is a wizard. But now and then he issues forth in the role of publicist, statesman, and social thinker—only invariably to make the gods laugh at his manifold ineptitudes and follies. Why a man who, if he kept his mouth closed, would command universal respect, should elect to make himself ridiculous by talking on subjects outside his sphere and beyond his knowledge is not easy to understand. Mr. Ford would do himself and the rest of the world an excellent service by confining himself to his knitting.

In 1925 Aaron Sapiro sued Ford for libel in what has been described by Victoria Saker Woeste as the first "hate speech case." Ford was in no mood for another court appearance given his disastrous showing in an earlier, unrelated lawsuit. Ford had sued the *Chicago Tribune* for libel after an editorial called him an "anarchist" because of his opposition to the American invasion of Mexico. During the trial, Ford was put on the stand and was humiliated for his ignorance of basic American history. At one point he uttered the infamous words "History is bunk." After that embarrassment, Ford was reluctant to be interrogated by Sapiro and caused numerous questionable delays in the trial. He finally settled the case with Sapiro by making a financial settlement to cover Sapiro's legal expenses. Ford also released a public apology, written by noted attorney Louis Marshall, that was published in the *Jewish Tribune*: "I sincerely regret any harm that may have been occasioned to the people of that great race and am anxious to make whatever amends are possible." Soon thereafter the *Dearborn Independent* ceased publication. There were many skeptics who questioned the sincerity of the apology. In any event, the damage was done and proved to be irreversible. Henry Ford was praised by Adolf Hitler in *Mein Kampf,* and in 1938, on his seventy-fifth birthday, he accepted the German Eagle medal from the Third Reich.

Decentralization and Hydroelectric Power

Ford's romanticized view of farmers and rural life mirrored his belief that cities had become unmanageable, as he told the *New York Times*:

> Cities have broken down. They cannot support their load. Centralization has been overdone. There is not a large city in the country where the burden on housing, sanitation, schools, lighting, transportation and telephone service is not too great. Every municipal problem can be traced to unnatural congestion. Cities are centers of social unrest and harbors of every passing craze. The city takes its food from grocery shelves and its opinions from minds too busy to think.

In Ford's view, the countryside provided more opportunities for a wholesome and fulfilling lifestyle, and he looked for ways to keep the farmer on the farm. He would do that by providing seasonal employment in rural villages through "industrial decentralization," and the key to achieving this was hydropower. Ford had a lifelong fascination with waterpower. As a child he experimented with a dam and waterwheel in his schoolyard and later built several small, but functioning, hydroelectric dams at his home. Working with Thomas Edison, he installed hydroelectric turbines at the powerhouse of his home in 1915, which was featured in a lengthy article in *Popular Science Monthly.*

Ford looked to Thomas Edison for more than technical advice. Edison was a mentor on a wide range of topics, the man he most admired and his closest friend. It was likely Edison who planted the idea for dispersed hydropower. Whatever the inspiration, Ford became the most visible advocate in the country for hydroelectric power, which he saw as nature's way of promoting decentralization. Industrial plants should be brought to the source of power rather than the other way around. Ford was not only a conceptual supporter, he had the resources to demonstrate its feasibility. "It is our idea," he said, "to develop the water power of small streams in the communities where they [farmers] are located and not transmit the power over long distances." He believed that farmers should harness every creek and brook that crossed their property. Ford was particularly taken with the Mississippi River, which he preached could "run the country" if the water could be harnessed. Hydroelectric technology had progressed to the point where it became economically viable on a larger scale. In 1918 Ford formally launched his "industry to the farm" program, committing millions of dollars to a "decentralization" strategy. Ford built a plant at Hamilton, Ohio, on the Little Miami River to turn out three hundred tractors a day. When the streams dried up during the summer months, he would release the workers to go back to their farms.

The following year, Ford took a highly publicized trip around the country looking for new factory sites. In California he underscored his intention to focus on sites that offered waterpower. He wanted to "dot the whole world with our factories" through his utopian Village Industries program. Old abandoned mills would be upgraded to accommo-

Henry Ford regularly went on camping trips with friends Thomas Edison, naturalist John Boroughs, and tire manufacturer Harvey Firestone. Ford believed that waterpower was the most environmentally friendly way to produce energy for his factories. From the collections of The Henry Ford (THF105476).

date modern industry. The Village Industries expansion used a completely unconventional approach, as described by John Robert Mullin: "it is a dictum of industry that production needs determine spatial requirements. Ford, in the case of the Village Industries, took the opposite view; that the size of the plant and the energy capacity of the river determined the product to be developed." Ford calculated that each horsepower generated could support the work of one employee. He developed approximately eighteen to thirty Village Industries plants—depending on who was counting and how the plants were defined.

Ford believed his Village Industries complemented the large urban factories. "A reciprocity can exist between farming and manufacturing," he wrote. "The manufacturer can give the farmer what he needs to be a good farmer, and the farmer and other producers of raw materials can give the manufacturer what he needs to be a good manufacturer. Then with transportation as a messenger, we shall have a stable and a sound system on built service." The Village Industries plants fabricated small parts and subassemblies such as screws, carburetors, and headlights that supplied the big factories in Detroit and Dearborn. They likely had more symbolic value than an actual economic benefit to the company. The financial records for the Village Industries plants were not even included in the company ledgers—they were always "Mr. Ford's" personal projects.

Ford was not alone at the time in supporting the concept of "decentralization" or its

Ford's admiration for waterpower led him to disperse or "decentralize" operations. He located small factories in the countryside near waterpower, with the goal of creating seasonal employment for farmers. The Nankin-Mills was one of Ford's smallest plants in the "Village Industries" program. Author's collection.

The size of a decentralized plant was dictated by the amount of waterpower produced by the adjacent river or stream. The Menomonie, Michigan, plant was a typical midsize facility. Author's collection.

Ford Motor Company Power Plant on Menominee River, Iron Mountain, Mich.—17

Several of Ford's decentralized plants were quite large, including the Green Island Plant on the Hudson River in New York State, which was the forerunner of the Twin Cities Assembly Plant. Author's collection.

FORD MOTOR CAR COMPANY, GREEN ISLAND, N. Y.   NEAR TROY.   76.

116479

Henry Ford sought to preserve rural values and culture by collecting antiques in a museum and restored village in Dearborn. His national search for antiquities led him to Minnesota, where he tried to buy the famed *William Crooks* locomotive. The family of James J. Hill declined to have it moved out of state. Here it is on display at the Union Depot in St. Paul in 1954. Photograph by the *Minneapolis Star Journal Tribune*. Courtesy of the Minnesota Historical Society.

linkage to hydroelectric power. Decentralization had become a central tenet of the City Beautiful Movement, which was favored by progressive city planners across the country, including those in Minneapolis and St. Paul. In retrospect, there is considerable irony in the fact that progressives of the period viewed decentralization as a laudable goal and the automobile as having positive environmental and public health benefits. Frank Lloyd Wright credited Henry Ford for being the inspiration of his visionary Broadacre City, the conceptual underpinnings of American suburban sprawl.

In addition to the small rural sites, Ford also acquired a number of properties with the capacity for larger hydropower plants, including Green Island, on the Hudson River in New York, which he discovered on a camping trip with Edison and Firestone. Ford built a single-story plant measuring 1,100 feet long by 120 feet wide to manufacture ball bearings. This decentralization project, and other similar ones, were larger and quite different in character than his Village Industries projects. Ford never fully articulated what constituted a "decentralized" plant, such as Green Island, and how those differed from a "Village Industries" plant. An observer of Ford noted that "because he moves by instinct he is trying to work out not by formulation but on the ground what he calls a sample of a better scheme. He began on the farm and he knows something real is to be found there."

The size of the workforce was clearly an important factor in defining his decentralized plants. Ford could create a Village Industries for just a handful of workers in a small town, but also simultaneously build large industrial complexes on rural sites using hydropower. Ford himself acknowledged the difficulty of maintaining a consistent definition. He wrote that his Hamilton plant had "grown in importance" to the point where "it employs 2,500 men and is (now) passing out of the class of village industries."

Even as Ford strived to support "The Farmer" and save rural America, he could not reconcile the fact that his automobile was working at cross–purposes with these goals. This conflict must have generated considerable inner turmoil, at least subconsciously. He responded, in part, by seeking to preserve the historic technological and transportation artifacts that were rapidly disappearing from small villages around the country. He became a voracious collector of "Americana," which he displayed in his huge museum

Ford considered his power plants to be works of art worthy of prominent display, as seen in this view of the power plant in Detroit's Highland Park facility. Author's collection.

in Greenfield Village, Dearborn, one of the first re-created museum villages in the country. Cost and size were of no concern as he bought and moved entire buildings that had historical significance or a personal connection. The search for artifacts extended to Minnesota. Ford wanted to acquire the famed locomotive *William Crooks* that was brought to the state in 1861. It "was considered a pet of the late James J. Hill during the last years of his life," who took great pride in being photographed alongside it. Hill's son Louis considered giving it to Ford if he was willing to display it in Minnesota, and even suggested sites at the Union Depot, or perhaps at the new Ford plant in Highland Park, St. Paul. The manager of the Minneapolis assembly plant, S. A. Stellwagen, actively pursued the sale and assured Ford's general secretary E. G. Liebold that "we will bring influences to bear from several other men who are personal friends of Louis W. Hill, and if it is at all possible to secure this locomotive for Mr. Ford, you may be sure that nothing will be left undone toward that end." But Liebold made it clear that Ford was only interested if the locomotive could be displayed in Dearborn alongside his huge collection, and that ended the discussions.

Ford's almost mystical belief in hydroelectric power has to be placed in the larger context of his views on energy, which he saw as a public trust. "In the organization of the Ford work we are continually reaching out for more and more developed power," he wrote. "We go to the coalfields, to the streams, and to the rivers, always seeking some cheap and convenient source of power which we can transform into electricity, take to the machine, increase the output of the workers, raise their wages, and lower the price to the public." Ford learned the business side of energy production as a young engineer at the Edison Illuminating Company in Detroit.

Ford needed an extraordinary amount of energy to run the largest manufacturing operation in the world, and this demand increased exponentially as thousands of electrical machines were placed at work stations, replacing the outdated belt and pulley system. Ford had good reason to place such an emphasis on energy—his entire company depended on it. He stated it clearly: "All our operations get back to the provision of power."

Navigation as Alternative to Railroads

Henry Ford had a remarkable ability to integrate seemingly unrelated ideas. His affection for "The Farmer," his enthusiasm for decentralization and hydroelectric power, his extraordinary environmental sensibilities, and his fierce dislike of monopolists—especially railroads and utility companies—coalesced into a powerful commitment to

During his campaign to secure the hydroelectric permit at the High Dam, Ford declared that he would promote navigation on the Mississippi River, which won widespread support, particularly with farmers. Ford gave the impression that assembled cars would be shipped in large quantities by barge, similar to those pictured here (not Ford cars) docked in Duluth. Courtesy of the Kathryn A. Martin Library Archives and Special Collections, University of Minnesota Duluth.

navigation. In 1915, the year after the Minneapolis plant opened, Ford announced plans for the River Rouge project on a two thousand–acre site on the banks of the River Rouge in Dearborn, Michigan. "I shall bring down the iron ore from Lake Superior in my own boats, when the river is widened enough," he said. "If the government will not widen it, I'll do it myself."

Navigation was clearly on Ford's mind as a company representative announced in 1916 that a $500,000 to $1,000,000 assembly plant would be built in Duluth. An article in a Virginia, Minnesota, newspaper claimed that "Low freight rates on Ford parts and accessories which the Great Lakes traffic affords is the lodestone which draws the factory to Duluth." C. C. Hildebrand, the Minneapolis branch manager, was quoted as saying, "An assembly plant here would receive parts not in carload lots, but by the shipload. A large crew of men would be employed here to assemble the cars ready for shipment to agents. By operating these assembling plants much is saved in freight charges." The article raised expectations for a huge economic boom, stating that the project would be so large that "There is a big probability that other factory branches will be supplied from Duluth after the establishment here." One Duluth company proceeded to build a large expansion onto its garage in anticipation of the new Ford plant.

David Lewis, a Ford historian, pointed out that "There was one problem—the plant was never built, and Ford never offered a precise reason why. But we do know that the company already had an assembly plant in the Twin Cities. A second plant was unneeded to serve the Upper Midwest." A second plant may have been unneeded but waterborne transportation had become an essential element of Ford's strategy for managing his supply chain and his efforts to create a vertically integrated, international company. An account described by David Halberstam makes that clear:

> Henry Ford went to Holland to dedicate a new plant at Rotterdam. "Mr. Ford, here is our new plant," Lord Perry, who was head of Ford in Europe, said proudly.
>
> "Where is the water?" the old man asked.
>
> "There isn't any water," Lord Perry replied.
>
> "Well, let's get out of here," Ford said "I don't even want to look at it." That had ended the ceremony. Ford had driven off, and they had torn down the plant and moved it to a deep water site.

Ford's experience with international navigation reinforced his commitment to connecting his far-flung domestic operations via inland waterways. Many commercial and political groups shared Ford's interest in inland navigation, particularly focusing on the Mississippi River. Ford had an adroit sense of timing on this issue—and many others—which enabled him to capitalize on momentum that was already coalescing. The federal government had been working to promote navigation on the Mississippi River throughout the nineteenth century. Those efforts received a major boost in 1907 when President Teddy Roosevelt declared that it was "the nation's duty to restore the Mississippi River to its rightful place as a great artery of commerce . . . This river system traverses too many states to render it possible to leave it merely to the states the task of fitting it for the greatest use of which it is possible. It is emphatically a national task for this great river system is one of our chief national assets." With inland navigation, Roosevelt found a powerful argument for a strong federal government, which he compared to his Panama Canal project. He established an Inland Waterways Commission, which launched a national publicity tour at Duluth and traveled to the Twin Cities, where he made a major address. Roosevelt joined the commission for the rest of the tour down the Mississippi River. The following year, the commission issued a report calling for developing navigation, in part because it would relieve congestion of the nation's rail lines. The communities along the Mississippi River welcomed the endorsement. Several years later, the commission organized a hydroplane tour to fly downriver from Minneapolis to New Orleans, with stops along the way to "obtain world-wide publicity for Minneapolis and the Mississippi valley, as well as the deep waterway movement." A Deep Waterway Convention met in Chicago where organizers pushed for a $200 million federal appropriation.

The United States' entry into World War I sidetracked these efforts, but it also opened the door for other arguments. Navigation could ease the railroad congestion, which was hindering war preparations. The business community in Minneapolis came up with a particularly novel angle—fears of possible German submarine attacks. They declared that "it would be next to impossible for any foreign power to halt transportation facilities on the Mississippi with its tributaries the Ohio and Missouri, offering equally safe and cheap inland trade routes to the East and West." Local business leaders pledged to organize and fund a Twin Cities navigation company that would establish barge service along the Mississippi.

Henry Ford, more than anyone in the United States, would benefit from the development of inland navigation. In 1921, he announced his intention to establish a fleet of barges to transport automobile parts from Detroit, via the Erie Canal, to his plant under construction at Green Island on the Hudson River, near Troy, New York. The barges, designed by Ford engineers, would be 150 feet long by 20 feet wide, with a capacity of 1,000 tons. Shipments would also go between the Green Island plant and the Kearny, New Jersey, plant, also under construction. All of these

31:—Giant Freighter passing under Raised Aerial Lift Bridge.

The Henry Ford passing through the Duluth-Superior Ship Canal.

Henry Ford had a large fleet of ships, which he used to connect his far-flung network of manufacturing and assembly plants. Freighters carried iron ore from Duluth to Detroit, and returned with shipments of coal from company-owned mines. The freighter *Henry Ford II* passes through the lift bridge in Duluth around 1924. Courtesy of the Minnesota Historical Society.

Ford Coal | Ford Coal

Ford Coal in Ford Coal Cars on D. T. & I. (Ford Owned) Railroad.   Portion of the Equipment Utilized in the Marketing of Ford Coal

Pond Creek Coal

Freeburn Seam, Stone, Pike County, Kentucky
Uses: By-products, domestic, steam, malleables

Characteristic analysis:

Ash	5.40%
Volatile Matter	33.09
Fixed Carbon	61.00
Sulphur	.51
B. T. U.'s	14,200

Banner Fork Coal

Wallins Creek Seam, Kentenia, Harlan Co., Kentucky
Uses: By-products, domestic, steam, malleables

Characteristic analysis:

Ash	4.00%
Volatile Matter	37.30
Fixed Carbon	58.00
Sulphur	.70
B. T. U.'s	14,200

Motorship Henry Ford II and Ford Coal on Company's Dock, Duluth † Minnesota.   This Boat and her Companion Ship, the Benson Ford, Transported More Than 1,500,000 Tons of Raw Materials on the Great Lakes Between April 15 and December 18, 1925

Ford stored a huge mound of coal on his dock in Duluth, which would then be shipped by rail to assembly plants. It would also occasionally be sold through car dealers. Author's collection.

sites required dredging to create a deeper channel, which Ford believed the government should underwrite. From his base in Detroit, Ford would be able to access much of the United States through the Great Lakes and several key canals and rivers. In 1922, Ford purchased a seventy-acre site on the Calumet River outside Chicago for a plant replacing one that had been built near downtown.

Ford acquired two freighters to ship coal from his Kentucky mines to plants in Upper Michigan and return with lumber to the River Rouge. Ford also built two six hundred-foot-long ore carriers, the *Benson Ford* and the *Henry Ford II*, which on its maiden voyage in 1924 transported twelve thousand tons of coal to Duluth, where it was unloaded onto a dock leased by the company. Ford had made a bid to buy the dock, which was rejected by owners. As a goodwill gesture some of the coal was sent to Minneapolis and St. Paul to "aid in maintaining reasonable prices and averting fuel shortages." On the return trip to the Rouge, the steamer transported Minnesota iron ore. Several news accounts reported

Lewis H. Brittin (*left*), the person most responsible for relocating the Ford assembly plant from Minneapolis to St. Paul, previously worked in Minneapolis promoting industrial development. In this photograph from 1920, he inspects an industrial tract with Douglas A. Fiske and A. M. Shelden. Courtesy of the Minnesota Historical Society.

that Ford had cousins who lived in Virginia, Minnesota, whom he visited after a trip to Duluth in 1914. The next year, an article in the *Virginia Daily Enterprise* described Ford's interest in purchasing a Mesabi Range iron mine and establishing a fleet of ships to transport the ore to Detroit.

Discovering the High Dam Site

Ford's interests in hydropower, decentralization, and inland navigation framed the search for a new location to replace the obsolete Minneapolis assembly plant. The new site would have to meet all of these basic requirements, plus it would have to be large enough to accommodate the assembly line, provide ample parking for workers, and have room for expansion. One location met all of Ford's criteria, but the process of acquiring the property took many interesting twists and turns and was remembered differently by those involved. In one version, R. E. Hilton, an official with the St. Paul Association, a business promotion group, overheard two Ford workers on a Minneapolis streetcar discussing how their company might have to move because it was running short of space. Hilton passed that information on to a key staff member of the St. Paul Association, Col. Lewis H. Brittin. In a later account Brittin recalled that he traveled to Detroit and met with Henry Ford, receiving encouragement to explore a site at the High Dam on the Mississippi River. The Army Corps of Engineers started construction of Lock and Dam No. 1 in 1911, which was also known as the High Dam. It included a foundation for a hydroelectric plant on the St. Paul side of the river and locks for navigation on the Minneapolis side. The hydroelectric plant was not finished because a number of complex policy issues had yet to be resolved. Ford must have been aware of the well-publicized and contentious discussions surrounding the High Dam site. Brittin arranged for aerial pictures of the dam and surrounding countryside and did feasibility studies for an industrial plant. He presented this research to Ford, who authorized Brittin to proceed with the project. At the time, Brittin explained to the *St. Paul Pioneer Press*: "Mr. Ford feels that with existing freight conditions with the Detroit plant at its present stage of development decentralization is most important . . . This plant will be an example of decentralization of a large industry that will be followed by many other large industries. It will be a thoroughly progressive plant open to educational institutions and in which students may take their shopwork." The High Dam location would meet all of Ford's requirements, and would also connect the St. Paul facility with his plants at St. Louis and New Orleans—if navigation on the Mississippi River could be developed.

Another newspaper account reported that Brittin visited Ford in spring 1921 to propose that he acquire the recently vacated Willys-Overland automobile plant on University Avenue at the city's border with Minneapolis. Ford reportedly declined the offer, "with a statement that he could build his own building but asked if there was any waterpower to be had." Other reports confirm Ford's specific interest in the High Dam site. An article in *Motor Age* magazine made it clear that discussions were already under way in the summer of 1922: "Announcement was made after a visit to Henry Ford by a delegation of Minnesota business men that he would build additions costing several million dollars to his factories near the high dam at Minneapolis and St. Paul. Ford was offered the water power now going to waste provided he could build a plant employing between four thousand and five thousand men."

However varied the accounts, there was one constant, the central role of Col. Lewis Hotchkiss Brittin. Although orphaned at an early age, Brittin attended an exclusive private school and studied at Harvard University but had to drop out in his second year to go to work. He later continued his engineering studies in New York and worked for a

L. H. Brittin was the principal behind the development of the Northwestern Terminal, the only industrial park in Minneapolis served by all the railroads. This building was one of several under construction in 1920. Several years later, St. Paul recruited Brittin to plan a similar project at the High Dam site. Photograph by C. J. Hibbard. Courtesy of the Minnesota Historical Society.

firm that specialized in industrial development. He spent five years in Mexico overseeing railroad construction projects for the firm. After returning to the United States, he worked for General Electric and was placed in charge of locating branch factories and warehouses, one of which was in Minneapolis. A group of local businessmen were so impressed with him that they offered him a job heading up the Northwestern Terminal, an innovative industrial park being developed in Minneapolis. Several years later, Brittin was hired by the St. Paul Association, which wanted to build similar industrial projects. Colonel Brittin, who received his military title for service in the Spanish-American War and World War I, was an extremely competent planner and energetic salesman. In his new position, he managed to secure Ford's interest, and reportedly a preliminary commitment, for the High Dam site in the "western suburb" of St. Paul. For St. Paul, it was an enormous coup to have a former Minneapolis official working on industrial development, made even more gratifying because he was about to relocate a major company from its cross-town rival. However, before a deal could be reached, Ford and St. Paul would have to resolve many thorny policy and political issues regarding the use of waterpower.

The High Dam had been the subject of intense scrutiny and controversy on both the local and national stages for more than seventy years. At that location, the river separates the Twin Cities, unlike upstream where it flows entirely through Minneapolis. The Army Corps of Engineers had jurisdiction over the Mississippi and all navigable rivers dating back to pre–Civil War times. It was responsible for maintaining a navigation channel with a minimum depth of four and a half feet from New Orleans to the head of navigation at St. Paul. With the river's width, ranging from three hundred feet in St. Paul to 1,400 feet at St. Louis, it was often difficult to maintain the needed channel depth during dry seasons. This made commercial navigation problematic, and shipments destined for St. Paul could often travel only as far north as Winona, Minnesota.

Rivers can provide both navigation and hydroelectric power, but maximizing both simultaneously is difficult. The shipping industry preferred a series of lower locks and dams that allowed for more gradual level changes. Hydroelectric companies, on the other hand, preferred higher dams, which allowed a steeper water drop, or "head," to power the turbines. The principal responsibility of the Army Corps was navigation - hydroelectric technology wasn't even commercially viable until the early twentieth century. In the absence of a comprehensive federal policy for navigation and hydroelectric power, projects typically had to receive special congressional approval and were undertaken on an ad hoc basis. The Corps generally opposed the building of hydroelectric or even dual-purpose dams. Hydropower supporters and environmentalists challenged the exclusive use of rivers for navigation, citing the pressing need to break the coal monopoly in America. They touted the environmental benefits of hydropower, known then as "white coal," as it was renewable, did not produce smoke, did not have to be mined or transported, and would not be depleted.

In the nineteenth century, Congress authorized private companies to build several dams on the Mississippi that would provide mechanical waterpower (prior to hydroelectric power), including at the St. Anthony Falls in Minneapolis and at Brainerd, Minnesota. In 1913, Stone and Webster, a private company, built a dam for hydroelectric power at Keokuk, Iowa. The Army Corps opposed this project because it opened the door for hydroelectric companies to share the river with navigation. In the absence of a clear federal policy, the various stakeholders would debate for decades over who could build a project on navigable rivers. Would it be for navigation or hydropower, who would control the rights to the power, how would it be priced, and, most controversially, would the utility be public or privately owned? These unresolved issues paralyzed federal action, stalling projects proposed for the Mississippi and other rivers. The bitter rivalry between Minneapolis and St. Paul immensely complicated the conflict locally.

Battle for the Hydroelectric Permit

The Mississippi River drops about one hundred feet from the Falls of St. Anthony in Minneapolis to the harbor in St. Paul. Below St. Paul the river had a channel depth of about four to six feet, which was generally sufficient for navigation. However, the nine miles upstream from St. Paul to Minneapolis had a depth of only two and a half feet. As a result, St. Paul became the natural head of navigation and developed as a regional transportation and commercial center. Minneapolis, on the other hand, used the river for waterpower at the St. Anthony Falls. Taking advantage of the abundant supply of power, Minneapolis built lumber and flour mills and developed as a manufacturing center. These different patterns of development were at the very core of their respective civic and economic identities. Shipping and manufacturing were theoretically complementary activities, but the cities could not achieve a cooperative relationship and regularly fought over the use of the Mississippi. Lucile M. Kane summed it up succinctly: "Each city aspired to share in the gift nature had bestowed upon the other." Minneapolis tried to attract navigation by clearing the river channels and offering financial incentives to shipping companies, but when that failed city leaders called for the construction of two locks and dams upriver from St. Paul. This would have made Minneapolis the new head of navigation, which St. Paul strongly opposed.

In 1894, Congress directed the Army Corps of Engineers to build two locks and dams in response to strong lobbying from Minneapolis. St. Paul dropped its opposition because it believed it could secure hydropower rights at the new dams. This would create parity between the rival cities—each would have navigation and hydroelectric power. St. Paul wanted a high dam, which was better for hydroelectric power and less desirable for navigation, but it agreed to two dams after an Army Corps official warned that "high dams sometimes break and that if a dam holding back six miles of water, 35 feet deep should give way it would sweep away lower St. Paul."

In 1903, workers began building Lock and Dam No. 2, also known as the Meeker Island Lock and Dam, just above what is now the Lake Street Bridge. While the dams were under construction, University of Minnesota professor Benjamin Groat published a report calling for one high dam that could allow for both navigation and hydropower. He claimed that one taller dam with a drop of thirty feet would generate considerably more hydroelectric power than two separate dams of thirteen feet. This report gave university officials, conservationists, and others supporting hydroelectricity an opening to lobby for a single high dam. Federal legislation in 1907 created another reason to reconsider the original plan for two dams. It called for increasing the depth of the channel along the entire length of the Mississippi River from four and a half feet to six feet. Lock and Dam

In 1911, the Army Corps of Engineers started construction of Lock and Dam No. 1, known as the High Dam. This view shows the massive walls for the locks during construction, located on the Minneapolis side of the river. Courtesy of the Army Corps of Engineers, St. Paul District.

The Army Corps used an Amberson-type design for the reinforced concrete structure of the High Dam. A series of arches enclosed a hollow space, which workers from Minneapolis would later walk through to get to the Ford plant before the construction of the Ford Bridge in 1927. Courtesy of the Army Corps of Engineers, St. Paul District.

No. 2 had just been completed, but Lock and Dam No. 1 was still under construction. The Corps needed to suspend work and review its design to ensure that it was compatible with the deeper channel. At that point, advocates for hydroelectric power pressed for one dual-purpose "high dam." Congress responded in 1909 and directed the Army Corps to undertake a review and established a board of three engineers to oversee the study.

The final report concluded that the Corps could readily modify Lock and Dam No. 1 to meet the requirements of the six-foot channel depth, and it confirmed that two smaller dams would not produce sufficient water "head." One new "high dam" would provide hydropower in a far more cost-effective manner. The engineering board recommended that the Army Corps construct the "high dam," with the extra costs for the hydroelectric structure to be paid by the operating entity. The Corps objected, maintaining its consistent preference for navigation, but it reluctantly held a public hearing in 1909 to determine if there was any interest in hydropower and to explore funding options. As it turned out, there was interest from the cities of St. Paul and Minneapolis, the state in the form of the University of Minnesota, as well as a private power company, Northern States Power (NSP). The public entities were alarmed by the interest of the private utility and were concerned that the federal government might consider privatizing the hydropower. They argued that the state had the exclusive right to control its natural resources, not the federal government. To bolster their prospects against the competing private utility, the two cities and the state agreed to form a joint venture known as the Municipal Electric Company.

After the public hearing, the Board of Engineers recommended to Congress that Lock and Dam No. 1 be raised to thirty feet and that the proposed Municipal Electric Company undertake the construction. NSP, the private utility, lost out largely because the state and cities controlled the riverfront land that would be flooded for the new dam. Given the clear recommendation of the engineering board, the Army Corps modified its opposition to hydroelectric power and argued that it alone should build the High Dam, even if it was a dual-use facility. However, this required new federal legislative authority, which was granted by the National Water Act in 1910. The legislation provided a license period of fifty years for the hydroelectric power, but did not specify the user fee, instead calling for "reasonable compensation."

The Corps reworked the partially completed Lock and Dam No. 1 and finished the new High Dam at a cost of $2 million. The dam is 574 feet wide and has a fixed overflow spillway. When the reservoir above the dam was filled in 1917, it submerged the original Lock and Dam No. 2, which had been completed at considerable expense just five years earlier. To ensure water safety, the top five feet of Lock and Dam No. 2 was removed. The pool from the new High Dam extended 5.4 miles upstream to the Northern Pacific Railway

Bridge. The newly created lake was large enough for a variety of recreational activities but it also created a significant environmental problem. At that time the two cities dumped raw sewage into the Mississippi River, which the new dam now blocked. This created, in effect, a noxious cesspool, particularly during the summer months when water levels were low.

The issues of operational control and user fees were debated by multiple stakeholders at all levels over the next three years as water continued to flow over the High Dam. This delay greatly rankled environmentalists and local officials, especially at a time when severe coal shortages forced the closing of businesses, reduced street lighting, canceled some streetcar service, and threatened government shutdown and layoffs. A St. Paul city council member estimated that the unused waterpower was equivalent to sixty thousand tons of coal with a value of four hundred thousand dollars per year. This wasted power, he added, was enough to operate from one hundred to two hundred manufacturing plants and light all streets in the city. The city council adopted a resolution demanding that the federal government install a hydroelectric facility at the High Dam or lease the equipment directly to St. Paul and Minneapolis.

In 1920, Congress established the Federal Power Commission, made up of the cabinet secretaries from the Departments of War, Interior, and Agriculture. The commission was charged with clarifying federal policy and administering a decision-making process. While the policy issues were slowly being sorted out on the federal level, Minneapolis, St. Paul, and the state university made very little progress toward creating the Municipal Electric Company. Minneapolis felt there was little sense of urgency to proceed with such an ambitious project during World War I. After the war, Minneapolis pushed for an enabling act at the state legislature in 1921, but its mayor, George E. Leach, charged that "The bill was put to sleep by a state senator whose law partner is the General Counsel for the Northern States Power," the private utility also seeking the permit.

The long-standing municipal rivalry between the two cities contributed to a breakdown in deliberations over the Municipal Electric Company. Rather than negotiate in good faith, St. Paul saw an opportunity to preempt Minneapolis and embarked on an audacious effort to secure the waterpower entirely for itself. On July 8, 1921, the St. Paul city council adopted a resolution authorizing the city to apply to the Federal Power Commission for exclusive rights to all hydropower at the new High Dam. This bold move caught Minneapolis, the state, and Northern States Power off guard. Just days before the October 18, 1921, public hearing at the Federal Power Commission, Minneapolis charged that St. Paul was secretly working with the Ford Motor Company and was "interested in getting the power rights for a private corporation." St. Paul refused to divulge its plan prior to its presentation to the commission, but its city attorney said that if St. Paul failed

The massive High Dam project required several years to complete. By 1914, the lock on the Minneapolis side was substantially finished, as well as the foundation for a future hydroelectric plant on the St. Paul side. This view looks east, showing the undeveloped bluff that would later become the site of the Ford Twin Cities Assembly Plant. Photograph by the *St. Paul Daily News*. Courtesy of the Minnesota Historical Society.

to get the permit for the hydropower, it would prefer "to have Minneapolis gain the rights rather than a private corporation." NSP denied it was a private company, claiming it was "semipublic" because it was a regulated utility.

During this period, the state of Minnesota, the third partner of the Municipal Electric Company, had become less engaged because of a change in leadership of the Board of Regents of the University of Minnesota. Additionally, the university's two staunchest advocates for the Municipal Electric Company resigned to support the other competing bidders. Northern States Power hired Francis S. Shenehon, dean of the College of Engineering, and St. Paul retained Adolph F. Meyer, assistant professor of hydraulics, as a technical expert. When the president of the university saw that the Municipal Electric Company was struggling to get organized, he reentered the fray by suggesting that the state bypass the two cities and take over the project. The head of the Department of Electrical Engineers supported a research role for the university and argued that a by-product of hydroelectricity was "the manufacture of artificial fertilizers and other products of

The completion of a hydroelectric plant was delayed for several years while numerous federal policy issues were resolved. The bitter rivalry between Minneapolis and St. Paul added to the delay and opened the door for Henry Ford to win the hydroelectric permit. This view from approximately 1924 shows the completed dam as it was before Ford had obtained the permit. Courtesy of the Minnesota Historical Society.

electrical furnaces and associated processes which might reduce the prices of such necessities to farmers and others." Rather than working together to form a partnership, the three public entities were now in direct competition.

St. Paul's application to the Federal Power Commission focused on the technical aspects of hydroelectricity, financing strategies, and plans for distribution of the power, and made no mention of the Ford Motor Company. It estimated that the High Dam could annually generate power equal to burning approximately a hundred thousand tons of coal. The city was prepared to finance the entire estimated cost of $11.4 million through its bonding power. The electricity generated would be for street lighting, water pumping, and public buildings. All surplus power would be directed to a new two hundred–acre "industrial district" that the city would develop on the bluffs above the High Dam. St. Paul proposed to use net profits from this development for "the specific purpose of upbuilding the public school system of the city." It proposed to purchase school equipment, remodel old buildings and construct new ones, and establish programs for vocational and industrial training and hygiene activities. Brittin developed the plan for the site with drawings furnished by prominent local architect A. H. Stem. It showed factories and had a detailed transportation layout, including an "extensive river terminal." It was similar in many respects to the Northwestern Terminal that Brittin had earlier developed in Minneapolis. While the city was preparing its application to the Federal Power Commission, it was already working with the Greater Saint Paul Committee, a business group, to quietly secure options on the needed land.

In presenting its case to the Federal Power Commission in October 1921, St. Paul went beyond touting the technical merits of its plan—it went right to the heart of the rivalry between the two cities, and stated:

> THAT Government Dam No. 1 was built primarily to give Minneapolis the advantages of river transportation and thus to transfer to it artificially the position of head of navigation on the Mississippi River, which position by natural right had hitherto been held by Saint Paul. Minneapolis, on the other hand, has enjoyed the important advantage of possessing within

In 1921, St. Paul decided to seek the hydroelectric permit on its own, abruptly ending its agreement with Minneapolis for a joint application. This drawing of the proposed industrial district by architect A. H. Stem was part of St. Paul's application to the Federal Power Commission. The proposal was prepared under the direction of Col. L. H. Brittin, and was similar in many ways to the Northwestern Terminal in Minneapolis. Courtesy of the Minnesota Historical Society.

its corporate limits the valuable water-powers of St. Anthony Falls, an advantage against which the City of Saint Paul has not hitherto had an opportunity to compete. In accordance with the principle of maintaining the parity of competing markets in transportation and industrial facilities, which principle has been well established by our Interstate Commerce Commission and State Commissions, in cases affecting the equality of competing markets, it is contended that Saint Paul should have an opportunity to maintain a parity with Minneapolis in the matter of water-power development by being permitted to derive such benefit as it can from the power which has automatically been provided in transferring the head of navigation of the Mississippi River from Saint Paul to Minneapolis.

St. Paul was stretching its argument by invoking the populist rhetoric of "trust-busting" in its rivalry with Minneapolis and the need for parity. In another dubious argument, St. Paul said that because the foundation for the powerhouse was built wholly within St. Paul, its application should be given preference. It did not mention that the lock for the High Dam was on the Minneapolis side of the river. Finally, it argued that it was the first to apply to the Federal Power Commission, fifteen days ahead of Northern States Power and forty-six days ahead of Minneapolis.

In its presentation to the commission, the Northern States Power Company claimed that it was the only applicant with actual experience in building and operating hydropower plants. It also argued that the Municipal Electric Company "ceased to exist as an entity when one of its constituent members—St. Paul—seceded." NSP conveniently overlooked the charge that it had used dubious means to oppose a bill in the state legislature to fund the Municipal Electric Company. The power company also criticized St. Paul for going it alone, "without the knowledge or consent of its colleagues," resulting in "securing such initial advantage by its unexpected filing of an application." Finally, NSP pointed out that it was the only entity that could assure distribution of power to both cities, underscoring the point that Minneapolis would receive no electricity under the St. Paul plan. The presentation by Minneapolis was short on details, primarily arguing that it had deeded city property to the federal government in 1915 for the ponding above the High Dam and was therefore entitled to half of the power generated by the dam. It also cited the original resolution of the Municipal Electric Company that called for power to be distributed "First to the grantor from whom the water power is acquired . . . , second to any state institution in such city or cities . . . , and third, any surplus then remaining in equal shares, to the cities."

Minneapolis viewed the agreement as a "treaty" and claimed it was startled that St. Paul applied for the permit. An official charged that this "hostile act" threatened "to take from Minneapolis what nature had given her." Douglas Fiske from the Minneapolis Civic and Commerce Association added that "This all happened because a certain promoter went into St. Paul in the spring of 1921 and conceived the idea that if the city filched the high dam power and founded an industrial district . . . it would bring about the undoing of Minneapolis . . . The promoter who conceived this highly immoral scheme has sought to transfer the cowl of St. Paul to the shoulders of Henry Ford to enable Ford, under the guise of a municipality to develop cheap electrical current for the use of his great enterprises." The unnamed promoter was, of course, Colonel Brittin, who had previously worked for Douglas Fiske at the Northwestern Terminal project in Minneapolis.

Minneapolis criticized St. Paul for withdrawing from the Municipal Electric Company and argued that it would be "immoral" for one city to control the power. Officials added that "It would be all the more unjust to give it to St. Paul with a population of 234,000 against 380,000 in Minneapolis." Minneapolis mayor Leach also criticized NSP, claiming that a representative from the company asked him to oppose a bill before the state legislature that would finance the Municipal Electric Company. During his appearance before the legislature, the mayor said he had to fight his way through the lobbyists of NSP and was allowed to speak for only four minutes before the bill was killed. On this point, St. Paul officials agreed with their Minneapolis counterparts, alleging that a company representative had also asked St. Paul to withdraw its support for the state bill. St. Paul mayor Hodgson charged that an NSP representative told him that the company did not place much value on electric power from the High Dam—their primary intention was to prevent the public sector from entering the hydropower business. The two cities could at least agree to put aside their mutual enmity for the purpose of attacking the private sector proposal. Leach argued that NSP already "has a monopoly . . . of the light and power of the state and declared that fighting for High Dam, No. 1, is the opening wedge to save this last great natural resource for the people, the rightful owners."

St. Paul agreed with Minneapolis that if NSP's position was upheld it would preclude the possibility of any municipality ever obtaining a license. It also dismissed the company's "solicitousness for the people and the Municipal Electric Company" when in fact it had "trained its batteries in opposition to the bill" that would have funded the collaboration. The three-way debate continued with NSP siding with Minneapolis in opposing the application of St. Paul. They argued that "water power development must be viewed as regional, not local," and that Minneapolis should have equal rights to the hydropower—which only NSP could provide.

Neil Cronin, the corporation counsel of Minneapolis, claimed that for ten years St. Paul had never disputed Minneapolis's entitlement to half of the waterpower. He argued that the underlying agreement had not changed just because the Municipal Electric Company had a temporary setback at the legislature. He also scoffed at St. Paul's notion that it was entitled to all the power just because the plant was physically situated within its borders, particularly since all the water came *through* Minneapolis, which meant that it should receive all the power. He concluded: "Is there any choice then, if a test is to be made, between our position and the syndicated interests represented by St. Paul and the almost monopolistic interests of the power company?"

Under questioning by the commission members, St. Paul officials admitted their plan would first distribute power to the industrial district, and only if there were surplus power would it go to municipal needs. Newspapers on both sides of the river took up the debate. The *Minneapolis Journal* wrote that St. Paul "had violated its solemn agreement of ten years standing, thrown over its two partners, and undertaken to grab everything." The editorial was particularly incensed that St. Paul wanted to use all the power "not to light the streets," but "to build up an industrial district for the benefit of private individuals and corporations." It concluded, "To the dishonor of violating its sacred obligations, St. Paul now adds a scheme that amounts to theft of the public's rights for the benefit of private enterprises which it expects to foster. And to clothe this scheme in a garment of respectability, it offers to devote the illegal profits thus obtained to improving the public schools of St. Paul!"

Minneapolis mayor Leach continued to press St. Paul to participate in the Municipal Electric Company, but the St. Paul city council had voted to prohibit its mayor from engaging in any action that would not further the city's own application. Because this was the first case before the Federal Power Commission, Leach urged that that it should receive particular consideration as it "would establish a policy and precedent that would be of national importance."

The Federal Power Commission reconvened in Washington on January 16, 1922, with the competing applicants in attendance. Minneapolis requested a one-year delay until the Minnesota legislature could take up its request to fund the Municipal Electric Company. In his opening remarks, Mayor Leach exclaimed, "I simply ask the United States to keep faith with the people of Minneapolis and the state of Minnesota. This dam was built by the government with the agreement that the power derived therefrom should go to the cities of St. Paul and Minneapolis and the University of Minnesota . . . To deny us our contract right simply because the Mayor of St. Paul refuses to join in the application is to punish Minneapolis for the omissions of St. Paul." Leach added he believed that St. Paul would likely rejoin the Municipal Electric Company if Minneapolis received the permit to operate the dam. The chair of the Federal Power Commission, Secretary of War J. W. Weeks, hoped to find a political solution. He asked Minnesota Senator Knute Nelson, who was in attendance, whether it might make sense to grant NSP a permit on an interim basis until the Municipal Electric Company became fully funded. Nelson protested, "You know

George Leach, the mayor of Minneapolis, strongly opposed St. Paul's application for the hydroelectric permit. The mayors of both cities participated in debates around the state to win support for their positions. Mayor Leach is shown here at the groundbreaking for the Minneapolis Municipal Auditorium in 1925. Courtesy of the Minnesota Historical Society.

that when a monopoly gets its 'claws' on anything it is hard to make it let go."

St. Paul continued to press for parity, arguing that Minneapolis already had a large hydroelectric plant at St. Anthony Falls while it had none. Chairman Weeks asked St. Paul's consultant, Adolph Meyer, how much of the power would go for municipal lighting, and was told about one-seventh. Weeks then asked if St. Paul would sell power to Minneapolis and Meyer answered, "I have the impression that Minneapolis has a more favorable rate than St. Paul for its city lighting. In any event, only a small proportion of Minneapolis could be reached." Robert F. Pack, the president of Northern States Power, complained, "Our company is between the devil and the deep sea. We are attacked by both cities, yet we serve both." He advocated for a comprehensive interconnected power system, claiming that "chaos would result if every municipality were allowed to sell its power." "Are you sure you are right?" asked Weeks, who went on to describe how the city of Los Angeles was selling its hydroelectric power throughout southern California. The applicants continued to debate whether it was better to be a socialist advocating for municipal ownership or a monopolist with interlocking corporate connections that extended "from Delaware to San Diego." The overwhelmed commission took no action and adjourned the hearing for a week.

During this recess, the staff of the Federal Power Commission disclosed their recommendation to award the license to NSP. Col. William Kelly, the chief engineer for the commission, stated: "To give a license to either municipality would be to give it exclusive use of a valuable resource to which the other municipality has equal rights." The staff report reviewed the history of the project dating back to 1911, noting that Minneapolis contributed about 75 percent of the land required for flowage, compared to 25 percent for St. Paul. It also concluded that "local jealousies prevented agreement on the terms of legislation" required to establish the Municipal Electric Company, and held out little hope for future cooperation. In a move that stunned observers, when the commission reconvened, it rejected the recommendation of its staff and supported the position of Minneapolis for a one-year delay. The commission hoped that during that time "the cities of Minneapolis and St. Paul and the University could get together and present a workable plan for ownership of the power." NSP officials were shocked at the last-minute reversal and complained that "if it is deemed advisable to let water still run and continue to waste coal, so be it."

Minneapolis mayor Leach was probably the only person at the hearing not stunned by the decision. The day before the Federal Power Commission met, he had secretly traveled to Washington to lobby the highest official in the land. He was rebuffed by President Warren G. Harding's secretary, but was undeterred, as he later wrote in his diary:

> I finally told Mr. Christian that I would be sitting on the steps of the White House until I did see the President, and I didn't think that would be a nice picture back home. He got ugly and told me they throw people in jail for disturbing the White House. I told him I would be a hero at home if they tried anything like that and maybe I would like it. I told Mr. Christian that I was going over to the Powhatan Hotel and check out and would return to the White House for the duration. The hotel was two blocks away and when I walked in the door, I was paged and Mr. Christian's voice came over the phone, saying the President's program had been changed so if I came right over, I could see him . . .
>
> After I was thoroughly instructed, I was ushered into the President's office with Christian hanging on my coat tails. I was presented and Mr. Harding, the handsomest and most distinguished looking President in the history of the country, got up from his desk to greet me officially, took my hand, put his other hand on my shoulder and said, "Mr. Mayor, what is all this talk about the High Dam in Minnesota"? I turned and looked at Mr. Christian and said I had been forbidden to mention it but "Mr. President, I cannot refuse an Executive

Order," and I proceeded to tell him the whole story. In the end he asked me what I wanted to do and I told him I wanted the Federal Power Commission at their meeting to give us a one year's delay so that I could put it up to the Minnesota Legislature for their final action.

Unfortunately, the postponement did not achieve the desired effect of encouraging cooperation between the cities. St. Paul continued to work on its proposal, but it also looked to hedge its hydroelectric bets if it did not secure the High Dam permit. In late July 1922, Brittin applied for a hydroelectric permit for a new project on the St. Croix River in Wisconsin, between St. Croix Falls and the Kettle River connection. This would have required condemnation authority, but it was also reported that "St. Paul interests" had already secured options for some of the needed land. Elected officials in Wisconsin mobilized to oppose St. Paul's plans.

Ford Announces Project and Files for Permit

Ford's interest in the High Dam site had been rumored for some time, fueled in part by newspaper accounts of visits by high-ranking company officials. Ford's chief engineer, W. B. Mayo, visited the site on September 13, 1922, and was very impressed. This was not a mere reconnaissance trip on Mayo's part, it was the beginning of a major public-relations campaign. "Mr. Ford feels that water transportation must . . . be used wherever possible. The high dam site is apparently the first opportunity . . . where navigation as well as power can be brought into existence," Mayo said. "Mr. Ford will not consider any site that does not have water transportation." He let it be known that great things were in store for Minnesota if Ford were to be given the hydroelectric permit: "Mr. Ford is interested in the Twin Cities as a production location. He has announced definitely that his organization is top heavy in Detroit and must be decentralized . . . If properly handled, the Twin Cities district can be a second Detroit."

Up to this point, Ford's role in the debate over the use of the High Dam was unofficial, but that changed on January 9, 1923, a year after the Federal Power Commission granted the postponement. Henry Ford announced plans for a $10 million assembly and manufacturing plant, promising "Ten Big Things" listed in the *St. Paul Daily News*:

> 1. The Ford factory of St. Paul, ultimately employing 14,000 men and having a payroll of $25,000,000 annually.
> 2. A new railway line to be built by the St. Paul road costing more than $2,000,000.

3. A new industrial district of some 700 acres south of the new Ford factory, built up along the new line of the St. Paul road.

4. A big barge line, wharves and river terminal on the Mississippi River to be built and operated by Mr. Ford.

5. Two new bridges across the river. One will be built by the St. Paul Road and the other by St. Paul and Minneapolis jointly, the latter crossing the river at St. Catherine ave. [Later Ford Parkway]

6. A complete, modern and up-to-date hydro-electric laboratory, donated by Mr. Ford to the University of Minnesota in the event the power from the high dam is used.

7. Shops of the Ford factory open at all times for the use of students of all the colleges of the Twin Cities in vocational training.

8. A new park of six and one-half acres, to be built by St. Paul on the Mississippi river boulevard, south of the Ford units to preserve the river view looking south and to mask the factory looking north.

9. The plant as a great magnet drawing all sorts of accessory and other supplemental industries to it by its activity.

10. An increased population, estimated at 75,000 people, divided between St. Paul and Minneapolis.

Following the major announcement of the new plant came the bombshell news that a month earlier Ford Motor Company had quietly applied to the commission for a one-year preliminary permit for the hydroelectric power. St. Paul officials quickly endorsed Ford's application over its own, saying that it "is but carrying out in a concrete way the plans submitted to the commission." Minneapolis moved to block St. Paul and Ford at the state legislature by introducing a bill to create its own municipal power company. Officials from St. Paul countered by embarking on a statewide campaign to win public support, portraying the Ford proposal as a way to break the impasse between the cities. They carried their message of regional benefits of the project to business and farm groups in Minneapolis, Duluth, Mankato, and Red Wing. The Ford plant, they claimed, would be a boon to the smelting industry throughout the Upper Midwest, as well as to the mining and rail industries. Ford representatives said they would build a new $6 million railroad line from the Twin Cities to Duluth to access raw materials and develop the Mississippi River as a major shipping channel, and balance the movement of goods downriver by bringing coal upriver to the new plant. This appealed to farmers whose income had declined more than 60 percent during the recession following World War I, even as the cost of living doubled. Ford committed to building the assembly plant even if he didn't get the permit, but he added that if he did, the project would be upgraded to a full manufacturing facility. This would increase employment from three thousand to fourteen thousand people. The stream of promises from the Ford group won support from residents all over the state. Who could oppose well-paying jobs?

Minneapolis had earlier alleged that St. Paul was secretly working with Ford and its suspicions were proven true. Business leaders were already working on acquiring the site for Ford's plant well before details were made public. A later story in the *Pioneer Press* disclosed the secret negotiations and reported that Henry Ford "would not take options on the land and would consider nothing but deeds . . . The magnitude of the undertaking may be realized when it is known that Ford would consider no more nor no less than the 167 acre tract. This was in possession of 97 owners in all parts of the country. The last deed came from New Orleans. The men who did this work were forced to supply the money for the land knowing if they failed to get it all they would have the site on their hands with their money gone. They knew they would face ridicule if the plans fell through."

Another article published in 1953 pieced together the sequence of events: "On November 6, 1922, the committee through Col. L. H. Brittin, its representative, gave Ford's chief engineer, W. B. Mayo, a promise 'of what it would do if Ford built his plant here.' A contract was drawn up between the committee, the Ford Motor Company and the Merchants Trust and Savings of St. Paul in which the site was agreed upon, and Ford put up $272,992.40 and the committee $42,028.40, a total of $315,020.80." One of the committee members said, "you will admit that it was a lot of men to keep a secret . . . Real estate agents, headed by Den E. Lane . . . scuttled out to get options on the land." Some citizens became suspicious of the land acquisition activity but the committee and the press maintained "Sphinx-like silence."

To bolster his chances for the hydroelectric permit, Ford mobilized his extensive corporate resources to win over the public, especially the farmers. He set up a huge display of Fordson tractors at the Minnesota State Fair. It featured "seventy-five Fordsons in constant operation and one hundred separate pieces of industrial and agricultural equipment being demonstrated daily . . . a continuous moving display in the 'bull ring' every minute of the day." At the close of the state fair, in October 1922, Ford announced an extravaganza for Minneapolis, featuring a "Big Parade" every day for a week showcasing "every conceivable type of body and trailer." Ford also unveiled his plan to build a major Farm Export Center in New York City to promote international trade and announced plans for navigation improvements for the Mississippi River.

Ford greatly increased company and dealer advertising in local newspapers during this period, including large ads in February 1923 promoting tours of the Minneapolis assembly plant. He promised to sell coal at cost to residents of the Twin Cities at a time of great shortages. He also distributed free educational movies to schools and commercial theaters, made by the company's cinema department, the largest company studio in the country. A newspaper ad for the Tower Theater in St. Paul, probably paid for by Ford, read: "See—the *Ford Age* Showing Remarkable Development of Ford Motor Company, Intimate Views of Henry Ford Himself." Ford used his extensive network of automobile dealerships to distribute company films, which were seen by an estimated four million people weekly around the country.

The Ford public-relations machine was in full force, and Mayor Leach couldn't even visit the fair or walk the streets of his city without being reminded of its potency. He stepped up his campaign by challenging the St. Paul mayor, Arthur E. Nelson, to a series of debates around the state. More than two thousand people attended the first debate at the Minneapolis Kenwood Armory, which was also broadcast live on the radio throughout the entire country. Mayor Leach concluded his remarks by attacking the Ford industrial system, "saying that Ford has a record turnover of labor and that his plants are highly developed speed-up systems." He added: "Waterpower is the key to replacement and the key to industrial progress for the coming generation. The power belongs to the people." Two thousand people attended the next debate at the Empress Theater in St. Paul on December 22, 1922, where Leach intoned:

> You have heard the eloquent prophecy of the magnificence that is about to descend on these two cities and the state of Minnesota from the bounteous hands of Mr. Henry Ford who wants us to turn over the High Dam to him. We have been made to see a beautiful picture—a vast and ornate factory spreading out over the dam site, tall chimneys belching forth their clouds of smoke—those black banners of Henry Ford. From either city long lines of happy and contented workers swarm to those places of ideal toil—how many of them I do not know—5,000, 10,000, 14,000. They are coming from the thousands of new homes they have built. A hundred thousand people have sprung up in the industrial home district of both cities. A beautiful bridge spans the Mississippi River. Street car lines pour forth their passengers. Real estate men have been made rich selling land. Contractors have been made rich building homes. Storekeepers are being made rich selling their wares. And all is peace and contentment. A happy prosperity has fallen upon us—and all from the bounty of Henry Ford.
>
> Why, ladies and gentlemen, that is just the way the slicker talks when he sells wild cat mining stocks . . . All this is promise—verbal commission—not a line in writing and not even a word from Henry Ford himself. This is simply what someone else tells you Mr. Ford is going to do.

The restless audience responded with catcalls and hoots, but when the St. Paul mayor spoke, the crowd cheered. Leach's aide cried foul, complaining that Ford dealers packed the house with their employees.

The Federal Power Commission was reviewing Ford's application for the High Dam at the same time it was considering another Ford application to buy a surplus federal hydroelectric plant in Alabama on the Tennessee River, known as Muscle Shoals. This was built by the federal government for military production during World War I. Ford proposed to build a seventy-five-mile-long industrial city. Because both projects had the same applicant and raised similar policy issues, their fates became intertwined. The Muscle Shoals project received national attention and was hugely controversial. In Minnesota, the High Dam project continued to simmer, with the mayors of St. Paul and Minneapolis debating each other around the state.

By most accounts, public sentiment in Minnesota supported the Ford proposal. The Duluth Chamber of Commerce came out in favor, as did the Farm Bureau, an important statewide organization. Even the major Minneapolis business groups, including the Minneapolis Civic and Commerce Association and the Lake Street District Association of Commerce, withdrew support for their city's application. These business groups had previously lobbied Ford to look at alternative sites, including the Overland Building, Fort Snelling, and a location near the state fairgrounds, likely the Northwestern Terminal developed by Brittin. But after meeting with Ford officials, they were convinced that they risked jeopardizing the development with its jobs and huge benefits for the entire region. To help gain the support of Minneapolis, St. Paul offered to pay half the cost of a new bridge making the plant accessible to neighborhoods in that city.

The battle between the two cities produced an unexpected and remarkable outcome—a vision for an integrated regional economy emerged in the business community. W. L. Harris of the New England Furniture and Carpet Company in Minneapolis declared:

> The establishment of this plant is a most significant indication of the desirability of the two cities getting together politically, economically, and in every other way. That should be the objective of both cities . . . It is time we quit competing and find out more points of natural affiliations as the financial and business center of the Northwest. We not only need more bridges across the river which separates us, but we need to bridge our differences with a view to becoming one big composite center even though we are separate municipalities.

A former Minneapolis mayor agreed: "Let us look at this in a practical common sense way, just as we would look at a problem in our private business. You can't grow if you play the dog in the manger. If you can't have the Ford in Minneapolis, let's have him in St. Paul." Even Douglas A. Fiske, Brittin's former boss at the Minneapolis Civic and Commerce Association, was won over and said: "Minneapolis wanted the Ford plant and worked for it. That is as natural as it was for St. Paul to go after it. But by the fact that God had located the best site on the St. Paul side of the river we had the short end of the argument from the beginning. Henry Ford made his decision and bought his land on the St. Paul side." Business leaders in Minneapolis abandoned their mayor en masse.

Ford's Labor Policies Become Part of Permit Debate

Running out of time and options, Minneapolis mayor Leach sought to rally public support by launching a desperate attack on Ford's labor policies, calling him "the feudal lord of Detroit." Rather than being an economic savior for the region, Leach railed, "a great part of the business of Detroit depends upon the condition of his digestion every morning. If he gets peeved at the railroads, the coal mines, the police force he is just as likely as not to shut down his factory for a month or six weeks until he can have his own way!"

St. Paul mayor Nelson had anticipated that Ford's labor policies might be raised and had already enlisted the support of William Mahoney, a key labor leader in his city. A group of community officials, including labor leaders from both cities, had earlier visited the Ford plant in Detroit to see how the workers were treated. They came away impressed from their meetings with top Ford officials, leading Mahoney to give tacit support for Ford's bid. Mahoney agreed with Mayor Nelson's report that the minimum pay for workers was $6 per day and that many men were making as much as $10, $15, or $20. Mayor Nelson and Colonel Brittin arranged for Mahoney to make a presentation to the Ramsey County Board, where he defended Ford's labor policies: "Ford's workers are happy and satisfied. Despite the fact that Ford makes a tremendous income yearly, he does it without exploiting labor and sells his product at a price that is reasonable and not profiteering, and his profit is made through efficiency in organization." Mahoney reflected further on some of the elemental issues labor unions faced then and would face in the future:

> The labor question is bigger than organized or unorganized labor. When we consider the Ford labor policy we must not compare it with ideals which have never been realized, but with conditions which prevail in other factories throughout the United States. We must judge the plant by whether the unions benefit by working in it. Ford is a practical man and he is making a real effort to make conditions better for the worker. His work speaks for itself . . . It is only in industries where labor is very strongly organized that the eight-hour day is an

accomplished fact, and 90 percent of the mechanics in Minneapolis today are not getting $6 a day, the amount Ford pays for common labor.

Mayor Leach continued to press the issue of Ford's labor policies, and resorted to challenging Mahoney to a debate. At a major event in Minneapolis, Leach again attacked Ford on the labor issue:

> Common laborer at $6 a day. Do you workers ever stop to think that you never hear of any other laborer in connection with Mr. Ford except common laborer? . . . Do you know how Mr. Ford made his billion dollars? Do you know wherein lies his wonderful efficiency—the efficiency that is the admiration and envy of every other manufacturer in the world? . . . It is simply this: that Henry Ford reduced all labor—all skilled labor—to common labor. Henry Ford makes a machine, sets it to work with a man—a common laborer—and that the machine and that man do the work of the skilled laborer.

Mayor Leach's arguments could not gain any traction. St. Paul managed to appropriate the "populist" argument, claiming that the power belonged to the entire state and should not be used for the benefit of just one city. This was a remarkable rebranding of its proposal that would give the hydroelectric power to Ford, a private corporation. Business groups and workers all over Minnesota picked up the populist argument and demanded their share of the benefits from the waterpower. The leader of the Farm Bureau said, "Minneapolis has no right by a referendum to tell 186,000 farmers of the state what disposition shall be made of the power at the High dam. This power does not belong to St. Paul; it does not belong to Minneapolis; it does not belong to Minnesota. It belongs to the entire country."

Seeing his hopes slipping away, Mayor Leach offered to lease Minneapolis's share of the power directly to Ford if his city was granted the permit. This further undercut the legitimacy of his attacks on Ford. The Federal Power Commission bluntly warned that "Minneapolis would lose all advantages for preference granted municipalities and states in the Federal Power Act if they intended to sublease the power to Ford or any other private corporation." Leach and his allies made their final desperate proposal—Minneapolis would withdraw its application if Ford would "agree in writing that any excess energy developed would be turned back to the municipalities," and furthermore "that the municipalities be given prior option to buy the Ford [hydroelectric] plant at cost if for any reasons its use were discontinued." The idea of a reverter clause was first introduced by NSP. Surprisingly, after Leach reintroduced the concept, St. Paul echoed its support that cities should have the option to acquire the hydro plant if Ford were to leave.

Unfortunately, these reasonable requests fell on deaf ears.

Mayor Leach then asked legislators from Minneapolis to modify his bill for a municipal utility to allow both cities an equal share of the power. St. Paul mayor Nelson asked why Minneapolis didn't just take over ownership of the privately owned hydroelectric plants at St. Anthony Falls if it believed in municipal ownership. The business community, which grew up around the Falls of St. Anthony, was quick to reject any call for public ownership. Douglas Fiske of Minneapolis declared, "Municipal ownership, I believe, is dangerous, uneconomic and unbusinesslike. Ford, on the other hand offers a businesslike proposition." Leach defended his proposal for municipal ownership by pointing out that St. Paul's original application for the permit called for the power to be used for municipal lighting. He could have added that there were numerous examples of successful municipal power companies throughout Minnesota and the United States, and that even Henry Ford had advocated for public ownership of utilities and a municipal takeover of the streetcar system in Detroit. But Leach could not shake the perception that he was a socialist. Mayor Leach's campaign for the hydro permit floundered from the start, with shifting and self-contradictory positions.

William Mahoney was a prominent labor leader in St. Paul and publisher of the *Union Advocate* newspaper. His support of Ford's labor policies helped Ford's application for the hydroelectric permit. He later deeply regretted his endorsement. Mahoney was elected mayor of St. Paul in 1932 on a campaign for municipal ownership of utilities. Photograph by Midway Studio. Courtesy of the Minnesota Historical Society.

The business community's rejection of Mayor Leach was particularly surprising because he had been specifically chosen in 1921 by representatives of the Minneapolis

IT'S EASY TO TELL WHICH WAY THE PUBLIC LEANS

As a desperate move at the end of the campaign, Mayor Leach proposed that Minneapolis operate a municipal electric utility at the High Dam, a position deemed socialist by many in the business community. This cartoon published on the front page of the *St. Paul Pioneer Press* on December 26, 1922, captured the sentiment. Courtesy of the Minnesota Historical Society.

Civic and Commerce Association to run against Mayor Tom Van Lear, a declared socialist. The nature of the strained relations with his sponsors was noted by Leach in his memoirs:

> At the peak of my struggle with Henry Ford the President of one of our banks called me in and told me to stop fighting Ford, that Ford had over a million on deposit in his bank and he said he had a telegram from Edsel Ford saying they must call the Mayor off. I declined to be called off and the banker accused me of either being a crook or a fool—I told him I might be willing to plead guilty to the last but never the first.

The Minneapolis bid ended on February 21, 1923, when the legislature defeated the High Dam enabling act just days before the Federal Power Commission was to meet in Washington. This left only NSP to challenge Ford, but it quickly withdrew from the competition. At the hearing of the commission, St. Paul, Minneapolis, and NSP supported the application of the Ford Motor Company. The state, through the University of Minnesota, held off endorsing the Ford proposal, because it continued to insist on receiving the surplus power no matter which applicant won the permit. The two cities agreed to expedite the construction of a bridge across the river. On March 3, 1923, the Federal Power Commission granted Ford a temporary permit for use of the High Dam, requiring that it apply for a permanent license within four months.

If there was any hope that Ford would take a more kindly view of organized labor after receiving strong support from William Mahoney and other labor leaders, those hopes were quickly dashed. The general secretary of the International Building Trades Unions wrote to Ford requesting a meeting to discuss his labor policies, saying, "Our experience with the so-called open shop idea has very forcibly impressed upon us that buildings erected with such a plan discriminate between union and non-union employees and in general such a plan shuts out entirely the opportunity for the organized building trades worker to secure employment." A Ford official responded: "The entire development at St. Paul is in the charge of Messrs. Stone and Webster, 147 Milk Street, Boston, Mass. And in line with the usual Ford policy, all contracts carry the open shop clause. It has always been the policy of this company to conduct its work on the open shop principles and we endeavor to see that there is no discrimination shown between union and non-union men on any jobs that are being put through for us. This same policy will be followed in connection with the St. Paul development."

During the fight for the High Dam permit, a *Minneapolis Tribune* editorial accused St. Paul and Ford of a "theft of the public's rights for the benefit of private enterprises." The editorial had clearly and accurately spelled out the policy implications of public versus private ownership, as did Mayor Leach throughout his campaign. Leach's call for public

ownership of the hydroelectricity disappointed his business backers, but
in laying out his arguments he articulated a thoughtful vision on the roles
of government, business, and labor
in the economic and political system.
Leach's disappointment was palpable
in his memoirs:

> The Ford interests made me many ver-
> bal promises namely that they would
> employ 5,000 men, that they would
> manufacture Farm Machinery and sell
> to the farmers F.O.B. Minneapolis, that
> they would ship their ore direct from
> Duluth, that they would put a line of
> barges on the river, that they would
> build a bridge so that Minneapolis
> men could cross at the plant and many
> others. Of course these promises were
> made through a representative. I don't
> suppose the Fords were a party to them
> but it won the public against me even
> though the only request I made was that
> they should put it in writing. I will leave
> it to the people of 1951 how well they
> kept their promises.

In the end Ford got the Dam and
Power for 100 years—the Northern
States Power got the surplus power. The people of Minneapolis and St. Paul got the privi-
lege of building the bridge at a taxpayers cost of over a million dollars.

SECOND ANNUAL PICNIC OF DALE SOCIALIST LOCAL Sunday, May 27, 1917

Speech by Thomas Van Lear Socialist Mayor of Minneapolis

Braham Brass Band will furnish music for the occasion

BASE BALL GAME Dale vs. Grandy

Other Sports GOOD PRIZES

Refreshments and Lunches on the Grounds

ADMISSION FREE

Come and Bring the Family and Have a Good Time

Dale can be reached from Grandy on the Great Northern or from Harris on the N. P.

Mayor Leach was rebuffed by the Minneapolis business community because of his "socialist plan" for public ownership of the hydroelectric power plant. This was particularly ironic because several years earlier he had been handpicked to run against a true socialist mayor, Thomas Van Lear. Courtesy of the Minnesota Historical Society.

On June 7, 1923, the Federal Power Commission formally granted the Ford Motor Company a fifty-year franchise to operate the High Dam power plant. Annual rent was set
at $95,440, which was to be revised in twenty years and every ten years thereafter. Ford
had to provide up to sixty thousand kilowatt hours per year to operate the federal locks

on the Minneapolis side. All surplus power would be sold to NSP, not distributed free to the cities as Mayor Leach had hoped. Ford was not as successful with his application for the Muscle Shoals project. After an incredibly bitter political process featuring charges of anti-Semitism and an alleged backroom deal with President Calvin Coolidge, Ford was forced to withdraw his application. He was successful in St. Paul probably because he opted to work through very competent local proxies and managed to avoid national political entanglements at the Federal Power Commission. Most important, Minnesota was particularly receptive to Ford's populist appeals to "The Farmer" and the many promises made to the local business community.

Colonel Brittin, the man most responsible for bringing Ford to St. Paul, was on hand in Washington to receive the license for the company. He declared that construction on the hydroelectric project would begin within weeks, managed by the national firm of Stone and Webster. This company had worked with Ford on other hydroelectric projects, including Green Island on the Hudson River, built with federal funds, and two plants in

Henry Ford's application for a hydroelectric permit at the High Dam was reviewed by the Federal Power Commission at the same time as his application for a project at Muscle Shoals, Alabama. Ford is seen here meeting with the chairman of the commission, Secretary of War John Meeks, seated at left. Author's collection.

Michigan. It had also built the dam and hydroelectric plant at Keokuk, Iowa, and even had a Twin Cities connection dating back to 1889 when it purchased Minneapolis General Electric.

News of Ford's winning the permit was prominently featured in the *New York Times*, which mistakenly identified the plant as being in Minneapolis, to the great displeasure of St. Paul mayor Arthur E. Nelson. In a letter to the editor, the irate official complained: "As a matter of fact, the Ford hydroelectric and manufacturing plant . . . is located entirely within the limits of the City of St. Paul. We are doing considerable municipal advertising at the present time . . . Necessarily we are interested in recognition of the fact that these large plants are actually locating in the City of St. Paul. I hope that in future articles . . . St. Paul may get the recognition to which, as the home of the Ford Northwest plant, we feel it is entitled."

With the hydropower license finally resolved, Mayor Leach reflected: "My fight started against the Northern States Power company and Ford came in at the finish and secured the power. I took a good licking in that fight and now I'm ready to cooperate with Ford and do all in my power to aid him develop his plant and district." But the resolution of the High Dam permit did not end the bitter rivalry between Minneapolis and St. Paul. Attention shifted to the building of the new "Ford" Bridge, which allowed the cities to continue bickering for the next several months about its location, design, and financing. Henry Ford pursued the site on the bluffs of the Mississippi River with a masterful campaign, believing it was a prize well worth the fight. Ford would demonstrate that as well with the design of his new building.

"The Finest Plant in the World"

Building the Twin Cities Assembly Plant

The bluff above the Mississippi River that would become home to the Twin Cities Assembly Plant was incorporated into the city of St. Paul in 1887. Previously it was part of an unregulated territory known as Reserve Township under the jurisdiction of the Fort Snelling reservation, a military outpost on the west side of the river. With few roads and no streetcar lines, the township had fewer than five hundred inhabitants as late as 1880. Its main access was a crude ferry from Fort Snelling. The area escaped much attention until it got caught up in a fight between Minneapolis and St. Paul over where to locate the state fair. In 1884, St. Paul and Ramsey County were pushing to have the fairgrounds in the Midway area, but Minneapolis officials suspected there was a secret plan to annex that location, thereby putting it within the boundary of its bitter rival. To break the impasse, Charles Loring, chairman of the Minneapolis Park Commission, proposed to the state fair joint committee that a "Union Park" and state fairgrounds should straddle the Mississippi River at the present-day location of Minnehaha Park on the west side of the river, and the future Ford Motor Company site on the east side.

More than a thousand acres would be set aside for the regional park on the west side surrounding the Minnehaha Falls. The east side had a "spacious level tract entirely suitable in its topographical character to the purpose of a state or union fair ground,"

This photograph, circa 1923, shows the undeveloped 167-acre site on the Mississippi River that Ford selected for his future assembly plant. St. Paul had just zoned the land for prime residential development, but the city quickly rezoned the property for industrial use. Author's collection.

with room for exposition buildings and racetracks. Some critics raised concerns about the locations "being remote from the established systems," particularly rail access, but the site on the east side of the river had the advantage of being outside city limits. As Charles Loring explained: "Each city is too jealous of the other to ever go inside the other's boundaries to attend a fair." The fair was ultimately placed at its current location on Snelling Avenue in Falcon Heights. The beautiful bluff on the Mississippi River would soon become the focal point of yet another battle between the municipal rivals.

By 1900, there were twenty-six dairy farms in the Reserve District supplying much of the produce for St. Paul. It was a tight-knit community with a number of immigrant farmers, including at least one who feared that "suburban sprawl" would disrupt their pastoral lifestyle. Rebecca A. Mavencamp wrote that a farmer sued to stop his neighbor from subdividing his property for a housing development. In July 1922, shortly before the announcement of the Ford plant, St. Paul designated the area for residential development as part of its first zoning code. City Planning Engineer George Herrold did not envision industry on the bluffs of the Mississippi River, even though industry traditionally had located along rivers. Herrold saw that land as ideal for prime residential development. The new zoning tool was generally aimed at

Ford was attracted to the natural beauty of the bluff on the Mississippi River and was determined to build a model plant that would complement the landscape. Author's collection.

separating land uses, keeping factories away from housing. Henry Ford was moving in the opposite direction, believing that well-designed factories could be compatible with housing and the landscape. Herrold was a visionary but also a realist who knew that the announcement of the Ford plant changed everything. He had little choice but to support rezoning the district to industrial use, but he remained committed to finding a way for it to be "the first area in the Northwest to be laid out along city planning lines." Herrold recognized the need to move carefully. Among other reasons, zoning still faced legal challenges - it was not upheld by the federal Supreme Court until 1926.

Henry Ford was enthusiastic about the location of his future plant, declaring it "The finest piece of ground in the country for my purpose." It met all of his criteria. It was away from the downtowns but close enough to find the needed workers. It was large enough for a single-story plant, had ample space for parking and expansion, and was near rail and barge service. Most important, it was one of the best sites in the country for hydroelectric power. On April 25, 1923, a month after receiving the hydroelectric permit, Henry Ford, his son Edsel, and other company officials made a surprise visit to the High Dam. "I wanted to be sure we not only would not injure any of the beauty of the location, but would so locate our plant and make it of such design that the beauties would be enhanced," he explained. "So I told the boys we'd lay the plans aside just as they were for a couple of days and I would go up there with them and see the ground myself." A reporter was on hand to capture Henry Ford's first look at his property:

> It didn't look very industrial then. In fact there wasn't a wisp of smoke to be seen—nothing but thickly wooded hills and moist dales, open patches of grasses beginning to grow green with the life of a new season, ravines running with spring's hastening water, and beyond the cleft waterway of the Mississippi, one of the most beautiful pictures in Minnesota's abundant gallery. Henry Ford pulled his heel out of the soft earth and swept his eye over the whole semi-circle. The expression in his serene face quickened with imagination. He heard the drum of steam exhausts, the detonations of dynamite, the straining of cables, the musketry of riveters, making a giant new plant for him, while to most folks living in the chosen city the whole project seemed like the circus giraffe to the farmer—"There ain't no such thing."

Henry Ford visited his property on April 25, 1923, and reoriented the layout of the building to face the Mississippi River. He is pictured, on the left, with P. E. Martin, vice president of manufacturing; Edsel Ford, president; Ernest Kanzler, production manager; W. B. Mayo, chief power engineer; and S. A. Stellwagen, Minneapolis plant manager. Photograph by *St. Paul Daily News*. Courtesy of the Minnesota Historical Society.

Viewing the river from the bluff, Ford declared, "This scene calls for a plant that will harmonize. I intend to put up a beautiful building that will in no way detract from its beauty." Henry Ford and his entourage drove across the Mississippi River to view the site from the Minneapolis side. Ford concluded that the orientation of the buildings should be changed from the plans already drawn up by his architect, Albert Kahn. Originally the classical facade was to face north, toward St. Catherine Avenue (now Ford Parkway). Ford wanted the main facade to face the river and the parkway. The change would require some reconfiguring, including changes to the rail connections, but none in his party would even consider questioning his decision.

The local press greeted the "auto king" enthusiastically and traded good-natured banter about a range of issues, from his presidential aspirations to whether he planned on buying a local railroad or newspaper. A reporter gushed that "Ford would like to become a permanent St. Paul resident," based on his statement that "If we stay here a few weeks we wouldn't leave." Henry Ford encountered a "deaf, dumb inventor" on his tour who approached with a written note. Ford and the inventor walked away from the group privately exchanging notes. The entire trip was a media sensation reinforcing the claim that Henry Ford was the "Best Advertised Man." His mastery of the local and national media

Government Dam and Ford Plant between St. Paul and Minneapolis, Minn.

This early schematic architectural plan showed the front facade facing north on what was then St. Catherine Avenue. Not only did the orientation change, the final design of the building was completely different than this first postcard illustration. Author's collection.

was critical to winning the license at the High Dam. Oswald Garrison Villard, owner of the *Nation Magazine*, observed, "In anybody else this would have been denounced as a 'grab' and a 'steal' deserving as utmost public condemnation," but for Ford, "there was only applause.

All news accounts stressed Ford's genuine desire to preserve the natural beauty of the site. "We've got to save these trees and give the birds some encouragement to make this an ideal spot, even if we do commercialize," he said. He was a serious "bird-watcher" who built hundreds of birdhouses on his Michigan estate, particularly for endangered species. One St. Paul paper reported that "members of the Ford party were deeply impressed with the scenic beauty" of the Ford site. "While they were here they mentioned it often, and they left for Detroit early Thursday evening more than ever convinced that the industry they bring must not mar the handiwork of nature." In addition to the natural beauty of the site, much was made of its proximity to the Mississippi River Boulevard. Parkways were a relatively new phenomenon, intended to bring people to nature and nature to people. They were an important element of the linear parks movement well established in the Twin Cities. Planner George Herrold believed he found a sensitive and willing partner in Henry Ford. He noted that the change to industrial zoning "was done with the understanding that the Company would do everything possible in architecture and in landscaping to preserve the River Boulevard." Ford approved setting the assembly plant back one hundred feet from the Mississippi River Drive, and four hundred feet from its northern boundary, to protect the surrounding woods. The rezoning also set aside fifty acres north of the plant and thirty-seven acres to the east for industrial and commercial purposes, which would include "a business center, hotels and boarding houses." Herrold felt there was enough undeveloped land around the plant for the model residential community he hoped to see built.

Fear of Land Speculation

A reporter covering Henry Ford's visit asked whether he intended to build a model town with workers' housing, as was suggested by an article in the *Wall Street Journal*. Minneapolis city council members took that report seriously because they insisted that as a condition of their support Ford would have to build half of the housing units in their city. Ford had constructed employee housing elsewhere, and even experimented with the notion of assembly-line houses, but he denied he would build any residential projects in the Twin Cities. William Mayo, Ford's chief engineer, spoke directly to the issue: "there will be no colonization scheme, no company stores, employees will be taken from the Twin Cities so far as possible, and home ownership would be encouraged." Henry Ford did express concern about land speculation and urged officials to take all possible steps to minimize it. He had long preached the value of home ownership and had created several programs to help his employees attain that goal. He had seen unscrupulous landlords in Detroit and other cities take advantage of his well-paid workers, many of whom were naive immigrants. With his "decentralization" phase, Ford saw a new kind of exploitation—speculators who swooped in to buy vacant land as soon as plant locations were announced. This was particularly rampant around his proposed Muscle Shoals project, where a number of real-estate developers were ultimately prosecuted for fraud. Land speculation was already under way in St. Paul. A newspaper article, published next to the account of Ford's visit, profiled a developer who was re-platting fifty acres on the southwest corner of Randolph and Snelling for 275 homesites. "Associated with the promoters," the paper noted, "are some of the same men who sold 500 lots at Flint, Michigan in three days at the time General Motors Inc., located there."

Real-estate ads were posted in the newspapers within days of Ford's announcement to build in St. Paul. One trumpeted, "Ford Is Coming—Buy Now with Prices Low . . . prices only $750. Reasonable Terms." Another wrote: "Ford Is Coming Properties Should Grow in Value"—and grow they did. One of the historic farmsteads owned by an early settler, John A. Stees, was sold and, according to real-estate experts, "the proximity of the new residential district to the Ford plant assures its rapid development." A ten-acre parcel on Otto Avenue jumped from $850 an acre to two thousand dollars an acre. Den E. Lane, the most prominent housing developer in St. Paul, predicted that he would "take care of" between four thousand and five thousand families within five years. "What the coming of Ford and other industries means to St. Paul," he added, "appears to be better realized outside of the city than it is right here; not a day goes by but that we do not receive letters from persons in various sections of the country asking for land, both residential and business property."

The most brazen ad campaign managed to turn Ford's own words into an endorsement for speculation. The developer of Hardenbergh Heights, a planned development six blocks from the Ford plant on Snelling Avenue, proclaimed, "HENRY FORD'S VIEWPOINT . . . There is nothing in the United States to equal the High Dam Site here . . . Does this mean anything to you, Mr. Wide Awake Business Man? If you believe that the Twin Cities will grow then you must also believe that this land will increase in value . . . It won't be long from now until many people will still be talking of the low priced lots they could have bought near the Ford plant in 1923." If Henry Ford could not curtail real-estate speculation, he suggested another option to a St. Paul reporter: "In these days of cheap cars it is easy for the worker who is being held up in the price of a home to live many miles away from his place of employment. They will shy away from high-priced property owned by speculators." Housing dispersal, together with industrial "decentralization" and the automobile, were the essential pillars of suburban sprawl.

Officials in St. Paul shared Ford's concerns about land speculation and worked to ensure that homesites would be affordable for workers. The St. Paul chapter of the American Institute of Architects and local realtors helped create plans for the new Highland Park neighborhood and guidelines for the South Minneapolis neighborhood across the river. They sought to prevent land from getting "into the hands of speculators who will hold it indefinitely with no improvements, and will ask prices so high as to make development of the district impossible." The city moved quickly to rezone and re-plat the land around the Ford plant and to install utilities. The entire cost of the new sewer system for the four-hundred-acre district was assessed against property owners. Colonel Brittin lobbied for speedy development to make sure St. Paul would not become the "back door" to the Ford plant. He warned that with the opening of the Ford Bridge, "the residential section just across the river will profit more from the Ford plant than St. Paul."

The new Highland Park plant was designed by noted industrial architect Albert Kahn, pictured in his Detroit office beneath a picture of the Pantheon. Although well versed in classical architecture, he rarely applied the style to industrial buildings. Courtesy of Albert Kahn Associates, Inc., Architects and Engineers.

Construction Begins

Ford had great confidence in Albert Kahn, his architect for the new plant in St. Paul. Kahn immigrated to Detroit from Germany in 1880, on the eve of the automobile boom. He was well versed in classical architecture, but also very knowledgeable about engineering and materials technology. With his younger brother Julius, who was an engineer, he invented the "Kahn Bar" for reinforcing concrete, which was sold through their company, Truscon Steel. In 1905, Kahn designed the first reinforced concrete factory in Detroit for the Packard Motor Company. This led to numerous commissions

Albert Kahn designed the Ford Engineering Laboratory in Dearborn *(above)*, which was built about the same time as the Twin Cities Assembly Plant *(below)*. The exteriors of the two buildings are remarkably similar. The Boston engineering firm Stone and Webster was credited as architect on the application to the St. Paul building department, but there is little doubt that Kahn was its principal designer. Courtesy of Albert Kahn Associates, Inc., Architects and Engineers.

from other automobile companies, including Ford, for both his Highland Park plant in Detroit and the River Rouge plant. Kahn revolutionized architectural practice by using a team approach, involving engineers and construction specialists early in the design process. Kahn, who was Jewish, maintained a cordial relationship with Henry Ford, in spite of his anti-Semitism campaign.

Stone and Webster, an engineering firm based in Boston with expertise in hydroelectric plants, played a significant role in the plant's design. Described as "design engineers" and "contractors," Stone and Webster were listed on the St. Paul construction permit as architects for the project, but there is little doubt that Albert Kahn was the principal designer. The building's Italian renaissance design was an almost identical copy of Ford's Engineering Laboratory designed by Kahn and built in Dearborn just months earlier. Because Ford never wasted a good design, as seen with the repeated use of John Graham's building motifs, he would have had no problem replicating a bigger version of the beautiful Engineering Laboratory on such a prominent location overlooking the Mississippi River. Kahn was listed as architect for several of the outlying buildings, including the Steam House and the Gas Producing Plant, and the interior renovations of the main building for the Glass Plant.

Job seekers arrived at the plant site well before construction began. Ford's policy was to hire locally, and he discouraged the "importation of labor," but there was little he could do to slow the influx of people who wanted to work for his company. Applicants also swarmed the Ford headquarters in Detroit, where they were redirected to the Saint Paul Association, which had to hire two special clerks to deal with the crowds. Eventually, the St. Paul group insisted on application letters rather than personal visits. After several thousand people applied in St. Paul, Brittin announced that Minneapolis would immediately get its own employment office. The *Union Advocate*, a labor newspaper, reported that the flood of "destitute persons" was overwhelming public charity and labor organizations, adding, "It is difficult to understand how anyone with intelligence could get the impression that there was any present or immediate future prospects of employment."

This extraordinary outpouring of interest occurred after Ford announced that he would build an assembly plant, but before the company had secured the hydroelectric permit, prompting Brittin to dangle one last enticement: "How many of those applications will be successful will be dependent in a large degree on the water power of the High Dam being granted to Ford because this will guide the decision as to whether the Ford plant will be merely an assembling unit employing 2,000 men or a factory employing 14,000." Upward of twenty-five thousand men from all over the country applied, but the company declared that "Preference will be given to bona fide residents of the Twin Cities, without regard to whether they live in Minneapolis or St. Paul." African American news-

The foundation for the hydroelectric plant was built a decade before Ford arrived and could not accommodate the new advanced turbines. Ford had to remove and rebuild most of the concrete structure. Author's collection.

papers carefully monitored hiring practices at the plant and urged community members to get prepared to apply. Henry Ford was well known for hiring minority workers in Detroit, but there were concerns that local Ford representatives might not be as receptive.

The first task for the Stone and Webster's engineers was to analyze the foundation of the hydropower plant built by the Army Corps just seven years earlier. They determined that much of it had to be redone to accommodate the most advanced turbines; more than three thousand tons of reinforced concrete had to be removed. The new power plant was built with a red-tile roof and classical detailing that complemented the architecture of the main assembly plant. The generator room extended the full width of the building, and with its thirty-six-foot ceiling and large windows, the interior was flooded with light. A traveling crane was attached to the ceiling to move heavy equipment, and a second crane was placed outside the generator room to remove debris from the river that could get trapped in the equipment.

By April 1924, workers had installed the first of four 4,500-kilovolt turbines in a deep concrete tube, and four eighteen-foot-tall Westinghouse generators above the vertical turbines. They were so large they had to be shipped on a customized rail car with a dropped floor so they could fit beneath bridges and tunnels. With a normal thirty-four-foot head of water, the plant could produce 18,000 horsepower. It generated and transmitted 13,200 volts of electricity to the assembly plant by underground cable where it was transformed to 440-, 220-, and 110-volt current. The plant started to produce electricity in July 1924 and has run continuously since, except during floods. Early Ford reports boasted

The hydropower plant was under construction by 1923. With its red-tile roof and limestone facade, the hydropower plant was designed to complement the main assembly plant. Author's collection.

that there was enough power to meet the needs of a city of seventy-five thousand people. Because the hydroelectric plant was completed before the assembly plant, Ford sold all the electricity to NSP in accordance with the federal permit. Even after the assembly plant was in full production, there was considerable surplus power. NSP was able to resell the power it bought from Ford at a substantially higher price, prompting a number of officials to call for the revocation or renegotiation of the permit.

Ford needed additional land just downriver from the hydroelectric plant to make a new "tailrace," or channel, for the water that traveled through the hydropower plant. The company bought a thirteen-acre island owned by NSP, which it swapped for the river frontage property below the Ford parcel, which the city of St. Paul had just acquired through eminent domain. The exchange included the proviso that any dredged materials from the tailrace channel be added to the city-owned parkland further to the south.

The attractive interior of the hydroelectric plant reflected Ford's reverence for power-generating equipment. A gallery was built on the second level to allow visitors to tour the plant. Author's collection.

The swap agreement with the city also stipulated "that no buildings are to be erected upon the land . . . whose top elevation is higher than Mississippi River Boulevard." The Steam Plant was later built on land that carried this restriction. This may explain why buildings constructed along the river were not placed on higher ground that could have better protected them from floods. There were published reports that Ford needed to buy additional land from the city to complete the shipping terminal, as well as three hundred more acres for storage space along the river. There was also a news account that "Col. Brittin will negotiate with Secretary Weeks for purchase of government land abutting the dam on which the steam auxiliary or stand-by plant of the Ford Motor Company is to be built." Another article in the *St. Paul Daily News* referred to the "combination steam and hydraulic power house on the St. Paul end of the dam." Brittin later received assurances that the federal government would sell Ford its shore land near the dam. It appears that Ford originally contemplated building the steam plant adjacent to the hydroelectric plant, but no further evidence for this has been found. It was eventually built further downriver on city land that was part of the swap agreement.

Stone and Webster drew architectural plans for the Ford project in phases that were put out to bid as a series of separate contracts rather than as a one complete package. This "fast-track" approach was likely needed to ensure that the foundation work would be completed before the harsh Minnesota winter. The first contracts for the substructure of the nineteen-acre plant were awarded to prominent St. Paul builder H. C. Struchen, who had extensive experience with concrete, including gunite, a process for spraying the material. According to the terms of the contract, the substructure work had to be completed by spring, which meant that Struchen would have to work throughout the winter. The contract was signed on a Saturday and by that evening Struchen's subcontractor, Clement F. Scully Equipment Company, was already on the site with two steam shovels. The crew was prepared to start the following day, except that "Mr. Ford it is known, has certain positive convictions on the evils of labor on the Sabbath day." Several additional steam shovels were brought to the site on Monday, December 10, 1923, as a crew of one hundred mobilized to get a jump on winter. The ground had already frozen to a depth of ten inches.

Struchen had more than a decade of experience in pouring concrete during winter, but nothing comparable to the scale of the new Ford plant, which had foundations almost three-quarters of a mile in length. Many doubted that Struchen could complete the job during the winter, including the project managers at Stone and Webster, but the work proceeded quickly. As workers dug the trenches, the crew followed and poured concrete before the dirt froze. Water for the mix had to be heated to 180 degrees and the sand to 100 degrees. Once workers poured the concrete, portable heaters had to keep it warm for

Ford "fast-tracked" construction of the Twin Cities Assembly Plant by parceling out the work in a series of separate contracts. H. C. Struchen was awarded the contract for the foundation work of the main assembly plant. In 1924, he started concrete work after the ground was frozen. Many skeptics doubted that the work could be carried on during the long Minnesota winter, but Struchen proved them wrong. Author's collection.

the first forty-eight hours. Struchen believed the extra cost of winter projects was offset by less expensive materials and labor during the off-season. Workers were paid $1.75 for a ten-hour day compared to $2.50 during the summer months. Struchen's company was an "open shop," meaning he hired both union and nonunion workers, but he usually paid nonunion workers more because he "admired their stand for freedom of choice." Struchen's views on unions would have certainly have found favor with Henry Ford and Colonel Brittin, but it was a deep disappointment to labor leaders, particularly William Mahoney, who wrote: "This situation is vigorously protested by the working people of the Twin Cities who did so much to secure the High Dam permit for Mr. Ford." He believed he had an understanding that construction workers would be paid along the line of his factory workers, and would work an eight-hour day. Instead, the contractors were working nine-hour shifts, with no overtime pay.

The *St. Paul Daily News* praised the fast pace of work, writing that its completion two weeks ahead of schedule "is the best news that St. Paul has received in a long time . . . as hundreds of laborers will have a chance to get employment this winter." Struchen had poured 3,500 yards of concrete with his crew of 235 men with temperatures often at twenty-five degrees below zero. Crews also dredged a six-foot navigation channel in the Mississippi River adjacent to the terminal, and poured a one-thousand-foot-long seawall.

With his outstanding work on the substructure, Struchen received additional contracts to drill tunnels connecting the main assembly plant to the power plants and terminal on the river one hundred feet below. In the first phase, Struchen built two tunnels,

After his impressive performance on the foundations, Struchen was awarded the contract to build several large tunnels that connected the power plants on the river to the assembly plant on the bluff, one hundred feet above. Struchen specialized in the "gunite" method of spraying concrete, which he used to line the tunnels. Author's collection.

This view of the rear of the assembly plant under construction is looking north to the grove of trees that Henry Ford personally ordered be preserved. Before roads were upgraded, materials were delivered by horse wagons. Author's collection.

each 776 feet long, 11 feet wide by 11 feet tall, leading from the river to a large chamber below the floor of the main plant. Next they drilled a vertical shaft, 36 feet by 25 feet, 100 feet down from the plant floor to connect with the tunnels below. This would hold an air shaft and two high-speed electric elevators large enough to transport finished cars and raw materials. The second phase of the project was an 880-foot-long tunnel connecting the future Gas Building on the river level to the future glass plant sixty feet above. A third tunnel connected the Steam Plant on the river to the main plant. The geology of the bluff consisted of a layer of loam and clay above limestone and shale and several types of sandstone. The upper thirty-five feet of the shaft was limestone, which contained some water pockets, but was solid enough to require blasting. The bottom of the tunnels was fifteen feet above the level of the river. The construction crew experimented with different methods of drilling through the soft rock. They discovered by accident that a jet of compressed air forced through a one-half-inch pipe could drill a hole four feet deep. The white sand was removed by horse-drawn carts and dumped behind the twenty-four-foot-tall reinforced concrete retaining walls being constructed along the river. A Fordson tractor smoothed the sand, described as "giant mounds, like an Alpine snow-slide," by dragging a "slip" back and forth. The excavated tunnels and shaft were sprayed with concrete, a technique Struchen used earlier on the Selby Avenue streetcar tunnel.

The contracts for the steel infrastructure for the redesigned hydroelectric plant and the new assembly building were divided between the St. Paul Foundry and the Minneapolis Steel and Machinery Company. Stone and Webster also selected general contractors from both cities, George J. Grant Construction from St. Paul and Winston Bros. from Minneapolis. Multiple companies were needed to meet the aggressive construction schedule, but spreading the work to both cities also had undeniable political benefits. Work started on the superstructure of the assembly plant on February 25, 1924. The fabricated steel was delivered to the site mainly by the newly extended "short line" of the St. Paul Railway, although horse-drawn wagons and trucks were also used.

Henry Ford was not sure there was room for an auxiliary steam plant along the river, but after inspecting the site, he decided to proceed. The Steam Plant would heat the main

During his visit to the site, Henry Ford decided there was enough room to build a Steam Plant along the river to supplement the hydroelectric power. He located it above the highest historic flood stage—but not high enough, as later floods would demonstrate. The enclosed bridge behind the Steam Plant carried steam pipes to tunnels that connected to the main plant. Author's collection.

assembly plant on the bluff and provide back-up electric power if the river was too low to generate hydroelectricity. Ford also believed that future expansion of manufacturing operations might require more electricity than the hydro plant could produce. The Steam Plant was located approximately a quarter mile downriver from the High Dam.

The construction contract for the Steam Plant was awarded to Stone and Webster in March 1924. Plant equipment included a 5,000 K.V.A. steam turbo generator providing 6,500 horsepower, and two McAleen boilers, each providing 1,361 horsepower. At 100 x 100 and 85 feet high, the

Railroad cars entered the Hopper House behind the plant and dropped coal to a conveyor belt below, which went through a tunnel under the assembly plant and across the bridge to the Steam Plant. The Oil House is in the background. Author's collection.

structure was large enough to accommodate a second generator if needed. Each boiler had a maximum capacity of 125,000 pounds of steam per hour and 237,000 pounds per hour at a temperature of 600 degrees. In addition to heating the assembly plant, steam was used for manufacturing processes. According to a later company memo: "The heating pipes, if extended in one long pipe, would reach from here to Duluth—175 miles."

Transportation Improvements to the Plant

During the campaign to secure the hydroelectric permit, Ford claimed he would use the river to bring coal to the plant and transport finished cars and parts out. Ford engineer William Mayo said that the company had been studying various types of barges to determine the model best suited for the Mississippi River. Ford would consider hauling freight from other companies, if necessary, to balance incoming and outgoing trips. Colonel Brittin, who went to Washington, D.C., to meet with Secretary of War J. W. Weeks regarding transferring some federal property along the river to Ford, also brought up navigation issues. He hoped to convince Weeks to have the federal government institute regular barge service between the Twin Cities and St. Louis, where another Ford plant was located. Brittin gave assurances that Ford would guarantee the necessary tonnage to make it profitable.

Ford was building a fleet of large freight vessels to transport materials around the Great Lakes and across the Atlantic. He was already shipping coal from Ford mines to Duluth, where it was stockpiled on a company dock. The coal would be transported from Duluth to the St. Paul plant by rail. Trains would enter the freestanding "Hopper House" up on the bluff, just east of the assembly plant, dumping the material on a conveyor belt that ran through a tunnel under the plant to a concrete bridge that connected to the Steam Plant. The conveyor belt could deliver one hundred tons of coal per hour over a distance of almost one-half mile. The coal would be pulverized to the fineness of flour and when fed into the furnaces would "flash into flame in the same manner that gas and oil will ignite." Given Henry Ford's obsession to be secure from energy disruptions,

Railroad tracks were depressed below the level of the floor of the assembly plant to allow for easier loading and unloading. Author's collection.

the Steam Plant was backed up by natural gas piped in from Oklahoma and two thirty thousand–gallon propane tanks, the largest installation west of Chicago. Years later Ford installed two huge storage tanks to hold one million gallons of fuel oil.

Colonel Brittin had studied options for new rail service and presented a detailed proposal to Henry Ford in late 1922. The new plant would need more than three hundred rail cars a day, so there was great interest by the rail companies. Brittin selected the Chicago, Milwaukee and St. Paul Railway Company to do a survey of possible routes, over the objections of the Minnesota Transfer Railway in the Midway. The St. Paul line concluded that tracks could cross the Mississippi River from Minneapolis at Minnehaha Falls. (This was never built.) Additional surveys mapped out detailed rail routes adjacent to the plant, some of which had to be adjusted after encountering opposition from property owners. About four and a half miles of tracks were installed connecting the plant to rail service running along West Seventh Street. Two lines were brought right into the assembly plant to accommodate thirty-eight rail cars on tracks that were partially depressed beneath the plant floor. Extra tracks were also installed south of the plant for outside storage. The thirteen miles of new tracks approaching the plant required considerable grading, including a twenty-five-foot deep cut almost a mile long. Several new temporary bridges were installed, including one that was 1,200 feet long and sixty feet high. Another had to separate the grades where the tracks crossed Cleveland Avenue.

During the campaign to win the hydroelectric permit, Ford agents "reliably reported" that a $6,000,000 railroad would be built between Duluth and the Twin Cities, "in the event he is granted the use of the power." Lewis Brittin was quoted as saying, "The report, which I have no doubt has foundation, justifies what I have said that the people of the Northwest have no idea the mammoth proportions to which the Ford program will grow if encouraged and given the opportunity." Plans for the proposed railroad were discussed at meetings of the St. Paul Association, the Minneapolis Civic and Commerce Association, and the Industrial Promotions committee of the Duluth Chamber of Commerce. There were even discussions about creating an alliance of St. Paul, Minneapolis, and Duluth businesses to develop the smelting industry. All the groups that heard the presentations supported Ford's bid for the hydroelectric permit, but the proposed Duluth railroad never materialized.

The Ford plant needed other local transportation improvements, some to enable workers to get to the site. Ford made land on the northeast corner of the site available to the streetcar company for a "turnaround" as part of the planned extension of the streetcar line. This came with the expressed provision that "no trees are to be disturbed." When Snelling Avenue was paved, the center was left open for tracks for the planned streetcar extension, which was to happen "as quickly as residential development allows." The

Randolph line was to be "double tracked," extending from Snelling Avenue to Cleveland Avenue, where it dropped south to Edsel Avenue (formerly known as St. Catherine's Avenue, and later Ford Road, and then finally Ford Parkway in 1924) and then directly west to the Ford plant. Officials from the Twin Cities had visited Detroit to study traffic congestion around the Ford plants and were impressed that the company established staggered work shifts to lessen the load on the streetcar system. They believed that a similar plan of releasing workers every fifteen minutes was needed locally so the plant "does not belch forth a crowd of workmen to jam the streets and streetcars every eight hours."

Before starting construction on the assembly plant, Ford cleared a large portion of the property south of Edsel Avenue for an equipment staging area and for parking. The avenue was also widened ten feet with the city purchasing a strip of land from Ford. Access roads were graveled to prevent vehicles from getting stuck in the mud. Randolph and Snelling Avenues and the Mississippi River Boulevard were paved and miles of new sidewalks were installed. A number of streets were also significantly widened. Otto Avenue (later Highland Parkway) went from 66 feet to 100 feet. Cleveland Avenue was widened to 100 feet, in spite of opposition from property owners who branded it a "fool's proposition." Fairview was widened from 66 feet to 86 feet, and West Seventh to 104 feet. A new "highway" was planned to link West Seventh Street directly to the Ford plant. Known as St. Paul Avenue, this 104-foot-wide diagonal connection had a gradual incline preferred by trucks, and was intended to keep vehicles away from the new housing.

All transportation plans assumed a new bridge across the Mississippi River that would connect the Ford plant to the neighborhoods in South Minneapolis. A joint committee of officials from St. Paul and Minneapolis convened to discuss its location and design. Ford's construction managers, Stone and Webster, and Colonel Brittin were responsible for overseeing the design of the approach roads leading to the new bridge. W. B. Mayo, a Ford official, pushed for a connection with Edsel Avenue and the new streetcar line. Officials at the Minneapolis Parks Board opposed this route because it would disturb the automobile tourist camp at Minnehaha Park. An architectural association was unhappy with the preliminary design of the bridge, and labor leaders lobbied for a "closed shop," an eight-hour day, and higher pay.

The most basic question was unresolved—who would pay for the bridge? During the campaign for the hydro permit, Ford was so supportive of the bridge that local leaders assumed that the company would contribute. Representatives of the Lake Street District Association clearly were left with that impression, saying that they "had visited Ford and that he had promised that if granted the water power rights, he would construct a bridge across the Mississippi at the high dam." In large measure because of that belief, the association supported the Ford proposal. Minneapolis officials finally put the question to

This view from 1926 shows the Intercity Bridge under construction. Now commonly known as the Ford Bridge, it allowed residents of South Minneapolis access to the Ford plant. Ford had left the impression that he would help pay for its construction, but the two cities ended up splitting the bill. Photograph by Hibbard Studio. Courtesy of the Minnesota Historical Society.

Ford directly, asking for a five hundred thousand–dollar contribution. Mayo rebuffed this solicitation, saying, "We feel that the construction of a bridge is merely the carrying of a road across the river and that it will be so greatly to the advantage in itself to both St. Paul and Minneapolis that the two cities will be amply justified in undertaking the entire expense on their own account."

Construction of the bridge started in 1925. Prior to its completion, workers at the plant from Minneapolis would occasionally walk across the frozen Mississippi River during winter rather than make the twenty-block trek to the Lake Street Bridge. There were reports that some workers walked through a narrow corridor in the dam until Ford put a stop to the practice. The new Intercity Bridge, more commonly known as the Ford Bridge, was completed in 1927. Officials lobbied hard to ensure that there would be one streetcar fare to riders coming from Minneapolis to the Ford plant.

The Most Beautiful Plant in the World

Construction of the main building of the Twin Cities Assembly Plant was substantially completed by May 1925. The beautifully detailed facade 1,400 feet in length faced the river in accordance with Henry Ford's directive. Because of its length, it was almost impossible to take in the long row of classical pilasters unless viewing from the other side of the river. Even the short side of the building, at 601 feet, was wider than the Mississippi River at that point. Observers felt its monumental appearance was befitting a civic building such as a museum or a library more than a factory. The structure had a total floor space of 841,400 square feet, making it Ford's largest branch plant, and it was powered by the company's largest hydroelectric power facility. One local paper praised the building as "the finest in the world," and marveled at the extensive conveyor lines that almost eliminated the need for trucking and handling. The building had large plate-glass windows facing the river, enabling visitors who were strolling the beautiful grounds "to see Ford cars change from a jumble of small parts into a completed automobile ready for delivery."

Henry Ford pledged that the plant would not detract from the beauty of its Mississippi River location and by all accounts he succeeded in spectacular fashion. The grove of trees that Ford had insisted be preserved was incorporated into a nicely landscaped park.

When completed, the classically designed Twin Cities Assembly Plant was described as "the finest in the world." Its large plate-glass windows allowed visitors to watch cars being made inside. Over 110,000 people attended an open house at the new plant during the week of April 4, 1927. This is a view of the showroom on the northwest corner of the building. Author's collection.

This 1926 aerial view looks north, showing the completed assembly plant, the Mississippi River Boulevard, and the two power plants on the river. Trains entered the building from the south east, and the parking lot is at the northeast corner. Construction had not yet started on the Ford Bridge. The grove of trees north of the plant was preserved, and the surrounding Highland Park neighborhood had yet to be developed. Courtesy of the Minnesota Historical Society.

City planner George Herrold wrote approvingly: "the company has carried out its part of the agreement in the finest way." In *The Machine in the Garden: Technology and the Pastoral Ideal in America*, Leo Marx wrote: "Within the lifetime of a single generation a rustic and in large part wild landscape was transformed into the site of the world's most productive industrial machine. It would be difficult to imagine more profound contradictions of value or meaning than those made manifest by this circumstance." If these contradictions could be resolved, it would be difficult to find a better example of the idealized "machine in the garden" than Albert Kahn's masterwork in St. Paul on the Mississippi

River. It was a new type of structure for the modern manufacturing era designed by a master architect who successfully integrated beauty, utility, and landscape. It also represented the fullest example of Henry Ford's personal beliefs and his ability to integrate those into his automobile-manufacturing operations.

In addition to being beautiful, the new building featured state-of-the-art mechanical systems. Windows on the sawtooth roof provided ample light and ventilation to the interior. These could be opened and closed by motors, as described by a Stone and Webster engineer: "it is as easy to open one hundred windows as it is to turn on the electric light in your home, for all you do is push a button and electric power does the rest." Radiators located at the ceiling level heated the plant. The building had a complete sprinkler system. Bathrooms were installed in mezzanines seven feet above the floor to

Management offices were nicely fitted with mahogany trim, leading workers to reference executive decisions as coming from "Mahogany Row." Author's collection.

conserve work space. Management offices were located in the northwest corner of the plant next to the show-room, featuring "appointments and finish that are about the last word in refinement, where every facility for convenience, comfort, and efficiency has been combined." The extensive use of mahogany wood paneling would later give rise to the term "Mahogany Row" by workers when referencing the plant managers.

An illustration of the hydroelectric plant at the Twin Cities Assembly Plant was featured in a national advertising campaign boasting of Ford's self-sufficiency. This advertisement ran in Twin Cities newspapers on August 17, 1924. From the collections of The Henry Ford (THF95511).

The Twin Cities Assembly Plant fulfilled many of Henry Ford's personal beliefs, among them the need for self-sufficiency created through vertical integration. He used an illustration of the St. Paul hydro-electric plant in a national advertising campaign boasting of his energy independence: "No market fluctuations affect the Ford Motor Company's materials, resources, men or machines. They are free from outside manipulation." By the time the plant opened, Ford owned and operated coal, iron, and garnet mines, timber lands and sawmills, coke ovens, foundries, power plants, blast furnaces, numerous by-products industries, wood distillation plants, glass plants, and silica mines. He also owned a fleet of ships, a railroad, and he was about to invest heavily in aviation.

Completion of Plant Brings Euphoria— and Job Seekers—to St. Paul

A local newspaper article proclaimed the opening of the St. Paul assembly plant as "the biggest single achievement and the forerunner of the biggest industrial boom in the history of the city." H. C. Struchen predicted it would create the need for thousands of workers and new houses. He had an explanation for this burst of building activity: "St. Paul's reputation as an open shop town is one of the biggest selling arguments possible so far as inducing Eastern manufacturers to locate here . . . for men have a tendency to migrate towards cities where they will not be handicapped by strikes." The city declared "Ford Week" and organized numerous festivities. A newspaper editorial proclaimed:

> Already 1,900 men are on the payroll of this new industry—men who are liberally paid. As the months roll by, operations will increase, more men will be added and more families supported. This same plant will carry in its wake many smaller manufacturers. These additional plants will have large payrolls. Community stores will appear and receive their share of the business. Our downtown merchants will gradually feel an increased demand for their merchandise. It spells a continuous expansion for St. Paul and its whole business zone.

Equipment or tools that could be salvaged from the Minneapolis plant were moved by tractor to the new assembly plant in St. Paul, and the vacated structure was put up for sale. Author's collection.

As the plant was nearing completion, a second wave of job seekers arrived looking to assemble cars for Ford. Crowds of applicants started to congregate at the site, with many camping out in a new "Tent City" described in the *St. Paul Daily News*:

> Today atop the bluffs along the Mississippi at the high dam is a village of tents—tents of those who have come hundreds, even thousands of miles to take advantage of the opportunity offered by the Ford plant development—one day, almost overnight like Aladdin's castle, this tent village will have become part of the great industrial center. Great engines will pound noisily on the spot where the tents are pitched—the thin wisps of smoke from the approved fireplaces over which these "pioneers" cook their meals will give way to the black clouds from many tall stacks. They are much like all other pioneers have been for many centuries on all lands, these folks who have left their homes to seek a new opportunity.

One of the camp residents, J. M. Cox, drove with his wife and six children from Johnson City, Tennessee, covering two thousand miles in nine days. As she busied herself washing her youngsters' clothes, Mrs. Cox, reflected:

> Yes it was a long way to come to work, but we thought it would be worth it. We wanted to get here right away so we would have a good chance to get in at the first sight of the thing—that way we can get settled a lot sooner . . . It doesn't matter how much if we have to live in a tent now and cook our food and do the washing outside—this won't last long, and some day when the plants are paying high wages and there is a lot of money to be made we won't be sorry that we put up with a little hardship at first.

Paul Bunk drove from Detroit with his wife and four children in a "house" mounted on a Ford truck. He had been employed by the Ford Motor Company but left Detroit because of the high rent. He said, "I don't have to worry about the rent now—there is enough room in the 'house' for all of us to sleep and most of the summer we can live outside . . . We can cook and bake over our fireplace here, and we can get along all right until winter just as we are now." The "first settler" found work as the night watchman for Stone and Webster. For the first few nights he had to sit out in the open until a construction shack was built. The campers who had set up in the woods appreciated the free accommodations but had to deal with mosquitoes, which were said to be particularly bad that summer. Smoke pots, known as "smudges," had to be set up in the evening to help keep insects at bay. One enterprising young man saw a business opportunity at the camp site, delivering more than two hundred bottles of milk a day with a wagon drawn by Shetland ponies.

Ford continued to make Model Ts at the Minneapolis facility until the new assembly

The first Model T car rolled off the assembly line on May 4, 1925, and was purchased by St. Paul dealer W. S. Williams. The Model T had lost favor with the public and was nearing the end of its nineteen-year run. Courtesy of the Minnesota Historical Society.

Several models of the enclosed Model T were displayed in the showroom. Fordson tractors were also assembled in the plant in 1926. Photograph by Hibbard Studio. Courtesy of the Minnesota Historical Society.

plant was completed. It was a significant improvement, with assembly lines that were a thousand feet long, compared to ninety feet in the old plant, and more than sixteen thousand linear feet of conveyers. The plant also had eleven paint-baking ovens from twenty to 250 feet in length, and some were wide enough to carry up to six conveyer lines. The first car produced at the Twin Cities Assembly Plant, a Tudor Sedan, rolled off the assembly line on May 4, 1925, to cheering crowds, including the mayors of St. Paul and Minneapolis, who led a ceremonial drive before the car was purchased by a St. Paul dealer, W. S. Williams. Attention was almost certainly focused more on the beautiful plant than the Model T car it produced, which was nearing the end of its nineteen-year run.

Ford initially used only one-third of the plant for assembly of Model T cars and Fordson tractors. Several months after the grand opening, the company awarded a $4 million

The increasing demand for enclosed cars with windows created a national shortage of glass. Ford invented a new method to produce long sheets of glass. At the St. Paul plant, high-quality silica was mined from tunnels beneath the factory floor and brought up by elevators and shoveled into the large furnace. The molten sand was then placed on long conveyor belts where it would harden and then be cut to size, as shown here. Courtesy of the Minnesota Historical Society.

contract to the Struchen Company to build a glass factory in the east craneway of the new building. At the time, there were major shortages of glass as demand for glass-enclosed automobiles jumped 60 percent by 1923. One analyst warned: "the ability to obtain plate glass supplies may be a key to the future of the automobile industry." Ford recognized this as a long-term problem and had already been experimenting with new ways to manufacture glass. Under the direction of W. B. Mayo, the company discovered it could produce sheets of glass in sections hundreds of feet long. Ford was the first automobile company

The glass furnace had to operate at very high temperatures to melt the silica. It was shut down only every three or four years for maintenance and repairs. Glass would then harden in the furnace and have to be broken out. Workers often took large chunks of the glass as souvenirs, and the rest was dumped in a landfill site on the river. Photograph by Norton & Peel. Courtesy of the Minnesota Historical Society.

to make glass; its plant in Pittsburgh was producing enough sheet glass for windshields and windows for one hundred thousand cars a month. The entire glass industry soon adopted Ford's innovative manufacturing techniques. The 1,400-foot length of the St. Paul plant was ideal for producing long sheets of glass. The plant also happened to sit on a large deposit of pure silica sand. Several years earlier, Colonel Brittin had the sand tested by University of Minnesota engineers, who found that it was pure enough for glass. He sent samples to the Ford labs in Detroit, which confirmed the results, giving Ford another reason to locate in St. Paul. Ford engineers described the quality of sand as the finest-grade silica they had found in the United States. One of Ford's environmental precepts was to place production near raw materials, thereby reducing the need for transportation. Mayo was convinced there was enough high-quality sand along the Mississippi and Minnesota rivers for hundreds of thousands of sheets of glass. Colonel Brittin predicted that the glass plant in St. Paul would have a huge economic impact, as it would furnish all cars made west of Chicago and likely add several thousand employees.

In late March 1926, the glass furnace was fired up and within a few months was producing 230,000 square feet of glass per month. Workers mined the silica from miles of tunnels beneath the plant and transported it on a miniature electric railroad to a five-ton elevator, which lifted the sand to the floor of the plant. The tunnels did not require forced ventilation because of the gravity flow of air, and the temperature was a constant fifty-eight degrees Fahrenheit year-round. Two concrete-lined tunnels connected to the power plants on the river as a safety precaution, and there were several emergency shafts.

In addition to the locally mined silica, other raw materials required for glass production were shipped to the plant by rail and stored in large bins. These ingredients would be weighed, mixed, and pressed into briquettes, another Ford innovation, and ready for the furnace. The glass furnace, which ran twenty-four hours a day, held about 650 tons of molten glass at a temperature of 2,750 degrees Fahrenheit. The gas burners in the furnace were located above the five-foot-deep container of molten glass. Raw materials were fed into one end of the ninety-foot furnace as glass would be drawn out the other end, producing sixty tons of glass a day. Approximately one million cubic feet of natural gas was needed daily to heat the furnace, and there were backup propane and oil tanks to ensure an uninterrupted supply. Glass production was shut down only every three or four years for maintenance and to replace the walls of the furnace. Residue of the glass collected on the bottom of the cooled furnace and had to be broken out in chunks. Many employees took samples of the beautiful blue-green glass as souvenirs and the rest was dumped along the banks of the Mississippi River.

Planning for Development in Highland Park

George Herrold's master plan for the Highland Park neighborhood included a three hundred–acre recreational area with an eighteen-hole golf course, an athletic field, "a timber canyoned picnic ground," and a large hillside park. His goal was one acre of parkland for every 142 people. The city formed a 5,466-acre park district to fund these improvements by property assessments, based on how close the property was to the amenities. The city acquired forty acres for a reservoir site. Herrold projected that High-

Located at
1814 Hillcrest Ave.,
Corner Fairview,
Lane's Highland
Park.

Open to the Public
February 12th to 25th
from 2 to 9 P. M.

Ample Parking
Space With Police
Protection.

Street Car Service---
Randolph-Snelling
to Otto.

Randolph-Hope,
Cleveland to
Ford Road.

Drive Any of These Routes---
Snelling to Ford Road;
Cleveland to Ford Road;
Fairview to Hillcrest

You Are Cordially Invited to Visit

ST. PAUL'S WINTER-BUILT DEMONSTRATION HOME NO. 2

Residential development did not occur in Highland Park as quickly as anticipated, and builders resorted to creative marketing strategies. Conrad Hamm built several Winter-Built Demonstration Homes to show that housing construction was a year-round activity, in much the same way as H. C. Struchen demonstrated several years earlier with industrial construction. Courtesy of the Minnesota Historical Society.

land Park would reach a population of 100,000, but he also calculated that the current zoning would allow a maximum of approximately 165,000 people. The new park proved to be enormously popular. A municipal pageant, "Cinderella Tale," was presented at the opening of the Highland Reservoir in 1926. It had 1,500 actors, many of them local schoolchildren, and attracted more than fifty thousand spectators.

Herrold's master plan called for the "A" residential category to have a minimum lot size of 5,000 feet, with a minimum frontage of 40 feet. Streets were platted to allow the most efficient placement of utilities. Long blocks, from 900 feet to 1,300 feet, were created in some areas to reduce the number of cross streets, minimizing traffic hazards. At the time, "workman's homes" cost between $4,500 and $6,000, and "businessman's homes" from $7,000 to $15,000. The average cost of a house in St. Paul was reported to be $13,160. Homeowners expected to pay approximately 25 percent of their income for housing with a ten-year mortgage, which would have required a minimum income of approximately $400 per month. By those standards, the typical Ford line worker would have been hard-pressed to afford his own home without having accumulated considerable savings. However, there were occasional affordable listings, including one that read: "the Ford Plant District, 5 room fully modern bungalow, garage, $3,500 $200 cash."

To achieve the goals of a planned community, Herrold enlisted support from a successful St. Paul developer, Den (Dennis) E. Lane, who had earlier worked with Colonel Brittin in quietly assembling the Ford site. An Irish immigrant, Lane had achieved success as early as 1910, developing bungalows throughout the Macalester Groveland neighborhood. He started his real-estate career while a student at St. Thomas College, and he claimed that by 1920 "he had designed, laid out, and named 50 percent of the St. Paul streets platted in the previous decade." By 1925 he had completed more than ten thousand property transactions. After World War I, Lane focused on the neighborhood around the Ford plant and platted the area now known as Lane's Highland Park addition. He likely gave the new neighborhood its name, Highland Park, which was indeed "high land," but was also probably a reference to Ford's industrial complex in Detroit.

Not much housing was built until well after the completion of the Ford plant, in part because of the extensive infrastructure work that was needed. One city commissioner complained that the amount the city was spending in the Ford district for streets was shortchanging other parts of the city. Mayor Nelson explained that the investment was necessary "so Ford workers can be persuaded to settle in St. Paul rather than Minneapolis." Struchen's demonstration of winter-building techniques for the Ford plant inspired a similar idea for the residential market. A "Winter-Built Demonstration Home" started construction in January 1927 at 1700 Hillcrest Avenue. It was a promotional effort by builder Conrad Hamm to encourage development around the Ford plant. Local newspapers promoted it as an opportunity to learn about new construction techniques and products. "Fifty firms and individuals are co-operating in the construction of this home," one ad noted, "and the public is invited to follow its construction as a practical course in modern building." Celotex panel boards were used in place of wood sheathing because they could be installed more quickly and offered better insulating value. Thousands of visitors toured the home, and saw the new modern products, including a built-in vacuum cleaner, washing machine, and electric refrigeration.

Lane's Highland Park subdivision of two hundred acres adjacent to the city park was put on the market on January 1, 1928. To prevent real-estate speculation, buyers had to agree to build their home within a specified number of months, and in exchange they were given a 50 percent discount on the land, priced at sixty dollars per lineal foot of frontage. Herrold wrote that the buyer received the reduction "in order to induce building and because he does not know what his neighbor's house will be like. The developer expects to make his money from the sale of the odd lots at a later time when the character of the neighborhood is fully established." Land was made available for two schools, and Lane pledged to offer sites at cost to any religious denomination that submitted building plans for a church.

Multifamily housing projects were also slow to develop around the plant. The Highland Village Apartments, one of the most significant housing projects in the city, was built at Cleveland Avenue and Ford Parkway in 1939. The complex just east of the Ford plant was a planned community of sixteen buildings with 265 units. Ford sold the property to the developers but retained mineral rights, allowing it to continue silica mining beneath the buildings. Retail development and a movie theater intensified activity at this intersection, making it the hub for the growing community.

Initially, there were expectations that the Ford project would spur development of a large manufacturing district around the plant. Marc Manderscheid has written of the unsuccessful efforts of the St. Paul Association to expand the industrial zoning district to bring in more manufacturers, but very few industrial companies located in Highland Park. The fact that the community developed as an upscale residential district is a tribute to the high quality design of the Ford plant. Proximity to the heavy industrial facility was not only not an impediment—it turned out to be an asset.

The Twin Cities Assembly Plant was designed at the same time as the surrounding neighborhood of Highland Park, which presented the opportunity for the industrialist and the city planner—two idealists—to work together. To a remarkable extent, the high aspirations of both Henry Ford and George Herrold were fulfilled.

Colonel Lewis Brittin, Ford Aviation, and the Arrival of Northwest Airways

With the completion of the Ford plant, the talented and ambitious Lewis Brittin moved on to his next challenge, promoting commercial aviation—which also happened to be a significant interest of Henry and Edsel Ford. As early as 1909, Ford had experimented with an airplane powered by a Model T engine. During World War I the federal government invested heavily in aviation, and Ford received a major contract to build the Liberty engine for the Curtiss airplanes. After the war, the federal government substantially withdrew from the aviation field, but Henry Ford continued to spend large amounts promoting the new technology.

Brittin believed that aviation was on the verge of becoming commercially viable, in part because the Ford Motor Company was planning to manufacture a large passenger aircraft. In 1925 Ford announced that it would help start a service between Detroit and Chicago by guaranteeing regular freight shipments of at least two thousand pounds, and would consider adding the Twin Cities if the venture succeeded. Brittin felt he could position St. Paul as an aviation hub. His close ties with Ford resulted in St. Paul's being included on the Edsel Ford 1926 Reliability Air Tour. Brittin wanted to establish an air-line service to take over contracts for delivery of airmail in St. Paul. He first tried to raise money locally but when that was unsuccessful he turned to his friends in Detroit. General Harold R. Harris, who was the president of Northwest Airways in 1953, described the effort:

> A long-distance telephone call to William Mayo, chief engineer for Ford at Detroit, brought an encouraging invitation. "Come here and tell your story," Mayo said. "I'll have thirty Detroit millionaires sitting around a table at the Detroit Athletic Club to listen to it." Colonel Brittin presented such a good case for his project that the Detroit group signed up. Northwest Air-ways—as it was then called—was organized as a Michigan corporation. It was capitalized at three hundred thousand dollars, and there were twenty-nine original stockholders. That was on September 1, 1926. It was pretty much a Detroit outfit."

Brittin was appointed vice president and general manager of the new airline. Among the stockholders was William B. Stout, a St. Paul native and prolific inventor, who set up an aviation company that was acquired by Henry Ford. Three days later, Northwest Airways was awarded a contract by the U.S. Post Office for the Twin Cities to Chicago airmail route. It was the sole bidder at $2.75 per pound. Brittin personally designed the logo of the new company, and by October 1, 1926, Northwest Airways was in operation. Brittin took the lead in establishing St. Paul's Holman Airport, named after Northwest's first pilot, Charles "Speed" Holman. Within three years, control of the airline was transferred to investors in the Twin Cities, and its corporate headquarters was moved to St. Paul. Brittin stayed on as general manager. In 1928, Northwest purchased two Ford Trimotor "Tin Goose" airplanes, designed by William Stout. These were the first commercial airplanes with all-metal construction, which provided some sense of security to passengers worried about safety, along with the Ford name on the tail. However, in 1929 a Ford trimotor crashed in Mounds Park shortly after takeoff from Holman Field, killing the pilot. Brittin was an extraordinary visionary and salesman. When promoting development around the St. Paul airport, he wrote: "These developments . . . do not come by rubbing Aladdin's lamp. They require careful expenditures of energy and thought." Several years later, Brittin's stellar business reputation was tarnished by accusations that he used "irregular" methods to procure Post Office airmail contracts, and then destroyed records subpoenaed by a Senate investigative committee. Brittin claimed he was innocent, but he was found in contempt of Congress and sentenced to ten days in jail, ending his career at the airlines. It was at that point the company changed its name to Northwest Airlines.

The Twin Cities Assembly Plant opened at a time of extraordinary prosperity for the

After the completion of the Ford plant, L. H. Brittin turned his attention to commercial aviation. He raised funding from Henry Ford and other company executives and organized Northwest Airways, later named Northwest Airlines. He also convinced Ford to include St. Paul on its Edsel Ford 1926 Reliability Air Tour, which featured caravans of planes barnstorming the country to demonstrate aviation safety. The planes attracted considerable attention when they arrived at Holman Field. Courtesy of the Minnesota Historical Society.

Ford Motor Company. In 1925 the company sold 268,411 vehicles, including cars, trucks, and tractors, about four times what it had sold just four years earlier. The opening of the plant also coincided with a major milestone for the auto industry, which now "ranked first in the value of its product, the cost of its materials, the volume added to manufacture, and wages paid." Industrialists like Henry Ford were creating the modern era. Remarkably, the average price of a car kept dropping even as wages for the workers kept rising. The design of the Twin Cities Assembly Plant reflected the national mood of optimism and exuberance and demonstrated the triumph of the Ford Motor Company and the entire automobile industry. Ford was so eager to show off the new plant that it held an open house with extended hours, "so that every man, woman, child in the Twin Cities and surrounding territory may have an opportunity to come in the afternoon or evening." More than 72,000 visitors streamed in to see the new assembly line and cars being made in a park. The following year, 84,000 toured the plant, and by 1937 more than 500,000 people had come from practically every state in the country. With the opening of the new assembly plant, the ten-story Minneapolis plant was put up for sale.

Henry Ford had many reasons to celebrate and feel secure about his company in early 1925 as he confidently turned his attention to other pursuits, including navigation, aviation, and a variety of environmental and historical projects. Unfortunately, his celebratory mood would not last. The Ford Motor Company was built almost entirely around the Model T car, which was rapidly losing favor in the marketplace. The next decade would bring enormous challenges to Henry Ford and his workers, and he could not afford to sit on his laurels.

From Model A
to M-8

The Great Depression and
World War II Years

The new Twin Cities Assembly Plant was a state-of-the-art manufacturing facility when it opened in 1926, but it was making an old-fashioned car, the Model T, which it had assembled in Minneapolis and around the country for almost two decades. In its first year, the plant assembled more than ninety thousand Model Ts, which supplied 750 dealers throughout the Upper Midwest. It also assembled almost three thousand Fordson tractors. The finished cars were shipped mainly by rail in spite of the fact that barges were 20 percent cheaper and Ford had pledged to use the river. Twenty-five Model Ts were shipped by barge downriver to Winona to be trucked to all dealers within a fifty-mile radius, sparking a flurry of publicity, but navigation never lived up to the much-ballyhooed promises. Ford's assembly plants downriver needed parts, which the Twin Cities plant did not make, not fully assembled cars. There was also little incoming shipping as Ford mainly used rail to transport raw materials and parts from Detroit. The Army Corps of Engineers built a second lock at the High Dam in 1932 with a nine-foot channel to stimulate river traffic, but even this did not significantly increase navigation.

Henry Ford had to be pleased with his considerable accomplishments when the plant opened in 1926. The Model T car was the best-selling vehicle in history, and his vision for a vertically integrated company controlling every aspect of automobile manufacturing was within reach. As the unchecked owner of the company, he was free to pursue his personal interests with his unlimited resources. One thing he chose not to do during this time, however, was to develop a new car. Ford believed the Model T would last forever and he was content with making only incremental improvements. He institutionalized this belief with a policy that required any new or modified part to be compatible with the original Model T. He followed this obsession to its logical conclusion by establishing a program for "remaking used cars on a scale commensurate with the making of new cars. The used cars are sent into Detroit and put through a repair process planned on the same lines as the manufacturing process." The general public, now accustomed to

When it opened, the new plant made basically the same Model T car that Ford had assembled in Minneapolis for more than a decade. The new plant's one-thousand-foot-long assembly line greatly increased production capacity. Author's collection.

New Model Ts are rolled to a barge on the river. During the campaign for the hydroelectric permit, Ford claimed he would use the Mississippi River for navigation. Except for a handful of cars shipped to Winona, Ford's plans were never implemented. Courtesy of the Minnesota Historical Society.

annual model changes, did not embrace the long run of the Model T. Ford dealers were particularly hard hit because they were facing stiff competition from the more fashionable General Motors cars.

The long run of the Model Ts and Fordson tractors proved, however, to be a boon for manufacturers of accessories and attachments. Henry Ford initially welcomed this huge aftermarket business because it enhanced the "universal" appeal of his vehicles. In 1922, Ford organized an exhibit at the Minnesota State Fair in collaboration with manufacturers of equipment, attachments, and implements for the Fordson. This concept had been tried several months earlier at his assembly plant in Long Island City, New York, in what Ford dubbed the First National Industrial Tractor Show. For its second year, there were displays of "over one hundred accessory items, including truck and tractor attachments, graders, snow plows, scrapers, cement mixers, sawmills," as well as "two types of gasoline locomotives especially adapted to Fordson tractor use and equipped for use on all standard narrow-gauge industrial railroads."

As the products multiplied, they became too numerous and complicated to test and approve. In addition, there was not enough space to display them in the existing car showrooms. Ford then experimented with promoting separate, specialty outlet stores around the country to carry the attachments. Locally, the Motor Power Equipment Company opened a store at 2512 University Avenue in St. Paul, and an outlet in Fargo. By 1925, it outgrew its facility in the Midway and erected a new building, designed by noted architect Clarence Johnston, on Ford Parkway across the street from the new Ford plant at 758 Mississippi River South, at the entrance to the Ford Bridge. An article in the *Pioneer Press* made clear the benefit of these stores for the average Ford dealer who was busy selling his monthly quota of cars:

> Here, at last, is a place where his particular customer can secure exactly what he wants for his particular job, be it hauling pulp wood, loading or unloading coal, or sawing wood. Here are the hundred and one items, which have heretofore been listed only in the directory grouped in one catalogue with descriptions and prices to go with them . . . At the warehouses of the Motor Power Equipment company, is kept on display every item sold, in so far as it may be possible, so that the customer may look over the item before he buys.

Eventually, Ford would have misgivings about promoting the accessory market. Attachments could damage the Ford vehicles and complicate warranties, and the company had increasing concerns that counterfeit parts threatened their lucrative parts business. An estimated seven million Model T cars were on the road in 1924 and the spare-parts business provided Ford 37 percent of its profits and significant revenue to dealers. Ready access to parts and trained service personnel was always an important part of Ford's appeal, particularly early on when cars frequently broke down on bad roads. By 1928, Ford had created a network of forty-five thousand independently owned service centers that met company performance standards and committed to using authentic Ford parts.

The Motor Power Equipment Company did not last long at its new building. By 1927, at least a portion of the building had been turned into the Ford Bridge Café.

Several industrial companies with close ties to Ford moved to Highland Park, including the Motor Power Equipment Company, which built a warehouse across the street from the plant. The Ford Bridge Café was later opened in the building. Courtesy of the Minnesota Historical Society.

Several other companies with business connections to Ford constructed buildings near the new plant. The Schurmeier Whitney Company, manufacturers of automobile and truck bodies, erected a one-story structure at 2277 Ford Parkway. This firm specialized in Ford vehicles and was previously located adjacent to the Ford assembly plant in Minneapolis. In addition, the McGee-White Corporation, which carried an extensive line of Ford accessory products, relocated from Minneapolis to a new structure at 2221 Ford Parkway.

End of the Model T

Leading up to the opening of Twin Cities Assembly Plant, the Ford Motor Company appeared to be flourishing. The Model T propelled the company to a 59 percent market share at its high point in 1921, followed by General Motors with 15 percent. However, GM would surpass Ford by 1927. The market for the Model T declined mainly because people didn't want to buy the same car over and over again. Consumers could have bought three new Model Ts over its nineteen-year run, as the average car lasted about seven years. Other companies had begun to change car models every year, which cultivated a style consciousness that made the Model T look very unfashionable, particularly to the increasing number of women buyers. The Model T's high body was designed for rutted roads and looked out of place on paved highways. Many drivers were embarrassed to be seen driving what had become a symbol of obsolescence. The Model T was considerably cheaper than other cars, with its Runabout model at $260 and Touring Car at $290 in 1924, but this advantage would erode as other companies became more efficient. Ford was generous in sharing his manufacturing innovations—and his people. A number of executives purged by Ford went to work for other companies, including William Knudsen, who went on to lead Chevrolet and General Motors.

Worried dealers met with Henry Ford and strongly urged him to make a number of changes to the Model T, particularly the ignition system. Ford snapped, "You can do that over my dead body . . . I think that the only thing we need to worry about is the best way to make more cars." Ford continued to lose market share to Chevrolet. In 1922 GM had a gain of 220 percent, compared to Ford's 27 percent. The Model T could not reclaim its dominant position at any price. In fact, Chevrolet could even raise its prices and manage to increase its market share against the Model T. Lower prices were not welcomed by dealers as it reduced commissions, and many top salespeople switched to other companies. Ford autoworkers were also not pleased with price cuts as they believed they were being pressured to produce more for less. In fact, the assembly line was speeded up as wages and benefits were reduced.

Ford's market share dipped from 57 percent to 45 percent, but Henry Ford was oblivious to the new reality. He attacked the marketing agencies for rigging sales tallies, and he criticized GM for introducing annual model changes, which he felt were wasteful: "This pressure to do a better job is very different from making a new style just for its own sake or to hoodwink people into imagining that what they have is obsolete. A business can be quickly destroyed by superseding one product by another which is no better, merely to induce fresh buying. This is breaking faith with the public."

By 1925, the automobile industry had changed from a growth model to a competition model. During the growth phase, cost and durability determined success and no one could match Henry Ford's obsession with lower costs. In the new competition phase, however, efficiency would take a backseat to management and marketing. Car companies needed different approaches to attract the more sophisticated buyer. Efficiency and data-

Workers in the plant posed for a group picture in the late 1920s. Author's collection.

driven decision making were now applied to back-office operations, and not just on the assembly line. Marketing was as important as manufacturing. Flexibility and teamwork were prized. General Motors' vision spoke to the new reality: "A car for every purse and purpose." Ford's approach was the opposite—his was the "universal" car fit for all, forever. He did not believe in model changes or market research. A buyer could take a Model T in any color "as long as it was black."

James Couzens, a partner of Ford who was responsible for the business side of the company during its successful early years, departed in 1915, creating a management vacuum. Ford's policies and actions increasingly became irrational and self-destructive. The goal of the Ford Motor Company was to fulfill the wishes of its owner, and his obsession was to build a reliable, inexpensive car. The goal of General Motors was to make a profit and enhance shareholder value, and its organizational structure was designed around that purpose. Having accomplished his goal of making a car for the masses, Ford felt he could spend much of his time and money integrating his hobbies and personal interests into the activities of the company. He was not particularly interested in profit and was personally oblivious to wealth. His wife once discovered a seventy-five-thousand-dollar check in his jacket pocket that he had forgotten about. Ford did not have an independent board of directors or outside shareholders. The company often priced its new products without doing an analysis of costs. It sometimes sold Fordson tractors and Model Ts at a loss. Personnel operated without titles or job descriptions, and were completely subject to his whim. He had no feedback loop to gauge sentiment in the marketplace, other than his dealers, whom he disdained. He wasn't interested in determining the needs of customers—worse, he didn't care. His factories and equipment were designed solely for efficiency and making a cheaper Model T. Most of his custom-designed single-purpose machines were so specialized they couldn't be reused even if the company wanted to change a design or introduce new models. Henry Ford refused to pull the plug on the Model T or modify management practices.

Henry Ford had changed. His wonderful twenty-five-track mind had become unhinged. He had come to believe his epic folk hero image and lost touch with reality. His strengths, which built the company, were now crippling weaknesses, particularly without the counterbalancing force of James Couzens and other managers. *Fortune Magazine* had it correctly diagnosed:

> A man cannot well be a museum director, an antique collector, a researcher in history, an educator, a promoter of aviation, a farmer, a health authority, a developer of hydroelectric power, a master of square dancing . . . and a political dabbler . . . and keep his full concentration on the manufacture of automobiles . . . There are too many people who will do what Mr.

Ford thinks and there are not enough people who can influence what Mr. Ford thinks. This keeps [Ford] out of touch with the world, with its markets.

Frustrated customers sent Henry Ford hundreds of letters a day. Trade journals were filled with critical articles, and dealers were demanding change. The manager of the Twin Cities district, S. A. Stellwagen, played a key role in communicating the frustrations experienced in the field. Edsel Ford appointed Stellwagen to a national committee of six managers who were described as "men of exceptional experience and energy . . . able to report with ruthless candor to Edsel Ford." He was among the most trusted and loyal branch managers in the company. After a meeting of two hundred salesmen and dealers in Denver in January 1926, Stellwagen sent a report to Edsel Ford "which declared that a new model was imperative, for a winner must always lead." Edsel used these reports to plead with his father to introduce a new car to replace the Model T.

Perhaps Ford was finally getting the message. Sales projections for 1927 showed a precipitous drop for the Model T, prompting a cryptic statement from Ford: "This little let down will give us an opportunity for closer inspection and will be in every way desirable. We are not contemplating any extraordinary changes in models, although, of course, the whole industry is in a state of development and improvement." Allan Nevins and Frank Ernest Hill described the public reaction:

> Rumor at once swept the nation. The entire history of the automobile industry holds nothing that parallels the public curiosity excited by reports that a new Ford impended . . . The public is burning with curiosity. What will it look like? How fast will it travel? What equipment will it carry? . . . Will he still undersell his competitors? All of these are questions heard every day in all quarters of the United States.

On the evening of May 25, 1927, the Ford Motor Company announced that it would build a new car, making the front page of every newspaper in the country. Henry Ford's decision was deeply difficult on a personal level, as revealed in his poignant statement, "The Model T was a pioneer . . . It had stamina and power. It was the car that ran before there were good roads to run on. It broke down the barriers of distance in rural sections, brought people of these sections closer together, and placed education within the reach of everyone . . . We are still proud of the Model T."

The day after the announcement, the fifteen millionth Model T rolled off the assembly line at the Rouge assembly plant. With Edsel and Henry Ford aboard, it was driven in a ceremonial procession to the engineering building in Dearborn. It was supposed to be the final Model T, but the announcement triggered a wave of sentimental buying that the company met by producing almost another half-million cars. Of the fifteen million Model Ts made, more than thirteen million were still registered in 1927.

Developing the New Model A

On his birthday in July 1927, Henry Ford contemplated the challenge of designing a new car: "Sixty-four today and the biggest job of my life ahead." He pushed aside his many interests to focus on the new car. His job was made more difficult because he had fired many of his best engineers, but he felt he could assemble a new team of designers from within the company. Ford had no personal doubts, and his self-confidence and legendary mechanical genius inspired those around him. Money was not an issue. He would spend whatever it took to make another car as revolutionary as the Model T. During the changeover, Ford promised a brief shutdown with minimal disruption, at first projecting a layoff of seventy thousand workers, which he later lowered to twenty-five thousand. Tens of thousands of employees and eight thousand dealers eagerly awaited the new car, as did millions of consumers. So many buyers were waiting that automobile sales slumped throughout the entire industry, impacting the national economy.

The Ford team was aware of the threat posed by the competition, particularly Chevrolet, which sold as many cars in the first six months of 1927 as the previous year. The *New York Times* wrote that "no presidential campaign of the decade, no sports contest aroused as much interest as the fight for the heavyweight national automobile championship between Henry Ford and General Motors." Alfred Sloan, the president of GM, visited the Twin Cities in October 1927 and in a well-publicized speech urged the public not to delay buying a new car. Chevrolet, he said, was a higher-quality car that should not be compared with the lower-priced car that Ford would make. Ford dealers, frustrated by empty showrooms, had to rely on their service department and the sale of used cars to survive.

Progress on the design of the new car was slow, but Ford had built a prototype by early August. Mass production would require retooling the entire Rouge plant and all assembly plants around the country. Virtually all 5,580 parts for the car were new and most had to be fabricated from scratch. The company could not salvage approximately half of the specialized single-purpose machines of the Model T era. The *New York Times* said it was "probably the biggest replacement of plant in the history of American industry." By May 1927, seventeen thousand skilled craftsmen—three times more than the company had before the shutdown—worked three shifts to convert the plants. Annual model changes proved to be a boon for tool and die workers needed to regularly replace the equipment. By October, 150 prototype cars were available for road tests, and the factories were being

Ford furloughed workers without pay when sales slowed or during a model changeover. During one break in the late 1920s, three furloughed workers decided to take a trip down the Mississippi River. They bought an old raft that was used to haul sand for the construction of the Ford Bridge and headed to New Orleans. They abandoned their journey along the way, sold the barge, and rode back to Minnesota on their motorcycles. Seth Lindsay is on the left and Ken Muxlow is in the middle. Courtesy of Ken Muxlow.

converted. On October 20, 1927, Henry Ford hand-stamped the first engine that rolled off the newly converted assembly line. The new car was named the Model A.

The world had been eagerly awaiting news, which Ford parceled out judiciously to build interest. He retained the country's oldest advertising agency, the N. W. Ayers Company, for the campaign. On December 1, 1927, full-page ads were placed in more than two thousand newspapers, including in the Twin Cities, with the news, "The New Ford Car will sell at a SURPRISINGLY LOW PRICE . . . The minute you see the pictures of the new Ford car, you will be delighted with its low, smart lines and the artistic color combinations. There, you will say, is a truly modern car . . . You will like the feeling of speed and power that the new Ford gives you—the comfortable, prideful feeling that comes from having a car worthy of any occasion."

The Model A could reach speeds of 55 to 65 miles per hour "with ease," with its forty horsepower engine. It could accelerate from 5 to 25 miles per hour in eight and one-half seconds, and could achieve 20 to 30 miles per gallon. The Model A had a low center of gravity with hydraulic shock absorbers as standard equipment, a new ignition system, new four-wheel brakes, and steel-spoke wheels. It also introduced tempered safety glass for all windows—an industry first. Ford could also highlight style. The Model A had "Beautiful, new low body lines . . . There is a bit of the European touch in the coachwork and contour." In other words, it was everything the old Model T wasn't. The car and the ads featured many things that Henry Ford swore he would never do.

More than one hundred thousand people rushed the showrooms in Detroit to see the new car. Mobs stormed displays in other cities and police had to be called in to maintain order. Within thirty-six hours more than ten million people saw the new model, and within two weeks customers placed orders for four hundred thousand cars. The Twin

After insisting for many years he would never abandon the Model T, Ford was forced to capitulate and develop a new car, the Model A. This 1927 marketing campaign for the new car was one of the most successful product launches in history. Author's collection.

Cities Assembly Plant was opened from 8:00 a.m. to 10:00 p.m. to show the new Model As, and streetcars had to be added to the Randolph line to accommodate the throngs. The new car was viewed by almost twenty-five thousand people the first day. Local dealers also ran their own large newspaper ads and extended their hours from 7:00 a.m. to midnight, although they had not even received the cars yet. The publicity surrounding the product launch was extraordinary. One newspaper marveled:

> With the simultaneous "unveiling" in all cities in the United States, as well as in foreign cities, of the new Ford models, Mr. Henry Ford takes his place as the master showman of all times. The mystery with which the new car has been surrounded, the tremendous interest aroused in this and other countries, and the huge volume of newspaper publicity which has attended the change of the Ford designs constitute an advertising feat which has never been equaled.

Publicity for the Model A generated enormous public interest, but the new cars still hadn't reached dealer showrooms. To speed up production, Henry Ford outsourced production of many parts, reversing a long-standing policy. Still, only one hundred cars per day were made in Detroit in early December—not even close to meeting the demand. An underground black market developed and some dealers sold the Model As at considerably marked-up prices. Those who were discovered by Ford lost their dealerships. It wasn't until February 1928 that dealers finally received all their models. Many were irate at the delays and loss of income. Some sued, and some went out of business, but most hung on. Ford helped improve relations by finally instituting a legitimate buyer financing program in May 1928, modeled after the GM program.

The plant closures caused by the changeover to the Model A had a devastating impact on employees, dealers, the community, and the economy. There were sixty thousand layoffs at Ford and thousands more at supplier companies because of Henry Ford's lack of foresight and planning. Detroit was especially hard hit, as the shutdown was responsible for almost half of its annual welfare budget in 1927. Many officials raised questions about the responsibilities of large corporations in meeting the costs of such disruptions.

During the plant's conversion, employees in St. Paul were furloughed without pay. They were greatly relieved to be back at work. Even with the periodic disruptions and tough working conditions, jobs at the Ford Motor Company were highly prized, especially as the country headed into the Great Depression. The plant had been completely retooled for the new Model As. For workers who spent their entire career making the Model T, this was a new experience, remembered by several who were interviewed in the late 1990s. Ken Muxlow described his work on the assembly line:

I started out making seat cushions on Model As. I used to "spit tacks." that is, hold the tacks in my mouth while I was hammering them. The tacks had to be sterilized for that reason. I also worked on installing the interior upholstery and fabric. One of my jobs was to cut out the fabric where the rear window was located. I still have a number of the oval fabric cutouts, which they were going to throw out. I saved a pile for rags.

It was usually an eight-hour workday, but if there was a shortage of parts or if there was a major machine breakdown, we were sent home without pay . . . There were a lot of tough jobs—they were all tough. Because if you didn't work hard, you worked fast. Between hard and fast, you take your pick. There weren't many guys who wanted my job.

Ken Muxlow's close friend Seth Lindsay also worked at Ford and described his work:

My first job was to put the passenger front door on Model A cars. I also repaired cars which had been dented up in the manufacturing process. Any worker who caused more than one or two dents would have found himself out on the front lawn with the other five hundred people looking for a job. I remember very clearly the design of the various parts of the Model A. It was very difficult to repair some dents because of the location of the gas tank cap in the middle of the front panel. I also worked at applying a lubricant treatment to car parts before they were installed. The poor condition of the roads caused most cars within a year to squeak terribly. My job was to brush a lampblack and Stanisol compound to the various car parts to help minimize the friction and noise.

Another job I did was to wet-sand the cars in between the undercoat of paint and the final coat. It was hot as hell working under the bright skylights during the summer. The heat also prevented the freshly painted cars from drying during a normal eight-hour work shift. The result was that we had to frequently put in a twelve-hour day to complete the work, and I don't think we were paid for the overtime.

One of the few African Americans hired during this time had the support of a most influential sponsor. In 1930, John Lee Banks was shining shoes at the St. Paul Hotel for one of his regular customers, Col. Lewis Brittin, who was then the general manager of Northwest Airways. Banks was very interested in aviation and Brittin gave him passes to fly with "Speed" Holman, the stunt flyer. "In 1930, right in the middle of the Depression, I told Colonel Brittin how I wanted to go work at the Ford plant," Banks said. "So he gave me a note to go see Mrs. High over at the Urban League . . . I went over, and she says, 'Well they aren't hiring anybody . . . but I know if you'll take this note out there that you'll get

John Banks was one of the very few African Americans hired to work at the plant before the modern era. Throughout his long employment he was active in organizing hobby clubs, exhibits, and social activities, in large measure to demonstrate that African Americans shared similar interests with white coworkers. He was a skilled photographer and led the Camera Club for many years. He is pictured here around 1950. Courtesy of the Minnesota Historical Society.

hired.' So I took it out there and they were laying off people left and right. But they hired me." Other minority workers were not as fortunate, as there was only one African American worker at the plant in 1936, presumably John Banks.

The initial success of the Model A brought economic stability to Ford, but the future of the company and its workers was not assured. It was priced significantly below the Chevrolet, in large part because Ford was selling at a loss. Production delays had cost Ford the sales lead to Chevrolet in 1928, but by 1929 Ford temporarily regained the lead. That year Chrysler had a big gain with its newly acquired Dodge brand. The October 1929 stock-market crash created considerable uncertainty, but Ford's massive retooling for the Model A helped the company to weather the Depression. Ford made $40 million in 1930, surpassing GM, but Chrysler's new cars, particularly the Plymouth, ate into Ford's market share. GM's management structure solidified its long-term competitive advantage over the autocratic and lumbering Ford organization. By 1931, Chevrolet had regained the lead with 42 percent of market share, and Ford sank the following year to third place behind Plymouth.

The Great Depression

During the early years of the Depression, industry sales plummeted 70 percent, and Ford lost $120 million between 1931 and 1933. The well-capitalized "Big Three" auto companies, Ford, GM, and Chrysler, managed to survive but many smaller manufacturers did not. There were 530 plants producing automobiles in 1929, but only sixty-eight by 1932. Ford turned to the commercial market and found success with sales of chassis for trucks and buses. Local companies typically made the vehicle bodies. Eckland Brothers in Minneapolis was one of the largest in the region and it advertised directly to Ford dealers: "Sell

Commercial Jobs in Fleets instead of one by one . . . Schools and bus lines need new buses . . . but they must be low in price and economical to operate and easy to maintain . . . that's where the Model AA Ford chassis equipped with a 14 passenger body by Eckland comes in." Eckland Brothers also built a number of bodies for house cars, the predecessor of the camper, which were becoming a popular novelty.

Ford had a grandiose vision that his bold actions could inspire others to help turn the economy around. He slashed prices on his cars and increased wages, but unfortunately others did not emulate this enlightened policy of economic stimulation. Ford's gesture proved to be too small to be effective, and with mounting losses he reversed course and lowered wages to four dollars a day, down from seven dollars. He also closed twenty-seven of his thirty-five plants, including the Twin Cities, which was shut from 1933 to 1935. Workers were not eligible for unemployment or other benefits, prior to unions, and had

During the Depression, Ford suspended all production from 1933 to 1935. With the slow recovery of the car market, Ford increasingly relied on the commercial market, producing chassis for trucks, buses, and specialty vehicles. This photograph shows a Sioux Line bus in 1934. Photograph by Norton & Peel. Courtesy of the Minnesota Historical Society.

to rely on family and friends for support during tough times. Marv Saline, the son of an autoworker at the St. Paul plant, recalled:

> During the 1930s my father had a very bad bout of rheumatism and couldn't work for four or five weeks. Of course, this was before the days of any kind of medical leave or benefits. One day my father was visited by two or three coworkers. On the way out, they threw an envelope on the table filled with cash. They had taken up a collection for my father at work—and it was a godsend. We never forgot that.

During the Depression Ford encouraged workers to plant vegetable gardens on acres of unused land behind the building. This practice continued at least until 1953, when this picture of the Janisch family was published in a company publication, *Ford at Fifty*. Author's collection.

Ford sometimes delivered coal to the needy. During the Depression Ford converted a large portion of the site to a vegetable garden for workers and their families. Bob Hansen, whose father Charley worked at the plant, recalled:

> I used to hoe there myself . . . You did like you would in your own home area, just planted your stuff and grew it . . . I must have been nine, ten, eleven years old . . . People would work there on the weekends and summer evenings. They [Ford] supplied the water, piped the water up there for them, and they plowed it for them . . . You had to supply your own tools. I didn't want any part of it. I didn't like to hoe. I did that under duress . . . like if you want to eat the food, you better hoe the food.

A company publication, *Ford at Fifty*, showed the garden still being used by employees in 1953. Julius Janisch and his wife and three children were pictured tending their plot, which reportedly yielded 310 ears of corn, thirty-two quarts of carrots, and seventy quarts of beans.

The Depression made it difficult for Ford to sell the shuttered Minneapolis plant, and the building was taken off the market in 1930. The following year, Ford converted the main floor into an enormous "display room" for more than one hundred commercial vehicles, including ambulances, funeral coaches, school buses, police trucks, panel delivery trucks, and dump trucks. A Minneapolis labor leader proposed that the empty plant be turned into housing for unemployed and homeless men. Minneapolis Mayor William A. Anderson, still bitter at the move of Ford to St. Paul, wrote to the company in 1932 "requesting them to make the building available for public relief." He held Ford "morally responsible as the construction of the plant had attracted many men here who were unable to find employment." A Ford security guard making the rounds of the

Ford was unable to sell the empty Minneapolis plant during the Depression, and a St. Paul newspaper tweaked Ford by suggesting it be rented out. The Minneapolis mayor and labor officials called for Ford to convert the building to housing for unemployed workers. Photograph by the *St. Paul Daily News*. Courtesy of the Minnesota Historical Society.

Ford used trucks to deliver cars to local dealers. A car transport carrier with new 1932 Fords with V-8 engines is shown parked in front of the Twin Cities plant. Railroads and trucking companies competed to develop transport carriers that that could ship cars more efficiently. Author's collection.

empty building was shot and killed, and the case was never solved. The next watchman understandably had some qualms about wandering around the empty ten-story building. Ken Muxlow recalled: "After I'd been there about a week, I asked them if I could carry a gun to protect myself. They raised Cain and they said, 'Absolutely not! If you need anything, there's a telephone.' I know telephone wires can be taken down pretty darned easy, so I will admit that occasionally, not all the time, I had a good pocket pistol and I had that with me—but, I never had to use it, thank goodness."

Having learned the lesson of staying with one car model too long, Henry Ford started working on a replacement for the Model A in 1930. A small team of engineers secretly worked at the historic Thomas Edison laboratory that had been moved to the restored Greenfield Village. Over several years they came up with a number of technical innovations, including the casting of a one-piece V-8 block. As sales of the Model A declined in

1932, the new V-8 was unveiled. After a slow start, largely because of the Depression, the car achieved reasonably good sales. Ford had come to accept the need for more regular model changes and worked on two-year cycles for the rest of the decade.

President Franklin Roosevelt, the New Deal, and Rise of Labor

By the time President Franklin Delano Roosevelt took office on March 4, 1933, industrial output had collapsed, the unemployment rate had reached 25 percent, farm prices dropped 60 percent, and banks were closed in thirty-two states. During Roosevelt's first hundred days, the National Industrial Recovery Act (NIRA) was passed to jump-start manufacturing. It was described as a "colossal experiment in self-regulation by American industry." Industry leaders on a sector-by-sector basis voluntarily agreed to standards of operation. The federal government suspended the enforcement of antitrust laws and established production quotas and targets for prices and wages. Business and labor groups could review industry agreements, and, if approved, they would be adopted as government policy. Labor unions were pleased with a provision known as Section 7A that made it easier to organize.

The National Automobile Chamber of Commerce took the lead in shaping the automotive industry agreement, but it did so without the help of Henry Ford, who boycotted the process. To get Ford's support for the agreement, language calling for the acceptance of labor unions was watered down with the inclusion of a "merit clause." Ford still refused to sign. He criticized government officials, "whose particular genius is to try to run other people's business . . . I was always under the impression that to manage a business properly you ought to know something about it." General Motors and Chrysler did sign, and flaunted their participation to embarrass Ford. They were just as strongly opposed to labor unions as Ford, but they felt that the "merit clause" in Section 7A gave them enough leeway to rebuff any organizing attempt.

The federal government could not force Ford to sign the agreement but it did have considerable leverage through its procurement policies. On March 14, 1934, the government announced it would stop buying Ford products, which quickly elevated Henry Ford to the most prominent opponent of the New Deal. "Before the New Deal could fully harness 'the wild horses of pioneer America,'" Allan Nevins and Frank Ernest Hill wrote, "this type of faith in a rugged individual would have to be modified." To challenge the ruling, the Ford Motor Company bid on a federal order for trucks issued by the Works Progress Administration. The government rejected the bid. Ford explained that he always intended to comply with the terms of the agreement but just refused to sign it. This was a distinction lost on federal procurement officials who declared that Ford's bid was not acceptable. Ford sued, and lost in federal court in June 1934. Roosevelt still hoped to avoid a fight with the popular Ford and continued to press him through a number of intermediaries, including Ford's close friend Thomas Edison.

Watering down the industry agreement certainly helped automobile manufacturers ward off unions, but they didn't need much help because of the lack of cohesion within the ranks of organized labor. Unions were considerably weakened by management's aggressive counterattacks and were in such a dysfunctional state they were not even a party to the negotiations of the NIRA sector agreement. With no unions participating in the discussions, the industry agreement permitted "company unions," which would make it even more difficult for labor. At the time, the Communist Party was the most effective group representing the autoworkers.

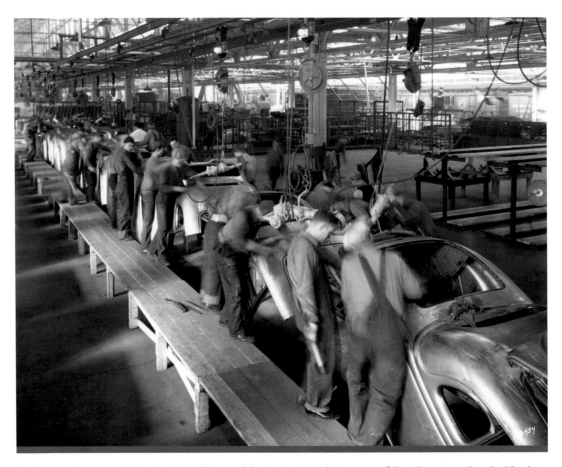

Workers on the assembly line in 1935. Photograph by Norton & Peel. Courtesy of the Minnesota Historical Society.

In 1935 the Supreme Court struck down the NIRA. Congress then passed the National Labor Relations Act, known as the Wagner Act, which was far more favorable to unions. This generated new hope in the labor movement and spawned a new cycle of organizing campaigns. In 1936, the United Auto Workers affiliated with the newly independent Congress of Industrial Organizations (CIO) and mounted successful organizing campaigns at GM and Chrysler, using a new tool—the sit-down strike. This emboldened union leaders to think about a full organizing campaign against their toughest challenge, the mighty Ford fortress.

As the economy started to improve after the Depression, Ford reopened the Twin Cities Assembly Plant. Joe Kucera, a draftsman hired that year, helped with the rebuilding:

> The Glass Plant was going to start up. So I waited in line with about six fellows for the interview with the plant manager. We were each given a drawing test. I had studied drafting, in the building construction program at Dunwoody—I got the job . . . For our first task we made layouts and sketches or retraced some drawings of the old glass plant . . . to bring it up to work with the new one. It was a major alteration. Actually, a brand-new Glass Plant. All the old equipment went out.

A new gas line was installed from the Steam Plant. Ford had to pay a 5 percent gross earnings tax on the amount consumed, presumably because it ran under the city parkway. Production resumed in January 1937, and the glass furnace consumed a million cubic feet of gas a day. Ford introduced a new sheet-glass manufacturing process utilizing the Colburn method. Production averaged more than a million square feet of "A" glass a month, which lasted until the World War II shutdown. The company made several other modifications to the Twin Cities plant after the Depression. The bathrooms, which were originally located at the mezzanine level, had to be raised five feet to make room for conveyors carrying car bodies and larger items. In addition, the Cooper Hewitt ceiling lights had to be removed. They had to be hung crooked to allow the mercury to flow to one corner and didn't provide great light. The new fluorescent fixtures greatly improved illumination at the work stations. Pete Koegel, the electrician who was hired for that work, recalled the antiunion sentiment of the plant manager: "He said to me, 'So, you'd like to work for the Ford Motor Company?' Christ sake! I'm getting less than fifteen dollars a week in 1936. Do I want to work there? I said, 'Yes, sir, I certainly would.' He said—this is his exact words, 'Are you any kind of union man of any kind?' What the hell? I'm a kid. I said, 'No, sir. I'm not no union man.' He said, 'It's a goddamned good thing! We don't want no union men around here.'"

Ford's Resistance to Labor and the Deterioration of Working Conditions

The New Deal gave legal protection to union organizing activities, but automobile companies would not go easily. Nelson Lichtenstein put it succinctly: "virtually every strike in the [automobile] industry signaled the destruction of the organization that had called it." One labor leader, Walter Reuther, was as determined to unionize the Ford Motor Company as Henry Ford was to prevent it. Reuther was elected to the United Auto Workers Executive Committee and organized thousands of workers on Detroit's West Side. He navigated the factional disputes of the labor movement through his tireless energy, his vision, and his messianic beliefs—a personality type that was remarkably similar to Henry Ford. On May 26, 1937, Walter Reuther and Richard Frankensteen led the UAW in a march against the Ford Rouge plant where they were met by a contingent of Ford service agents in what became known as the "Battle of the Overpass." Reuther and other union organizers were severely beaten by the agents, who also pummeled bystanders, including reporters, photographers, and women. Newspapers and magazines published a number of iconic photographs of the battle, one of which received a Pulitzer Prize. These images exposed to a shocked nation what the Ford service department had become—a gang of thugs. The union was galvanized: "Today the world has seen the true character of the Ford Motor Co. We don't intend that it shall forget it." Henry Ford's carefully cultivated image was unraveling, and his response was to strike back at the media, canceling all advertising contracts with *Time, Life,* and *Fortune* magazines. While Ford's image took a beating, Reuther emerged as a fitting rival, a dedicated and brave labor hero. This was not their last encounter; the epic final battle was still several years away.

The UAW documented the illegal actions and built a case for the National Labor Relations Board (NLRB). In a scathing decision, the board ruled that the Ford Motor Company was guilty of numerous violations of the Wagner Act and ordered it to reinstate fired union organizers, pay back wages, and stop interfering with organizing efforts. Henry Ford rejected the decision and responded with a flurry of appeals. Labor unrest spread from Detroit to the branch assembly plants, including Dallas and Kansas City, where bloody battles ensued. Ford's response in Kansas City was to shut the plant down for three months and threaten to move operations to Omaha. This so alarmed the city manager that he flew to Detroit and pledged that the Kansas City police department would shift from a neutral position in the labor dispute to one supporting Ford's antiunion activities. The protracted skirmishing over the next several years weakened public and legal support for the NLRB as many unemployed workers resented companies being shut down by strikes.

Under Ford's relentless counteroffensive, cracks developed in labor's unified front, which he further exploited by adopting a "divide and conquer" strategy. He secretly negotiated with various labor factions simultaneously, and even created a sham company union. While Ford was having short-term tactical success in keeping the unions off balance, the NLRB continued to document the abuses. It reported: "The River Rouge plant has taken on many aspects of a community in which martial law has been declared, and in which a huge military organization has been superimposed upon the regular civil authorities." The Rouge plant had approximately ninety thousand workers, and reportedly had eight hundred "storm troops" for "keeping order," and around nine thousand company spies. All Ford facilities, including the Twin Cities Assembly Plant, had some elements of this security apparatus. Joe Kucera remembered seeing a security guard hiding among the heating coils in the ceiling. He also recalled that working conditions deteriorated significantly during the labor strife: "One time I was by the ovens and the guys started complaining that it was hot around where

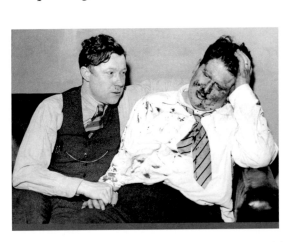

Ford's benevolent attitude toward workers disappeared during the Depression. Henry Ford vowed to never accept unions, even after the United Auto Workers organized General Motors and Chrysler. There were numerous bloody conflicts between the two sides, including the highly publicized "Battle of the Overpass" in 1937. Ford security forces pummeled UAW demonstrators, including its leaders Walter Reuther and Richard Frankensteen. Photograph courtesy of the Walter P. Reuther Library, Archives of Labor and Urban Affairs, Wayne State University. *News-week* magazine cover from author's collection.

This worker spray-painted a car body mounted on an overhead conveyor in 1935. He did not have respirator equipment and the room appeared to lack much in the way of ventilation. Surrounded by fixed window sash, it must have been quite warm in the summer. Photograph by Norton & Peel. Courtesy of the Minnesota Historical Society.

the oven painted the car bodies. The guys were really complaining. Old Bill Swallow who was head of paint said, 'Hell, it ain't hot. We ain't carried nobody out yet.'"

Another worker, Chet Brokl, had to sand car bodies before the final painting. Because it was a wet-sanding process, he was outfitted with rubber boots and aprons. It was very tough work, even for a self-described tough farm kid. "One day," he said, "I looked down at the running water in the trough and noticed that it had turned blood red. I looked at my hands and discovered I had sanded clear through the rubber tape and had rubbed off large areas of my skin. I re-taped my hands, but not before my foreman came over. 'Keep on sanding,' he shouted, 'or you know where the door is.'"

More frequent model changes increased the amount of new equipment and technologies that were introduced, often on a trial-and-error basis. Ford tried a mechanized sander the size of a small watermelon, held by two hands. At first, Brokl thought this was a great improvement, but after a few hours holding the eight-pound tool, he reconsidered. "It was vibrating and shaking terribly, like a hydraulic jack," he said. "I would occasionally put the sander down to use the squeegee to test for paint scratches, and rest my arms. By the end of the shift, I could hardly move. Within a few days the bicep muscle of my right arm was so swollen it looked like a baseball. I had lost all feeling in the arm, and couldn't close my hand. I couldn't hold a tool or a utensil." Brokl lived with his family and feared they would notice him eating with his left hand because he couldn't hold a fork in his right hand. He worried they would tell him to quit his job. Eventually, Ford did improve the tool. Another time Brokl worked with a new type of primer paint that gave him rashes all over. He visited the Ford doctor and was told "Keep at it. You will get used to it, and it will disappear."

Working conditions deteriorated further when Henry Ford hired Harry Bennett, a

The assembly line had become a movable platform by 1935. A Ford time-studies man by the window closely observes workers, looking for ways to speed up operations. Photograph by Norton & Peel. Courtesy of the Minnesota Historical Society.

known thug with underworld ties, as his right-hand man. John Kenneth Galbraith wrote that Bennett, "along with his satellite prizefighters, punks, ex-football players . . . and assorted baccalaureates of the Michigan penal institutions, eventually made the Ford Motor Company into an industrial charnel house." Bennett would even come between Henry Ford and his only child, Edsel, who was the nominal president of the Ford Motor

This group photograph from the 1930s shows what appears to be the entire workforce in front of the Twin Cities Assembly Plant. Courtesy of Ken Muxlow (who appears somewhere in the picture).

Company. In doing so, Bennett and Henry Ford not only destroyed what little remained of a filial relationship but also marginalized one of the company's most rational and competent managers.

Preparing for World War II

The unsettled mood caused by the Depression and labor turmoil took a new turn with the war in Europe and the increasing likelihood that the United States would be drawn into the conflict. President Roosevelt began the nation's first peacetime military draft in October 1940 and established a weapons-procurement program. The rapid advance of the German army left England as the last major combatant in Europe. Roosevelt pledged support and declared that the United States would become the "arsenal of democracy." He signed the Lend-Lease Act in March 1941, which enabled the United States to supply England with materials essential to its defense. Given the need for military preparedness, the government desperately wanted to work with the Ford Motor Company, one of the largest industrial concerns in the world. However, military planners in Washington were concerned about the company's dysfunction, as David Halberstam describes:

> Henry Ford remained locked in the past. He grew more erratic and finally senile. At the end of his life he believed that WWII did not exist, and that it was simply a ploy made up by newspapers to help the munitions industry. No one could reach the old man anymore. It was a spectacular self-destruction, one that would never again be matched in a giant American corporation. It was as if the old man, having made the company, felt he had a right to destroy it.

Ford's harsh labor policies, his pacifism, his animosity toward Roosevelt, and his perceived sympathies for the Nazis made it difficult to enlist him in the military preparedness effort. Despite these obstacles, the Ford Motor Company received a contract in August 1940 to manufacture four thousand Pratt & Whitney eighteen-cylinder air-cooled airplane engines. The contract also allocated $14 million for construction of a new plant at the Rouge complex. Linking military contracts to the construction of new plants was not unusual, prompting one military procurement official to complain, "every time the government approached the mass-production industries with the placement of contracts, industrial brass said, 'We will take on that job providing you give us a new plant.'" The military awarded the engine contract before Ford agreed to accept a union, prompt-

ing strenuous objections from the UAW. Union leaders accused Ford of massive labor violations and also of being a "Nazi sympathizer," especially after he received a medal from the Third Reich.

Ironically, the federal official in charge of military procurement was William S. Knudsen, who, after being dismissed by Henry Ford, went on to run General Motors. Given the sense of urgency for military preparation, there was little desire to stop Ford's participation over labor issues. The government was so determined to involve the company that President Roosevelt indicated at a press conference that "the government is

A 1938 Standard Tudor and a 1938 half-ton truck chassis are on display in the plant's showroom. Signs in the background promote the Ford V-8, sixty horsepower engine, which was designed to save fuel. Author's collection.

prepared to take over the plants of the Ford Motor Company if, for defense reasons, this was deemed necessary." Ford proceeded to build a new plant to make the airplane engines, but to meet the contract deadlines had to spread production around to its branch plants. The Twin Cities plant received a contract to produce more than thirty parts for the Pratt & Whitney engines, including pistons, pump assemblies, cam support assemblies, and oil pumps.

While preparations were being made for war abroad, labor battles continued at home, with Ford blocking the UAW at every turn. Internal strife and mismanagement continued to weaken organizing efforts, but the union kept reporting Ford's illegal activities to the NLRB and pressured the federal government to bar it from bidding on any military projects. Ford's delaying actions finally came to a legal end in February 1941 when the Supreme Court issued a clear-cut victory for the UAW in upholding the actions of the NLRB. Henry Ford was unbowed, however, and refused to accept the law of the land. He insisted that he would "never submit to any union" and repeated his charge that "the outside forces" were out to get him.

A month later, a spark ignited the final explosion. The firing of a union organizer at the Rouge plant prompted fifty thousand workers to walk off the job on April 1, 1941. It was a spontaneous strike, but the union was ready, and quickly barricaded all the roads entering the Rouge plant. Battles erupted between the Ford Service Department guards, who had machine guns, and the rock-throwing workers. After several days it was clear that for the first time local law-enforcement officials would not come to Ford's aid. He had no choice but to capitulate and agree to union elections. Given the convoluted labor situation that Ford helped create, workers had three choices on the ballot: the UAW affiliated with the CIO; the UAW affiliated with the AFL; or no union. The UAW-CIO won with 70 percent of the vote. By all accounts, Henry Ford was an emotionally and physically broken man just a few months from his seventy-eighth birthday. He had already had a stroke and was speaking incoherently on occasion, but he still refused to sign a labor contract, even knowing that the federal government had an option of taking over management of the company to complete the defense contracts.

Ford would listen to only one person—his wife Clara. She was extremely distressed that his behavior threatened the very survival of the company that she hoped would be passed on to their son Edsel. Clara reportedly gave her husband an ultimatum: either sign the labor agreement or she would leave him. Henry capitulated, and on June 20, 1941, he signed what turned out to be the most the generous labor contract ever won by the UAW. It included a "union shop" and "checkoff" system, meaning that the company would directly withhold monthly union dues and assessments from workers' pay.

During these weeks of high drama in Dearborn, the company closed the Twin Cities

The Mercury 8 car was assembled at the Twin Cities plant in 1939. This brand was introduced by Ford in 1937 to fill the price gap between Ford and Lincoln and to compete with GM's Buick and Oldsmobile. Courtesy of the Minnesota Historical Society.

Assembly Plant and furloughed its 1,700 workers because the Rouge plant was not shipping parts. Everyone knew Ford had company spies at the plant and that involvement in organizing efforts would likely lead to dismissal. Many workers, especially those with families, were reluctant to take that risk. Local organizing activities took a backseat to the national efforts, but some preliminary organizing efforts occurred. John Banks recalled hosting the national UAW organizer in his living room, who was sent to the Twin Cities to lead the local effort. Joe Kucera described another meeting in Minneapolis:

> It came out that we were going to have a union and a group organized a meeting over on Twenty-eighth and Lake. It was a Plymouth garage. I was in the drafting department so I

didn't go inside. The draftsmen were not part of the group then. But I was there watching them. The guys were going in. It was a pretty fair crowd. As the guys were going in, old Dorsey and Elliot, plant manager and assistant, were riding around the place. All they wanted to do is see who was going in. A millwright was fired, but they hired him back. But then, when we started meeting at other places, I went.

The Twin Cities Assembly Plant reopened on April 27, 1941, several weeks after the national labor agreement in Detroit. For the national contract to apply to the St. Paul plant, a majority of local workers had to agree to be represented by the new UAW-CIO. On June 27, more than 1,200 workers attended an evening meeting and nine hundred signed union membership cards, giving it the needed majority. On July 18, 1941, CIO-UAW charter No. 879 went into effect, giving workers at the Twin Cities plant assurance that they were covered under the terms of the master contract signed in Dearborn. The new UAW Local 879 opened an office at 444 Rice Street, St. Paul, and proceeded to elect officers. Several weeks later, a Twin Cities delegation, led by Joseph Mattson, met with Ford representatives in Chicago to learn the details of the union contract negotiated in Detroit.

The labor wars were winding down as the military buildup intensified. It was only a matter of time before car production would end and the plant would be converted to military production. In April 1941, as the River Rouge plant was being reprogrammed for the war effort, William Knudsen, chief of the Office for Emergency Management, announced that automobile companies had voluntarily agreed to reduce production of cars by 20 percent to ensure industrial capacity for the military effort. GM canceled its planned model change for 1943 but said it would continue with production of its 1942 cars. These restrictions resulted in a huge rush of orders for the 1941 models. After many years of struggle to win the right to represent workers at the Ford Motor Company, the union had to abruptly redefine its mission. Its first job now was to protect its members as the plant was converted from civilian production under Ford to military production under the Office of Emergency Management (OEM). Labor leaders at the local, state, and federal levels lobbied to keep autoworkers employed in defense industries as car production was phased out. On December 7, 1941, eight months after the signing of the UAW contract, Japan attacked Pearl Harbor and the United States entered the war. Under heavy pressure by the government, manufacturers canceled automobile production completely to prepare for military contracts. Most workers were furloughed after the Twin Cities plant stopped making cars, but some were kept on to make boxes for shipping glass. Workers' concerns about employment were real, but the prospect of military service was more pressing.

In retaliation for America's support for England, Germany unleashed its submarines and sank an unarmed American merchant vessel outside the combat zone. The Nazis sank approximately five hundred ships during the first six months of 1942, resulting in the deaths of far more Americans than at Pearl Harbor. The Ford Motor Company was particularly vulnerable because its sizable maritime fleet was shipping materials to its branches throughout Europe, including Germany and England. In July 1941, the United States moved to "federalize" the Ford fleet for the Lend-Lease program to transport materials to England. Ford protested that many of the vessels were designed for inland navigation and not intended for transatlantic travel, but to no avail. A Ford official remembered: "There was a time when telegrams or letters seemed to arrive almost daily . . . directing the company to turn over certain ships, 'no questions asked.' They advised where and when the transfer of Ford vessels was to take place and under what conditions. The ships were either bought outright or taken over on time or 'bareboat' charters. The company cooperated fully, even though it left the movement of its own materials to the Rouge Plant in doubt." Ford ships and maritime employees "paid heavily in this slaughter." The casualties went largely unreported at the time because of the government news blackout.

The War Years

Over the next several months the Ford Motor Company received orders for a variety of military items, including the "Jeep," a small reconnaissance truck, a "swamp buggy" that could operate in soggy terrain, airplane gliders, several weapons systems, and the B-24 Liberator Bomber, one of the largest contracts of the war. Ford constructed an enormous plant at Willow Run, Michigan, financed by the federal government, to build the planes. The bombers that came streaming off the assembly line needed a variety of modifications before being used in combat, which were to be done by "modification centers" around the country. The army contracted with Northwest Airlines in February 1942 and built two new maintenance hangers at the Holman Airport in St. Paul. A number of Ford mechanics were assigned to this project during the war. Ford and other companies around the country, including the Northwestern Aeronautical Corporation in the Twin Cities, also received a contract to build wooden gliders. Ford took the lead on manufacturing the new glider and built a prototype that was sent to other contractors for study.

In the summer of 1942, Ford and several other car manufacturers received a "seemingly impossible assignment . . . to design a vehicle with all the speed assets of an automobile, firepower of a light tank, armor, and enough equipment and crew accommodations for a scouting trip of several days." Ford designed several versions of experimental light-armored vehicles, and built a small number of T-17s and T-22s at the Twin Cities

Automobile companies received military contracts in the lead up to WWII and gradually phased out of making cars. On February 1, 1942, two months after Pearl Harbor, the government imposed a complete ban on car production.The production of the M-8 armored vehicle, pictured here, was assigned to the Twin Cities plant. Author's collection.

Assembly Plant. None of the vehicles met the requirements of the military. Ford then designed the M-8 armored vehicle and built prototype models at the Rouge plant, which the military accepted. Ford assigned production of the armored vehicles to plants in the Twin Cities and Chicago. To expedite production, the M-8 used existing equipment as much as possible—the driveshaft and axel assemblies were essentially the same as those on Ford trucks.

The Twin Cities Assembly Plant had to be modified to produce the M-8 and the Pratt & Whitney airplane engine parts, and $10,500,000 was added to the military contracts for that purpose. A fence was installed inside the plant for security purposes running north and south, creating two separate production zones. The M-8 was assembled on the east side, which had the taller ceiling height of twenty-six feet for the crane bay. This additional space was needed to install the mounted gun turrets, and it also opened directly to an oval test track at the rear of the building. The Pratt & Whitney engine parts were assembled on the west half of the plant, which had a ceiling height of fourteen feet. More than thirty separate parts, including pistons, pump assemblies, cam support assemblies, and oil pumps, were made. These separate projects even had different schedules, with one operating two shifts and the other three. Well over half—perhaps 80 percent—of the workers on the aircraft side were women, which required the installation of more women's bathrooms. Loretta Jackson remembered that the women had to wear uniforms, a "horrible kind of overalls." The clerical workers had to wear a jacket and navy blue slacks, safety shoes, and white socks. Jackson recalled that the normally monotonous routine on the assembly line was disrupted one day by "two women fighting over one guy . . . the good ones were all gone."

The military enforced very tight security at the plant. Only top management officials could cross from the M-8 side to the aircraft engine side. During the war, windows were

More than five thousand armored vehicles were made in the Twin Cities under very tight security. As evident in the banner, patriotic fervor ran high as virtually every worker had loved ones serving in the military. Author's collection.

The M-8s were made on the east side of the plant and were driven directly out to a newly installed oval test track at the rear of the plant. Author's collection.

With the shortage of male workers owing to the war, large numbers of women were hired to assemble parts for Pratt & Whitney airplane engines. Author's collection.

blacked out for security reasons, and traffic on Mississippi River Boulevard was detoured around the plant. There were also contingency plans to use the tunnels under the plant as an air-raid shelter, which one report said "could sleep some 13,500 or seat 30,000." The large underground chambers could have been turned into an emergency hospital if necessary, with the "baby railroad" carrying medical supplies.

On December 8, 1942, Governor Harold Stassen toured the plant and was pleased with the progress: "Only a month since the conversion was approved, finished products are already being turned out." Bob Hansen, a young process engineer at the time, was impressed with the quality of the work: "We had the opportunity to get into the new operations on machines which we didn't have. We did the tool developing and tool grinding for milling machines, shaping machines. They all had to have specially designed tips, so they'd cut the right grooves." Meisel gears for the pumps, and much of the war production, were machined with tolerances of one thousandth (.001). Ford built a new freestanding clean room within the plant for the precision work, with air vents that went directly through the roof.

The M-8 was a six-wheel armored car. It could operate with four-wheel drive, or six-wheel drive in rough terrain, but it was not nearly as mobile as a tank with continuous tracks. Its two front tires provided the steering mechanism and its rear four tires were fixed. The deep-treaded tires were bullet proof and self-sealing. The vehicle weighed eight and one-half tons and could travel at speeds of up to sixty miles per hour with a range of three hundred to four hundred miles. The M-8 had a seventy-five-gallon fuel tank with a liner that would seal itself if pierced by a bullet.

A Ford memo described the M-8 as "powerful enough to bowl over a good sized tree." It was loaded with short- and long-range radio equipment, making it an ideal escort and reconnaissance vehicle. Offensively, the armored car could "pack a terrific wallop" with 37 mm cannon,

Assembly work for the Pratt & Whitney engines was done on the west side of the plant. A security fence separated it from the M-8 production on the east side of the plant. Author's collection.

Senator Harry Truman and a group of federal officials toured the Twin Cities plant in 1942 to inspect the military production. Pictured from left to right are Senator Kilgore, Senator Wallgren, Senator Joseph H. Ball, Senator Harry Truman, Charles Sorensen (executive vice president of Ford), Senator Mead, Hugh Fulton (chief counsel for the Truman Committee investigating the national defense program), and unknown. Courtesy of the Minnesota Historical Society.

which was powerful enough to pierce Japanese tanks but not the better-armored German tanks. It also had twin machine guns mounted in the turret. Its crew of four carried four carbines, six land mines, and a full complement of hand grenades. The M-8 had a hull of heavy armor plate that functioned as a framework or chassis, but it was not thick enough to withstand a direct hit by an antitank shell. The underside also lacked sufficient armor to protect against land mines. Its best defense was speed and agility, but its innovative design provided some protection against heavy machine-gun fire. None of the exterior surfaces were completely horizontal or vertical, and this lack of right angles made it more difficult for bullets to pierce. If attacked, the crew could enclose the windshield with an armor plate and switch to a periscope for visibility. A companion utility command vehicle, the M-20, was also made at the St. Paul plant.

The rapid conversion to military production created a severe shortage of skilled workers around the country. The plant superintendent, H. C. Dorsey, described the need for welders: "We never did have more than a dozen welders at any time; yet in preparation for our scheduled production of M-8's we had to have over 400 welders trained and accepted according to rigid Army Ordinance standards. This was done in our welding school, where they were trained by welders from our Detroit Rouge plant." During their training period, the workers were paid regular wages. After passing a test, they could work as a certified welder attaching plates to the two tanks. "One was a two-engine job and about a seventeen tonner and the other one was about a ten tonner, lighter weight," recalled Joe Kucera. "First they built the bigger ones, not too many, then the smaller ones."

After the hull was welded, workers attached the wheels, springs, and other parts. The vehicles were then put on a "towline," where workers added turrets, instruments, and cannons. The M-8s received several coats of olive drab paint. The last coat was applied after the road tests, including a one-hundred-mile drive on the rear test track and additional runs over rough terrain. The Ford plant shipped more than two thousand parts along with the finished M-8s, packed in a thousand wooden boxes that were custom-made in St. Paul. Parts were moved on a sophisticated conveyer system through a variety of "cleaning, dipping, and drying steps," directly into the freight cars located on tracks within the plant.

The production of M-8s was top secret for almost a year and a half before local

"Coffee-break" at Plant No. 4

A large number of welders was needed to make the M-8, and with the worker shortage Ford had to set up a welding school at the plant. John Rouen was among those who received training. His picture appeared in the company publication *Ford at Fifty*. He was later surprised to see his image being used to sell coffee and other commercial products in national magazines and on billboards. Courtesy of the family of John Rouen.

Ford carefully packed finished M-8s on trains under very tight security precautions and shipped them under wrap to their destinations. Author's collection.

reporters could write about the project. Ford opened the Twin Cities Assembly Plant to the press on March 18, 1944, after thousands of vehicles were shipped to Europe, where they were already being used in battle. Reporters took a ride on the test track, prompting one to write: "It handles like an automobile, proved by the fact that girl drivers are as able to handle the unit as men." Years later, several retired autoworkers remembered one of the women drivers who drove so fast around the concrete track that she flipped a vehicle. "I think the guys got her into that . . . They kept saying, 'You're kind of slow on your test runs,'" said one. "They kept needling her until she hit a curb too fast and went over it." She was not hurt, but the incident highlighted the changing workforce during wartime.

The St. Paul plant manufactured more than six thousand M-8s by March 1944. Combined with its production at the Chicago Ford plant, the M-8 became the highest-volume armored car ever made. Primarily used for reconnaissance missions in Europe and Japan, it "helped spearhead the attack" of the Normandy invasion and the European Offensive. The relatively quiet vehicles became known as "Patton's Ghosts," as they were able to sneak up on the Germans.

Even the formal entry of the United States into the war could not contain the difficult labor-relations problems. The government created a dispute resolution process and several new agencies to help bring labor peace, but both industry and labor continued to press for advantage. Businesses called for a suspension of organizing campaigns, in the name of "national unity," but as one observer wrote, "Labor would no more give them that than cut off its strong right arm." "Labor is making sacrifices everywhere," said one autoworker. "Our brothers and sons are dying in the trenches. Can anyone show any sign that the men who sign checks have made any sacrifice?"

Leaders of the UAW, who were asked to sign a no-strike pledge, responded with a proposal titled "Equality of Sacrifice," which included:

1. An end to war profits.
2. No luxuries in wartime.
3. No war millionaires.
4. A check of rising costs and inflation.
5. Rationing of all food, clothing, housing, and other necessities.
6. Security allowances for men in the armed forces.
7. Adjustment in wages to meet living costs.
8. A moratorium on debts.
9. Participation by labor in production planning.
10. Far-sighted planning for the postwar recession.
11. Payment of wages over forty hours to be in non-negotiable war bonds.

The UAW believed that waiving time-and-a half pay for overtime, and accepting war bonds in lieu of cash for overtime, demonstrated a significant contribution to the war effort. Reuther proposed a cap on executive salaries of twenty-five thousand dollars, which was about eight times the annual wage of a fifty-hour-a-week war worker. The Equality of Sacrifice proposals became the conceptual framework for labor's demands for the next half century. The government's efforts to impose a truce on labor skirmishes were not entirely successful and the strong feelings persisted throughout the war. A congressman from Michigan called the CIO "Communistic" and demanded that the government take over striking plants, a move that the Communist Party would probably have welcomed.

Industry executives argued that there was little point in sending American troops abroad if striking workers back home sabotaged their efforts. A labor supporter countered, "There is no use in America producing defense materials if it is a nation of slaves." Labor officials claimed that the number of strikes against defense facilities was very small, representing less than 1 percent of plants. In a speech in St. Paul, Secretary of Labor Frances Perkins rejected the notion that strikes were hurting the defense preparations, and claimed that there was four times more loss because of industrial accidents on the job. An official with the American Legion criticized those who believed in "time-and-a-half patriotism." A letter to the editor countered: "We are being no more disloyal than the big business men who last year insisted on guarantees of expansion costs and profits before they would start their big defense projects rolling. We are willing and proud to make equal sacrifices for America's defense, and we are the ones who, when it comes to that, will defend her with our lives."

Henry Ford had suffered several strokes and his henchman Harry Bennett was intent on filling the leadership vacuum in the company. The most capable executive at the company was Edsel Ford, but his paranoid father had marginalized and cruelly humiliated him over the years. His health suffered as a result, and he died on May 26, 1943, at the age of forty-nine of complications from stomach cancer, undulant fever, and, by the observation of many, "of a broken heart." The day before Edsel's funeral, Henry Ford made the startling announcement that he would return as president, which he had relinquished to Edsel in 1919. Ford was eighty years old and his health was so poor that his doctor strongly advised him to retire. Military officials had come to rely on Edsel, and were very concerned about the ability of the company to fulfill its military contracts. Edsel's only child, Henry II, was on active duty with the navy, but the military released him in the hope that he would return to the company to help fill the void.

Military contracts ensured the survival of Ford and other companies during the war, but dealers were not so fortunate. The slack demand during the Depression years had given them little cushion to fall back on. Most manufacturers, including Ford, stopped making cars during the Depression, and then again during the war. To survive, dealers relied almost entirely on service and repair work, and the sale of tires, batteries, and accessories. Dealers also had to scramble to find mechanics during the war as the military had drafted most of the skilled workers.

Ford suspended production during the Depression and during World War II, causing considerable hardship to dealers. They had to rely on the sale of used cars and service work to survive; many, including the Woodhead Company on Lake Street in Minneapolis, had to borrow money to keep their business afloat. Henry Ford was notoriously unsympathetic to the plight of dealers. Courtesy of John Woodhead.

Ford made little effort to support dealers during these difficult times, and, if anything, the company intensified operating control. The 1939 franchise agreement with the Woodhead Company on Lake Street in Minneapolis gave Ford the right to unilaterally terminate it with sixty days' notice. It also required new accounting systems and financial reports to the company every ten days. Woodhead had to keep an inventory on hand equaling 10 percent of the projected annual sales. Requests for new vehicles had to be submitted to the company by the tenth day of each month, but Ford was not held liable if it did not make a shipment. Dealers had to pay cash for the new merchandise unless otherwise authorized by the company. The agreement also spelled out the need for the dealer to "contemplate" owning his building, which would prove problematic for Woodhead, who was renting.

John Woodhead had to suspend dividend payments to shareholders during the Depression and needed to take out several loans to keep his business afloat. The new measures created enormous hardships that were highlighted by *Forbes Magazine* in an article titled "How Ford Dealers Are Treated, As Told by One of Them": "Is it surprising

Henry Ford's grandson, known as Henry II (or "the Deuce"), was released from service in the navy to oversee military production at the company during the war. The founding patriarch had become senile and was seen as an increasingly disruptive force. Henry II first had to wrest power away from his grandfather and then from the henchmen that Henry Ford had installed. Author's collection.

During the war, virtually every industrial plant in Minnesota was converted to military production. With the war winding down, companies hoped to apply their sophisticated manufacturing techniques to civilian production. A trade exposition called the Production for Victory Convention was held in January 1944 at the Minneapolis Auditorium, offering local manufacturers an opportunity to showcase their technical expertise. Among them was a complete Pratt & Whitney engine with parts made at the Ford Twin Cities plant. Author's collection.

that the number of Ford dealers wanting to quit is constantly increasing? . . . Not in any other organization in the world has so much work, worry, and humiliation been visited upon men who are financially able to own and manage their own business affairs, as has been heaped on the shoulders of the ordinary Ford dealer."

Henry Ford remained president throughout the war, but Harry Bennett basically ran the company. Bennett had pushed Henry II to the side, greatly upsetting Henry's wife Clara and Edsel's widow Eleanor. They were determined to wrest control of the company away from Bennett and to install Henry II as president. When Ford balked, Clara was again compelled to give Henry an ultimatum: either appoint Henry II or she would sell her share of the stock to an outsider. Given Henry Ford's failing health, he had little choice but to comply. The eighty-year-old patriarch and the twenty-five-year-old grandson finally met to complete the transfer and Henry II, knowing of the difficulties faced by his father Edsel, insisted he run the company with complete autonomy. On September 25, 1945, the company founder resigned from the board, and Henry Ford II became president. The grandson now had both the title and assurances that he would be free from interference, but he could not feel secure until he was able to consolidate his position within the company.

More than three thousand workers were employed at the Twin Cities Assembly Plant during World War II, far more than during peacetime. By the end of the war, the plant produced more than 800,000 pistons; 35,000 cam supports; 100,000 pump assemblies; and 250,000 gears for the Pratt & Whitney engine. In late January 1944 an extraordinary exposition was held at the Minneapolis Auditorium showing the extent to which military production had transformed industry in Minnesota. Scores of companies displayed their military products at the Production for Victory event, which included a complete Pratt & Whitney engine with parts made at the Twin Cities plant. This exhibit was a celebration of wartime contributions, but it was also a way to showcase their hopes for the postwar economy. Millions of people served in the military during the war, and many more worked in the defense industries, including huge numbers of women and minorities who joined the workforce. The country endured hard times during the Depression and made enormous sacrifices during World War II. The Greatest Generation in Minnesota had proudly done its part, and it was now time to transition back to civilian life, to a sense of normalcy—and, everyone hoped, to prosperity. It was also time for the new president, Henry Ford II, to take charge of his company.

Ascent of the Autoworkers

The Postwar Boom and Challenges

When the war ended, there were about twenty-five million cars on the road, and most were more than ten years old. People wanted new cars and Ford was eager to meet the pent-up demand. Several hundred workers, including many returning veterans, were brought back to the St. Paul plant during the summer of 1945 to start the plant's conversion from military to civilian production. Ford shipped three hundred new 1946 model cars from Michigan to the Twin Cities to showcase its new lineup. After the new production equipment was installed, the new vehicles rolled off the assembly line, starting with school-bus chassis, followed by trucks and cars. The glass plant started up on July 6, 1945.

Soldiers, many without jobs or permanent housing, returned home to families they had not seen in years. Under federal law, veterans could return to their jobs at the Ford plant and keep their union seniority, receiving credit for their years in the military. Some of the women who had been working at the plant wanted to stay but did not have the same protections. There were only 1,800 job openings at the plant, down from the three thousand during the war. During the war, women were viewed as important contributors, portrayed as Rosie the Riveters, but demobilization abruptly changed this perception. Now they were seen as competitors to men for jobs in an uncertain labor market. According to polls taken at the time, most women wanted to continue working, but there was enormous pressure for them to return home. "All of a sudden, in every medium of

This aerial view shows the Twin Cities Assembly Plant after World War II, with the oval testing track for the M-8 armored vehicles still in place. The remnants of the employee gardens from the Depression also remain. The corner of Ford Parkway and Cleveland Avenue was sold for the Highland Village Apartments, which were constructed in 1939, but Ford retained mineral rights for the land, enabling it to mine sand for the glass plant. A larger parking lot was installed in the northeast corner of the plant, and landfill to the south of the Steam Plant was starting to level off the riverbank. Other than that, the plant had changed very little from its opening in 1925. Author's collection.

Henry Ford vertically integrated operations to protect his company from outside disruption. His timber holdings and sawmills in Iron Mountain, Michigan, furnished the siding for the "woodies" that were popular after the war. This picture shows the car bodies being unloaded inside the Twin Cities plant in 1947. Author's collection.

popular culture," wrote Doris Kearns Goodwin, "women were barraged with propaganda on the virtues of domesticity."

During difficult economic times, there was resistance to women working. During the Depression, a number of states passed laws prohibiting married women from working if their husband had a job. The UAW had little interest in expanding employment opportunities for women, and on more than one occasion opposed women's participation. During the war, the government instituted protections for women, including equal pay for equal work. This sentiment, however, was not widely shared by autoworkers. Recognizing the problem, UAW president Walter Reuther said, "Industry must not be allowed to settle the labor problem by chaining women to kitchen sinks." Maury Maverick, a federal official at the Smaller War Plants Corporation said, "Women have learned too much to go back . . . [they] will either be out hooting it up or doing something constructive so we have to be doing something to make it so they can work."

Most women at the Twin Cities Assembly Plant left voluntarily, but not Verna Welsch, who lost her husband in a car crash a month before their son was born. For her, the well-paying Ford job was a necessity. She was assigned a variety of difficult jobs after the war, which she believed were intended to force her to quit. In one incident she believed her rib was broken by a not-so-friendly bear hug from another male worker. She remembered one particularly difficult day, where "they put me down on body build washing floor pans. I had to get all the wax off so that the paint would stick and jiggle them apart and turn them over. It was hard." In another instance she was assigned to cleaning parts with chemical solvents that her coworker across the line splashed on her, causing an allergic rash. One day the men in the department were watching her closely, but they abruptly

Cars became more streamlined after the war, as seen in this picture of a 1947 Ford coupe displayed at a Minneapolis showroom. Photograph by the *Minneapolis Star Journal Tribune*. Courtesy of the Minnesota Historical Society.

Americans went on a car-buying spree after the war, and Ford took advantage of every opportunity to celebrate company milestones. Pictured is the fifty-thousandth car made at the Twin Cites plant in 1948. Courtesy of the Minnesota Historical Society.

left, perplexing Verna. She assumed it was because they didn't want women workers, but when the men returned, one said, "That's not it at all. We went up and put our money down on a bet to see how long you would stay." Verna responded: "Seeing you were so nice to come and talk to me, I hope you put the largest amount because I'm going to stay here till they carry me out on a stretcher!" In 1946, Verna and a number of women were assigned to the instrument panel line, which was similar to their wartime work on the Pratt & Whitney engines.

Years later, Al Hendricks, a union official in both St. Paul and the International UAW in Detroit, acknowledged that "both the union and management made it so a lot of them quit, the way the guys treated them and the mentality that they were taking men's jobs that come out of service." When car production resumed, Hendricks encouraged women to apply for better jobs as they opened up. "Verna Welsch was a very bright woman.

I told her, 'There's a stock status job open . . . Put your name in for it.'" Verna declined, believing she had little chance for the job, but Hendricks put her name in anyway. She came out on top in the test score and worked in that position until she retired in 1974. In 1957, the *St. Paul Pioneer Press* profiled the four remaining "Rosie, the Riveters." One who "stuck it out" said she received a good wage but the challenges she faced were very real, as the article stated: "They are vastly outnumbered by their male counterparts, some 450 to one . . . The present assembly line is not geared for employment of women, except in the jobs these four do."

During the war, women made enormous contributions working in factories. Those with families were able to place their children in nursery schools and day-care centers that had been set up with federal funding. After the war, Minneapolis mayor Hubert H. Humphrey lobbied to keep these programs in place until all veterans had returned and found employment. He also pushed to have the government fund housing programs to address the serious shortage.

Henry Ford II Brings Change

The United States had changed enormously during World War II, particularly in the area of labor relations. Henry Ford II, largely untested at the age of twenty-five, was chosen to lead the company. Walter Reuther once told him, "You were smart, Henry, you chose the right grandfather." But no one really knew how smart or tough the new leader was. Young Henry very quickly demonstrated his ability to navigate through the thicket of factional camps by firing the dangerous Harry Bennett. David Halberstam observed:

> Part of the reasons for his toughness stemmed from the special circumstances of his childhood. For Henry Ford might have been raised in one of the two or three grandest houses in America, but a dark shadow hung over it nevertheless. He had just been a boy during the years in which his grandfather systematically crushed his father, destroying first Edsel's emotional and then his physical health, and he was shielded from as much of the tragedy as possible. But the residual impact was always there, a father ruined by a grandfather, a mother determined to never let this happen to her own children. For what happened in his home was evidently evil; it was very close to filicide.

Henry II flaunted his privileged life but still managed to come across as a "common man." He was as well liked on the shop floor, where he was known as "the Deuce," as he was in corporate suites, halls of Congress, or museum boards. Halberstam noted: "At the height of tensions between labor and management, he could walk down a Ford line and still be hailed, worker after worker rushing over to shake his hand. He said the things they would have liked to say, and even more important, lived the life they would have liked to lead."

Early in his tenure, Henry II made a surprising decision. He brought in two new leadership teams with different experiences, styles, and approaches. He mediated between the two groups and received a world-class education in the process. In 1946 he brought in Ernest Breech, a successful executive at GM with a background in accounting and manufacturing, to straighten out the accounting mess left by his grandfather. Ford also hired a group of ten brilliant young technocrats who worked together at the Statistical

The Custom Tudor was the most popular Ford model in 1949, shown here being washed at the Twin Cities plant. Author's collection.

Control Center of the Army Air Force. As a team, they were pioneers in developing data-driven, operational, and logistical systems for the military buildup and would become immortalized as "the Whiz Kids." Over the next several decades, two became presidents of Ford, and most of the others would rise to top executive positions. Its most famed member, Robert McNamara, went from the presidency of Ford to lead the Department of Defense under Presidents Kennedy and Johnson during the Vietnam War.

As executive vice president, Ernest Breech was the most powerful man in the company after Henry Ford II. When he started in 1946, the company was losing $10 million a month, but from 1951 to 1960 it earned $5.5 billion. Breech could rightly claim much of the credit, but the pent-up demand for automobiles after the war made the job easier. Times were so good that the Big Three automakers, Ford, GM, and Chrysler, had, in effect, a "shared monopoly." The absence of competition strengthened the hand of the finance people who had little interest in cars. To the Whiz Kids, manufacturing was incidental—finance was where their creative genius could shine. They did not like to visit factories or branch plants and had little interest in product design. They especially disliked the marketing division and were reluctant to attend dealer conventions or mingle with car salesmen. A huge tension developed between the finance and manufacturing people, and the "bean counters" won. Manufacturing, which had been the strength of the company, now took a backseat.

The older Henry Ford had been in failing health for several years and he withdrew from the management of the company. He died on April 7, 1947, at age eighty-three, with his wife Clara at his side. Earlier in the evening, the River Rouge flooded the local power station, knocking out all power to his house. The man who had a lifelong obsession about power left this world with candles and kerosene lamps by his bedside.

Henry and his new team of managers reaped the benefits of the shared monopoly. He attracted top talent and boosted the morale of employees. He established training and apprenticeship programs, created a suggestion program, which paid workers for good ideas and made promotions from within the ranks. Ford also strengthened relations with communities where plants were located. The superintendent of the Twin Cities plant, Bob Elliot, recalled that he and other plant managers received a letter in 1946 from Ford urging him to be "a good industrial citizen" of St. Paul. "I hadn't the faintest idea what he meant by a good industrial citizen," but he did some research and discovered that the plant made very few purchases locally. Elliot then hosted a meeting of the Twin City Association of Purchasing Agents and gave them a tour of the company supply rooms. By 1949, the Twin Cities plant reported a tenfold increase in local purchases of goods and services. In 1954, Ford estimated it had a $22 million economic impact in the Twin Cities in wages, local purchases, transportation expenses, and taxes. A decade later, Ford was

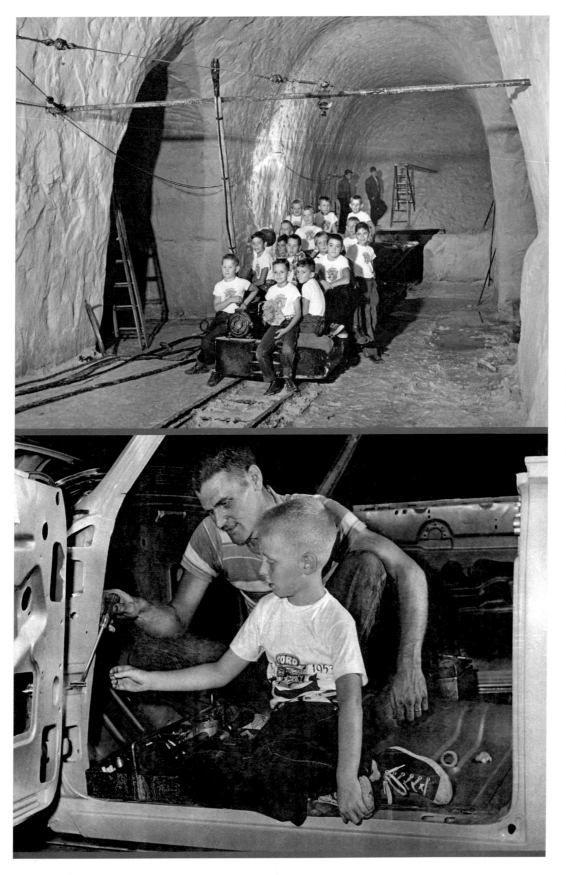

The Ford Motor Company always welcomed visitors to its plants, particularly the children of employees. The Twin Cities plant had the highest number of visitors after the Rouge plant in Detroit. In addition to seeing cars being made, visitors were often treated to a tour of the sand mines under the plant (*above*). One of the most popular activities for workers was the annual "Bring your child to work day" (*below*). Many families had several generations working at the plant. Author's collection.

A worker at the Twin Cities plant smoking on the job. To get off on the right foot with workers, Henry Ford II introduced a number of new policies that proved very popular. He lifted the ban on smoking imposed by Henry Ford, who was an ardent antismoking advocate. Author's collection.

purchasing supplies from 270 businesses in the Twin Cities, including an $18 million-a-year expenditure on Minnesota iron ore. Ford also took a more active role in community affairs, offering free cars for the "Welcome Wagons" program and free driver's education lessons, sponsoring industrial arts and other educational programs, providing plant tours, and making its property available for community activities. In 1953 Ford leased a portion of its property to a Highland Park Little League club, creating enormous community goodwill.

Ford developed particularly close ties with Minnesota-based 3M, which supplied masking tape and other products for the paint department. 3M staff regularly visited the plant, bringing samples of experimental products and talking to the Ford painters about how to improve and develop their products. Roger Okerstrom was having problems cutting tape and suggested a way to incorporate the blade into a sliding bar on the dispenser. 3M quickly adopted the suggestion.

Henry Ford II endeared himself to many workers by permitting smoking at the plants, reversing a company policy established by his grandfather. Henry Ford was a fervent opponent of smoking and had penned a booklet titled *The Case against the Little White Slaver* in 1914. Although smoking was banned, some workers chewed snuff, including one in St. Paul who turned it into a high art form. He "had a technique like you couldn't believe," remembered Bob Hansen. "He chewed snuff all the time but he couldn't spit on the floor. When everybody saw Art going down the aisle, everybody went this way because every once in a while he'd go whoosh! And a fog of tobacco . . . saliva was floating around there. You had to just swim through it."

Working Conditions at the Twin Cities Assembly Plant

Joe Kucera recalled Henry Ford II's impact: "Working conditions improved very much. When Ford was here he saw that we didn't have a cafeteria. He said, 'A cafeteria should be installed immediately.' The next day I started drawing plans for a cafeteria. Up until then people sat down onto a bench, sat down by your job or on a bale of cushions or you went outside and had a smoke and eat your sandwich." Enon Olson also remembered the transformation: "the way I understand it, Henry Ford II had told the managers . . . 'I want you to treat the people like you want to be treated yourself.' He wanted to turn things around, which was a long road. He had to get rid of a lot of the old school. I'll never forget when the plant manager come walking out of the office. He says, 'Shit! They train you for thirty years to be a son of a bitch, and now they want you to change overnight.'"

Working conditions at the plant improved considerably, but life on the assembly line was still no picnic. Prior to 1949, workers had no designated time for a bathroom break or to stretch the muscles. If a worker had to go to the bathroom, he would race up to a toilet in the mezzanine and then race back to the line to catch up with his job as it moved down the line. As one worker described it:

> I would go to the bathroom immediately before my work shift in the morning and right after lunch, so I could get through the workday. Even so, during the shifts I usually had to dash over to the bathroom, give a squirt and race back before being noticed. To keep up with the assembly line, I would speed up to "get ahead" of the line before I took my bathroom break, and then catch up when I returned. I had another problem with these quick bathroom breaks. When I was working with the lampblack and Stanisol, my hands were completely black and oily I didn't have time to wash up while in the bathroom, so my trousers around my zipper got very blackened and dirty.

William Brengman started in the cushion department in June 1950, right out of high school. His training period lasted only an hour. The work was fast-paced and not something he wanted to do all his life—but for a young kid, the money was good. Later he was assigned to putting the window regulator in the door:

> This was the first operation after the unit had come out of the paint oven. The bodies were so hot. They would burn anything that touched the metal. You had to reach inside the door skin to put in this window regulator. Your arms and fingers were just full of little burn marks. If you didn't like it, there was always somebody out there out at the gate who was looking for a job. Every morning I'd be coming over the hill in Highland Park and just as soon as I would see those stacks of the plant, I'd just kind of get sick to my stomach.

Roger Okerstrom recalled that temperatures in the paint booth would rise well above one hundred degrees during the summer. The workers placed buckets of ice in front of fans, and also took lots of salt tablets. The union later won an agreement to suspend work if the temperature reached above one hundred degrees, but Okerstrom doesn't recall the plant being shut down. During his thirty years at the plant, he saw several workers die on the assembly line. "They just push them aside and keep the line going. They wouldn't even shut it off. They never shut the line off. Put another man in his spot and carry the guy out."

The Twin Cities plant was not immune to industrial accidents, the most tragic of which was the electrocution of a sheet-metal worker in 1949. Cuts, broken bones, and bruises were more common fare. Accident reports were written up after each incident and directed to the full-time plant safety inspector, who was a mechanical engineer. "His pet peeve was ladders that would be broken or cracked," remembered Gene Roedl, a retired nurse at the plant. "If he saw it, he would break it up in front of the supervisor and the supervisor would pull his hair out."

For emergencies, the plant had a hotline phone system, which could be dialed from

This 1939 view shows workers using air-powered chisels to dislodge sand from tunnels beneath the plant, which would be brought up to the furnaces for glass manufacturing. After World War II, workers were required to wear respirators. Photograph by the *St. Paul Dispatch*. Courtesy of the Minnesota Historical Society.

multiple locations around the plant. Hearing the alarms, the skilled tradesmen dropped everything, jumped on the crash truck, and raced to the emergency. Two full-time nurses and a part-time doctor backed them up. The medical team did some procedures right in the plant, including stitching up cuts that happened regularly, especially when the glass plant was operating. Loretta Jackson, who worked in the office, recalled being worried about her husband, who worked on the assembly line. After every accident she would run to see if the trail of blood came from her husband's unit.

Doctors and nurses also were responsible for very basic medical exams for new hires—height, weight, maybe a blood test. Roedl recalled what they would be looking for: "Usually hernias. People would deny ever having any back problems and you would see a great big scar down the middle of their back." In the 1960s, as carpal tunnel syndrome became prevalent, Ford would move workers to a different job. If the foreman was not cooperative and the problem worsened, the worker could file a disability or compensation claim.

The Twin Cities Assembly Plant manufactured glass, except during interruptions caused by the Depression and World War II. Because of the heat in the furnaces, workers had to wear an asbestos suit, and received a twenty-minute break every forty minutes. The sand for the glass came from tunnels beneath the plant. In a typical eight-hour shift, two or three miners extracted approximately thirty tons of sand. They wore hard hats and respirators, and had to complete physical examinations annually, including chest X-rays. Compressors located on the plant floor powered the mining equipment below. Workers used a handheld air-powered chisel with a metal nozzle to undercut the sand starting at the top of the tunnels. A miniature train on rails would remove the sand, while workers knelt on a walkway next to the train as they shoveled the sand. Two tunnels, separated by about sixty feet, were mined on alternate days, one for loosening materials and one for loading the dropped sand into dump cars. This was done as a health precaution, to let the air clear before workers extracted the sand.

Al Hendricks described his experience working in the sand mines:

> The temperature is fifty-two degrees the year round. The air is real heavy. You worked very little and you'd sweat like the dickens. Because the humidity is real high, they told you to work slow and work comfortable. And, if you had to go to the bathroom go upstairs! . . . We were digging back, toward Highland Park. There are miles and miles of tunnels. The tunnel we were working on had pins up in the ceilings and electric lights running in there. We didn't have a map, we just went down and followed the track and the lights.

Cheap power produced by the hydroelectric plant was essential for making glass, but Henry Ford's vision for a power plant on the Mississippi River carried some risk, even though it was located considerably above the historical flood stage. In 1952, the worst flood of the Mississippi River in history knocked out the steam and hydroelectric plants and shut down production for a week. Following the cleanup, Ford filled in the bank, partially covering the lowest level of the Steam Plant. In 1965, warnings of an even worse flood prompted plant officials to take extraordinary measures. Trucks dumped enough sand to fill fifty-five thousand bags, which were placed around the power plants and the entrance to the tunnels. The company encased the entire lower level of the Steam Plant with a new concrete wall, and fully braced the interior of the building. Engineers were determined to maintain production, and ordered an array of backup steam units, generators, and air compressors, and extra supplies of oil and propane gas. The company also stockpiled extra parts and materials, assuming that its supply chain would be disrupted.

With the increasingly dire warnings from the weather service, Ford installed a temporary overhead power transmission line to the plant in case the hydro plant was shut down. The Army Corps predicted a river crest at 738.9 feet, which proved to be exactly correct. In 1952, fifty-eight thousand cubic feet of water per second flowed over the dam. In 1965, it was one hundred thousand cubic feet.

Ford located the Steam Plant above the highest-known flood stage, but the flood in April 1952 proved that height inadequate. Even two dikes could not keep water from flooding the screen house (where river water was filtered) and the lower levels of the Steam Plant, disrupting operations for a week. Ford later filled in the riverbank, partially covering the lower level of the Steam Plant. Author's collection.

Ford was more prepared for the flood of 1965, which was even worse than the one in 1952. The river almost completely submerged the screen house as well as the lower levels of the Steam Plant. Water levels were basically the same on both sides of the dam. In spite of the massive flood, Ford's advanced preparations allowed the plant to operate without disruption; however, the spring floods of 2001 disrupted power for twenty-three days. Author's collection.

The river crested so high that the river had the same level of water on both sides of the dam. The Hydroelectric Plant and the Steam Plant were shut down, and it was necessary to do a "controlled flooding" of the Steam Plant with clean water to equalize the pressure of the rising river. Ford assigned workers to shore up the basement of the Steam Plant, but union officials stopped the operation until better safety precautions could be implemented. There was a near disaster at the Hydroelectric Plant when six or seven workers tried to dislodge large chunks of ice on a catwalk on the upriver side of the plant. Several union officials just happened to be walking by and saw the pressure building up next to the catwalk and ordered the workers off—just before the ice snapped it.

Workers had sandbagged the entrances to the tunnels but unfortunately did not account for the portable generators that were being used in other portions of the inter-

A wave of ice chunks from the spring thaw in 1965 was strong enough to crush the catwalk on the north side of the hydroelectric plant. Workers on the dock who were trying to break up the ice jam narrowly avoided serious injury. Author's collection.

connected tunnels. Carbon monoxide backed up into the hydro plant and other areas of the plant and many workers were overcome. They had to be carried up the steep stairs on stretchers to waiting ambulances. The nurse, Gene Roedl, said, "We had arrangements so that we could tap into commercial oxygen tanks. It was nip and tuck. There was no way of getting these people out from down there except up about fifty steps up the bank." Fifteen workers were sent to Midway Hospital.

Power from the temporary overhead lines and portable steam generators kept the plant running throughout the "Twenty Days of Crisis," and advanced planning helped maintain deliveries throughout. The main railroad yards in St. Paul were under eleven feet of water and were out of commission for several weeks. Alternate yards could not accommodate the tall railcars used by Ford because of low utility lines and bridges, and many trains had to be rerouted to the Minnesota Transfer Yard in the Midway. Roads were also flooded throughout the region and bridges damaged, making trucking difficult. Engineers at the Ford plant worked around the clock to find alternate routes for their heavy trucks and secure the needed permits. Because of the transportation logjam, they also had to temporarily store cars in nearby parking lots.

Considerable fill was later added along the river to protect the buildings and prevent land erosion. The lower level of the Steam Plant was buried and a new entrance was installed at the second floor. Given the seriousness of two major floods, plant engineers seriously considered building a new steam plant up on the bluff to the east of the assembly plant that would have incorporated the existing Hopper Building, but Ford executives overruled that recommendation.

Walter Reuther and the United Auto Workers Union

Many returning autoworkers had seen the devastation of war firsthand. Pete Koegel was in Japan on submarine detail and was responsible for helping secure what was left of Hiroshima shortly after the bomb blast. Chet Brokl commanded a tank under General George Patton and received several Bronze Stars for bravery. The returning soldiers resumed work at Ford, but as very different people in a very different country. To them, the labor wars were over and they were not about to be pushed around by abusive straw bosses. Vast swaths of the economy were unionized. The returning soldiers demanded to be treated with respect, and they also expected to share in the benefits of America's new prosperity. Chet Brokl recalled, "When I returned to Ford after the service, my job was to load and unload the rail boxcars, which were towed right into the plant. By then, the autoworkers were unionized, and I could hardly believe how things had changed."

The worker shortage created by the booming postwar economy gave organized labor unprecedented leverage, which Walter Reuther, president of the UAW, applied with gusto. Lee Iacocca, onetime president of Ford and later the chair of Chrysler Motors, described the labor leader's negotiating style: "Reuther would actually sit down at the negotiating sessions and draw a picture of a pie. 'It's the job of management to bake this pie,' he'd announce. Then he'd point to the various segments of the pie and explain—as if he were talking to school children: 'This much goes for raw materials, this much for overhead and rent, this much for executive salaries, and this much for labor. We're here today, gentlemen, because we're not entirely satisfied with the way this pie has been divided. We want to cut it up just a little bit differently.'"

Reuther was not interested in "just another nickel in the envelope." He wanted a whole new envelope that included such things as a guaranteed annual wage, cost-of-living increases, supplemental unemployment benefits, and a broad array of health and pension benefits. "He was messianic about the union," Halberstam wrote. "For him it was . . . an instrument of justice with which to temper an unjust world. It was not just about getting better wages; it was about leading lives of greater dignity. The UAW was not just a union, it was a community, and its job was to make the larger community of which it was a part a more decent, more tolerant place. He believed . . . in the attainability of a better society." During World War II, he pushed for what became known as the "Reuther Plan," based

Walter Reuther, president of the United Auto Workers, was the strategist behind the remarkable advances of labor in the postwar period. With his abundant energy and ability to function with very little sleep, he often wore down his management counterparts during marathon negotiations. Courtesy of the National Automotive History Collection, Detroit Public Library.

on models developed by British labor groups. This classic European socialist program established a guaranteed annual wage for workers, the pooling of industrial capacity, and the participation of workers in the management of companies. Throughout his entire career, Reuther never wavered in his hope to institute this system in the United States.

During the war, the UAW pledged that it would not strike, but after the armistice it moved quickly to make up for lost time. The UAW struck GM in November 1945, raising concerns by the Army Corps in St. Paul that a possible strike at the Ford plant could shut down the hydroelectric plant. It wrote Local 879 in November 1945 that "No standby source of power is maintained at the locks" and urged that in the event of a strike the hydropower plant stay open.

Reuther was one of the first labor leaders to negotiate multiyear contracts, which provided more stability, starting with a two-year contract in 1948, followed by a five-year contract in 1950. He introduced the concept of "pattern bargaining"—the UAW would pick one car company for major negotiations, to achieve an agreement that could then be used as the basis for contracts with other companies. As long as there was parity, companies were more likely to give in to Reuther's demands. This was labor's version of "whipsawing." Reuther had boundless energy that allowed him to stay focused during the protracted labor deliberations, which often lasted weeks and months.

Reuther had several bedrock negotiating principles. He viewed seniority as the most fundamental right because many other benefits were tied to tenure. Prior to the UAW, companies could fire workers for "the punishable crime of growing old." Those over the age of forty were thought to be unable to keep up with the fast pace of the assembly line and were the first to be laid off and the last to be rehired. The seniority clause reversed that with "First one in, last one out." Reuther's second overarching principle was the need for parity between salaried and hourly workers. He saw a "class distinction" in workers' pay; line workers were paid by the hour and had little job security but management workers were salaried and received a number of benefits, including pensions. As a result of UAW pressure, the National Labor Relations Board determined in a groundbreaking ruling that unions had the right to bargain for pension benefits. In September 1949, the UAW negotiated a pension package of one hundred dollars a month, which included Social Security payments of $32.50 a month.

Even as he was pressing auto companies for a variety of fringe benefits, Reuther understood, as very few others did at the time, the potential pitfalls of that strategy. He wanted health and pension benefits to come directly from the government so as to not put automakers at a competitive disadvantage with foreign companies. His approach was to first negotiate the benefits, but then push the companies into supporting the federalization of the benefits. Within twenty-four hours of Ford's signing the pension agreement, Congress raised Social Security benefits for all Americans, thereby lowering Ford's costs. Reuther believed he was negotiating not just for his autoworkers, but for the entire middle class.

By 1953 the UAW benefit packages included an annual improvement factor, cost-of-living allowance (COLA), medical insurance, the first noncontributory pension plan in the industry, and a variety of training programs. Eldorous L. Dayton wrote of Reuther's push for the guaranteed semiannual layoff pay in the spring of 1955, "We decided General Motors was the easiest place to get money from, because it has the most, but the most difficult to pioneer with principle. Ford is the easiest place to make progress on principle. So we decided on the strategy of implementing the principle we expected to establish at Ford with the money we get from GM." Reuther understood that young Henry Ford was trying to recover from his grandfather's legacy of hostile labor relations.

The UAW benefited greatly from the car companies' complacent attitude. After the war, executives started to receive annual bonus payments linked to short-term financial performance of the company, and finance people were worried about work stoppage above all else. Lee Iacocca wrote in his memoir that concern over losing the bonus

The pace of work along the crowded assembly lines at the Twin Cities plant in 1948 was intense. The car being assembled here is the 1949 Custom Tudor. Author's collection.

because of a strike factored into their willing acquiescence to the demands of the unions. To offset the growing costs of labor and maintain profitability, management increased the price of cars, and reduced investment in research, product development, and factory maintenance. These decisions, which would have been anathema to Henry Ford, would eventually make the companies vulnerable to serious competition from foreign auto-makers.

Increased labor costs did widen the gap with foreign workers, but Reuther argued that there were enough profits to absorb the wage increases without raising prices. In 1957, he tried to get Ford to lower car prices, and even offered to take that into consideration when negotiating wages. He also tried to get Ford, a privately held company, to open its books as part of a larger strategy to argue for a more equitable redistribution, but the company declined. Reuther attacked high corporate salaries and bonuses, an argument he could credibly make, as he was drawing a salary of seven thousand dollars at a time when the president of Ford was making $459,000.

Although Reuther knew that expensive labor agreements would make the companies less competitive, it is also clear that he willingly went along with the free-spending ways of his corporate counterparts. David Halberstam explained: "it was an essentially monop-olistic union in an essentially monopolistic industry. The pass-on became a norm of the industry, and the UAW, voluntarily or no, accepted it. It was a world without illusion. The company and the union had an investment in each other. Bigness begat bigness . . . Their relationship was about power and well-respected boundaries." The new standard of living secured by the UAW led to the explosive growth of the American middle class, which benefited companies as much as the workers. In 1962 the manager of the St. Paul plant estimated that "in 1912 it took an employee sixty-nine weeks to earn the price of a new Ford, today it takes him only twenty-five weeks."

The Collective Bargaining Process and Work Standards

When Ford accepted the UAW in 1941, it ceded some control to a collective bargaining process designed to create a more harmonious workplace. The International UAW dele-gated considerable power down to local chapters, each of which typically represented one larger work site or several smaller plants. Members of UAW Local 879, which represented the autoworkers at the Twin Cities Assembly Plant, elected officers by secret ballot and set goals and procedures for the union and priorities for contract negotiations. National labor leaders negotiated agreements, but these were based on recommendations from union locals and ultimately had to be ratified by a majority of local bargaining units.

On issues relating to a particular work site, union locals negotiated a separate agreement with their plant management. One of the most contentious issues in St. Paul was the four, ten-hour-day work schedule, which was approved. Monthly membership dues amounted to two hours' pay, which Ford automatically deducted from workers' paychecks.

The president of the local union was also the chief administrative officer, overseeing meetings, committees, finances, and other duties defined by the UAW constitution. The building chairman was responsible for collective bargaining and headed up the bargaining committee, which consisted of representatives from throughout the plant. Committeemen were elected from a particular area within the plant and were responsible for administering grievances for approximately three hundred people, among other tasks. (This position is often referred to as shop steward in other unions.)

The UAW Local 879 in St. Paul received its charter when Ford signed a national agreement with the UAW in 1941. Rank-and-file workers were given the right to vote on proposed national contracts and to negotiate local contracts, which could include such items as installation of locker rooms or a milk-vending machine. Bob Killeen, a union leader at Local 879 (second from left), enjoys the new milk-vending machine. Author's collection.

During negotiations for the first labor agreement, Ford offered to pay the salary of most union officials at the same rate they had been receiving as company employees. This proposal was strongly debated, as some union officials feared it could create divided loyalties, but it was accepted.

Union locals organized national and regional associations to facilitate closer interactions among plants. These were originally based on geography, but later by plant type. Seventeen Ford assembly plants, including the one in St. Paul, formed a labor group that met regularly to compare notes on manpower levels and major issues. The first elected chair of the assembly sub-council was Bob Killeen, who was building chairman of Local 879 and one of the most influential labor leaders in Minnesota. There was apparently

The Big Three automakers had a "shared monopoly" after the war, and Ford had brisk car sales in 1955. The Customline model, shown here, was one of the more popular cars. Company profits rose significantly, along with workers' income. Photograph by the *Minneapolis Star and Tribune*. Courtesy of the Minnesota Historical Society.

little competition or rivalry among the plants, even as the company often tried to pit one against another. Comparing notes had its benefits. At one meeting Killeen learned that spray-painters in Dearborn were paid for time needed to put grease on their face and get prepared with their overalls. "So I came back and jumped right on that one. It was a short time later that we had preparatory time here. There are all kinds of examples like that."

Economic benefits were very important to the workers but these were not as immediately impactful as improving the day-to-day working conditions on the assembly line. Perhaps the biggest flash point revolved around the issue known as "work standards" or "production standards." Ford sought to maximize individual workloads, aiming for the ideal utilization rate of 100 percent. In other words, a worker could not waste a single motion or lose one second of effort, or have any letup in the pace for the entire day. Time-studies experts, with stopwatches, cameras, and notepads in hand, observed workers for hours at a time, looking to eliminate the slightest wasted motion. Any perceived letup in effort would justify the assignment of additional tasks, or the possible rearrangement of machines and equipment to increase efficiency.

In 1949, the year Bob Killeen started working at Ford, the national UAW negotiated a major breakthrough on work standards. The contract agreement stated: "Such production standards shall be fair and equitable and shall be set on the basis of normal working conditions, the quality of workmanship, and the normal working capacities of normal experienced operators, with due consideration to fatigue and the need for 'personal' time. It is recognized that disputes on production standards shall be resolved at the plant level wherever possible." If no agreement could be reached, the union had the right to file a grievance, or even to strike.

Ford divided workloads into a series of discrete tasks that could be done in approximately seventy-five seconds as the car moved along the assembly line. These "standard units," or "modules," could be shifted around to maximize output or reduce the number of employees. The UAW felt that "Fordism" had crossed a line, creating an inhumane work environment. Many would try to find relief by "gaming the system." A new worker on the line was told: "Any idiot can do the job; it takes a smart person to do less." Bob Killeen recalled the cat-and-mouse contest played with the fifteen time-studies men at the Twin Cities plant:

> The company would change things throughout the year, trying to put more work on a guy here and there, eliminating people, one or two on the line. We used to spend a great share of our time policing that. First of all, we had our people indoctrinated about how to fumble and stumble when the guy was standing there and not be obvious. They'd get the standard written up, maybe three or four pages . . . with all the times . . . and ratings. This guy was working 70 percent . . . while tightening up the screws on the fender. Taking the fender off the conveyor and putting it on the car before he attached the bolts, he did that at 90 percent. It was very seldom that they ever had anybody at 100 percent. They wanted 100 percent, but we never accepted that.

Joe Kucera, who moved heaters and radios from the service stock to the assembly with a handcart, loaded twenty-five when he knew he was being watched by a time-studies man, but fifty otherwise. This gave him an extra twenty-minute break.

The occasional breakdown on the assembly line would give workers unscheduled relief. "A [car] body drop in the paint ovens . . . was usually good for twenty minutes," said Killeen. "The foremen would all go nuts . . . we'd all sit there smiling, praying that it would take a long time." The paint ovens were very hot and foremen had to put gloves on to lift the car bodies back on the chain, but this was one instance where the union did not complain about foremen working. Sometimes workers would spot a wobbly body about to fall and did nothing about it, eager for a break. The company would try to get workers to "push the bodies" to keep up with production, but the union refused to go along. Ford attempted to withhold pay during those unplanned shutdowns, or charge it against the relief time that was later negotiated, but the union opposed that. However, if a breakdown occurred close to the scheduled lunchtime, the company was able to require workers to take an early break.

Worker resistance would sometimes turn to sabotage. "Management's difficulty of proving sabotage allowed workers . . . to get away with individual, intermittent acts of resistance," wrote Craig Zabala, an economist and former autoworker. "This 'freedom' had two functions: it allowed workers an emotional outlet for their frustration with alienating work and unfair manager actions, and it gave workers, on occasion, an informal bargaining weapon to use to try to fight the speedup and other unwanted management policies." Slowdowns and "working to rule" did not usually involve physical damage, but sometimes that occurred. Workers at the Twin Cities plant sometimes scratched car bodies, installed the wrong tires, or placed empty beer cans in door cavities knowing they would rattle. A car was once assembled with two doors on one side and a single door on the other. In the 1950s, a number of disruptions on the chassis line caused Ford to station a supervisor under the pit to find out the cause. "All at once, click, I heard a bolt, nut, come in and fall right into the links and then cut out the conveyor," said Joe Kucera. "I finally realized it was being done on purpose. We didn't catch the guys; there were about four of them doing it, but they saw the bolts I'd picked up and they knew then—and that stopped."

The 1949 contract allowed workers to request a dialogue with management if they felt the workload was not "fair and equitable." Plants almost always produced several different models simultaneously, making it challenging to develop consistent work standards. A four-door car had twice as many door handles to install as a two-door, but the speed of the line would not be slowed down. At a typical assembly plant, there could have been 378 options of colors, body designs, engines, transmissions, and other parts. The union wanted to create a balanced, fair, and consistent workload. A speedup occurred not just when the assembly line moved faster, but also when a worker had to perform more tasks on each passing unit.

Killeen spent considerable time monitoring production standards and fighting speedups. "They were speeding up the line after they'd have a line breakdown. Instead of running thirty-nine an hour . . . it was sixty." Killeen insisted that the company produce line speed charts that spelled out the pace in "inches per minute. It had the center of one body to the center of the other." If the line was speeded up, the company had several options: add workers, increase the spacing of the units, reduce the speed of the line, or temporarily stop the line. Killeen negotiated a provision in the Local 879 contract requiring Ford to install a storage line for cars that fed into the main assembly line. This would build up an inventory of cars that could be mixed to allow a proper balance of workload.

Disputes over work standards could bog down both the union and the company and Killeen felt it was important to keep an eye on the big picture:

A station-wagon body is lowered on the chassis. During the 1920s, the large windows on the west side of the building provided essential light but were later screened to shield workers from the hot sun. Temperatures in the summer could reach above one hundred degrees, and the only cooling came from large overhead fans. Photograph by the *Minneapolis Star Journal Tribune*. Courtesy of the Minnesota Historical Society.

Now, the company would tighten up its work standards and you might increase your production by 6 percent in a year in some plants. Six percent is nothing. If you started treating people decently and respected them and cooperated and showed them that you cared about them, it's not unusual for a company to get 35 percent productivity in a year and far exceed anything we ever had on the work standards. It's amazing how much change that will make, just by treating people decent. We used to fumble and stumble and challenge . . . and we'd get a lousy 2 percent better.

Contract agreements helped create a more collaborative approach for addressing the work standards issues. When Ford introduced a new car model, the assembly line started out slowly to allow workers to become familiar with their new assignments and the company to test its assumptions for work standards. Sometimes, after the work standard had been mutually agreed upon and the line brought up to full speed, the company made other adjustments to the workload. This made it more difficult for workers to settle into a routine and would sometimes throw off the balance on other parts of the line. In the 1970s, the union and the company agreed to essentially "freeze" work standards 120 days after completion of a model change, but still allow for some reasonable adjustments. Disputes over production standards could be challenged through the grievance process, but most important from a union perspective, they were also "strikeable during the term of a contract."

Job Classifications and the Grievance Process

The job classification system emerged as another contentious labor-relations issue. Henry Ford introduced job classifications as a way to give the appearance of worker mobility and advancement—"to have you nickel your way to the top." Over time, the union recognized that classifications were tied to seniority rights, its most cherished principle. For a seniority system to work, it had to be based on a clear delineation of job duties—not just length of service. Otherwise, companies could randomly lay off workers without taking into account training and work experience. Unions used the classification system as a negotiating tool. Classifications "became so costly because we started building fences around all these things," said Killeen. "To get promoted . . . you might have to move five different people because you promoted one guy. But, we had to have them . . . to protect us from the bad foremen who had a bad weekend."

Job classifications spelled out specific work duties, but there were other levels of job categories. Unskilled workers were assigned to the assembly line. Skilled workers, such as

The suits, ties, and hats of management officials made them conspicuous among the rank and file. Here an official at the desk observes the Customline nearing completion. Photograph by the *Minneapolis Star Journal Tribune*. Courtesy of the Minnesota Historical Society.

electricians or pipe fitters, were responsible for maintaining the equipment and building systems. Known as "maintenance workers," they had to pass a professional licensing test. They composed approximately 10 percent of the workforce and were represented by the UAW along with the unskilled workers. Over the years, other unions would occasionally "raid" the plant in an effort to represent the skilled workers, but the UAW was successful in rebuffing those jurisdictional disputes. Skilled workers were given some special privileges within the UAW constitution, including the right to vote as a separate group on contract ratifications.

Unskilled workers were divided into subcategories of designated, undesignated, or general labor pool. A designated worker had learned some of the more complex operations on the assembly line, such as spray-painting, welding, metal finishing, or door fitting. Undesignated workers mastered less demanding skills such as installing glass or building seat cushions. All other positions were assigned to the general labor pool. These categories became important mainly during layoffs, as the company wanted to protect the designated positions that it believed were essential for production. The union wanted a rigid seniority system, arguing that Ford should train senior workers from the labor pool for the designated positions.

Complex labor agreements gave rise to differences of interpretation. There were several ways to resolve these differences, starting with the grievance process, which was created to interpret and enforce the labor agreements. A grievance is a complaint filed about individual workloads, line speeds, or an abusive foreman. The very first UAW labor contract with Ford in 1941 spelled out how to administer the process. The aggrieved worker had to first take up the matter with his immediate foreman or supervisor. If that failed, the worker could then request a meeting between his company foreman and his union representative. If that did not resolve the matter, the grievance would be written up and brought to a hearing at the local plant. Both sides would try to establish the facts of a particular incident and resolve the matter. If a grievance could not be resolved at the plant level, it went before a hearing with an impartial umpire. A final decision could result in a disciplinary action against a plant foreman, termination of a worker, or the remedying of some specific problem.

Loretta Jackson, who worked in the management office, recalled an employment manager asking her to attend one of the first grievance meetings at the plant: "'Take your notebook and pencils and come with me and write down everything they say.' I walked in there and he didn't introduce me to anybody . . . They started talking about grievances. So I put numbers over their heads. When I came back in, he said, 'Can you transcribe it?' I said sure. So I sat down and pounded the typewriters and I had the numbers." A photograph was taken of the meeting, which Jackson used to keep track of the people, which she included with her notes. The manager asked, "What are the numbers?" She answered: "Those are the people you didn't introduce me to." Over time, Jackson became an acknowledged expert on contracts and both sides respected her as a neutral party. The grievance hearings generally ruled in favor of workers. The vast majority were complaints against supervisors working out of title. The contract allowed foremen to show workers how to do a job, but not to actually do the work, which was a violation that could result in a fine.

The dispute resolution process did not always work as designed. Foremen would sometimes tear up grievances right in front of workers, which prompted a heated response from the union committeemen. Shouting matches occurred right up through the formal hearing in the plant. Sometimes, workers would file phony grievances. Sometimes the

Loretta Jackson attends one of the first grievance hearings at the Ford Plant. Union officials are seated on the left and company officials on the right, including Jackson, who worked for management and was taking notes. This hearing occurred in 1943, and windows appear to be blacked out for security purposes during the war. The officials are holding a check, which was delivered by workers as their contribution to the war fund. Courtesy of Loretta Jackson.

For a ratification vote or an important meeting, the union hall would often be standing room only. Some workers who could not fit into the hall had to peer through an open window in the rear. Courtesy of UAW Local 879.

formal grievance would be ignored. In one incident, a worker was sent home for taking a bite out of a pear he had placed under his work stool. Workers, many of whom had returned from military service, were fed up and decided to take action. On one occasion, Al Hendricks and a second worker on the line "shut the switch off . . . and walked all the way down the south end and told the people 'Get off.'" This stopped the line and triggered a rush of union and management officials to the line, including the plant industrial relations manager. Hendricks recalled the fallout:

> Bob Killeen came up as building chairman and he told us, "Under the contract, I have to tell you to go back to work." While he was doing this, he was winking at us because, under the contract, the union cannot be involved in a wildcat strike. He was doing what he had to do . . . but at the same time, he was winking, telling us not to listen to him. So, we stood there while

he told us three, four times to go back to work and, then, management huddled . . . Jensen [Ford's industrial relations manager] looked at his watch and he says, "If you don't go back to work in fifteen minutes, you can go home." We all put on our coats and went home and they had to shut the plant down. That was the first wildcat strike that shut the plant down.

One of the Ford supervisors had apparently seen Hendricks lead the rebellion and was determined to make an example of him. However, the union local interceded and worked out mild discipline for the entire group. During the transitional period after World War II, the UAW and Ford were both struggling to bring some semblance of control and order to the tense workplace.

In virtually every negotiation, the UAW fought for more relief time. In 1949, Ford agreed to provide morning and afternoon breaks, using "relief men," or utility workers, to fill in for workers on break. One utility position was created for every nineteen workers. This was particularly welcomed when workers were regularly putting in ten-hour days.

Workers had a thirty-minute unpaid break for lunch, during which time the assembly line was shut down. Most people brought lunch from home and just pulled up a stool or a box and ate near their workstation. Lunch carts also circulated around the plant. Later, an open section of the plant was set aside as a cafeteria offering hot meals. Local 879 got Ford to extend the hours of the cafeteria to allow workers on multiple shifts and long days to have breakfast and evening meals. Management officials had a separate full-service dining room, but that was eventually eliminated to promote better relations between the "hourlies" and the "salaried."

Al Hendricks and Bob Killeen both began at Ford in 1949, and both went on to be UAW leaders. Labor relations drastically changed from the time they started to the time they retired. Killeen said of the early years, "Every day you knew the minute you walked in to cross the threshold, it was a fight, from the time you got there till you left."

In 1956, Adlai Stevenson, the Democratic nominee for president, toured the plant. Bob Killeen looks on at the center of the photograph. Courtesy of the Minnesota Historical Society.

A shorter workweek was a priority in the 1958 negotiations, a position strongly supported by the Local 879 officials shown here. Bob Killeen is standing in the back row, second from left. Author's collection.

Both young labor leaders played by the unwritten rules of the rough-and-tumble world of labor organizing. Hendricks, who got his start with a wildcat strike, was elected as a committeeman and worked his way up the ranks to building chairman. He eventually moved to the International UAW in Detroit, where he served alongside Walter Reuther. Killeen was involved in a number of organizing campaigns throughout the Twin Cities and was once seen in a television news report brawling with "scab" workers outside a company the UAW was trying to organize. Because he was doing this on Ford time, he almost lost his job.

Local 879 held its early membership meetings at American Legion halls, alternating between Minneapolis and St. Paul. To make it easier for the workers, the union decided to build a hall across the street from the plant, and to pay for the building with a special assessment of fifty cents a month. Bob Killeen and Ray Busch toured union halls at other plants and modeled their building after the one in St. Louis. Construction started in 1953 on their building at 2191 Ford Parkway. Over the years, a number of important labor and political leaders attended programs at the hall, including Walter Reuther, who visited in 1955, Victor Reuther, Senator Paul Wellstone, and many international labor activists. In 1979, the hall was dedicated in memory of Ray Busch, who spent several decades in leadership positions at the local, including serving as president from 1950 to 1967.

Working Conditions and Opportunities for Advancement

Of all the complex issues Walter Reuther and the UAW faced, the hardest was to give workers some sense of control or security in a work environment that offered none. Neither the company nor the union could eliminate the inevitable booms and busts of the economy, but Reuther was determined to reduce the worker's sense of powerlessness. He won the right to bargain over plant closures, the right to transfer to another plant if laid off, and he secured guaranteed pay for furloughs and time remaining under the labor agreements. He also pushed for training programs, believing they would not only help keep plants open, but also create marketable skills for workers if plants closed. The commitment to education and training was firmly established in 1941 when the UAW created an Education Department and instituted a variety of training programs. "Education is the heart of the labor movement," declared the UAW. "Deny workers the opportunity to education and you have denied them the possibilities of enjoying the blessings of human liberty and democracy."

The Ford Motor Company had a reputation for hiring young, strapping farm kids with calluses on their hands—no skills needed. Older retirees from the St. Paul plant remember that showing the palms of their hands was their principal employment test. One said with a chuckle, "Maybe it was the strong back, weak mind thing." As late as the 1950s, there were still several workers at the plant who could not read or write. At its main plants in Detroit, and to a lesser extent at the branch plants, Ford also hired a large number of immigrants who spoke little or no English. A lack of skills was not seen as an impediment. Ford did provide some minimal training for new hires, but most could learn their job on the assembly line in an hour. Even though workers may have lacked specific trade skills, many had grown up in an environment that prized hard work, mechanical tinkering, and independent thinking—a background not unlike that of the company's founder.

These attributes had little value on the assembly line, and options for advancement were fairly limited. A highly prized job was utility worker, which allowed people to move around doing different tasks on the line. Learning new skills gave some additional security, but Ford's rigid employment system limited advancement options. Management workers were "salaried," and production workers on the assembly line were "hourly." The gap between the two was huge. Protocols and environmental cues were used to define the differences and institutionalize the gap. Each group had separate entrance doors, parking spots, security arrangements, time-keeping systems, attire (both formal and informal), and even the manner of payment was different. Hourly workers were paid in cash as late as the 1940s. "Hourlies" had to wear metal badges with their employee number and punch in on time clocks until the 1970s. One of the more despised requirements for "hourlies" was marching through tight railings, similar to cattle gates, when exiting the building. Hands had to be held high as guards checked for stolen property. One worker from the hydro plant had a comical mishap when passing through the railings. He had caught a fish from the docks while on duty, which he tried to sneak out by hiding it under his jacket. As he raised his arms, the fish dropped off his belt, causing great amusement but no discipline. The dehumanizing railings were later removed.

Theft was not uncommon. There were rumors of new cars being driven out the door, but more often small parts were smuggled out, or things like tires were thrown over the fence. In one odd case, a worker was caught taking paint home every night in his lunchbox thermos. He reportedly had taken enough over the years to paint his entire house.

There was little socializing or fraternizing between the salaried and the hourly staff, but there was some good-natured bantering. Del Peterson, who was a process engineer, recalled an encounter when walking around the plant with another engineer on a hot July day: "So, Jake and I walked down to the coffee machine. We just walked [from] the air-conditioned office with our nice white smocks on and all of that . . . and here comes a bunch of pipe fitters who had been working on a spray booth . . . This one fellow . . . called 'Hacksaw Pete'—made a lot of noise about just about everything. They were coming to the coffee machine also. The guy starts on me: 'God-

There were significant differences in how "hourly" union workers were treated compared to management workers, and a variety of protocols and environmental cues underscored those differences. Hourlies were required to wear numbered metal badges. The early badges used the name "Twin City," a term sometimes used by businesses in the 1920s. Author's collection.

Hourly workers were required to exit the plant through these narrow metal railings. They had to hold their arms up so security guards could inspect for possible theft of materials or tools. Author's collection.

damned engineers, all they got to do is sit around all day in an air-conditioned office and us poor guys are out here busting our butts and we're all just sweating and dripping.'" Del's colleague put his quarter in the coffee machine and without missing a beat responded, "Well, you should have listened in geometry class."

"Hacksaw Pete" was not a salaried manager with an air-conditioned office, but, as an hourly skilled pipe fitter, he certainly would have listened in his geometry class. Skilled workers, including electricians, plumbers, pipe fitters, welders, and millwrights, held a considerably higher position in the hierarchy than a regular hourly worker on the assembly line. They were paid more and had more job security. The best way for a production worker to get off the assembly line was to become a skilled worker. Opportunities for that transition expanded as the company needed to hire more skilled workers to operate the increasingly complex equipment—but workers had to first find a way to learn the skills.

Henry Ford, who was largely responsible for "de-skilling" the workforce, nonetheless believed the company had a responsibility to provide some education. He himself started out as an unskilled apprentice at a machine shop in Detroit. In addition to

View of management offices in 1938. Author's collection.

providing basic training for assembly-line work, Ford also offered self-improvement programs through his Sociological Department and "Americanization" programs, including
English-language classes taught by volunteers. In 1916 he established the Henry Ford
Trade School, which provided free vocational training to underprivileged boys. Students aged twelve to fifteen worked as machinist apprentices at the Highland Park plant
under top-flight instructors. This blend of classroom education and "on-the-job" training
became the model for many vocational training programs. The Ford family also founded
and funded more than fifty educational institutions around the world, including high
schools and community colleges. After World War II, Ford, and many other companies,
offered tuition assistance, and a number of employees at the Twin Cities plant received
their high-school diploma through this program.

Ford employees who wished to learn a skilled trade could attend a number of excellent vocational schools in the Twin Cities, including Dunwoody Institute in Minneapolis
and the Mechanic Arts High School in St. Paul, which was founded as the Boys Vocational School. By the 1960s this institution was renamed the St. Paul Technical Vocational

Institute, but was more popularly known as "the TVI." (In recent years, it became St. Paul College.) The two world wars brought an awareness for the need for military preparedness and the importance of a skilled workforce. The military provided technical training directly to enlistees and civilians working in vital industries, as well as to returning veterans. Ford and other companies that had military contracts were also given federal funding for training programs. During World War II, Ford set up a welding classroom in the St. Paul plant for workers, many of whom were middle-aged and had previously assembled V8 cars. "It takes from six to eight weeks," said a company official, "to teach an old dog new tricks." Students learning machining worked on the job alongside a skilled operator until they became proficient.

Except during wartime, Ford generally looked outside the plant to hire skilled workers, but this policy changed in the 1950s when the company experienced labor shortages. Bob Killeen had lost his bid for reelection at the union and had to return to the assembly line. Hoping to get off the line, he used his well-honed negotiating skills to convince the company to institute a new policy allowing for more upward mobility. Killeen had earlier gone to Minneapolis Vocational to become a machinist and when a machinist's job opened up in the plant, he bid on it. He had seniority, but because he had no prior machinist work experience he had to file a grievance to persuade the company to hire him. "They thought I would disrupt everything," he said. "Just to the contrary . . . I did my job as well as I could and they were very happy with it." Others on the line took note, including William Brengman, who started on the assembly right after high school. He left for the navy during the Korean conflict, where he was trained in foundry work and machining. After the war, he returned to the assembly line at Ford. He, and several others at the plant, went to the St. Paul Technical Vocational Institute in the evening on their own time and expense. Over a three-year period, Brengman learned machining and he applied for a machinist helper position when it became available. "The union and the company kind of went along with that theory," he said. "We created our own . . . 'upgrader program.' We could do the job even if we didn't have a formal apprenticeship program."

Many of the protocols that distinguished hourlies from management workers were phased out, but separate entrance doors remained to the end. Author's collection.

Brengman's tooling experience did not fit within the existing tool and die job classification or any other category—a new classification was needed. Brengman turned to his building chairman, Al Hendricks, who was preparing to join the national contract negotiations in Detroit. Hendricks brought along some of Brengman's blueprints and a tool he made for a key cylinder's operation. He was able to create a new classification known as toolmaker. Brengman explained:

> [It had] the same rating as what an electrician makes at Ford and which was one of the higher pay scales . . . There were some bitter feelings among some of the people in other trades because we got this classification. These people were established, maybe steamfitters or pipe fitters, some carpenters, some millwrights, that had been working for Ford for years and years. And here some upstart machinists come along and get a classification as toolmaker, which was ten or fifteen cents more an hour than they were making.

Killeen and Brengman had become skilled workers because they went to vocational school on their own initiative. Killeen and the union wanted to extend that option to line workers who were unable to go to school. He saw a possible avenue through the model changeover process. Installing new equipment and tools for the annual model changes was an intense, complex effort lasting from several weeks to three or more months. Ford generally hired outside contractors for this work to supplement the plant's skilled maintenance workers, but because of the tight schedule, the company often brought in some production workers to help during the shutdown. Killeen argued that this could enable unskilled workers to amass enough on-the-job training to qualify for a skilled position. "Changeover is all you need," said Killeen. "You worked as a changeover for a number of years and knew what was going on and if they needed a plumber or a machinist or whatever, you got the job as a journeyman."

The Ford Motor Company was not enthusiastic about on-the-job training programs, probably because of its complex administrative requirements and concerns about setting a precedent. Local 879 proposed strengthening the changeover program to require some class instruction, but this still did not satisfy the company which was committed to a formal apprenticeship system. The National Apprenticeship Act, which was enacted in 1937 as part of Franklin Roosevelt's New Deal program, was modeled in part on the Henry Ford Trade School. The Ford Motor Company established a formal apprenticeship program in 1967. States administer the private apprenticeship agreements; in Minnesota, four thousand hours of work experience are required to be qualified.

Killeen, who was later reelected as a union officer, had a lot invested in the "upgrader program" and he fought to get it accepted. He explained that when Ford hired "from the outside . . . they didn't have to train any workers. The fact is they were jumping over some poor production worker that had worked . . . all those years." It became increasingly difficult for production workers putting in long days, and working an irregular and unpredictable schedule, to find the time or energy for vocational classes. The union did not oppose the formal apprenticeship program but pushed to keep the "upgrader" as an additional option, allowing a line worker to qualify if he could accumulate enough experience on multiple changeovers. "I wanted a two-path program," said Hendricks. "The 'upgrader program' is there and then we brought in the apprenticeship program; so we have two paths for people becoming a journeyman. They both have to take the state license tests."

An informal training program was also created at the Twin Cities Assembly Plant that enabled workers to keep current with technological innovations. Two employees, both coincidently named Robert Johnson, took the lead. Robert "Cubby" Johnson was a master electrician active in Local 879, and R. W. "Bob" Johnson was the plant engineering manager. "We needed to set up training that was specific to our needs," said Cubby Johnson, "above and beyond what St. Paul Vo-Tech or Dunwoody or somebody else could supply." He traveled to Detroit and other plants to meet with his counterparts and inspect learning centers. He was excited about the prospects and found an unused bathroom in the mezzanine level measuring sixteen feet by ten feet, which he converted to a makeshift training center. He scrounged up equipment, including an early black-and-white computer that had a "canned program in it that you loaded with tape," and a U.S. Air Force World War II videotape program. Master or journeyman skilled workers from the plant gave informal tutorials to other workers in the new training center. Vendors came in to give presentations on their latest products, and some companies set up demo trailers in the parking lot. The video library grew, and workers could access it at their convenience. Cubby believed the program worked because it was a shared effort: "In the eleven years I was there, I never had a budget. I never knew where the money was coming from. I knew where it was going, because I would say to Bob [Johnson], 'I need this and I need that.' 'Give me a day or two.' He'd be back and he'd say, 'Yes, I got it. You go ahead and order it.' I never knew what a training budget was."

While Henry Ford II's more conciliatory attitude toward employees helped calm labor relations in the short term, labor leaders and company officials continued to jockey for advantage at every opportunity. Any proposal by the company had the potential for becoming a labor-relations flash point, even something as seemingly innocuous as a suggestion program. A company publication, *Ford at Fifty*, described the roots of the suggestion program: "In the good old days the industrial worker did as he was told and usually kept his opinions to himself. Nobody cared about his ideas. When Henry Ford II and his new top management reorganized the Ford Motor Company, this wall of silence between the executives and the workers was broken down as quickly as possible." One of the ways the company did this was to set up a formal suggestion program in 1947, which invited workers "to give out . . . original ideas for improving Ford's manufacturing and management methods." The company would pay workers for ideas that improved the design of the car or the manufacturing process, or improved the workplace. The cash award generally amounted to one-sixth of the savings to the company up to a maximum of six thousand dollars.

Leaders at UAW Local 879 opposed the program, fearing it would undermine their authority by encouraging direct communication between workers and management. They also feared that productivity gains could eliminate jobs. The UAW Local 879 newsletter in November 1951 spelled out the concerns:

> Maybe you think that Mr. Ford's suggestion plan is okay, but if you do you are making a serious mistake. By offering suggestions to eliminate operations you are, in the long run, making Mr. Ford richer and yourself—Joe Worker—poorer. In fact you may suggest yourself right out of a job. Mr. Ford has a lot of smart cookies up in the front office accumulating a shine on the seat of their pants. If you want to make Mr. Ford richer then let them be the ones to dream up ways to eliminate YOUR job. Why should you help them?

These concerns were not unfounded, as another article complained the following year: "Glass Department Suggestion Cost 20 Jobs. Because of the suggestion made by someone in glass, the new method of cutting, layout, and inspection of glass is being experimented with, and if successful will eliminate some 20 jobs. We hope the suggestor is one of those laid off." In spite of union opposition, many workers submitted suggestions. By 1955 Ford had distributed well over a million dollars to workers around the country. In one year, 94 percent of the 4,700 employees at the Chicago stamping plant submitted suggestions, and more than a thousand workers received more than $380,000 in awards. Workers, who were once told to not think, were now having a significant impact on the design and manufacture of automobiles.

In St. Paul, the company placed suggestion boxes around the plant, making it convenient for workers to participate. Roger Okerstrom took a blank application home in 1959 and his wife typed up his simple suggestion: "Paint wagon tail gate sides the same as body color." The company had been masking the sides and bottom of the inside of the tailgate, and his idea would have eliminated the need for that step. Ford implemented the idea around the country, saving each plant between forty thousand and fifty thousand dollars per month. Okerstrom won the first 1966 Galaxie 500 four-door hardtop made

TWIN CITIES FORD NEWS   October 21, 1964

'Big Bats' Boom in 1964

LEAGUE LEADERS . . . Four Twin Cities homerun sluggers rattled suggestion hits to all fields to cop 1964 Idea Award championships. The fearsome foursome are Francis Conroy, top money man since start of plan ($5,095.86); Frank Long, top batting average (6 for 6 in ideas accepted); Harris Brengman, top suggester (23 ideas), and Al Lindstrom, top man in awards ($612.42).

In 1947, Henry Ford II instituted the suggestion program, which paid workers for ideas and innovations that saved the company money. Ford promoted this program heavily for a number of years through its plant newsletters. Author's collection.

in the plant, and he and his family were treated to lunch at a nearby restaurant. Verna Welsch, one of the women who continued to work after the war, won twelve awards, including the suggestion that the instrument panel's wiring should be color-coded.

The suggestion program waned over the years, mainly because Ford lost interest. The company did not increase the amounts of cash prizes or commit staff to review suggestions or estimate cost savings. Its attention had shifted to employee involvement programs, which were more collaborative in nature and did not offer cash prizes. The union's resistance also contributed to the program's decline, even though Ford consented to have any worker who lost his job through new innovations to be transferred elsewhere. Roger Okerstrom was an active member of UAW Local 879 but he supported the suggestion program. Winning the big prize meant so much to him and his family that it was featured prominently in his obituary forty-six years later.

Managing the Twin Cities Assembly Plant

Assembling cars is like a gigantic three-dimensional puzzle with ten thousand parts arriving simultaneously at a precise spot on a moving target to be put together by workers with the proper training and tools. Ford could take four or five years to develop a new car, and this involved many experts from different disciplines. The idea for a new car started with the Product Planning Team, which had expertise in market research, design, engineering, manufacturing, and finance. Ford then brought in stylists and design engineers to create a prototype car, followed later by the work of manufacturing engineers who planned and coordinated all aspects of the production system, including materials, parts, tools, equipment, manpower, materials handling, physical plant, and storage.

A portion of the ten thousand to fifteen thousand parts for a new vehicle was stock items from previous years, but a number were new components designed by mechanical engineers and fabricated as prototypes. The parts that Ford produced in-house often required new machines and tools, which also had to be designed and built. As parts became more complex, much of the design and engineering work and manufacturing shifted to outside vendors. Company experts in purchasing and supply chain management oversaw the bidding process. They generally consulted with suppliers on design, cost, and schedule, before finalizing the bid packets.

Process engineers in Detroit designed the system and instructional materials for the workers explaining how to assemble the parts of a car. Ford then sent these "process sheets" to St. Paul and other plants, with materials' specifications and drawings on how to weld, screw, bolt, glue, or snap the parts together. Engineers in Detroit regularly interacted with their counterparts at the branch plants, who often had more practical experience in assembling cars. Bob Hansen and Del Peterson were Twin Cities Assembly Plant process engineers who had also worked in Detroit. They recalled the intense pressure to finish the process sheets as the deadline for unveiling the new model car approached. The illustrated sheets were indispensable for training line workers. "You could really do the operation," said Hansen, "with very little training by just having the [process] sheet." In more recent years, process sheets became digital and were placed at computer stations on the assembly line near the foremen and workers. After being trained with the process sheets, renamed Quality Deployment Sheets, workers had to sign off indicating that they understood the task.

No matter how thorough the advance planning, plants would often have problems when starting up production of new models. Outside suppliers sometimes shipped batches of substandard parts. With the moving assembly line, workers could not just stop and wait for a new part, so process engineers and machinists in the plant had to improvise. Hansen described one project: "We got a new shipment in and we found out on the first one that it wasn't going to work because it had a gap in it . . . You had to make sure the doors would fit it . . . [we] had to scribe the whole body with an exact line that the molding was on and you had to get the machinists, the tool and die maker, to come over with a drill fixture and reengineer that before you start up the next morning."

Some parts couldn't be installed as designed. "I was responsible for a lot of the tooling that was used with power tools, weird kinds of sockets and things," recalled Del Peterson. "A lot of the designs were made by people who did not understand the clearances required for using power tools as opposed to hand tools. So, one of my little deals was trying to cook up every kind of crazy socket there was to get around those goofy corners." He added:

> In many cases there was no time to sit down and do things the way they tell you that things are done in school. If you need a hand tool to hold a piece of chrome while somebody is running a screw in the thing from the other side, you can't sit down and start drawing this. The cars are running down the line. You go down and see Fred Arenz in the machine shop and you just cook something up on the spot. Once you get something working, you tell him, "Make thirteen more of those." Then you were in business.

The pressure of the moving assembly line and meeting the daily quota sometimes took a toll on managers. Bob Hansen recalled that when the line once went down, the production manager "took his hat off and threw it in the floor. 'Goddamn it,' he said, 'we ain't got time to think about it. We've got to *do* something.'" In another incident, one excitable foreman got upset about problem doors. "He'd take the door off and get it on the floor and he'd stomp on it." Hansen remembered another door problem: "They had an assembler tool but there was so much variation in quality that the only way you'd get that door to fit was you'd slam it shut with that block in there and you'd spring it one way and spring it the other way. Then you'd spring it up and spring it down. And it worked." Years later, Del Peterson still had a widely circulated cartoon that said, "Jeez! We finally got the sonuvabitch closed, and *now* we can't get it open!"

Process engineers also designed conveyor systems to bring parts and subassemblies to the assembly line. These systems combined stock items and custom-designed elements, including baskets, hooks, or saddles, that would be fabricated and installed on-site. Conveyor lines on the floor had to be designed to lift and turn the larger and heavier parts, like the car bodies. Powered by an electric motor, the speed of the conveyor belts could be adjusted to produce varying numbers of cars, typically forty to seventy units per hour. As the manufacturing process became more specialized and automated, conveyors took on more complex, interactive functions. Tools that tightened bolts even had sensors built in that could measure torque. Some of these tools would later have the ability to shut the line down if a problem was detected. With the increasing complexity of conveyors and tools, more of the design and fabrication was done by outside suppliers.

The material-handling engineers designed the systems that moved parts to the assembly line. They calculated the number, size, and sequence of car parts and developed a plan for where and how they would be stored. Parts were usually kept in reserve areas before being moved to the assembly line. They could be moved by forklift, hand truck, or tow tractors that pulled trailers with bins. There were also semiautomatic delivery systems, including driverless trains that ran along electric wires embedded in the concrete floor, and automated robotic storage retrieval systems. The St. Paul plant's ceiling height was fourteen feet, which was considerably lower than industry standards, so engineers had to be creative. The usage rate and desired level of inventory dictated the amount and location of storage space. Generally, the St. Paul plant had a two-to-five-day supply of parts on hand, which were delivered by rail or truck, or occasionally by plane. "Hot items," essential to keeping the assembly line moving, could be ordered by 7:30 in the morning and flown in from Detroit by noon.

The Traffic Department was responsible for getting parts and raw materials into the plant and moving finished cars out. By the 1960s, the plant received up to six hundred thousand pounds of parts each day from around 150 different vendors. The days of unloading heavy shipments by hand were long over, as the company introduced labor-saving equipment. Approximately 60 percent of the finished cars were shipped by truck to dealers. If the distance was more than three hundred or four hundred miles, Ford usually transported the vehicles by rail. This method became more cost-effective in the 1960s when railroads introduced tri-level cars that could carry twelve to fifteen cars. There would occasionally be shortages of railcars, which would back up the inventory of com-

Quality control became a major problem from the late 1950s on. This cartoon, widely circulated at the plant, showed the all-too-real difficulty of making cars with defective parts. Author's collection.

pleted cars. At one point, more than seven thousand vehicles had to be temporarily stored in the parking lots at racetracks in Hudson, Wisconsin, and Shakopee, Minnesota. Local 879 suggested that Ford should make railcars at the plants it intended to close. Only about 12 percent of the vehicles assembled in the Twin Cities in the 1960s were sent to Minnesota dealerships. Other destinations included Colorado, Idaho, Illinois, Iowa, Kansas, Michigan, Missouri, Montana, Nevada, New Mexico, Oklahoma, Oregon, Texas, Utah, Washington, Wisconsin, Wyoming, and Fairbanks, Alaska, a distance of 4,018 miles. Car models that were made in other plants around the country for Ford dealers in Minnesota were sent by rail to the plant, where they were unloaded and moved to a waiting area for delivery trucks. With production of the Ranger pickup, the Twin Cities became an export plant, shipping vehicles to Canada, Norway, and many other countries.

Industrial engineers focused on the human elements of car manufacturing—the workers. They assigned each task itemized in a process sheet to a worker on the assembly line and made sure each was performed in the most efficient, safe, and reasonable way possible. Industrial engineers in Detroit created a "white book" to project a reasonable time for each assembly task. The goal was to "balance the line" so that the flow of materials was synchronized with the capabilities of the workers on a schedule that met production targets. Company "time-study" experts monitored production in the plant, in collaboration with the UAW.

The plant engineering department was responsible for the physical elements of the assembly building, the grounds, hydroelectric plant, and steam plant, as well as all tools, equipment, and conveyor lines. "Plant engineering," according to Bob Johnson, a retired engineer, "consisted of many amazing, talented, and hardworking supervisors, skilled tradesmen, and plant services crew. They did fabrication, installation, and could fix anything but a broken heart." The plant engineer was responsible for planning building expansions, as the assembly plant grew from approximately 840,000 square feet to more than 1.3 million square feet. In 1956, because of a shortage of production space, Ford moved its parts inventory for dealers to a new Parts Depot building on a twelve-acre site at St. Anthony Boulevard and Northeast Marshall Street in Minneapolis. Ten years later, a new warehouse was built at the assembly plant for production parts. The most significant alteration to the main assembly building, and certainly the most unfortunate one aesthetically and historically, was the removal in 1968 of three-quarters of the original classical facade facing the Mississippi River, and its replacement with a windowless wall of ribbed cast-concrete panels. The new section protruded sixty feet from the original structure, a "modernization" that allowed for more storage space along the final assembly line.

Retired plant engineer Ralph Cook recalled that engineers considered and rejected one

In 1968 most of the original classical facade was removed to expand the plant to the west. All that remained of the original facade was the main entrance, the showroom, and the north wall. Author's collection.

expansion idea that could possibly have saved the plant from being shut down years later. Ford explored building a stamping plant on-site to reduce the time and expense needed to ship bulky parts but concluded that there was not enough space. On-site stamping plants had become standard in new assembly plants, and the lack of one in the Twin Cities was cited as a factor in its closing. Ford had sold off some of its property over the years, including a parcel at Cleveland and Ford Parkway for the Highland Village Apartments, and a four-acre parcel at the northeast corner of the site for a shopping center. It also donated a parcel for senior housing. It is not clear, however, if those parcels would have been large enough for a stamping plant.

Plant engineers also designed and built a number of projects within the plant. An improvised training center was installed in the ceiling between the open-web steel joists, as well as a weight room and exercise lounge. The original bathrooms in the mezzanine level had to be raised five feet to make room for conveyors. Staff from the department also built the plant cafeteria and a number of special-purpose clean-air rooms. The low ceilings were especially problematic for the material handling engineer, who had difficulty installing the maze of conveyors belts and navigating the forklift trucks. He turned to the plant engineer for help. When Bob Johnson started at Ford, company policy prohibited the cutting of the ceiling joists—all overhead conveyors, piping, and tooling had to be attached with clamps fabricated by a plant "blacksmith." That policy was relaxed and joists were cut and rebuilt as needed to install equipment. Johnson recognized that the low ceiling height was a challenge, but he did not believe it was a major factor in closing the plant.

The plant manager oversaw all operations at the Twin Cities Assembly Plant and had responsibility for all hourly and salaried workers. In recent years, the company's policy was to rotate managers every several years, but in the 1950s and 1960s they had longer tenure and more status and power. Del Peterson described one manager named Dorsey. He "had his desk kind of against one wall and in front of the desk on the tile there was a marked-off spot . . . When anybody in the plant—a foreman, a superintendent, anybody—came to see him about anything, they took their hat off, went into the office, and they stood on that tile for their interview. The boss was really the boss in those days and there was no doubt about it." Dorsey's favorite aphorism was "If you can't have your own way, there's no sense being boss." Peterson and other engineering staff once did a major layout plan for the painting ovens, drawing the partitions right on the floor. Dorsey looked at the mark on the floor and said, "I don't want that spray booth and oven there." He drew a line with his foot on the floor a foot away and said, "Put it there." In those days, the plant manager ran the plant and could tell Detroit, "No, that he didn't want to do it that way and he didn't do it that way."

Dorsey, who was widely known as "Napoleon," once punched his human resources manager with a paperweight during an argument. The authoritarianism eventually gave way to a more collegial approach. Henry Ford II introduced a new system that decentralized the decision-making process, shifting considerable responsibility to the local plant manager. Plant managers were given more autonomy for meeting production quotas and were empowered to run the plant almost like an independent business. Local plants would be "charged" for parts produced by other Ford plants, and had to track a variety of other production costs. One of the more highly regarded managers in St. Paul was Tom Brand, who moved on to the Chicago Assembly Plant, where he was profiled in Studs Terkel's best-selling 1972 book *Working*.

The plant manager led an eleven-person operating committee that met weekly. The plant comptroller gave detailed reports of output for the previous week, and the total costs per vehicle broken out by the body, paint, trim, and chassis subgroups. These results were compared to projections prepared by Ford staff in Detroit, as well as reports from other plants around the country. Departments within the Twin Cities plant that did not "make the numbers" or "make cost" were held accountable. Local management also tracked warranty charges of vehicles after they left the plant to measure quality. This complemented the quality testing done in the plant, which included a "teardown" analysis of random samples of bodies to ensure that welds were being done properly.

Model Changes and Beginning of Automation and Robotics

Model changes were a particularly intense time for the engineering staff. In late July 1965, the plant was shut down for three weeks for the changeover to the 1966 models. Most of the workers went on their summer vacation, but about three hundred people remained behind to prepare for the new cars. A Ford press release described the process: "The plant's thousands of tons of machinery and equipment are gone over with a fine tooth comb," said P. E. Boudreau, manager of plant engineering. "In addition to installing new equipment and tooling for the 1966 models, the changeover period gives us an opportunity to inspect, repair, clean, polish, paint and prepare for another year of production." Workers inspected five miles of conveyors, the paint spray booths and ovens, automatic welding fixtures, and special tools such as giant holding devices that fit body parts together to ensure perfect welds. Bob Hansen explained: "A 'tool' is anything from a household screwdriver to a floor pan press welder capable of making 125 spot welds per minute. Over two thousand small power tools must be examined." Retooling the assembly lines would generally involve relatively modest changes, but even a seemingly small modification, such as adding a decorative stripe of paint to the car, could require tearing up of a section of the floor to make way for the paint crew. More significant changes, as in the case of assembling a completely new vehicle, would sometimes require major changes, or even a new building.

Having a cadre of skilled workers was more critical as automation and robotics were introduced to the workplace. During the 1965 changeover, a group of very talented skilled tradesmen, working with the encouragement and support of plant management, created some fixed automated welding tools for the body shop. Cy Winkler, a legendary toolmaker, received a cash payment through the suggestion program for a handheld welding gun and other customized jigs that were early examples of automation. Skilled workers and plant engineers also worked with the Graco Company in Minneapolis to develop the first generation of automated sprayers later adopted at other Ford plants. Al McGregor remembered the paint robots from the early 1970s:

The plant expanded enormously from its original construction in 1926. Notable additions were the huge paint complex to the rear of the plant and several warehouse buildings. The original grove of trees admired by Henry Ford was replaced with parking lots. The wharves along the river, rarely used for navigation, were overgrown with trees. The area south of the Steam Plant became a landfill dump and was capped with a concrete slab for parking. Senior housing and fields for Little League ball clubs occupy the southeast corner of the property. Author's collection.

I think there were four of them. One of them was used to open the door of the vehicle. Then the second one would paint inside. They were looked upon with a lot of suspicion by most of us who worked around them and on them. They didn't necessarily do a very good job. They were kind of the forerunners of some of the things we have today that are much, much, much better. Eventually, they threw those particular robots away and began doing it by hand again. I suspect that a lot of us made snide comments about robots, but it's the wave. You either get with the program or get run over.

Robotics brought automation to a new level as the machines could be programmed to do multiple functions over time—it was no longer a single-purpose machine. Workers appreciated robots and automated machinery that could do the "dirty, dangerous, and dreary" tasks, but as with all new labor-saving technologies, there were concerns about being displaced. Manufacturers embraced the prospect of shifting work away from humans, but Walter Reuther pointed out one downside of that strategy. In the 1950s, he was touring a Ford plant that featured a number of robots and a company official "with a slightly gleeful tone in his voice" asked, "Walter, how are you going to get those robots to pay your union dues?" Reuther quickly retorted, "How are you going to get them to buy your cars?"

Ford often selected the Twin Cities plant and its high-quality workforce to test new equipment. The introduction of new machinery was often a trial-and-error process and things did not always go as planned. A Norwegian company, Trallfa, made the first robot for the plant. It was installed by plant electricians in the paint booth, under the supervision of a Norwegian engineer. After the engineer left, the robot broke down and the tradesmen at Ford had the difficult job of repairing it. Cubby Johnson recalled, "After much consulting with manuals, one of the electricians said, 'Let's just slap it in the control panel with a lutefisk, it should work then'!"

While the process engineers were getting the plant ready for the new models, material handling engineers were examining "dunnage"—boxes, bins, or racks—designed to store sheet metal and other parts for the new models. The 1966 models had about twelve thousand parts and J. T. Lamont, manager of production control, said, "Our job is to see that the right part reaches the right place at the right time and in the right quantity. The process is continuous. When we stop ordering parts for the 65s, we begin taking in parts for the new models." A trickle of parts for the 1966 Galaxie 500, LTD, Country Squire Station Wagon, Fairlane 500, and Mercury models began entering the plant before the first week of changeover, turning into a landslide when each new model's production was in full swing. Lamont added: "Our daily absorption of parts increases rapidly during changeover and reaches a peak of fifty boxcars and four hundred thousand pounds of truck freight daily during the last few days before regular production."

Ford engineers used production forecasts for ordering parts and materials. The right "production mix" in 1965 was an assortment of sedans, hardtops, station wagons, and trucks. About 650 vehicles would be assembled simultaneously, and it would take about a day and a half for the complete car to work its way through the system. The first twenty-two cars to come off the assembly line were "preproduction" units that would be taken apart and inspected by the engineers. Tolerances would be checked and necessary adjustments made during the "tooling prove-out." When the last of the old models was made, all the surplus parts and materials, including surplus radios, windshields, lights, and the like, were scrapped or made available as service parts in the "balancing-out" process.

The considerable overlap between engineering specialties, and the constantly changing manufacturing process, required a great deal of interaction and coordination. The manufacturing engineering manager oversaw three departments: Process Engineering, Industrial Engineering, and Plant Engineering. Ford once considered creating a more decentralized engineering approach within the plant and selected the Twin Cities for a demonstration project. Engineering staff and skilled workers were assigned directly to four major subgroups: body, paint, trim, and chassis. These production groups and engineering staff had considerable autonomy. The experiment produced uncertain results and was abandoned, but Ford tried again several years later. The number of subgroups was reduced to three—body, paint, and chassis—and with the kinks worked out the decentralized approach was expanded around the country.

Detroit recognized the expertise of the manufacturing engineers in St. Paul and other branch plants and there was a constant interaction and exchange. As new models were developed, plant engineers from around the country would go to Detroit to make recommendations during the design process. Prior to production, engineers visited the designated pilot plant in Detroit for a final inspection of the model to learn what they needed to do to get their plants ready. Sometimes Ford would designate one assembly plant to take the lead for manufacturing a new model. Personnel from other plants would travel to the plant to observe the rollout. Some of the launches did not go smoothly. Bob Hansen remembers one: "It was awful. You had all the conveyors there and all the people around. They weren't operating. They wouldn't operate. There would be eighty, ninety people around a body and they were trying to get information and see what's going on. You didn't have any room . . . You could have some peculiarities in your own plant. That's what you were down there for, to find out if there is anything in that new model that's going to screw up your own plant layout or your plant tooling or anything else." Turnaround time for preparing the St. Paul plant was very short, sometimes only a few days, which was why a number of engineers and production people also made the trip to the pilot plant. Another purpose for the frequent trips to Detroit, according to Bob Johnson, was to communicate with the finance people about the cost implications of redesigning the layout of the plant for the new model. Detroit officials had architectural plans for the

St. Paul plant and there would sometimes be lively discussion about what improvements were necessary and the budget.

Engineers at the Ford plant had an enormously difficult and stressful job. There was an unrelenting pressure to keep the assembly line moving and to meet the daily quota of cars. Every day brought a different challenge. During changeover periods, the engineering and maintenance staff worked especially long hours, typically twelve-hour weekdays and eight hours on weekends. Several engineers said they worked for an entire year without a single day off—including Christmas and New Year's Day. Ford became their family. After a long, hard day they would go home for a late dinner, eat, sleep, and turn around for work the next day. Bob Johnson managed to squeeze an extra eight years into his thirty-year career at Ford as he accumulated more than fifteen thousand hours of overtime. The engineers were well paid and had excellent benefits, but the workload and stress caused many to retire by the age of sixty.

Surplus Hydroelectric Power

Automobile companies and workers prospered in the decades after World War II. Car sales were brisk, and contentious labor-relations issues were gradually being sorted out through the framework of negotiated agreements. The good times brought a sense of normalcy and optimism to the several generations who worked in the 1950s and 1960s. Although the Twin Cities Assembly Plant assembled millions of cars, trucks, and tanks, it did not develop as a major manufacturing facility as many had hoped, even though there was abundant hydroelectricity. Ford initially used only about 12 percent of the power generated. A small portion of the surplus went to operate the federal lock and dam operations, and the balance was sold to Northern States Power (NSP). According to the terms of the federal permit, the hydropower plant was required to operate at full capacity.

An internal Ford memo from 1949 reported that the utilization of the hydroelectricity was lower than expected because the company did not produce "radiators, batteries, springs . . . other miscellaneous items," as originally envisioned. However, a promotional flyer distributed at the plant in 1927 listed limited production of both radiators and batteries. Photographic evidence also shows some battery production. The flyer also stated that "A Steel Wheel manufacturing plant is planned for installation in 1927 so that more than the maximum electric current produced by the water power will be needed by the Ford Company manufacturing operations." But this did not happen. As a result, the Ford hydropower plant was the largest nonutility distributor of energy in Minnesota for a number of years. The sale of the surplus power to NSP was a significant source of revenue for the company.

Even though the St. Paul plant did not become the major manufacturing facility that was envisioned, building expansions and the introduction of new high demand tools and equipment, notably the electrostatic painting process, required more electricity. Investments in technology after the war were expensive, offset in part by the need for fewer—but more skilled—workers. Making automobiles had seemingly settled into a more predictable routine: engineers were solving problems with new technologies, workers and management were negotiating labor contracts, advertising departments were churning out cute ads, and customers kept buying the fancy big cars. But it would soon become clear that there were many things other than technology and marketing that impacted the car business. Things were about to get considerably more complicated.

An Uncertain Industry

Slumping Sales, Labor Unrest, and the Ranger Pickup

Americans went on a car-buying spree after the war, and the Twin Cities Assembly Plant made some of the most popular models, including Crestliner, Crown Victoria, Fairlane 500, Del Rio, Starliner, Country Sedan Station Wagon, Country Squire Station Wagon, and Galaxie. Manufacturers designed bigger cars with bulkier engines and more horsepower. With the discovery of new oil fields and the availability of cheap gas, the race was on to load up as much weight and superfluous design elements as possible. Engineers, designers, and industry executives turned their backs on Henry Ford's most basic tenets—technological innovation, efficiency engineering, and environmental sustainability. The focus was now on marketing and merchandising, with little concern about quality or keeping the price down.

In 1956, at the height of the golden age for the American automobile industry, the Ford Motor Company "went public" with the largest stock offering up to that point in history. The buoyant mood made it difficult to recognize the looming threats from abroad. Volkswagen introduced the "people's car" to the United States in 1949 but sold only two vehicles. This rose to three hundred units in 1950, and to a hundred thousand a few years later. A Ford executive was not concerned about "the little German toys," saying that Ford produced more cars in one day than Volkswagen did in a year. Volkswagen had been

In 1956, Ford celebrated the manufacture of its two millionth car in Minnesota, a 1957 Victoria. Photograph by the *Minneapolis Star Journal Tribune*. Courtesy of the Minnesota Historical Society.

offered to the Ford Motor Company after the war, but Henry Ford II declined. Executives were confident, wrote Alton Doody, that "American drivers would continue to want bigger, plusher, flashier, more powerful cars," but they were wrong. By 1955 Volkswagen was selling more than one million cars a year, and went on to sell more than sixteen million, surpassing the Model T.

Japanese cars, as had the Volkswagen, arrived with little fanfare. In 1959 Nissan exhibited at the Los Angeles Auto Show and sold only a few cars, which was not surprising given that Japan was best known in the United States for manufacturing cheap toys. But the company continued to improve the design and quality of its automobiles and its sales gradually increased. Nissan's founder, Yoshisuke Aikawa, was enamored with Henry Ford and had visited Detroit in 1908 to learn from the master. After World War II, General

Douglas MacArthur was appointed to oversee the Japanese reconstruction program. He took a very enlightened and sensitive approach, and wrote its new postwar constitution, broke up the traditional industrial monopolies, supported trade unionism, and oversaw the restart of industry. He also brought American management experts to Japan, many of whom had been spurned by American companies. William Edwards Deming, a pioneer in developing quality control systems, found a very receptive audience in Japan for his theories. Nissan and other companies embraced the quality movement and the concept of continuous improvement.

Even though American carmakers monopolized sales, they would rarely pass up an opportunity to further strengthen their hand with protectionist measures. None was more notorious than the "Chicken Tariff," which would have a direct bearing on the Twin Cities Assembly Plant. In 1962 the Kennedy administration accused poultry farmers in Europe of blocking chicken imports from the United States. The Europeans complained that the American poultry factories were decimating their industry, and exporting, in the words of one columnist for *Atlantic Monthly*, a "battery-bred, chemically fed, sanitized, porcelain-finished, money-back-if-you-can-taste-it bird." Europe imposed tariffs, costing American poultry producers billions (adjusted valuation) in lost revenues, which led to considerable political pressure to retaliate. In December 1963, President Lyndon Johnson announced a tariff on potato starch, brandy, and light trucks, saying the value of these imports was approximately equal to the value of the blocked chicken trade.

Audiotapes released thirty years later reveal a more complete picture. Johnson was concerned that Walter Reuther and the UAW were about to call a national strike that would have hurt his election prospects and he was heard pressing for a no-strike pledge. Reuther responded by asking for federal assistance to stem the tide of foreign imports, particularly the Volkswagen. Soon thereafter, the federal government imposed a 25 percent tax on imported light

The plant manager and workers watched a 1962 Fairlane come off the line. Author's collection.

Dealers who survived the Depression and World War II were able to recoup their losses in the boom years. The signs in the window of the Midway Ford dealership on University Avenue in St. Paul capture the sentiment: "Fabulous!" "Exciting!" The showroom was packed with station wagons, which were popular in the early 1960s. Courtesy of the Slawik family.

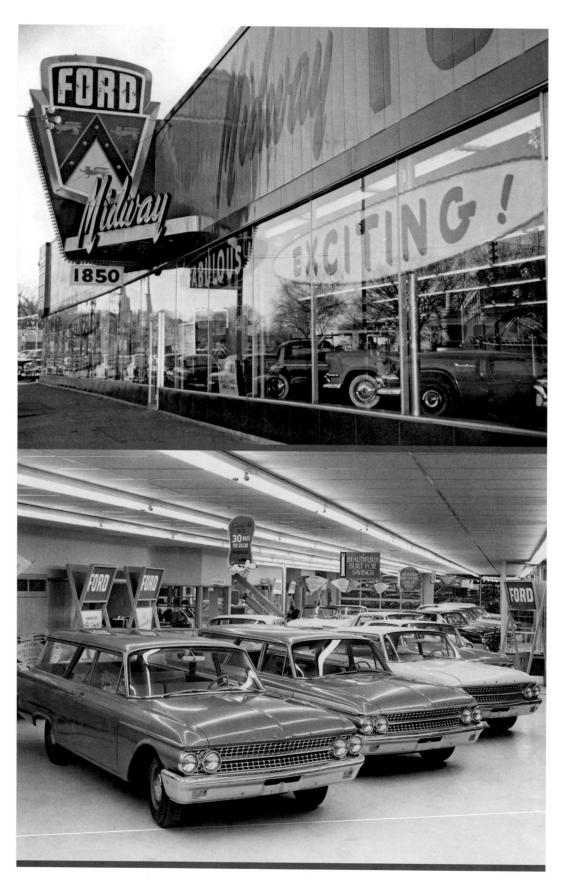

trucks. The "Chicken Tariff" did not specifically target Volkswagen, as it had to conform to the technical requirements of the international trade talks, but Volkswagen light trucks were among the items taxed. With the tariff, American automakers had secured a virtual monopoly on the light truck market. The UAW did not strike in 1964, and Lyndon Johnson won the election in a landslide.

Three years later, Arab nations imposed an oil embargo on the United States in retaliation for supporting Israel in the Six-Day War. A dramatic spike in gasoline prices led many Americans to rethink their love affair with big cars. When the Arab countries imposed a second oil embargo, small imported cars flooded the American market. "It was no contest," wrote Robert Shook. "The Japanese cars sold like hotcakes, and, to the delightful surprise of their purchasers, *they were good cars*, with far fewer problems than those made in the United States. *Made in Japan* was no longer synonymous with shoddy merchandise." Americans liked the overall design, precision manufacturing, operating efficiency, and durability of the imported cars. The Japanese understood the most important elements of success: "Know your customer, and provide a product that *exceeds* their expectations." Ford and the other American car companies were coasting along with the false security of the shared monopoly, while Japanese companies were implementing the quality control measures of Edwards Deming.

The "Reckoning"

The day of "reckoning," as David Halberstam so aptly called it, had arrived. The expensive, inefficient, shoddy American cars, fueled by cheap gasoline, built with high-wage union labor at substandard manufacturing plants run by finance people, were about to meet Ralph Nader, the Environmental Protection Agency, oil embargoes, Volkswagen, Datsun, and Honda. All the underlying assumptions of the industry would be tested and all would fail. Economic forecasters at Ford did not foresee the disastrous confluence of events in the 1970s and 1980s. Ralph Nader questioned the safety of American cars in his 1965 book *Unsafe at Any Speed*, which highlighted problems with the Corvair compact manufactured by General Motors. Rather than responding directly to Nader's claims, GM hired private investigators to uncover damaging personal information. When Nader discovered their clumsy campaign, he filed a lawsuit and won a significant judgment. The episode tarnished the reputation of the largest American car manufacturer and the entire industry. It also led to the enactment of the National Traffic and Motor Vehicle Safety Act of 1966, which mandated seat belts and other safety features. University of Minnesota Professor James "Crash" Ryan, who was credited with inventing the seat belt, was singled out by Nader in his book as the only automotive engineer who "has squarely and persistently challenged the automobile manufacturers to build crashworthy vehicles." Throughout his career, Ryan had looked for allies in the auto industry, including Ford, without much success.

As a backdrop to these automotive problems, the nation was being torn apart by the Vietnam War, political assassinations, race and gender conflicts, substance abuse, and serious political unrest. These frustrations contributed to a sense of alienation among the workforce, which led to discipline problems on the shop floor. Times had changed since the ardent prohibitionist Henry Ford fired any worker caught drinking on the job. By the 1960s, the medical staff at the Twin Cities plant was dealing with a serious substance abuse crisis and took a different approach. Any employee suspected of drinking was given a breathalyzer test on the premises. Company policy was rehabilitation, but if that failed, the worker would eventually be discharged. In 1985 fifty workers entered treatment programs, most of whom had cocaine addictions. The company established an Employee Assistance Program to provide on-site counseling for substance abuse, gambling addiction, and other personal programs, and established meeting times for Alcoholic Anonymous. Although coworkers and the union were sympathetic, there was real concern that impaired workers could create a dangerous work environment for all. Local news media would occasionally report on the drinking problem, including one highly publicized television exposé showing autoworkers drinking in the parking lot while on break.

The dramatic decline in quality was a serious problem afflicting American auto companies. A popular urban legend was to avoid buying cars that were made on Monday because of the high absentee rate or sloppy work done after the weekend. The word *FORD* was caricatured as standing for "Found on Road Dead" and "Fix or Repair Daily." It was reported that even company executives did not want to drive their own

The Twin Cities plant made some of the best-selling cars of the 1960s, including the Galaxie. The assembly line could accommodate a mix of cars with different colors and finishes, and even different models. Author's collection.

Young families with kids propelled the sale of new cars. These are likely children of workers at the plant. Author's collection.

cars. The decline in quality was certainly no surprise to workers. Virtually everyone at the St. Paul plant interviewed for this book had stories about being ignored when reporting quality concerns. One informed his foreman about a tailgate rattle and was bluntly told to stop checking. Another reported that the level of the bumpers was off by an inch or so. The foreman inspected and recognized that it was not just one car but a long line of cars with the same problem. He told the worker to let them pass unless the bumper was off by an inch and a half. Sometimes executives visiting from Detroit made the decision to approve faulty parts. On one occasion, a paint foreman pulled a car off the line because the fender and the door colors were not an exact match. Roger Okerstrom recalled that a top Ford official executive happened by and said to the manager, "Uh, it doesn't look off color to me, does it look off color to you?" The foreman then said, "Nope," and the car went back on the line. Al Hendricks, from Local 879, claimed that Ford talked a big game about quality but did not follow through. He remembered a foreman in body build who made workers stretch out the spot welds. Another worker described the difficulty of installing the hood when the parts didn't fit: "You just had a big mallet, a big hammer, and you would pound here and there and get the thing to fit proper so it would close and open right. We just beat the thing in there so it would fit. Once you got it in, you'd hope it would open and close." The really bad cars were marked up and sent over to "the hole" to be fixed. Often, more than one hundred were backed up at the hole, which meant the workers had to put in longer days.

Workers resented being blamed for the decline in quality. They drove the same cars and had the same problems. "We wanted to be involved in the quality," said Al Hendricks. "Management told us it was none of our business." Bob Killeen added, "All workers that I ever knew didn't like putting something on a car that didn't work. But after a while, when you'd bring this up with your supervisor about this bad car or that bad car and they'd say, 'Forget about it, Killeen, you just put on the door handles and forget about that. It's not your job. We pay engineers for that.'" Quality control inspectors—"foremen who carried 'OK' stamps in their pocket"—routinely approved cars that were rejected on the assembly line. Meeting the production target for the day was more important than quality.

In frustration, the International UAW urged workers to write up a list of the offending foremen, which was collected into folders and presented to Ford executives. In 1979 they sent a letter to Ford officials bluntly stating that "it is not the UAW worker who is lacking in his work and pride, but management's quest for the bonus dollar that has caused the quality of our product to diminish." Top executives claimed they were unaware of the problems, and tried to deflect blame. Management officials at the local level often had a better understanding of the problems. In an unguarded moment, the manager of the Twin Cities plant was quoted as saying, "As far as I am concerned, Ford assembly division management is out of control in attempting to reduce manpower in the plant. The UAW has a much more realistic view of how many people it takes to make a quality truck."

During the boom years, buyers put up with the shoddy American cars, but when the high-quality imports arrived, customers left in droves. Ford went into a tailspin, with sales dropping by 50 percent. Henry Ford II stated it bluntly: "We made some bum cars." A Ford vice president later said, "We were building the cars the way we wanted to build them rather than the way our customers wanted. It wasn't just Ford; all the domestic automakers did the same thing because we had a monopoly. We were doing that for seventy years." An industry survey showed that Ford had the worst quality record of the Big Three. In 1979, Ford recalled more cars than it produced and over the next four years lost more than $3 billion, an amount equal to 43 percent of its net worth. The *Los Angeles Times* declared ominously that "The giant Ford is now on its knees." It closed nine plants and laid off 250,000 workers. GM was also reeling, and its chairman, Roger Smith, said, "We're up to our ass in trouble and we've got to start doing things differently. We're behind our foreign competition right now in quality, in technological design, in plants and facilities, and yes, even in our management . . . in 1980 the little girl with the lemonade stand down the street made more profit than all of us—GM, Ford, Chrysler, and AMC together."

Because of the Chicken Tariff, the American auto industry maintained a near monopoly on light trucks, SUVs, and minivans, capturing 86 percent of the market, compared to only 64 percent for cars. The government eventually scaled back the import tax on SUVs and minivans, but these vehicles continued to be defined as light trucks and received tax incentives and regulatory exemptions. Auto executives and the UAW continued to push for restrictions on imports, and received considerable political support during the 1980 presidential campaign. The protectionist sentiment, while politically popular, was hard to justify. American car companies, led by Ford, had operated in countries around the world for more than seventy years and dominated sales, often in the face of intense nationalistic opposition. American executives privately admitted that restrictions on imports would only provide short-term, illusionary relief. Even more problematic, and certainly more hypocritical, American companies were dramatically increasing investment in Mexican plants along the U.S. border—even as they were pressing for restrictions on imports.

The Japanese agreed to voluntarily restrict the number of imports, but not to the level called for by the UAW and Ford. Pressure increased on the Japanese companies to

Cars came streaming off the assembly lines of the St. Paul plant and were counted by the millions. This is a 1966 Galaxie LTD. Author's collection.

build manufacturing plants in the United States. The UAW pushed the slogan "If you sell it here, build it here." The president of Local 879, Samuel Pavnick, wrote to President Jimmy Carter in 1980: "If the Japanese and other nations of the world wish to do business in the United States, they must invest in plants and equipment here." The UAW would later deeply regret that position. Carter was in favor of foreign companies locating in the United States, but for environmental reasons—he sought to find alternatives to American "gas guzzlers."

Embracing Edwards Deming and Quality Control

The American auto industry's spectacular collapse was mostly self-inflicted. European and Asian competitors overcame many of the same global challenges. Their cars were traditionally small and energy efficient owing to long-standing government policies that taxed horsepower and gasoline—unlike American policy, which essentially encouraged big cars and cheap gas. Automobile manufacturing constituted almost 20 percent of the American economy, and its demise brought about a period of intense national introspection. NBC broadcast a documentary titled *If Japan Can . . . Why Can't We?* that attributed the success of Japanese manufacturers, in large part, to the work of quality expert William Edwards Deming. The documentary received considerable attention in the corporate suites at Ford, where officials were scrambling to discover the secrets of the Japanese companies.

Donald Petersen, CEO of Ford, personally requested a meeting with Deming, knowing that the quality guru insisted on dealing directly with the top executive. At their first meeting, Deming was emotional at the prospect of working with the iconic American company after having been rejected in his homeland for many years. He hoped that success at Ford would encourage other American companies to adopt quality techniques. Deming was blunt about Ford's culture and the way its managers operated, talking not about quality but about management. He said that "management actions were responsible for 85 percent of all problems in developing better cars." He framed the discussion in the context of employee relations. Management must eliminate fear from the workplace and give workers the opportunity to do a better job. "It all sounded so logical," Petersen wrote in his autobiography, "because it seemed to me that Dr. Deming's philosophy is rooted in basic concepts of human behavior, such as trusting your fellow man and living by the Golden Rule. Everything he says starts with the importance of the human being and moves on from there."

Deming argued that workers on the assembly line needed to be engaged, but given

Ford's checkered labor-relations history, he knew that would be a challenge. Conditions at Ford had regressed almost to the level of the darkest days of the 1940s, prompting the UAW on several occasions to employ its principal tool, the national strike. There was a walkout in 1961 over production standards and a company proposal for a two-tier pay scale for workers. In 1967 the union led a sixty-eight-day national strike over line speedups and employee benefits, costing Ford the production of five hundred thousand vehicles. The bitterness at the Twin Cities Assembly Plant during a 1976 strike was extraordinary. "It is typical for strikers to talk disparagingly about their employer," wrote Randy Furst of the *Minneapolis Star*, "but at the Ford Motor Company in St. Paul it is more than mere animosity. Many of the workers express outright hatred for management and conditions on the line." Workers complained that management was trying to make up for declining sales by speeding up the line, instituting mandatory overtime, and creating unbearable working conditions. Several workers said the pace was so intense that they could not even open their hands in the morning until they were soaked in ice water. The president of Local 879 said that if a national strike had not been called, there would have been a local walkout. The UAW had amassed a strike fund of $175 million, which was enough to survive a sixteen- or seventeen-week walkout. The strike shut down 102 facilities in twenty-two states, including the Twin Cities plant. It was settled after one month, largely to the benefit of the workers. This would be the last national strike against the Ford Motor Company to this day.

Deming advised Ford that there were no simple solutions. Change required a commitment from everyone to implement the process of "continual improvement" as measured by comprehensive statistical data. Manufacturing was a system, not bits and pieces that could be manipulated into improved outcomes. He preached patience, warning that improvement would take years. Leaders of the United Auto Workers union, like the top management of Ford, recognized the crisis and agreed with the need for change. The painful reality was that Ford and other American automakers were closing plants and laying off workers, and the relentless foreign competition was not about to let up.

In 1980, at the height of the recession and slump in sales, Phillip Caldwell replaced Henry Ford II as chairman of the Ford Motor Company. Robert Shook describes Caldwell's very first board meeting: "he scribbled a note on a piece of paper and proceeded to read it aloud: 'Quality is the number one objective of the Ford Motor Company.' At first there was a silence. Then each of the board members nodded their heads in agreement. This single small act shaped the course of action that was to follow." Tariffs and tax gimmicks could not stem the tide of foreign imports or improve the quality of the American cars. But as Dr. Deming warned, the transformation to quality would take time. Ford's market share continued to drop, from 24 percent in 1978 to 16 percent in 1982, and even slipped to 14 percent in one quarter, keeping just ahead of Chrysler. In 1982, the company paid no dividends for the first time since it went public. Shareholder equity dropped 40 percent and ratings of its commercial paper and creditworthiness sharply declined. Nonetheless, Ford stayed with the commitment to quality and continued to invest in its manufacturing assets. Ford also concluded that it had no choice but to adopt the Japanese model of Total Quality Management (TQM) and Employee Involvement (EI).

A joint delegation of company and union officials visited Japan to get a close-up look at the operations of the "the competition." The trip helped promote a sense of solidarity between Ford and the UAW and officials ahead of the contract talks of 1982 and 1984. Those negotiations, which were described as unusually cordial, produced the Employee Involvement program offering more training opportunities, a profit-sharing plan, concessions from the union on wages, cost-of-living increases worth $1.2 billion, better job security, and a role in the decision-making process for plant closures. Ford had precedents to Employee Involvement, including the suggestion program dating back to 1947, and, to a lesser extent, the "Partners in Progress" (PIP) introduced in 1963. These programs were based on the premise that workers could make meaningful, intelligent contributions. PIP was a top-down effort by Ford, while the UAW and Ford jointly developed EI. Unlike the suggestion program, neither PIP nor EI distributed cash awards directly to workers. The underlying rationale was that improvement suggestions would help the company and therefore be good for employees.

EI was more proactive and collaborative than the suggestion program, with labor and management working side by side. In effect, workers had two tasks: to perform their assigned job well, and to improve the way their job was being done. It was also hoped that a more respectful and collegial work environment would provide a more fulfilling work experience. The EI system did not eliminate the suggestion program—workers were still eligible for a cash award for their individual ideas.

For EI to succeed, supervisors had to share the management role with workers, giving them the responsibility and authority to act as problem solvers. Under the Team Concept, management created small working groups closest to the point of production to study opportunities for continuous improvement. EI required employees to do multiple tasks, with management and labor from different departments and ranks working together. This challenged the job classification system with its hundreds of rigid categories. The new methods created considerable anxiety and resistance from both management and labor. Supervisors felt their authority was undermined. Rank-and-file workers feared that the Team Concept and EI would eliminate not only the job classification system but also seniority rights, which had become even more important with ongoing plant closures. National union leaders, however, felt they had little choice but to collaborate with Ford.

In 1979, the UAW declared, "The new position of the UAW was based on an understanding that the union would develop programs to improve the economic and social conditions of the workforce while also addressing employer concerns about productivity and efficiency. The UAW made it clear that it understood the connection between quality, customer satisfaction, and job security." A number of rank-and-file workers opposed concessions and collaboration in general, which they derided as "jointness." One worker put it simply: "There is the company and there is the union. You do not smudge that line." Some workers believed that profit-sharing plans and signing bonuses would limit pay raises.

For two Local 879 officials with a long history of militant unionism, the transition to collaboration was stunning. Al Hendricks and Bob Killeen were nearing the end of their careers and were alarmed that many of the gains they had helped create were being swept away with the collapse of the auto industry. Both concluded that a new approach was needed. Hendricks had been promoted from Local 879 to the International UAW in Detroit. He served six terms on the National Bargaining Committee assisting Walter Reuther on some of the most important labor negotiations in American history. He became a strong supporter of the Employee Involvement movement and served on the Ford–UAW Joint Committee. He also played a key role in implementing a number of training programs, including one at the Twin Cities plant. These were jointly funded and administered by the company and the union. In the 1982 landmark contract that created Employee Involvement, the UAW agreed to forgo five cents per hour of a pay increase in exchange for Ford's spending that amount on a worker education and training program.

The Development and Training Fund was set up as a separate nonprofit entity, and the pilot program in the Twin Cities provided tuition assistance for any UAW member who wanted to go to school or college. "People used it for most anything," said Hendricks. "Some people went to umpire's school. Some went to diving. Some went to small-engine repair and started a shop in the backyard. You've got to look at this educational thing and go back to Walter Reuther's speech of making a 'total human being.' That stuck with me all the way through this, that a person should have the right to continue on with his education to take him as far as his ability will carry. It should not be a right of economics but a right of a human being and citizen."

The additional training opportunities also helped workers prepare for the inevitable job layoffs. This education benefit was available *only* to the unionized workers—not to salaried or management employees. Hendricks noted the irony that the "hourlies" may have been better prepared: "You go to the unemployment line, they're all standing there together and they're all looking for jobs. There isn't one guy that's one damned bit better . . . There are no different lines there." Hendricks also linked the educational

Over their long careers with UAW Local 879, Bob Killeen and Al Hendricks moved from militant activism to a more collaborative approach with Ford, even as younger union leaders were turning more radical. Killeen, at the podium on left, and Hendricks, with papers at right, are on the stage of the Local 879 union hall. Courtesy of UAW Local 879.

and retraining programs to another important benefit negotiated by the UAW—more advanced notice for plant closures. This would give workers more lead time to pursue retraining options. Lead time would also give workers an opportunity to prepare with customized training if the company planned to install new equipment or machinery, or even to build a new plant. The UAW believed that training programs were good not only for workers but also for the company. For the EI program to be successful, the company needed workers with more skills and a positive attitude.

Bob Killeen became one of the leaders in the Quality Movement in Minnesota. Governor Rudy Perpich appointed him to a commission on the economic future of the state, where he was elected chair of the Subcommittee on Productivity and Quality. One of its members, Lou Schultz, was a management consultant who worked with Deming, and he educated the commission members on Total Quality Management. "We decided," said Killeen, "to ask the governor if we should set up some kind of 'quality college,' some organization within the state, to teach workers, educators, business what the whole quality movement was about." Perpich established the Minnesota Council for Quality and named Killeen cochairman along with Roger Hale from the Tennant Company. An executive on loan from Control Data was appointed to administer the council.

Killeen got to know Deming personally and worked with him on several projects around the country. The UAW applauded Deming's comments about the need to eliminate fear and to instill a more respectful workplace and his opposition to using work standards as a measuring tool. "That's crazy," he said. "Substitute the statistical process control so the part, when it's made and it's shipped, you know every part is right." Killeen remembered parts inspections when he started: "It used to be one guy's job to pick every one up, lift it out of the box, and look for defects. They don't do that [now]. That job is gone." Killeen went around the state and country preaching the quality message, which was shared by many corporate executives. He reflected on his early labor battles, including fights over the classification system, which "bit the companies in the rear end. They were costly, no question about it. I now understand the situation better." He believed that the world had changed dramatically after "the reckoning." Killeen and Hendricks had become cheerleaders for collaboration.

The Unity Caucus and New Directions Oppose Collaboration

While senior UAW leaders in Detroit were moving toward collaboration with Ford, many workers at Local 879 and other locals around the country were going in the opposite direction. They banded together in St. Paul as the Unity Caucus and a decade later nationally under the banner of the New Directions movement. The dissidents believed that the International UAW had lost its will to fight concessions, speedups, and layoffs. They felt the union leadership was no longer the solution but part of the problem. Unhappy members preferred the more strident days of the 1940s when strikes, sit-ins, slowdowns, and a variety of aggressive organizing activities led to the recognition of the UAW. Those struggles also led to a "social contract" between Ford and the UAW, and the government. When auto companies accepted labor unions, they received a legally binding framework for limiting strikes and other labor actions. Unions received the right to negotiate for wages, benefits, and working conditions and gained a process for resolving disputes. Unions also received another enormous benefit—companies collected dues directly from employee paychecks.

Labor had agreed not to strike during World War II, but right after the war embarked on a broad campaign of strikes. Business leaders mounted a counteroffensive and secured political support to rewrite the rules. The Taft-Hartley Act of 1947 restricted a number of union practices, including jurisdictional strikes, wildcat strikes, secondary boycotts, and picketing. Additionally, the federal government was empowered to end illegal strikes, and states were given the right to pass "right-to-work" laws, which prohibited closed shops. Labor power was further trimmed by Supreme Court decisions and rulings of the National Labor Relations Board (NLRB) that outlawed sympathy strikes and gave management the right to hire permanent replacement workers if a strike was deemed illegal. Companies reeling from the economic slump after "the reckoning" moved aggressively to undo the social contract. Labor historian Peter Rachleff captured the shift: "When corporate management and government officials withdrew from the social contract that tied them to 'business unionism,' the system . . . collapsed like a house of cards." According to union dissidents, companies looked to cut costs by speeding up the assembly line, reducing the number of workers, scrimping on quality, cutting wages, outsourcing, laying off workers, and closing plants.

Layoffs were not a problem at St. Paul, as strong demand for the F-Series trucks required a second shift in 1978. Ford had little difficulty hiring workers during a time of high unemployment, even as wages and benefits were being reduced. The new workers were mostly assigned to the second shift, as those with higher seniority preferred the first shift. The day and night shifts at the plant started to take on very different characteristics. The early shift was mostly older white men, while the night shift was younger, had more women, and was more racially diverse. People on both shifts were anxious to keep their jobs, but the younger workers on the night shift had less tolerance for the authoritarian regime—a reflection of the general frustrations spawned by the Vietnam War. The new workers, however, were careful to not signal their frustrations until after completing their ninety-day probationary period. During that time, workers would have to go along with the intensified workplace imposed by Ford.

Several of the new hires had different motivations. They were members of a variety of radical political organizations assigned to infiltrate the plant to build support for their ideology. For many people, the antiwar movement led to a rejection of the entire American political and economic system, which they expressed by joining groups such as Students for Democratic Society (SDS), or communist organizations of a Marxist, Leninist, Trotskyist, or Maoist stripe. Their goal was radical change, and one way to accomplish that, they believed, was to "turn to industry," to organize and convert workers. Among the national leaders in this effort was Jack Barnes, head of the Socialist Workers Party, which he joined as a student at Carleton College. Several well-educated and committed radicals from around the country signed up for the second shift with the intention of organizing industrial workers. They had degrees from the University of Iowa,

In 1978 the St. Paul plant stopped making cars and switched entirely to trucks, assembling the hugely popular F-Series Trucks and Ranger pickup, seen here at a later date. Courtesy of *Highland Villager*.

University of Florida, University of Minnesota, and Dartmouth College, among other schools. They were trained and directed by a hierarchy of national leaders and operated within highly structured groups. They held weekly meetings within their "cells" and reported regularly to their respective national or regional leaders. Rob McKenzie, an organizer at the plant who went on to be president of Local 879, said that national leaders discouraged workers from running for union office for fear they would get so bogged down in handling grievances and other duties that they would eventually lose interest in "the revolution." These fears were not unfounded. Lynn Hinkle, a union committeeman on the night shift, recalled that he had to spend considerable time on such things as finding common ground within his group of three hundred workers on what music could be played aloud on the radio that was respectful of different tastes and cultures. Hinkle, who was raised "dirt poor" in Kansas City, Kansas, attended Dartmouth College, where he became a Marxist-Leninist and full-time student organizer. He moved to Minneapolis in 1969 and worked as a community organizer in the Powderhorn neighborhood in

In the 1970s and 1980s, the workforce at the plant was disgruntled over deteriorating work conditions, giving rise to dissident labor activists. Tom Laney, who gained a large following, is in the center here, with Harry DeBoer, at right, a former Trotskyist who was one of the leaders of the Minneapolis Teamsters strike in 1934. Laney's activism was grounded in Catholic social teaching, not political ideology. Courtesy of Tom Laney.

Minneapolis and founded *Common Ground* magazine before working at Ford. He also became one of the leaders in the Twin Cities Worker Organizing Committee.

The more Ford pressed the workers by speeding up the line, the more workers were open to resistance, whether motivated by ideology or through a personal sense of fair play. Many unhappy workers gravitated toward Tom Laney, who had emerged as a traditional trade-union leader in the plant. He started at Ford in 1972, although he was already familiar with the Local 879 union hall where he attended anti–Vietnam War rallies. Laney formed the Unity Caucus to fight speedups and other abuses. He was a charismatic leader, motivated by personal indignation at the company's escalating pressure—not politics. He was known for his fiery temper and well-honed sense of righteous indignation. Laney was raised in a Catholic family in a small town in Wisconsin, where his father was a respected doctor. He attended a seminary for a while where he was imbued with Catholic teachings on social justice. He served in the army and completed some college before finding himself at the Ford plant in the unlikely role of dissident labor leader surrounded by a cadre of trained communist radicals on a different mission.

These differences in motivation were not impediments to the dissidents working together—at least initially. Laney was respected for his early organizing work and took on the role of mediator to hold the factions together. Working cooperatively, the dissidents organized meetings and distributed newsletters and leaflets. When Laney discovered that Ford was using competition between the first and second shifts as a spur to speeding up the work, he brought both shifts together so workers could compare notes and organize resistance. With his boundless energy and persuasive personality, he developed a considerable following. Laney was elected committeeman in 1978 and was responsible for representing a group of about three hundred workers on the night shift. As labor conditions continued to deteriorate, his visibility and stature soared within the plant, and even nationally. He, and other dissidents from Local 879, moved to the forefront of national efforts within labor to resist concessions, oppose outsourcing, and reshape the workplace. In so doing, Laney was often at odds with union leadership on both the local and national levels.

One of the turning points in the labor battles came from the 1979 taxpayer bailout of the Chrysler Corporation in the form of loan guarantees amounting to $1.5 billion. Politicians, editorial writers, and the general public were clamoring for savings and concessions from "the company," which included workers, in exchange for the loan. The UAW agreed to do its share by accepting wage reductions of three dollars per hour and other contributions valued at $462.5 million. A report done several years later by the Heritage Foundation showed that in spite of the sacrifice, almost half the workforce was cut during the loan period. Autoworkers also soon realized that management's contribution intended to demonstrate "equality of sacrifice" did not work as heralded. The report stated: "Despite the fact that Chrysler lost nearly $500 million in 1981, the Salary Reduction Program ended that year, and executive salaries were restored to their 1979 level. Moreover, the company made retroactive payments to its executives for about two-thirds of the income they lost while the program was in effect." For the UAW to have agreed to reopen Chrysler's labor contract and make significant concessions was unprecedented. Even worse, in agreeing to a lower wage for workers at Chrysler than at Ford or GM, the UAW abandoned its practice of "pattern bargaining" that Walter Reuther used so effectively to whipsaw companies. Carmakers could now use the wage differential to whipsaw workers, and in very short order Ford and GM were demanding concessions comparable to that of Chrysler. Jerry Tucker, a UAW organizer from St. Louis, had long preached that the main purpose of unions was "to take workers' wages out of competition," but this policy abruptly ended with the Chrysler pact.

In St. Paul, Ford intensified pressure on the workers to speed up and in October 1979 nearly four hundred employees were fired or quit. The Unity Caucus, according to an article in *Labor Notes*, "encouraged workers to resist the speedup by timing line speeds, checking the space between cabs, and trying to establish an informal system of line stewards. Their slogan was 'Walk, Don't Run.'" Ford management, and the compliant leadership of Local 879, recognized that Laney and the Unity Caucus were emerging as a serious threat. Ford launched a campaign of surveillance, harassment, suspensions, and firings. When Donna Lapinski was seen wearing a Unity Caucus T-shirt and passing out flyers, she was reassigned to the paint department at the far end of the plant, inaccessible to others. She, and other workers who were harassed, suspended, or fired, were angered that Local 879 did not support their grievances. Caucus leaders knew that if they could not even protect their own members from harassment and terminations, they would be finished as an organization.

About ten members of the Unity Caucus retained Rick Macpherson, a Minneapolis labor lawyer, who filed a complaint with the National Labor Relations Board. Years later, Macpherson remembered: "The case highlighted what Ford and the Local were willing to do to make sure Tom Laney would never be president, and that the Unity Caucus would not achieve power . . . The harassment was blatant." During the discovery phase of the trial, it became clear that Ford had a better collection of Unity Caucus flyers than did its own members. "People knew there was surveillance," said Macpherson, "but had no idea as to extent they were being watched."

The high-stakes trial lasted several months. Dissidents in the Unity Caucus believed that the leadership of Local 879 was actively supporting Ford by helping line up witnesses against them. In the spring of 1981, the presiding judge at the National Labor Relations Board in Minneapolis issued a strong verdict in favor of the Unity Caucus, finding that the management at the Twin Cities Assembly Plant was guilty of engaging in unfair labor practices in 1978 and 1979. *Labor Notes* reported: "Some of the practices include threatening and disciplining workers for talking with their union committeeman, filing grievances, or discussing line speeds and workloads with other workers." Ford was ordered to reinstate one fired worker with back pay, clear the records of two others, and "post a notice in the plant that it would no longer engage in certain unfair labor practices."

The campaign of harassment backfired on Ford as the verdict made Laney a hero to the workers in the plant. Not long after the verdict, he was fired by Ford for "threatening a member of supervision." Laney believed that the punishment he received for that incident was excessive and motivated by his opposition to the "concessions contract" that had been proposed by the International UAW. Before the ratification vote, the president of Local 879 had warned Laney that he would be charged with misrepresenting the contract. Rank-and-file members of Local 879 rebuffed their leadership and rejected the proposed contract, even as it was approved by most locals around the country. Laney was eventually reinstated at Ford after a long grievance process.

Laney was involved in another high-profile dispute before the International UAW Public Review Board. In 1980, Ford announced that it would close an assembly plant in Los Angeles. Upon hearing the news, LeRoy Griffin, the building chairman of Local 879, wrote in the *Autoworker*: "The Los Angeles UAW officials and their membership have been plagued by a self-proclaimed Marxist-Leninist group which has created severe problems for most of the union officials—as well as the company! We have seen over the past years at the Twin Cities [plant] the same tactics and methods of disruption that played a large part in shutting down the Los Angeles assembly plant." The dissident leader at the Los

Angeles plant, Ron Delia, took strong exception to Griffin's comments and called it "red-baiting." Laney, who supported the dissident group in LA, invited Delia to attend the annual Local 879 picnic at a Minneapolis park, which outraged the leadership at Local 879. More than one hundred members of the local were waiting for Delia and disrupted his talk. The next day, the president of Local 879, LeRoy Griffin, wrote to the LA union: "It was made clear to the rump group that Local 879 would not tolerate the infiltration into our local or our area of dissidents from another location . . . Brother Delia was told to 'get his ass out of the Twin Cities area' or face the consequences." Griffin followed this up with an article in the *Autoworker* titled "Blown Away" in which he claimed that Laney and his group were "blown out of" the park. The membership of Local 879 was now at war with itself.

Laney filed a complaint with the International UAW over the uncivil behavior of his local leadership, which he believed was a violation of the UAW Code of Democratic Practices. He was unsuccessful in the early rounds, but a year and a half later the board declared: "The facts . . . convince us beyond any question that the free speech rights of Thomas Laney and other members of the local union . . . were grossly violated." The board also underscored its commitment to the importance of free speech in union matters: "It is apparent that the democratic traditions espoused in the Codes of Ethical Practices could not long survive repetition of the subversion which occurred here." For the second time, Tom Laney had taken the protest outside his local and scored a major victory.

Labor's problems would greatly intensify after President Ronald Regan fired striking air traffic controllers of the PATCO union in 1981. Business leaders felt increasingly empowered by the changing political environment and were no longer worried about strikes. In fact, they welcomed them as an opportunity to fire the workers and destroy the union. Peter Rachleff observed "Companies were willing to tolerate only those unions which agreed to act not as advocates for their members, but as agents for the corporate agenda—by accepting concessions and job reductions and by promoting union–management cooperation in place of an adversarial relationship." In the minds of many workers, the International UAW had become a tool of Ford. One activist said the UAW had taken the attitude that "If you can't beat them, join them. We'll never be able to win another strike, so our only hope is to cooperate with the bosses in advance . . . by becoming junior partners." The concessions kept coming, and the dissidents saw no end to the "controlled retreat." Some argued that UAW leaders were more concerned about keeping their jobs and union dues than protecting the interests of workers. They also believed that Ford's push for a variety of "joint committees" had an ulterior motivation. These independent entities allowed the company to financially reward UAW leaders who supported collaboration, with no accountability to their members. Frustration mounted.

Union members enjoyed the Local 879 annual picnics. Author's collection.

"Why do I need a union to negotiate a wage cut for me?" asked one worker. "I can do that just fine for myself." In the 1980s, union membership in the country declined from twenty-four million to seventeen million. It was described as the bleakest decade for American workers in history. Labor's slide had turned into a rout.

Buoyed by his victories at the NLRB and the UAW National Review Board, Laney announced his candidacy for president of Local 879 as part of a Unity Caucus ticket. He campaigned against EI, quality circles, the Team Concept, and labor–management cooperation in general, which he claimed was mainly intended to co-opt the voice of the workers. He paraphrased Benjamin Franklin in describing collaboration: "It was like two wolves and a lamb voting on what to have for dinner." Workers would not share in the benefits of increased productivity: they would be laid off because of those gains. Dissidents also believed that Ford would take employee suggestions and implement them at nonunion plants, making them even more competitive. More than 250,000 jobs in the

American auto industry were lost during the previous decade, and the Unity Caucus ridiculed the notion that Ford had their interests at heart. They felt workers had made many efforts over the years to improve quality and were ignored, and they believed it was disingenuous for management to suddenly be waving the quality banner. In 1984, Laney and his team were elected. On January 15, 1985, at the first meeting of his executive team, Laney passed out an eight-page outline of the "Pastoral Letter on Catholic Social Teaching and the U.S. Economy." He was determined to take Local 879 in a new direction. He was not a political ideologue, but he was shaped by a value system that may have had more in common with his communist allies than he would admit.

"The Solidarity of lineworkers was a powerful force," Laney wrote, "and each time the company cut jobs out of the line and passed the work to those jobs that remained . . . we managed to leave this extra work undone. Within a couple of weeks the cut jobs were reinstated, the war was ended, civility returned." Aggressive action, and even acts of civil disobedience, had returned to the playbook. For precedent, Laney pointed to the massive sit-in strike at GM that created the UAW. Gregg Shotwell, a national dissident leader and

Tom Laney helped form the dissident labor group Unity Caucus and won the presidency of Local 879 in 1984. He is pictured here in the middle of the first row with his leadership team. Courtesy of UAW Local 879.

friend of Laney's, described the militant attitude of the early union leaders: "Back in the day, there wouldn't have been any discussion when 41 workers were fired. Production would have slowed to a gut-shot crawl. One car less for each worker fired. The code, '41 for 41,' would have spread like a virus, infecting every twist and turn, lift and tote, down the line." For Laney, the concept of solidarity applied to other unions and social-justice causes. He was tireless in providing "strike support" for other campaigns, even before he became president. He joined the fight against farm foreclosures, and supported Cesar Chavez's efforts to unionize farmworkers—Chavez stayed with the Laney family when campaigning in Minnesota. In 1981, Laney picketed on behalf of striking cafeteria workers at Carleton College in Northfield, Minnesota, where he befriended a young professor named Paul Wellstone. Under Laney's leadership, Local 879 provided strong support in 1985 to the P-9 meatpacking union at the Hormel plant in Austin, Minnesota. The P-9 strikers were given a rousing rally at the UAW 879 Hall in St. Paul. A Twin Cities support committee was formed and St. Paul autoworkers joined the picket lines in Austin. They sent food caravans to striking workers and supported boycotts against Hormel and its corporate partners.

The strike received national attention and considerable sympathy and support, but it was difficult to overcome the anti-worker sentiment of the 1980s. Rudy Perpich, the Democratic-Farmer-Labor (DFL) governor of Minnesota, called in the National Guard in 1986 to break up the strike against Hormel and allow access by "scab" workers. It was reported that Perpich consulted with several labor leaders before proceeding, including Bob Killeen from the UAW. Ford workers ended up on both sides of the final face-off. Several were in the National Guard that had been called up for duty. They were directed to shoot tear gas into the crowd of picketers, which included a sizable number of their fellow workers from the Twin Cities Assembly Plant. One striker said he was sure that the Ford National Guard members were intentionally missing their targets.

Laney's solidarity with other unions would sometimes be reciprocated. In 1985 there was a bottleneck unloading new cars from the tri-level railcars, which the union blamed on a shortage of workers. Ford was under intense pressure to get these cars to its dealers and decided to reroute the trains to the Milwaukee Road Terminal where they would be unloaded by Teamster workers. Laney had earlier supported Teamster strikes and developed a sense of solidarity with them, which they remembered. The Teamsters refused to unload the cars and they were sent back to the Ford plant.

Union locals and dissident workers who opposed concessions were disciplined by the International UAW leadership. One analyst observed that while the union locals operated in true democratic fashion, things were very different in Detroit: "Dissent on policy was barely tolerated, and opposition to anointed candidates ruthlessly crushed." Increasingly, the fight was between the UAW leadership and reformers at all levels. Autoworkers at Ford plants in Canada refused to go along with concessions, and when the International UAW tried to exert control, they seceded. In 1985 they formed their own national labor organization, the Canadian Auto Workers. This further intensified pressure on American UAW officials, who were now dealing with a serious internal rebellion by New Directions. This group was founded by Jerry Tucker, a union leader in St. Louis who had built a reputation nationally for several successful organizing campaigns. He had risen from head of his local to regional director in the International UAW. He opposed concessions and advocated for a variety of strategies that echoed those of Laney's Unity Caucus. Knowing that a strike was not a viable option, he argued, "Don't let the bastards provoke you into striking! Stay inside. Learn to 'run the plant backwards.' Trust the knowledge and ingenuity of the rank and file to figure out how to make the plant ungovernable while mobilizing new forces and new allies to support you at the bargaining table."

Tucker put the responsibility for action on the workers at the local level, on the shop floor—and not through the national UAW leaders. He asked, "Where are the possible bottlenecks in production?" "What are the crucial points in the production process?" "If we are to tame management by using our intimate knowledge of how work gets done, where is the tip of the spear?" The New Directions group also rallied around the concept of "horizontal solidarity," which harkened back to the philosophy of Walter Reuther. The UAW should represent the interests of the entire working class and the community, not just its members. It should link up with other campaigns promoting social and economic justice. Believing they had inherited the founder's mantle, New Directions leaders did not see themselves as "dissidents" but as adherents to the original vision. They sneeringly referred to the international union as "the New UAW." Tucker formally broke with the International UAW leadership and ran for president, which Laney and his colleagues strongly supported. Tucker's rebellion threatened to tear apart what was once the most powerful union in the world.

With the labor movement reeling from its internal conflicts, companies were preparing to deliver the knockout blow. Eliminating the strike option and forcing concessions significantly weakened the UAW and other unions, but the new threats of "outsourcing" and "offshoring" threatened their very existence. American multinational companies created almost as many jobs in Mexico from 1986 through 1990 as they did in the United States—and this was four years before the North American Free Trade Agreement (NAFTA) was even implemented. American companies invested heavily in an area in Mexico along the American border, known as the Maquiladora, which was established as a free-trade zone. Mexican autoworkers were making around 10 percent of their American counterparts. After NAFTA went into effect in 1994, imports jumped 235 percent and the United States lost three million manufacturing jobs.

Ford did not reduce prices of cars made in Mexico to reflect lower labor costs. In fact, there were studies that showed the wage differential had relatively little impact on the price of the imported car. Even if prices were reduced, it probably would not have been the determining factor in a buyer's decision. It was about quality, not price, as Henry Ford learned chasing the Chevrolet with his lower-priced Model T. Workers were particularly irate that executive bonuses and compensation packages did not figure into the conversation about "competitiveness." The threat to close plants in the United States and transfer operations to Mexico and other countries was very real, and it cast a shadow over all labor negotiations. It became clear that car companies would not relent until American labor costs competed with those in foreign countries.

Tom Laney argued that "ten-dollar-a-day" workers in Mexico eliminated a hundred thousand American jobs over the previous decade. "The UAW doesn't have a clue about

Widespread frustration over a variety of political, economic, and cultural issues in the 1980s and 1990s led to unrest on the plant floor and on the streets. Local 879 autoworkers marched in many demonstrations with banners proclaiming their support of the labor struggle, including this one in St. Paul. Author's collection.

what to do about NAFTA." Laney believed that labor unions should be organized internationally, to keep pace with American car companies: "We should provide funding for democratic reform in [Mexican] unions. It would increase wages and benefits and make the labor market a little more level." He led efforts to create alliances with his Mexican counterparts and sponsored exchange trips between the countries. He also decried the abysmal human-rights record in Latin America, where labor organizers at Ford and other industrial plants were routinely beaten, jailed, and sometimes murdered. Leaders at the International UAW strongly opposed Laney's international organizing efforts and criticized the fourteen thousand dollars in Local funds spent on exchange visits between Minnesota and Mexico. Solidarity, to Laney, had a moral and even a spiritual dimension: "The UAW was telling us that some of us had to go and the rest of us had to work harder to compete first with the Japanese and later with everyone who needs a decent job. In 1982, we lost the fight for Solidarity amongst ourselves. We lost the fight for Solidarity with the Japanese. In 1984, we lost the fight for Solidarity with our own Canadian members as they abandoned the UAW's dog-eat-dog philosophy. In the 1990s we lost the fight to stop the assassination of Mexican Ford workers. Basically, we lost the fight for the respect and love one worker has for another. We lost the fight for the Christian belief that God wants us to be fulfilled by our jobs. All of us."

Laney's comments about assassination were referring to the 1990 murder of Cleto Nigmo, who worked at a Ford plant in Cuautitlán, Mexico. He was part of a sit-in strike protesting a new labor contract that had been accepted by his "official" union. Ford had unilaterally canceled an existing labor agreement and laid off its 3,700 workers. The company then substituted a replacement contract with substantial wage cuts and other concessions. This prompted the workers to disaffiliate from the state-run union. Ford favored the "official" union and opposed efforts to create a locally controlled, democratic union. On January 8, 1990, more than one hundred armed men stormed the plant to break up the strike. Eight workers were shot, including Nigmo, who died several days later.

Workers at Local 879 were among the first in the country to hear about the incident. They had been monitoring labor and human-rights abuses in Mexico and Latin America through several unlikely channels. Bert Rubash, a millwright at the plant and an early technophile, found a way to connect to an international "peacenet" communications system. He learned of Nigmo's murder and, with the assistance of Spanish-speaking workers at the plant, understood that this was far more consequential than "an intra-union dispute," as described by the *New York Times*. Rubash was one of a group of extremely intelligent and committed activists at Local 879. He went on to earn degrees in physics and French literature from the University of Minnesota. Another activist, Donna Lapinski, was a graduate of the University of Minnesota who spoke Spanish and taught English in

Tom Laney lost his reelection bid to head Local 879 but was later elected committeeman and remained active in the union. He supported labor rights in Mexico as the answer to globalization and made several trips befriending labor leaders in the early 1990s. He is pictured with Raul Escobar and his family. Courtesy of Tom Laney.

Mexico for several years before starting at Ford. She was one of the complainants in the lawsuit decided by the NLRB. As a result of that experience, she went to law school and is now practicing immigration law.

A parallel channel to Latin America had opened through a network of Catholic social-justice activists. In 1980, four Catholic clergy were executed in El Salvador by "death squads" who were trained at the School of the Americas at Fort Benning, Georgia, an American combat-training school for military personnel from Latin America. An American priest, Roy Bourgeois, was doing ministry work in Bolivia and had known several of the victims. He was expelled by a dictator who was also educated at the School of the Americas. Bourgeois launched an international campaign to close the School of the Americas. On Thanksgiving Day 1989, he brought his campaign to the St. Paul Cathedral, where he went on a twenty-day hunger strike. Bob Killeen, a devout Catholic, joined Bourgeois at the cathedral to show solidarity. Killeen had visited several Latin American countries and learned firsthand of the oppression. He joined Veterans for Peace in Minnesota in its ongoing campaign to close the School of the Americas. Although retired from the union, he helped organize UAW demonstrations at the Minnesota state capitol opposing the military juntas. Labor activists believed that these murders and other repressive actions were intended to stifle labor democracy at a time American manufacturers were shifting production to Latin America.

A third channel to news from Latin America came from the sizable number of retirees who had moved to warmer climes along the Mexican border. Their local newspapers often had accounts of events just a few miles south, which retirees would send back to Local 879. These varied channels of communication before the age of the Internet enabled leaders at Local 879 to become knowledgeable about working conditions in Latin America and the implications of free trade. Because of personal connections to people on the front lines, they certainly had a more complete picture of events than leaders at the International UAW, and probably even than the American media at the time.

Local 879 mounted a remarkable campaign during the next several years to publicize the murder of Cleto Nigmo and to push for improved conditions for Mexican autoworkers. This developed into one of the first organizing campaigns in the country around the issue of human rights and fair trade. In October 1990, Tom Laney and Jose Quintana, from Local 879, visited the striking workers at Cuautitlán and made plans to bring several leaders to Minnesota. Later that year, Ted LaValley, the president of Local 879, used the festive occasion of a Ford Q-1 (Quality) Award presentation at the Twin Cities plant to speak of Nigmo's murder to the assembled leaders of Ford and the International UAW. He minced no words: "Does Q-1 by itself bring plant security? No. We've seen right here in the U.S. plants have been closed that have gained the Q-1 recognition. Nor does it mean labor relations problems will go away . . . where at Cuautitlán, Mexico, which also has a [Q-1] flag waving over their complex, there's blood on the floor inside that plant." Earlier

Leaders in the UAW and other unions opposed American foreign policy in Latin America, which they believed favored American corporate interests over the human rights of workers. The UAW led a rally at the Minnesota state capitol protesting American involvement in El Salvador in the 1990s. Courtesy of Tom Laney.

in the award ceremony, an official from the International UAW spoke to the large group and said workers should look "to protect the profits of the Ford Motor Company." This was not the message Ted LaValley, Tom Laney, and other leaders at Local 879 wanted to hear. They were committed to the more confrontational path taken by strikers in Cuautitlán, Mexico, and the Hormel plant in Austin, Minnesota. Their fight was not just against the companies; it was against their own international unions.

On January 8, 1991, the first anniversary of Nigmo's death, two thousand workers at the Twin Cities Assembly Plant wore black ribbons with his name, demanding an explanation from Ford for his murder. These were made by the Canadian Auto Workers as an expression of solidarity with their NAFTA partners. Later that month, Local 879 organized a conference at Macalester College titled "Competition vs. Solidarity in an Era of Free Trade," attracting experts and activists from around the country. This was billed as the first conference held on North American trade issues. One of the speakers, David Morris, succinctly explained the challenge: "Businesses always search for the weakest social contract." The Minnesota Fair Trade Coalition grew out of that conference. In April 1991, a busload of activists from Minnesota, including Tom Laney, Ted LaValley, and Rod Haworth from Local 879, went to Chicago to testify at the U.S. International Trade Commission hearings on NAFTA. After the hearing, Laney and LaValley flew directly to Mexico to meet with anti-NAFTA organizers. In March 1991, several workers from the Cuautitlán plant were brought to Minnesota by Local 879, but it took some effort, as they were initially denied travel visas. A staff person in Minnesota Congressman Jim Oberstar's office explained the holdup to Laney: "Tom, the State Department is saying these men are Communists." Laney responded: "Well the world's biggest Communist [Mikhail Gorbachev] is now touring St. Paul and people seem to love him. All I can tell you about our Mexican friends is that they make perfect sense to Union people." The workers from the Cuautitlán plant were finally given visas.

When introduced to a huge rally at the Local 879 union hall, one official said, "We went to Mexico thinking that we could help these workers, that we could teach them how to organize their union, but when we got there, we discovered that our Mexican brothers understood unionism far better than most of us did." When in St. Paul, the Cuautitlán workers also met with Paul Wellstone, the newly elected senator. Laney and other members of Local 879 were early and strong supporters of candidate Wellstone, who formally launched his campaign in 1990 at the Local 879 union hall. Laney hosted a fund-raising event at his home, and autoworkers painted the famous green bus that Wellstone used to travel around the state. Senator Wellstone followed up the meeting with the Mexican autoworkers with strongly worded letters to the U.S. State Department and the president

More than one hundred armed men broke up a sit-in strike at a Mexican Ford plant in 1990. They shot eight workers, killing Cleto Nigmo. Local 879 led the planning for an international memorial event on the first anniversary of Cleto's murder. Ford workers wore ribbons and armbands in the plant that read "Solidarity and Struggle for Justice. Cleto Nigmo Remembered Jan. 8, 1990." Courtesy of Tom Laney.

Tom Laney met Professor Paul Wellstone at a Carleton College rally supporting cafeteria workers who were on strike. When Wellstone ran for the U.S. Senate in 1990, Laney and Local 879 were early supporters and painted his green campaign bus. Laney is at far right; Bob Killeen, long retired from the union but still active in political causes, is third from the left. Courtesy of Tom Laney.

of Mexico inquiring about the murder of Cleto Nigmo and the broader issue of human rights violations.

In April 1991, representatives from Local 879 made a presentation at the *Labor Notes* national convention in Detroit on labor conditions in Mexico. In May, Tom Laney, Jose Quintana, and Bill McGaughey, a Minneapolis fair-trade activist, filed a complaint with the office of the U.S. trade representative charging human-rights violations by the Mexican government. McGaughey was later selected as an international observer for the court-ordered union election at the Cuautitlán plant, along with Skip Pepin of Local 879. On May 9, 1991, a group from Local 879 attended the Ford annual shareholders meeting in Detroit and Tom Laney spoke about the murder of Cleto Nigmo and raised questions about Ford's culpability. The shocked Ford CEO, Red Poling, denied that Ford had any responsibility. A second conference on fair trade was held at Macalester College in September 1991. Leaders from New Directions attended, including Jerry Tucker and Pete Kelly, who asked, "When American workers agree to work for three bowls of rice a day, what will happen when someone else in the world agrees to work for two?"

The strategy of Tom Laney and Jerry Tucker to take a more confrontational approach in the United States to stop plant closings and concessions and to push for better wages and labor standards overseas did not work. Multinational corporations continued to expand abroad, and tariffs continued to be reduced or eliminated. Capital and jobs fled the United States at an alarming rate. Laney, Tucker, and other dissident leaders were rejected by union members afraid of losing their jobs. Workers made it clear that they were willing to accept lower wages and other concessions to keep their jobs. The International UAW consolidated

Tom Laney and Local 879 arranged for several dissident labor leaders from the Mexican Ford plant, including Raul Escobar and Jose Martinez, to meet with the newly elected Senator Paul Wellstone, who took up their cause. Courtesy of Tom Laney.

its grasp on power and intensified its cooperation with Ford, but this did not end the plant closings. Doug Fraser, a retired president of the UAW, wrote: "Where industry once yearned for subservient unions, it now wants no unions at all."

Ford Taurus-Sable

Most union locals around the country participated in the Employee Involvement program—but not Local 879, which voted to withdraw its support in the mid-1980s. Ford would have to implement it without its help. The value of EI to Ford was clearly demonstrated in the development of new Taurus-Sable cars, which was well documented by William Shook in his book *Turnaround: The New Ford Motor Company*. The Taurus was a completely new car, built by a completely overhauled company. Ford committed in 1979 to be competitive again and invested $5 billion in the turnaround, revolutionizing the company and the American auto industry. A team approach was used for design and development, involving people "upstream" and "downstream," including company officials, workers, suppliers, dealers, and even customers. The development proceeded *concurrently*, not *sequentially*. Early in the process, the Taurus team visited the Atlanta assembly plant and received more than 1,400 suggestions from line workers, more than half of which were adopted. Ford even consulted with collision repair mechanics on the design of the Taurus, which helped make it easier and cheaper to fix. The Taurus was introduced in 1986 and became the best-selling midsize car in the United States. It had an outstanding customer satisfaction rate—more than 94 percent said they would buy another Ford car. The Taurus was named one of the top ten cars in 1986, 1987, and 1988, its first three years, and received car of the year honors in 1988. This was a stunning turn-about for an American company. Taurus assembly plants were running two ten-hour shifts to meet demand for the first time in thirty years. In 1987, Ford earned $4.62 billion, an industry record, vaulting past General Motors for the top spot. It maintained the lead for the next several years. Ford averaged about twenty-two worker hours to assemble a vehicle, compared to thirty-six worker hours for GM, which went on to close twenty-one factories and eliminate seventy-four thousand jobs. The Taurus likely saved the Ford Motor Company, including the Twin Cities Assembly Plant, and the Employee Involvement program was given most of the credit.

Ford CEO Donald Petersen later wrote a book, *A Better Idea: Redefining the Way Americans Work*, which included a number of EI case studies, including a section on St. Paul. At the Twin Cities truck plant:

> A group of employees in the plant's paint area formed a dirt-in-paint team in mid-1988. The team included hourly maintenance workers, outside suppliers, and a couple of salaried supervisors. When the team was formed, quality surveys showed that more than 6 percent of the trucks produced at the plant were affected by dirt in their paint. The team studied the quality surveys in depth and used statistics to isolate the source of the dirt where possible. In late 1989, the team invited the supplier that provided the company with air filters to join the team as an active member, and he provided the expertise to rid the air in the plant of dust and dirt that might contaminate the paint. The team also decided to buy new tools and equipment, including a laser dirt counter that identifies the location and sources of dirt and a hardened steel wedge to remove dirt without creating sanding dust. They also purchased a humidifier system to clean the air and Kanibo sponges to swab the vehicle bodies. By June 1990, the percentage of trucks with dirty paint dropped to less than one percent; the number of trucks with defects related to dirt in the paint plummeted by 76 percent in two years.

Members of New Directions saw no reason to let up in their fight against EI, still convinced that the benefits of "jointness" were short-term and illusory. Their movement represented a very small percentage of the UAW membership, on both the national and local levels, but their intensity continued to spur debate. At a labor conference in St. Paul in early 1993, it was reported that most of the three hundred–plus in attendance felt that

Ford continued to invest in the Twin Cities plant, installing a new paint shop in 1985 with sophisticated environmental equipment. Courtesy of Dan Huseby.

cooperative worker–management initiatives were "all bad news for union members." But national UAW representative Tom Schneider argued that the joint education, health, and safety programs were "overall . . . good for UAW employees and good for Ford Motor Company." He added that in the recent UAW presidential election the New Directions candidate drew only 5 percent of the vote. "I don't believe you have to have a continuous adversarial relationship with management. I think they [New Directions] prefer the hammering on table and swearing at each other of the '40s and '50s, but that's not applicable today." Jim Buckman, executive director of the Minnesota Council for Quality, concurred, saying that opponents of worker-management programs were "living in the past." Given the precarious economic conditions, most workers felt they had little choice but to go along with the Employee Involvement program. The industry was too fragile and there was too much fear. Rod Haworth, president of Local 879 and once a member of New Directions, eventually came around to support a more collaborative approach, but he was cautious: "Partnerships are fine, but both sides need to be partners from an equal power base . . . then the union not only has the ability to say 'yes,' it also has the ability to say 'no.'"

As Ford and the UAW continued to circle each other looking for some tactical advantage, car sales continued to slide. Momentum from the success of the Taurus could not be sustained because the company reverted to the historical pattern of forgetting or ignoring the important lessons learned. The cycle of boom and bust continued. For the workers, competition with Japanese auto companies became bitter and personal. In a widely publicized report, a high-ranking Japanese official said that American workers were lazy, that many can't read, and that they were basically the subcontractors for Japan. He added: "If America doesn't watch out, it is going to be judged by the world as finished." This caused considerable anger at the St. Paul assembly plant. "This right now for me is war," said one worker. "For me it was a slap in the face, an insult. When he said that, he was going after my job. Most Americans will see this as a major insult, and the Japanese will rue the day they started talking like this. There's going to be a backlash."

Local 879 president Rod Haworth added: "It's a very arrogant, nationalist thing they are saying. It's a ploy to separate us, to cause divisions among the American people. There already is this great prejudice against the American auto worker because of the wages we make—as if it is a sin to make a living wage. Now they are throwing fuel on the fire—at the same time they're [the Japanese] having problems with worker stress and worker suicide." At its annual summer picnic, Local 879 displayed a junk Toyota and invited people "to plunk down a dollar to take a swing at the enemy vehicle with a sledgehammer."

In 1941, American companies made 75 percent of all cars in the world, but by 1990 this had dropped to 20 percent. Shifting production to other countries to save on labor costs didn't solve the problem because those savings weren't even applied to lowering the price of the car. Outsourcing also enabled those countries to learn the technologies and skills needed to eventually develop their own domestic industry. President Ronald Reagan sought to make American exports more competitive by devaluing the dollar, but this enabled foreign investors to use the cheap dollar to buy up American assets. In sum, policy makers tried a lot of gimmicks but nothing worked. Robert Perrucci wrote there was a failure to institute the "traditional and accepted way of seeking new markets, investing in research and development, and developing more efficient technology." The U.S. Department of Transportation analyzed the decline of the American auto industry and published a scathing report titled "The U.S. Automobile Industry, 1980." Making cars had become a collaborative effort involving the auto companies, the union, and the government—and the report assigned blame to each for the sorry state of the industry. It debunked the claim that wage disparity between American and foreign autoworkers was the main cause of the problem: "The greatest source of Japanese advantage is structural:

process and product technology which yield major productivity gains. U.S. management must commit major resources to matching those productivity accomplishments if our industry is to regain competitive health."

Some critics, including Perrucci, felt that American companies "had no intention of trying to compete with the Japanese to recapture market share." Car companies only wanted to make higher profits on the share of the market they controlled. To distract from this strategy, and to keep up the pressure on foreign automakers, union officials, corporate executives, and politicians promoted the notion that it was time for those companies to build cars and trucks in the United States. "Thus were born the transplants," wrote Perrucci, employing a term widely used to describe foreign companies setting up plants in the United States.

Foreign manufacturers recognized the economic benefits of bypassing tariffs and saving on transportation costs, as well as the political benefits of bringing jobs to the United States. Wages at the first six transplant companies in the United States were considerably lower than those paid by American auto companies. Only two plants were unionized. The Japanese "just-in-time" manufacturing system required "production networks" to cluster around their plants, which further magnified the economic impact of the transplants. Suppliers had to make deliveries within two to eight hours. They were mostly nonunion, Japanese-owned companies, and they typically hired nonunion contractors to build their plants. It was estimated that for every new job at a transplant company, two American jobs were lost. This did not deter competition among the states to attract the transplant companies.

Economic Development Incentives for Plant Locations

By 2005, more than twenty "transplant" companies had opened plants in the United States, mostly along the I-65 corridor running north–south from Michigan to Alabama. Foreign companies knew they were attractive economic development prizes and they shopped around for financial incentives, which often led to bidding wars between "entrepreneurial states." Pennsylvania won a Volkswagen plant with 2,500 workers by providing $71 million in low-interest loans, rail and highway improvements, job recruiting, and tax abatements. (That plant was later closed.) In at least one case, American tax dollars given to a Japanese transplant depleted retraining funds for laid-off American workers. For American unionized autoworkers, competing with low-wage foreign companies was one thing, but to compete against foreign companies making cars in this country was a disaster. Appealing to patriotic instincts was ineffectual, as the line between foreign and

Congressman Bruce Vento is shown around the plant by Ted LaValley from Local 879. Courtesy of Tom Laney.

American cars became impossibly blurred. The *Minneapolis Star Tribune* asked, "Is it preferable to buy a car from a U.S. Company that is made in Canada or Mexico, where cheaper labor doesn't help laid-off U.S. workers, or to buy a Japanese company's car made in the United States, where U.S. auto-workers make a living?" This became "a confounding argument to the buy-America types."

American companies learned from their foreign competitors and asked for similar subsidies when expanding or relocating. When GM announced plans in the mid-1980s to build a $3.5 billion Saturn plant with six thousand workers, offers came pouring in from twenty-seven states with generous "giveaway packages." The intense recruiting campaign culminated on national television with Phil Donahue hosting GM chair Roger Smith and seven governors in a "Let's Make a Deal" format. Minnesota governor Rudy Perpich, who was among those participating, said, "This is probably the biggest prize to come along in a decade." Perpich's offer to GM reportedly amounted to a staggering billion dollars in benefits, including $30 million to acquire a proposed site in Cottage Grove, a waiver of sales tax on equipment or materials, and a waiver of taxes on property and corporate income. For good measure, it included nearly $100 million in mortgage subsidies to assist in executive relocations, as well as a day-care center for employees. Finally, Perpich offered to create a Center for Advanced Manufacturing Studies to be managed by the University of Minnesota and a $20-million vocational school for Saturn employees. Reporters questioned the fairness of offering benefits that were not available to existing companies in the state or the equity of subsidizing mortgages for high-income executives. Minnesota's bid fell short and GM decided to build at Spring Hill, Tennessee. (Perpich's offer to build a manufacturing and training facility could possibly have been the basis for a similar proposal a decade later to keep the Ford plant in St. Paul.) Perpich's Saturn campaign took place within months of his calling in the National Guard to break up the Hormel strike. In his efforts to recruit GM and other companies, he was determined to make Minnesota appear more business-friendly.

Economic development officials generally perceived unions as liabilities as foreign companies made it clear they intended to locate in right-to-work states. The percentage of unionized workers in the United States dropped from a high of 35 percent in the mid-1950s to single digits. The plummeting membership in the UAW depleted its coffers, but the union stayed committed to a cooperative approach with Ford. Presumably, it accepted the reasoning of economist Michael Rothschild, who wrote: "The worst crime against working people is a company that fails to operate at a profit." Without a strong and competitive company, the UAW feared there would be no jobs and perhaps no union. After the 1973 oil embargo, Ford and the UAW lobbied together for exemptions from mileage standards and regulatory exemptions for light trucks. In 1984, Chrysler introduced the minivan, which it was able to define as a light truck, making it exempt from mileage standards. In 1990, Ford launched the SUV boom with the Explorer model, which also received favorable regulatory rulings and tax incentives. Small trucks and large cars were the mainstay of the American auto industry, and for the next two decades the auto companies and the UAW worked together to defeat attempts to lessen tax incentives or environmental exemptions. The *New York Times* published a report in 1997, "License to Pollute," that documented this web of special federal protections only available to trucks and SUVs. Many of these exemptions, regulations, and tax breaks are still in effect, although the impact is reduced with the arrival of the transplant companies. In an ironic twist, Ford and other American companies that are producing vehicles abroad for the domestic market are subject to the "Chicken Tariff."

F-Series Trucks and Ranger Compacts

The Twin Cities Assembly Plant produced trucks, along with cars, from the time it opened in 1926, but in 1978 it was converted to all trucks. Employees were extremely fortunate to be assigned the F-Series pickup trucks and Ranger compact trucks, which were consistently top-selling vehicles. These vehicles were also more profitable per unit than cars. Sales of trucks in the United States doubled during the 1980s to five million, and Ford captured an impressive 30 percent market share. The Ford F-Series and Ranger pickup trucks were among the top-selling vehicles in North America, and the F-Series ranked number one for ten straight years. The Twin Cities plant produced 20 percent of Ford's trucks, working two ten-hour shifts to meet the demand. In spite of the strong sales, Ford complained that five Japanese companies were illegally dumping small trucks on the American market, selling them for 10 to 48 percent less than in their home market. In 1990, the Twin Cities plant turned out 164,000 Rangers and F-series trucks, averaging nine hundred units per day. That year the company upgraded the plant, making it the only "swing plant" that could build three models—the F-Series, Ranger, and Ranger Supercab.

The Twin Cities plant supplied Rangers to the entire North American market, while a plant in Thailand supplied the rest of the world. The origin and evolution of the Ranger truck illustrated the ways in which the global economy transformed manufacturing. In the 1960s, Ford invested in Mazda, based in Hiroshima, Japan, and it increased its ownership share to as high as 33.4 percent. Ford was mainly interested in learning the secrets of Japanese manufacturing, but it also had a special interest in Mazda's small pickup trucks called the B Series, which started production in 1961. Ford copied this model and introduced it into the North American market in 1972 under the name Ford Courier. A decade later, Ford modified the design, changed its name, and in 1982 started making Ranger pickups at its Louisville and Edison, New Jersey, plants. (Ford had already been producing an F-Series truck with the name Ranger, which it appropriated for the compact pickup.) The Edison plant made both the Ranger and the virtually identical Mazda B truck. The Mazda B was also produced in Thailand and sold throughout Asia, sometimes under the Ford Ranger brand. By 1987, the Ranger had become the best-selling compact pickup truck in America, a distinction it held for eighteen years.

The market for the Ranger truck was strong but volatile, requiring Ford to regularly adjust employment levels. In 1989, Ford temporarily laid off two thousand workers in St. Paul and three thousand in Louisville because of slow sales. The Twin Cities plant went from two ten-hour shifts to two eight-hour shifts for the first time in six years, and the plant was idled for a month at the end of 1990. By March 1991 the plant had been idled

The Twin Cities plant was the only Ford facility that could build three truck models: the F-Series, Ranger, and Ranger Supercab. Author's collection.

nine of the previous sixteen months. To meet market demand Ford sometimes shifted production of models from one plant to another. The Ford Explorer, for example, was made in Louisville at a plant that also made Ranger trucks. When the company decided to increase production of the hugely successful Explorer, it moved Ranger production to two other plants, in Edison, New Jersey, and St. Paul. This meant that the best-selling F-Series trucks, which St. Paul had been making for more than thirty years, would be dropped in 1992. Workers were concerned, as Ted LaValley of Local 879 explained: "If there is only one line, the operation of the plant is totally dictated by sales on that one unit." More models meant more security. The Local negotiated an agreement with Ford to leave the F-Series assembly-line equipment in place just in case there might be future need.

In 1991, as the Twin Cities plant prepared to stake its future solely on Ranger compacts, the American auto industry had a manufacturing "overcapacity" of six million cars, leading to a new round of plant closures around the country. The final full-sized truck made in St. Paul was the Northland Edition pickup, which was designed to commemorate the seventy-fifth anniversary of F-Series trucks. The plant closed for

In the 1960s, Ford acquired a significant financial interest in Mazda, a Japanese company, and the Twin Cities plant built Mazda pickup trucks, which were essentially the same as the Ranger. Workers must have had conflicted feelings about making trucks for their Asian rivals, as evidenced by the racially offensive sign greeting the first Mazda produced at the plant in the 1980s. Author's collection.

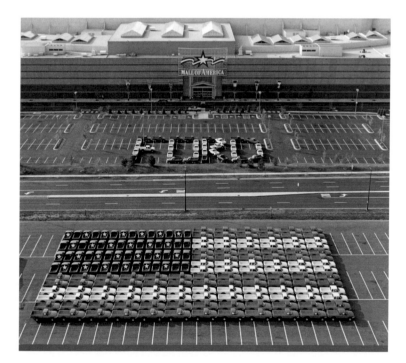

The Ranger pickup truck was enormously popular, and Minnesota dealers celebrated the iconic best-selling vehicle with a display of red, white, and blue Rangers in the form of a big flag parked at the Mall of America in Bloomington, Minnesota. Author's collection.

four months for a $96 million retooling for the new compact pickup. The first extended-cab Ranger STX rolled off the line in April 1992. It featured a four-liter V6 engine with a four-speed automatic transmission. It also had "fully articulated bucket seats, a full console, power windows and locks, a sliding rear window, jump seats that fold out of the sides of the extended cap, air conditioning, a package with a stereo-cassette, cruise control, and tilt steering." The auto reporter for the *Minneapolis Star Tribune*, John Gilbert, couldn't contain his hometown pride: "We can't be certain that the Rangers built in St. Paul are a cut above the rest. But deep down, we're pretty sure they are." The Ranger was the best-selling compact pickup truck in the country, and the Twin Cities Assembly Plant produced about half of the models sold. Strong sales prompted Ford to hire additional workers in St. Paul. In 1996, Ford made 157,415 Rangers, and that figured doubled by 1998. That year approximately 1,800 workers assembled approximately forty-seven vehicles per hour. More than six hundred separate tasks occurred on the assembly line, and by then most of the jobs were computerized.

During the 1980s, Ford distributed more than $24 million in profit sharing, averaging twelve thousand dollars per worker. During that time, autoworkers at GM and Chrysler received little or no profit sharing. Ford workers did not receive bonuses from 1991 to 1993, but in 1998 they received a record payout of $4,400. "It makes you feel good," said one worker, "to get a nice check like that. When management and workers get together, we can maybe get a little more." Another said, "I can't tell you how many times people will walk by, pick up a loose screw on the floor and say, 'profit sharing.'"

With the decline of the American auto industry, union members rejected more militant labor positions in favor of collaboration with Ford. However, they continued to support progressive causes, including civil rights, equal employment opportunities, and environmental sustainability. Many talented artists worked at the Ford plant, including Richard Magnuson, who drew this cover for the Local 879 magazine. Author's collection.

While most were enthusiastic, some workers felt that the payments were just the return of hourly raises that they had given up in early contracts. Additionally, compensation from profit sharing was not added to base pay, which would have compounded over time with pay raises. Tom Laney saw other problems: "a genuine cooperation would necessarily include my right to an equal share in the design, investment, and direction of the industry with voting and traditional striking and grievance rights." Hard work by those on the assembly line was only one of many variables determining whether the company was profitable, and workers had very little input on the other variables. If the company was unprofitable because of bad management decisions or excessive executive compensation, the workers were out of luck. Worse yet to workers, Ford could claim lower profits by investing in plants overseas, rather than those in the United States. In effect, American workers were being asked to help pay for the outsourcing of their own jobs.

Mandatory Overtime

To meet demand when sales were strong, Ford adopted a policy of mandatory overtime rather than adding more workers. This reduced costs for employee benefits, as the company could basically have one benefits package for the equivalent of two workers. It also greatly reduced costs for furloughs and terminations. In 1955, employees worked six nine-hour days. In 1984, they had to work five ten-hour days and often had to work two Saturdays a month. One autoworker complained that while everyone else in the world worked fifty-two weeks a year, they had to work more than seventy weeks. The mandatory overtime policy was a significant departure from Henry Ford's highly publicized rollout in 1922 of the forty-hour workweek. "Every man needs more than one day a week for rest and recreation," read the press release. "The Ford company has always sought to promote ideal home life for its employees. We believe that in order to live properly, every man should have more time to spend with his family, more time for self-improvement, more time for building up the place called home."

Workers putting in fifty-eight-hour weeks were generally happy for the "fat paychecks," and many were making upwards of eighty thousand dollars a year or more. They were grateful for the job as it got them past one financial milestone at a time—a kid's college tuition, a daughter's wedding, medical bills, and an occasional family vacation. Ford paid well and families were able to enjoy comfortable middle-class lives. With savings and a generous pension plan, they were financially secure, but the extra hours took a toll. Family events were difficult to plan and workers missed many birthday parties and Little League games. Wives of workers sometimes resorted to bringing children to the grounds

Ford permitted the Little League to use its property for baseball fields, which was greatly appreciated by the community. Courtesy of *Highland Villager*.

of the assembly plant so they could talk with their fathers through the open swivel windows. One of the sad ironies is that workers could see families enjoying Little League games on the ball fields that Ford leased to the community, while they themselves rarely had that opportunity. Rod Haworth said, "You are caught between that desire to spend more time with your family and at the same time to have an increased income to enable you to do other things. It's a Catch-22." One worker complained, "Who the hell wants overtime in the summer? People are begging for days off and to get vacations. There can be too much of the extra money." A standing joke at the plant was that someone had "a used boat to sell that's hardly ever used." Workers would occasionally find relief from the grueling schedule with unforeseen shutdowns, which occurred even during high-demand times. The Gulf War in 1991 dropped sales by 90 percent. Supplier strikes, weather disruptions, or product recalls also resulted in shutdowns. In 2000, Firestone tires had two safety recalls that stopped production for more than three weeks.

Mandatory overtime was very demanding physically. Putting in a normal eight-hour shift on an assembly line is tough enough, but turning the same bolt for ten hours a day, six days a week, took a toll, physically and mentally. Accidents and injuries increased, and disability claims rose significantly. Many workers claimed they felt the residual effects of the physical stress for the rest of their lives. To cope with the sixty-hour workweek, workers looked for opportunities to relieve the pressure. Retiree Lynn Hinkle recalled the infamous "cuckoo incident," which still brought him peals of laughter many years later. A worker on the line resented being harassed by a foreman over petty issues, and after one incident he yelled "cuckoo" repeatedly while circling his temple with his index finger. His coworker across the line picked up the chant. It quickly spread across the entire plant, as hundreds of cuckoo birds joined in. For the next several days, every time a worker had a problem with his foreman, the chant would start up again. The company felt compelled to put the insurrection down and issued what became known as the infamous "Cuckoo Memo." Bored workers occasionally entertained themselves by shooting blasts of air from their pneumatic tools. An unpopular foreman became a favorite target as workers tried to dislodge his ill-fitting toupee.

Union leaders opposed mandatory overtime not only because of the physical and mental toll, but also because it resulted in fewer employees. The UAW argued that if overtime were eliminated, twelve thousand laid-off workers could be put back on the job. But rank-and-file members made it clear they wanted extra hours and overtime pay. In one embarrassing incident, a UAW leader in Michigan organized a rally at the state capitol to oppose mandatory overtime and not one member of his local showed up. But with the increasing spike in accidents and injuries, even Ford concluded that excessive mandatory overtime had reached its limits. The company created a new category of employees, known as Temporary Part Time (TPT), which paid less and offered no benefits. The UAW leadership went along with this two-tier plan, reversing a long-standing, bedrock principle of Walter Reuther. The concept of worker solidarity held sacred by the founders of the UAW, and later leaders like Tom Laney, was fast eroding. Fully vested union workers made it clear whose interest they really wanted to protect. They were not willing to give up overtime pay to make room for new workers. They would accept two tiers of workers, and even three tiers, to protect their own interests. The historic slogans of the UAW—"One for all and all for one" and "An injury to one is an injury to all"—were no longer the rallying cries of a feared adversary but the quaint relics of a fractured workforce.

Strong sales of the Ranger pickup and consistently high rankings for productivity and quality at the Twin Cities Assembly Plant led Ford to continue investing in the facility. In 1990 it was one of the first plants to receive Ford's Q1 Award. The Twin Cities plant was ranked the most productive truck plant of the Big Three in the 1996 Harbour Report, and ranked first for quality in the 1997 J. D. Power annual report. In that year, the plant produced 157,415 Rangers. In 1999, the Louisville plant stopped making Rangers, and in 2004, the Edison plant closed and production was shifted to the Twin Cities plant, along with its plant manager, Mona Rinehart. She was known as "Mona the Closer," which workers in St. Paul took as a bad omen. However, that year Ford invested $28 million to convert the plant to add the production of Mazdas. The Ford partnership with Mazda led to significant cross-fertilization with a number of other models, including the Laser, Escort, Telstar, Probe, and the best-selling Explorer. This corporate collaboration ended in 2011 when Ford sold its stock back to Mazda.

Ford's continued investment in the physical plant in St. Paul reassured workers but raised some concerns in the Highland Park and South Minneapolis neighborhoods. The scale and character of manufacturing changed quite a bit since the plant opened in 1925. Residents complained of an odor from a new paint facility completed in 1985 and sued Ford for violations of the Clean Air Act. Ford agreed to add more equipment

The Twin Cities Assembly Plant expanded considerably over the years. An automated parts storage building proved very contentious because it was taller than permitted in a restricted scenic district along the Mississippi River. Author's collection.

and to monitor the problem. Several years later, Ford sought to build an eighty-foot-tall computerized warehouse that was twice the height permitted for buildings in the protected corridor of the Mississippi River scenic district. After numerous public hearings and some not-so-subtle threats from Ford that it was needed to keep the plant open, the permits were granted and the warehouse was built.

Even with plant expansions, high rankings for quality and productivity, and a strong-selling model, autoworkers never felt really secure about their future. In the volatile automobile industry, plants were opening and closing all the time, and there were always fears that the next plant to close would be theirs. That time was rapidly approaching.

The End
of the Line

The Closure of the Twin Cities
Assembly Plant

"Hey, kid, you're crazy coming to work here," said a coworker to Del Peterson on his first day at Ford. "They're going to be closing this place." Sixty years later, Peterson recalled, "That was June 1949." Most of the workers at the Twin Cities plant, no matter when they started, had heard rumors the plant might close. Uncertainty was an inevitable part of the automobile business, but cultivating insecurity was seemingly a company labor-relations strategy. The *Minneapolis Star Tribune* reported that a Ford executive, Mark Fields, said "he wants to create 'a sense of crisis, but not panic,' arguing that Ford workers will find motivation in fear."

It usually starts with a rumor. Bob Killeen recalled that Local 879 leaders were summoned to a meeting in Governor Wendell Anderson's office around 1975. They were told that the governor had heard through a connection that Ford was planning to shut the plant down, and he offered to help. The plant stayed open. "I know he was involved in it," said Killeen, "but I don't know what he did." Anderson did indeed have several connections in Detroit, including with the CEO, Henry Ford II. When he became governor in 1971, Anderson selected a Ford made at the Twin Cities Assembly Plant as the official state car. Sometime later he attended an economic summit in Washington, D.C., with business leaders and other elected officials, including sixteen or seventeen governors.

Henry Ford II spoke, and afterward Anderson responded that unlike most other governors in the room who had Cadillac limousines, he had the pleasure of riding in a Ford. Henry Ford came over later and thanked him for the kind words. In addition to making an important friend at Ford Motor Company, Anderson also had close ties to the UAW, both locally and nationally. When UAW leaders visited Minnesota, they sometimes stayed with Anderson at the governor's mansion.

Fears of Plant Closure and the New Training Center

With seemingly random closures, shutdowns, and furloughs, autoworkers have little control over their jobs or their schedules. Car companies can be cruising along on a wave of prosperity and suddenly end up in the ditch. No one feels the ebbs and flows more than workers on the assembly line. Any time Ford announced plans to build a new model, anxiety rose at assembly plants all over the country as workers weighed what it meant for them. In 1995, Ford announced a four-door version of the Ranger truck, sparking fears locally that the Twin Cities Assembly Plant would be closed. The St. Paul plant had been making Rangers exclusively for three years, but the popular truck was also made in Louisville, Kentucky, and Edison, New Jersey.

Rob McKenzie, president of Local 879, felt that aggressive action was needed to bolster the chances to make the new four-door truck. With his professional demeanor, McKenzie took an unlikely path to the presidency of the union. He was raised in a small town in southwest Iowa and went to the University of Iowa in 1970, where he joined a fraternity and became an ardent fan of the Hawkeyes football team. His academic major was American studies, which included classes in Marxist theory. Like many college students of the time, McKenzie went to antiwar demonstrations and was galvanized by the 1968 Chicago Democratic National Convention and the killing of protesters at Kent State University. He joined the Revolutionary Union, a Maoist Communist group, and followed its call to infiltrate industry. After graduation he worked at the Ford Chicago Assembly Plant from 1975 to 1977, then transferred to the night shift at the Twin Cities Assembly Plant in 1978. He married another radical activist and by the age of twenty-six had a child. His revolutionary fervor was gradually redirected to the immediate challenge of improving working conditions in the plant. During this time, McKenzie studied industrial electronics at St. Paul College, preparing for a different kind of revolution—robotics. He became a skilled tradesman active in the leadership of UAW Local 879, holding a number of elective offices before becoming president.

McKenzie's preliminary discussions with state officials suggested that direct public

UAW President Rob McKenzie at the Ford–UAW–MnSCU Training Center as it neared completion in 1999. He worked tirelessly to secure bonding money from the state for the project, which was hoped would give Ford added reason to keep the plant open. Courtesy of *Highland Villager*.

support was unlikely as it was perceived to be "corporate welfare." The new Ranger model would need significant plant retooling, which the St. Paul plant could accommodate in the space vacated by the F-Series trucks. But it would also need considerable training for the assembly line workers to operate the new high-tech manufacturing equipment. Perhaps there would be some interest in funding training programs, or even a new training center? This, it could be argued, benefited the workers of the state as much as the company. McKenzie and other union officials knew the value of educational partnerships that Ford had established with local colleges, and they had been wondering how to make those programs more accessible to members who were working ten-hour days. They decided it was time to push for a full-fledged educational center at the plant. Such a facility, McKenzie reasoned, would give St. Paul an edge in producing the new model Ranger.

The state of Minnesota and the University of Minnesota had an interest in educational programs at the Twin Cities Assembly Plant dating back to deliberations over

The Training Center (now demolished) had classrooms, computer and technical training labs, robotics and automation equipment, and a large meeting hall. Courtesy of TKDA Architects and Engineers.

the Hydroelectric Plant in the 1920s. Minnesota's aggressive bid for the GM Saturn project in 1985 included a proposal for a Center for Advanced Manufacturing Studies staffed by the University of Minnesota, and a $20 million vocational school for Saturn employees, so the idea for an educational collaboration had already been raised. With concerns mounting about the possible closure of the plant, Governor Arne Carlson set up a task force in 1995 to look for ways to secure its future. A decade after the unsuccessful Saturn bid, state officials had again come to believe that a modest investment in a training facility could help ensure Ford's continued presence in Minnesota and create a well-trained workforce.

The UAW, the governor, and the Minnesota State Colleges and Universities (MnSCU) developed a plan and presented it to Ford officials in Detroit and to Minnesota legislators. The state approved a bonding allocation of $5 million for a training center to be built on Ford property. McKenzie recalled, "I spent every day all day for six weeks lobbying for the state money to build the Center. The five million dollars wasn't approved until the last day of the legislative session." Ford and the UAW agreed to each provide $2.3 million to match the state funds. With a partnership agreement and financing plan in place, a project team toured UAW–Ford training centers around the country. Workers in St. Paul were enthusiastic about the benefits of a training center. "I want off this line," said Liternia Dotson. At the age of forty-two and having raised three children, she wanted to trade her job attaching air bag sensors to something involving computers. She was not even sure she would stay at Ford.

Even as momentum was building for the new training center, rumors continued to swirl that Ford would close the plant. The *Detroit Free Press* reported in late 1997 that a decision had already been made, which the company quickly denied. McKenzie was skeptical of the report, citing the plant's high quality rankings and the fact that Ford had committed to the joint training center, but Fred Zimmerman, professor of manufacturing at the University of St. Thomas, took the speculation seriously: "It's a good plant, but it's an old plant and it's a small plant, and it's one of the few that sits on saleable real estate. It's probably worth more dead than alive." The beautiful site on the Mississippi River would be one of the most attractive development sites in the region, with a potential value of $50 million to $100 million, in addition to the considerable value of the hydroelectric permit.

TKDA Architects of St. Paul designed the new UAW-Ford-MnSCU Training Center and construction started in February 1998. The state would own the building and could use it for 20 percent of its operating hours. Ford would own the land under the center, which was attached to the northeast corner of the plant, and would lease the building from the state. A four-person board of directors, including representatives from the UAW, Ford, Minnesota State Colleges and Universities, and the Minnesota Department of Administration, would oversee the project. The project, according to McKenzie, was the only educational training institution of its size and scope to be managed jointly by a corporation, a union, and a government entity on a local level. He described it as "an experiment in industrial relations," which may have understated its extraordinary symbolic value. After a century of labor turmoil, the union, the company, and the government had become genuine partners on a project they all perceived to be mutually beneficial. To remain competitive, a

Many jobs in the plant required basic knowledge of computers, as seen in this photograph from 1999. Courtesy of David Parker.

well-trained and motivated workforce was needed to implement Ford's program for continuous improvement. The company, the union, and the government needed to work together to make that happen.

The new two-story forty thousand-square-foot Training Center opened in February 1999. It featured Kawasaki robots and automation equipment, a machine shop, a woodworking shop, an auto diagnostic bay, paint repair bay, labs, and a 180-seat auditorium with state-of-the-art audiovisual and teleconferencing equipment. It also had eight classrooms, three computer labs, three technical training labs, a student lounge, and offices. Educational partners included all of the universities in the MnSCU system, as well as the engineering and manufacturing programs at the University of St. Thomas. The center offered a wide variety of classes, including business plan development, economics, management fundamentals, interpersonal communication, and cultural anthropology. It also housed the Ford–UAW apprenticeship program for electricians, millwrights, toolmakers, plumber/pipe fitters, industrial light-truck mechanics, welders, sheet-metal workers, and stationary steam engineers. Previously, apprentice trainees had to take classes at area technical schools.

The new center was open several nights a week until midnight to make the programs as accessible as possible. While many classes were for personal development, some were for Ford. In 2004, for example, the state awarded a $399,305 training grant to help expand continuous improvement programs at the plant. Retirees were also able to take classes at the training center, a benefit provided by Ford and the UAW. The company also provided computer classes at the training center and Internet access at home for less than five dollars per month. In 2000, Ford offered each of its 350,000 worldwide employees computers and ink-jet printers at deeply discounted prices. A Ford spokesperson said she hoped workers would become more comfortable with computers on the job if they used them at home.

Too Far from the Supply Chain Corridor

The programmatic and geospatial relationship between an assembly plant and its suppliers evolved over time. During Ford's first decentralization phase, assembly plants were built along rail lines in urban centers to reduce costs of shipping a fully assembled car. As Henry Ford moved toward vertical integration, the company added navigation as a means of connecting production facilities that were scattered around the world. The introduction of annual model changes required a greater variety of parts and a more rapid production schedule, which impacted plant location decisions. In 1960, tri-level railcars were introduced, which significantly reduced the cost of shipping fully assembled cars, which diminished the advantage of decentralized plants. Production was consolidated in the middle of the country, and plants on the coasts were closed. With the departure of founder Henry Ford, the company gradually increased the percentage of parts that were made by outside suppliers. The transition away from vertical integration toward outside suppliers was difficult. Initially, Ford used its vast purchasing power to press vendors mainly on price—not quality.

Suppliers felt that Ford had little interest in their economic well-being or appreciation for their intellectual property. Morale sagged, and many of the best suppliers left Ford to work for the transplant companies. The quality of Ford cars declined in large part because of inferior parts made mostly by outside suppliers. In 1997, Ford was paying almost $5 billion a year in warranty costs. Ted LaValley, the Local 879 chairman, complained, "Divided out per unit they are paying as much in warranty as they are paying us for building them . . . When is local management going to understand quality will reduce the cost per unit?" In his monthly president's report, Rob McKenzie wrote: "Ford has a lot of nonunion and anti-union suppliers who don't care about their own workers or the quality of the product they push out the door. If Ford chooses to ignore the problem we all end up paying for it . . . In the long run, the best hope of preserving jobs in the auto industry lies in unionizing the auto parts industry."

Ford clearly used its purchasing practices as a labor-relations tool as workers at nonunion shops were paid less. Early on, workers had some success in fending off Ford's outsourcing policy. At the height of the "Buy American" campaign, Ford shipped car jacks made in China to St. Paul, where the workers refused to unload them. The plant manager had little choice but to send them back and replace them with American parts. But Ford was committed to outsourcing and this policy was further accelerated with the introduction of "modularization," or "modular build." A single supplier made a package of components and put them together as a sub-assembled unit ready to be installed. Ford claimed this was an efficiency measure, but the UAW saw this as a union-busting tactic. In 1985, Ford took a circuitous route in St. Paul to introduce modularization. It shipped Ranger engines by truck to the Space Center, a warehouse near the Midway, where workers affiliated with the Teamsters Union attached thirty-four parts to the engine. Ford also sent dash panels by rail to the Space Center, to be trucked down to the Owatonna Tool Company in Owatonna, Minnesota, where a nonunion workforce would assemble and paint the dash panels and glove-box doors. Tom Laney, who was president of Local 879 at the time, pressed them to stop the work, with some success.

By the mid-1980s, upward of 70 percent of car parts were made by outside suppliers. In 1999, Local 879 tried to organize Johnson Controls in Hudson, Wisconsin, which made

Workers put together a dashboard module in 1999. Courtesy of David Parker.

car seats for Ford. The union complained that Johnson Controls held "captive meetings" subjecting workers to antiunion messages and scare tactics and starting rumors that the plant would close if workers supported the UAW. The organizing effort failed. "If you see someone from Johnson Controls in our plant," McKenzie wrote, "ask him or her why that company hates union workers so much."

In 2002, a second organizing campaign at Johnson Controls succeeded, but workers would earn less than those in the assembly plant. The differential in pay rates generated tension among workers, particularly because both groups were represented by the same union, which made things more complicated. The UAW justified the two-tier system because there were two different companies. With that logic, Ford would have every incentive to keep spinning off projects—which it did. In St. Paul, it spun off the job of loading and unloading cars on the tri-level trains, claiming that other plants had agreed to that practice. No project was too small. In 2001, dealers requested that covers be made for about one thousand vehicles, which Ford outsourced to the Budget Rental Company, even though workers at the plant asked to bid on the project.

The shift from vertical to horizontal integration was accelerated by the introduction of shorter development cycles. Parts had become increasingly complex, and Ford could not match the expertise of the specialized suppliers. It shifted more of the responsibility for research and design to suppliers, which in turn demanded longer-term purchase agreements to cover their increased costs. To amortize their research costs, suppliers also needed to work with multiple manufacturers and not be totally dependent on one company. These trends required Ford to have a much closer relationship with its suppliers, both programmatically and physically, and these ties reinforced a natural "clustering" effect. American companies moved toward the Japanese system, with suppliers locating within a four-hour delivery radius. A manufacturing corridor, known as "Auto Alley," developed as American and transplant companies and their suppliers located along the I-65 and I-75 highways, running south from Michigan through Ohio, Kentucky, Tennessee, and Alabama. The typical modern assembly plant today is located on a four-lane freeway with approximately 120 suppliers within 150 miles.

Getting a supplier to buck the trend and move a factory closer to the Twin Cities

A view of the complex equipment on the assembly line in 1999. Courtesy of David Parker.

Assembly Plant was a challenge, as seen with the example of Tower Automotive. Tower was a "preferred supplier," meaning it had a collaborative, long-term relationship with Ford. In 2000, Ford gave Tower specifications for a large order of truck frames and other parts. To fill the contract, Tower would need to install expensive new equipment to coat the metal components. This prompted the company to compare the cost of renovating its Milwaukee plant to constructing a new plant near St. Paul. During this exploratory process, Tower executives met with development officials in Minnesota and Wisconsin, but, according to news accounts, "declined to discuss what kind of financial help or subsidies the company might be seeking." In the midst of Tower's analysis, Ford revised its manufacturing plans and asked Tower to make frames for the entire output of Ranger trucks, including those built at Edison, as well as other parts for the Dearborn plant. This tilted the geographic advantage back to Milwaukee. Tower then opened discussions with its plant workforce about labor issues, prompting a reporter to ask "whether the company is asking for concessions to keep open the plant there." "That would be speculative," a company official responded. "We've agreed not to negotiate in the press." Tower did not build in St. Paul. Today, it is a $2 billion company based in Livonia, Michigan, with thirty-one production facilities strategically located near its customers in North America, South America, Europe, and Asia.

Continuing Decline in Quality

Ford lost more than $6.4 billion in 1998 and 1999 and announced that it would lay off thirty-five thousand workers and close five unspecified plants. The next contract, a four-year national agreement, was ratified in late 2003. Edison, New Jersey, and two other plants were to be closed in three years. Tom Laney said that the Edison workers should have seized the plant. Edison was the only other facility that made Ranger trucks, so that work would likely be shifted to St. Paul, and perhaps also the Mazda pickup trucks they were making. Ford also awarded the Twin Cities Assembly Plant the four-door Ranger project. While this spared the plant from closure, the news sparked little celebration in St. Paul, where workers spoke of management incompetence. "Ford's rapid decline from a high profit company ready to overtake GM in market share to the poor position we find ourselves in today," wrote Rob McKenzie, "will probably be studied by business schools in the future." The Big Three automakers lost an additional 10 percent market share to the transplant companies, and for the first time dropped below 50 percent. The center of the American auto industry "is now Kentucky—not Detroit," said McKenzie. "No issue is more important today for unionized autoworkers than quality."

While Ford was celebrating the quantity of cars being made, the company was paying less attention to quality. Frustrated owners often took their complaints to the streets—in this case, parked right in front of the Twin Cities Assembly Plant. Courtesy of *Highland Villager*.

Ford's profits plunged in late 2001 largely because of the precipitous drop in quality. Kari Altema, a worker on the assembly line, put the blame squarely on management in a conversation with the *Star Tribune*: "The one thing I never would have thought I would hear from a supervisor was, 'Let the dealer fix it!' That's right, 'Let the dealer fix it!'" Problems with suppliers were also unresolved. A survey of companies in 2005 revealed that Ford had the worst relationship with its suppliers of any company in any industry—not just in the auto industry. Consumers had come to demand quality, which they could more easily monitor through data provided by an increasing number of third-party analysts and agencies. Ford did not sustain the continuous improvement programs of the late 1980s or the lessons from developing the Taurus. A steep drop-off in sales prompted "a game of musical chairs" to see which of Ford's seventeen assembly plants would close. The company considered a number of factors, including the age of the plant, the age and length of service of the workforce (which would impact payout packages), worker productivity, the cost of energy and shipping, taxes, and proximity to suppliers. In St. Paul, there was another important criterion, the value of the land. The beautiful site that was once so compelling to Henry Ford had become a liability. One analyst said, "for a cash-strapped automaker, whatever the land would fetch would be a windfall." On the plus side, the St. Paul facility had its own hydroelectric power and scored very well on production-related criteria.

Ford had an agreement with the UAW to not close a plant during a contract period unless it was previously listed in the labor agreement. Because most contracts had terms covering several years, this gave workers considerable lead time to plan their futures. Workers also had other benefits to soften a possible plant closure, including termination packages, transfer rights, and retraining benefits. Union critics believed that these agreements were overly generous, but the UAW insisted they should be seen in the context of a highly volatile industry with an unprecedented level of workplace insecurity.

Working on the Ranger assembly line, 1999. Courtesy of David Parker.

Some benefits, however, may have been harder to explain. In its 1999 contract, Ford agreed to provide Family Service and Learning Centers at all its plants, as well as concierge services, which would "connect time strapped employees with such services as plumbers or carpenters," or would "send someone to wait for the cable installer." Ford had reason to go along with this unusual perk because it made it easier for people to work fifty-eight hours per week. The company did have another option, of course: to hire more workers and go back to the forty-hour workweek.

Although the contract assured that the St. Paul plant would remain open for at least several more years, local autoworkers were concerned that no new models were announced for production after 2007. Ford's market share had fallen from 24 percent in 1993 to 17 percent in 2005, the lowest since the late 1920s. The company was using only 79 percent of its North American plant capacity and announced plans to lay off between twenty-five thousand and thirty thousand workers. It also intended to close an additional fourteen plants, including seven in North America.

With sales of Rangers continuing to decline through 2006, Ford laid off almost four hundred workers in St. Paul and reduced the work schedule. A Ford spokesperson said, "We anticipate the need to align capacity with demand later this year," which sounded like additional cuts were in the offing. That Ford had still not announced any new models for the Twin Cities plant after 2007 heightened anxiety.

A devastating blow for the plant came from a most unlikely and unforeseen place: the federal tax code. Under a significant revision of the tax code in 2004 the tax incentives for trucks would apply only to vehicles weighing more than six thousand pounds. Because the Ranger weighed less, it was now at a competitive disadvantage with the larger pickups. Sales of Rangers dropped 30 percent, prompting Ford to suspend production at the St. Paul plant and furlough its workers for five weeks. State Senator Ellen Anderson, an ardent environmentalist, complained: "Our plant in St. Paul is being directly hit by this federal policy that encourages [consumers to buy] gas guzzlers that weigh three tons." By 2005, Ranger sales slipped to third place behind Toyota and Chevrolet. It was an abrupt shock to many that a few sentences in a tax bill could jeopardize a plant with an annual payroll of $132 million.

Efforts to Save the Twin Cities Plant

The increasing signals that Ford might close the St. Paul plant prompted renewed engagement by political leaders. The state planning department, under Governor Jesse Ventura, outlined a forward-looking strategy in an Op-Ed article in the *Minneapolis Star Tribune* in 2001. Jack Uldrich and Rolf Nordstrom argued: "Rather than wait for 1,800 layoffs and then react with the customary angst and inevitable hand-wringing that usually follow such events, Minnesota can, with a little forethought and ingenuity, instead turn this into a huge opportunity. How? Invite the Ford Motor Co. to transform its Twin Cities Assembly Plant in St. Paul into a flagship facility capable of producing hybrid, gas and electric-powered vehicles, and eventually fuel-cell cars and trucks." Their article was reprinted in the Local 879 newsletter. Five years later, union officials and others proposed a similar plan for a variety of environmental projects, including electric, flex-fuel, and hybrid vehicles.

There was some cause for optimism. The Ford Motor Company had created a Midwest Ethanol Corridor project to promote the use of E-85 fuel. The Big Three automakers had stepped up production of flex-fuel vehicles, which helped them meet their Corporate Average Fuel Economy (CAFE) standards. Light trucks were mandated to get at least 20.7 miles per gallon, and passenger trucks 27.5 miles per gallon—but flex vehicles only had to

Worker using a compressed-air power tool in 1999. Courtesy of David Parker.

get 35 miles per gallon. Even the gas-guzzling Ford Explorer qualified by 2001. More than two hundred thousand flex-fuel Ranger pickups were made, mostly in St. Paul. Minnesota was a major player in the biofuel industry in part because of a state law that required a minimum of 10 percent ethanol in all gasoline. The state also provided a number of subsidies and tax credits. By 1999, Minnesota was producing more than 162 million gallons of ethanol a year. Cargill, Inc., a major Minnesota agribusiness, entered the market "because of the strong public policy commitment to the industry," and became one of the top five producers in the country.

In January 2006, Governor Tim Pawlenty and Commissioner Matt Kramer of the Department of Employment and Economic Development traveled to Dearborn to meet with Anne Stevens, chief operating officer for Ford Americas. They wanted to explore ways to keep Ford in Minnesota, although not necessarily at the site of the Twin Cities Assembly Plant. The state's approach was based in large measure on the environmental proposals that had been circulating. Pawlenty proposed that the state and Ford partner in creating a research center for alternative fuels such as ethanol and other biofuels. This initiative seemed to align with Ford's stated intention of producing 250,000 hybrid cars by 2010. In a major speech in 2005, CEO William (Bill) Ford Jr. urged Congress to increase tax incentives to drive innovation that would make the country less dependent on foreign oil and help manufacturers convert older plants into high-tech facilities. Governor Pawlenty said he hoped to match incentive packages being prepared by other states, but cautioned, "Don't jump to the conclusion that I am just going to throw cash out there. It would have to be something that also had mutual interest and benefit to the state of Minnesota." Pawlenty was hopeful, but he was not confident. "We have to face some basic facts," he said. "If you look at the natural trajectory of the plant and its product, it is not on a positive course currently."

Workers at the plant braced for the worst. Marvalene Johnson, who was on the instrument panel line, said, "As far as I know they have already written us off. I don't think it's [Pawlenty's initiatives] going to work." Another indicator of the glum mood in the plant was that there was a noticeable increase in the number of "For Sale" signs on company bulletin boards offering snowmobiles, boats, and furniture. Some in the community were hoping for more aggressive action from the governor, but the state's measured approach found favor with the *Minneapolis Star Tribune*: "In all this, Pawlenty seems to be cleaving to the right principle: Any public investment should produce durable assets for Minnesota, not just a subsidy to Ford. That was the idea when the state invested in a big training facility at the site some years ago, and it seems to be driving the governor's strategy on flexible fuel research now."

Ford executives told the governor that no decision had been made on the fate of the plant, encouraging local officials to expand the range of environmental options for the company to consider. As one gesture of its seriousness, the legislature proposed one hundred thousand dollars in funding to Minnesota State University, Mankato, for a plug-in hybrid research project. This proposal was partially based on a 2007 suggestion by David Morris from the Institute for Local Self-Reliance. He suggested that the plant be "the centerpiece for a bold new transportation initiative—a battery-powered vehicle, charged from a household socket, with a backup biofueled engine." Ford was aware of the legislation, but responded coolly: "We believe that the hybrid model that is in the market today, which we offer on our Ford Escape and our Mercury Mariner, is the most suitable application for the majority of consumers and the way they use their vehicles." A Ford lobbyist opposed the legislation, but both houses passed it unanimously. Ford's attitude was particularly upsetting to environmentalists because the company already had some experience with building an electric Ranger in California to comply with the state's mandate for alternative-fueled vehicles. That mandate was lifted in 2003 as a result of pressure from Ford and GM, and the car companies quickly repossessed and destroyed the leased electric Rangers.

Minnesota officials spoke with Ford executives several times after their meeting in January. Ford was scheduled to make a major announcement about its restructuring plans on January 23, 2006, and was expected to unveil the list of plants to be closed. Workers on the assembly line, who huddled around radios that day, were deeply disappointed, as Mike Meyers of the *Star Tribune* explained: "Criticized by some in the past for being hesitant to address the company's problems, Ford management seemed to deliver on that reputation for tentativeness Monday by not naming all of the plants it will close. The hesitation leaves thousands of workers in a fog about their future." In a three-hour news conference, Ford reaffirmed its intent to close fourteen plants by 2012, but named only five plants for closure in 2008—not including the Twin Cities. It added that it would list two additional plants for closure by the end of the year. "We dodged a bullet," said one St. Paul worker. Another said, "Actually, I feel like crying. Just the whole impact around the country on people, their lives and their families. It's sad because we're eventually going to get axed, too." Union president Rob McKenzie put the announcement in a broader context: "Unfortunately, this is another day in the continuing story of the destruction of the American middle class. Our view is if we don't do something about health care costs and trade policy, we're going to see many more days like this." The company's retrenchment plan was projected to save $6 billion by 2010, and with Ford's announcement its stock jumped almost 5 percent.

"It's a serious situation for them to not identify the other two plants," said University of Colorado management professor Wayne Cascio. "I don't know where they got that advice, but it's not good advice." He believed that fear might be a short-term motivator, but that it was corrosive in the long term. University of St. Thomas professor Sunil Ramlall agreed, saying that Ford "miscalculated if they think workers whose jobs remain in peril will remain in top form . . . There is a huge price to be paid. It's going to affect the workforce morale, which ultimately will affect their productivity." In 2006 there were approximately two thousand workers at the St. Paul plant with an annual payroll of $140 million. The average employee was earning a base pay of $27 an hour, amounting to $56,000 a year, working a four-day, ten-hour schedule. Economists estimated that each job at the plant supported nine other jobs. The plant generated between $9 and $10 million in state payroll taxes, and $1.3 million in annual property taxes to Ramsey County.

With anxiety mounting over Ford's plans, some pressed for a reuse option that would create more jobs than a biofuel research center. Governor Tim Pawlenty was unmoved: "A state or local unit of government can't chase around industries and subsidize them all on the theory that we're going to insulate them from changing world market forces. However, we can and should engage them in partnerships where it makes sense for the future of that company and the state."

St. Thomas professor Fred Zimmerman argued that the state should have done more earlier, citing as an example the possibility of supporting an integrated metal-stamping operation. Bulky items made from rolled steel had to be shipped in from considerable distances. Hoods, doors, floor pans, dash and instrument panels, and other stampings had to be shipped from Chicago. Most of the plants built by Japanese transplants, Zimmerman pointed out, had on-site stamping plants, something that Local 879 had been seeking. Years earlier, engineers at the Twin Cities Assembly Plant studied the feasibility of building an on-site stamping plant, but this was rejected because of a lack of space. There was considerable talk as far back as the campaign for the hydroelectric permit in 1924 that Henry Ford would invest in a smelting plant on the Iron Range, which would have made a stamping plant more likely. This did not materialize, but hopes were raised in 1963 when Ford invested in the Oglebay Norton taconite plant in Eveleth, Minnesota, and again in 1999 when Ford partnered with Minnesota Iron and Steel in a $1.3 billion taconite mine and production facility at Nashwauk. This plant did produce "automotive quality" flat rolled steel, some of which was shipped to the St. Paul plant.

With the continuing uncertainty regarding the status of the St. Paul plant, a second meeting of Ford and state officials took place on March 30, 2006. This was reportedly at the request of the "technical gurus" at Ford who were interested in discussing ways to broaden the usage of ethanol. The fate of the Twin Cities plant was not discussed during the two-hour session.

Pressed steel doors in storage shelves. Courtesy of Dan Huseby.

The Dreaded Phone Call

On the morning of April 13, 2006, Jim Eagle, the bargaining chairman of the UAW Local 879, received the phone call from Ford that he had been dreading. He was informed that the plant would be closed in June 2008. Eagle gathered other officials in the union hall, prepared a memo, and walked across the street to the plant to give the devastating news to the workers. He did so hours before the official announcement from the company, even though he had been asked to wait. He shrugged, "If I had been a manager they would have fired me." A Ford spokesman said, "The decision is final. The plant will be idled in 2008," although the exact date was not set. There had speculation for years that the plant would close, but many workers were in shock when it finally happened. "There was some crying and some anger," said Eagle. "And some people just didn't believe it." "We were really quite surprised," said Rob McKenzie. "This is not the outcome we expected." One worker at the plant said he had been hearing rumors of the plant closing since he started in 1970: "I grew old at the Ford Motor Company. I'm still in shock. It's a very sad day." McKenzie put the announcement in a larger context: "In the end the forces of deindustrialization, globalization, a broken health care system, and bad management overcame the valiant effort of the Twin Cities Assembly Plant workforce to save this factory." One distraught worker walked into the union office in the plant and killed herself with a gunshot to the head.

As bad as the news was, workers at least had almost two years to prepare for their next job. Many were already gearing up to pursue more education. With the closing date set for 2008, union leaders focused on the upcoming contract negotiations with the hope of protecting workers as much as possible.

A number of people, including some at the plant, believed that Local 879 should have done more to save the plant by modifying its labor agreements. John Killeen, a forty-one-year-old autoworker and Bob Killeen's son, felt that the union could have offered to waive some work rules and reduce the number of sick days to save the company money: "We needed to change the workforce idea that we could continue down the same path in terms of how we approach doing our job. That things were so bad was not communicated to the plant floor. People didn't understand." Union officials at the local level did have some latitude to negotiate such issues as job classifications. Other workers strongly argued that the UAW had already agreed to pretty much everything Ford asked, going back to the contracts of the early 1980s that established Employee Involvement and profit sharing. Every contract since then gave additional concessions. The clearest indicator of the union's compliant attitude was that there were virtually no workers at the plant who

Worker operating power equipment in 1999. Courtesy of David Parker.

had ever participated in a strike. The last UAW national strike was in 1976. The strike was no longer a union weapon.

State officials believed they did all they could and doubted whether any combination of tax cuts, rebates, or other financial incentives could have saved the plant, but some were not so sure. Fred Zimmerman said, "A monkey with a lobotomy could have seen this coming a mile away. There are efforts that should have been started eight or nine years ago. Minnesota has neglected the health of its industry as a policy issue. They seem to be far more interested in stadiums for the Gophers or the Vikings than they are having a viable place to work for people." The state economist was not as alarmed, saying the closing would not have a major impact because the auto industry represents only 0.1 percent of the state's economy. Even though the decision was termed "final," several state legislators weren't so sure. Representative Matt Entenza said, "The economy will change. Auto demand will change. The question is: Are we prepared as a state to get together to help save this plant? I think we have to be." In early 2007, alarmed legislators, working with UAW Local 879, introduced a resolution calling for a five-year moratorium on the sale of the property, but this was defeated.

The day Ford announced the closing of the Twin Cities Assembly Plant, the city of St. Paul formed a task force to help guide plans for the redevelopment of the prime 122-acre parcel. "We hope we can create a mix of residential and retail business opportunities in that area," Mayor Chris Coleman said, "because we think it's important to retain a portion of those jobs or equivalent jobs there." He held out hope of attracting a technology center or some light manufacturing. The property was zoned industrial, but a conversion to residential or mixed use would significantly increase its value for redevelopment. This seemingly gave the city some leverage. Redevelopment prospects were complicated, however, because the level of contamination was unknown. In addition, the site had restrictions on building height because it was in a protected scenic river district, as well as within the flight path of the Minneapolis–St. Paul International Airport.

Several months after the announcement of the plant closure, Local 879 and Ford sponsored a job and educational fair at the Training Center. Almost the entire workforce showed up to talk with state employment specialists and representatives from twenty-six universities and colleges. Doug Toenjes, who worked at the plant for eighteen years, said, "We are just getting an idea of our options. If we have to check out two years from now, we have to start our schooling, and we have to see what else is out there. By the time the plant closes, there may not be other manufacturing jobs around."

In mid-December 2006, Ford started the process of selling off the Hydroelectric Plant with an invitational bidding process targeted to utility companies, government agencies, and investment firms. District Energy of St. Paul and the Metropolitan Airports Commission were among the bidders, as was Xcel Energy, the successor to NSP, which fought for the permit eighty years earlier. The bid packet included a request from the city of St. Paul to obtain "a portion of the output from the facility for a planned 'green' community." Some—including the Green Party, which advocated for public ownership—had hoped that the city would take a more direct role in preserving the hydropower plant for the public. Local 879 complained that selling off the hydropower plant would reduce its potential as a manufacturing site. Ford had explored selling the hydroelectric facility in 1999, which the union strongly opposed: "Any potential buyers of the Hydro should be aware that UAW Local 879 will make that purchase as difficult as possible." At that point Ford dropped the idea. When the issue reemerged six years later, the political climate had changed considerably, with the union in a much weakened position. In the initial fight over the permit, Minneapolis Mayor George Leach proposed in 1923 that a reversionary clause be attached to the license that would transfer it back to the Twin Cities if Ford were to ever withdraw. This was not done, and in 2007, neither Minneapolis nor St. Paul made an effort to stop the sale.

On May 29, 2007, Ford announced that Brookfield Power, from Quebec Province, Canada, had won the bid for the four-acre hydro plant with a reported offer of $50 million. Brookfield operated 140 hydroelectric plants on fifty rivers throughout North and South America, including a ten-megawatt hydroelectric power plant at St. Anthony Falls in Minneapolis. A union representative, Lynn Hinkle, again criticized the sale: "I think it's hard not to see this as something that takes away one of the best assets of the entire site." Some environmentalists and white-water rafting enthusiasts opposed the sale of the hydropower facility for a different reason. They advocated for the removal of the dam and the return of the Mississippi River to its natural state.

Termination Packages for the Workers

Under the terms of the union contract, workers with the highest seniority had first rights to a voluntary buyout if Ford took that route for "force reduction." The company was concerned, however, that if too many senior workers opted for the buyout it would deplete the plant of its most experienced people. If Ford took the layoff route, rather than the buyout, it would start from the "bottom up," with the junior workers being discharged first. Ford executives took considerable time finalizing termination plans, leaving workers in an uncertain state. Ford reported a third-quarter loss in 2006 of $5.8 billion, and sales slipped to fourth place by the end of the year, behind GM, Toyota, and DaimlerChrysler. Ford moved up its plans to close sixteen plants. Executives reiterated their intention to reduce the workforce "on a voluntary basis." The company hoped to reduce thirty thousand jobs nationally through a buyout plan, which represented about 40 percent of its workforce.

The UAW and Ford worked together to prepare the termination plan, finally announcing eight different buyout packages, which varied by a worker's age and length of service. Each worker received a DVD explaining the options. In October, Ford set up tents on the grounds of the Twin Cities plant to distribute information and answer questions, and gave workers six weeks to make a choice. Under one option, workers could take a lump sum payment from $35,000 to $140,000 depending on age and length of service. Workers with ten years' experience received the highest amount, which was reduced as workers approached retirement age. There were also options for a mix of education benefits and cash payments amounting to half of a worker's normal salary. Health benefits and life insurance would continue to be covered for a period of time, and workers would

maintain normal pension rights. These buyout provisions were considerably more generous than those offered workers at the Edison, New Jersey, plant, which closed just three
years earlier.

Some workers were not enthusiastic about the buyout option. Curtis Lee, who had
transferred to the St. Paul plant after being displaced from the Ford Wixom plant, said,
"It's $60,000 after taxes. And after six months you have to pay for your health insurance.
That's a big factor. We make $50,000 now, so that $60,000 isn't a whole lot of money."
Workers who accepted a buyout could not collect unemployment insurance for two
years. In addition, it was unclear if employees would be eligible for services from the
Dislocated Worker Program, which is funded by a dedicated state payroll tax. Minnesota
officials initially ruled that workers who accepted the buyouts would be viewed as leaving
voluntarily. The union challenged this interpretation, claiming that Ohio and Michigan
had declared workers under similar circumstances eligible for the training programs.
An Ohio official declared, "We ruled that the separation is a lack-of-work separation.
The fundamental purpose of the buyouts was to reduce the work force." By June 2007,
Minnesota reversed course, declaring autoworkers eligible for the program.

Workers who declined the payout option kept their right to transfer to other plants,
but this was risky given the wave of layoffs and plant closings. Transfer rights, a major
benefit negotiated by the UAW in 1982, allowed displaced workers to receive priority for job openings at any Ford plant around the country. Implementing this benefit
proved somewhat complicated. Workers hired in 1983 at the Twin Cities plant were later
"bumped" by transferees. They filed a lawsuit claiming breach of contract and the case
went all the way to the Supreme Court. Over the years, the Twin Cities plant had far more
workers transfer in than out because of the strong market for the F-Series and Ranger
pickup trucks.

Newly hired transferees sometimes had difficulty fitting into the tight-knit group in
St. Paul, which had a long tradition of hiring locally, often from within the families of current or former workers. Some "preferentials" felt like outsiders when they arrived. Most
were asked to pull up stakes and move hundreds of miles on five or six days' notice, and
many left their families behind for weeks or months. They sometimes showed up to the
union hall unannounced, looking for help finding an apartment. Some found temporary
accommodations in homes of workers and some ended up sleeping in their cars until
they got settled. One worker said, "I grew up in Newark. My family grew up in Newark. I
never lived more than five minutes from any of my relatives. Now I'm 1,300 miles away.
My wife said she's not coming out here ''cause there's nothing here but grass, weeds,
and trees.'"

Many transferees were black or Hispanic, and they arrived at a predominantly white

Ranger trucks on the assembly line. Courtesy of Dan Huseby.

Worker examines parts from overhead conveyor. Courtesy of David Parker.

plant. On occasion, they were met by racial taunts—including a cross burning on the assembly line in 1985. In at least one instance, a preferential worker was so upset at what he perceived as hostile treatment that he pulled a gun on a Ford official and made "terroristic threats," landing him in jail. Michael T. Favata, a transplant who worked at the plant for ten years, later wrote: "They always had one of the best in quality, but they treated us transplants from Michigan, Alabama, and from other plants that closed in the early '80s really bad. It was management and the locals that made life unbearable for most of us! I lasted ten years of hell in that place." When Tom Laney was in office, he worked hard to welcome the new workers, instituting a "buddy system." He blamed management for exacerbating racial tension by ratcheting up concerns about quality in a way that questioned the work ethic of "outsiders." He saw this as a wedge issue that further intensified anxiety about the plant closing. Laney welcomed the fact that many of the "preferentials" came from plants that had much more militant unions and brought new energy to his local. At the time, he reminded members that the preferential hiring program would be there if they ever needed it in the future. Approximately 260 workers in St. Paul signed up for transfers, and sixty found positions in other plants. Sheator Robinson worked at the Twin Cities plant for nineteen years and wanted to continue working until she received her full pension. She accepted a position at the Kansas City assembly plant, which made the F-15 full-sized pickups, as well as the two hybrid sport utility vehicles. She said, "That's kind of the wave of the future. I think it's a safe plant."

Many workers found the array of separation packages overwhelming. "I'm starting all over again," said Tracy Ausen in tears to a *Minneapolis Star Tribune* reporter. "You try to put on a brave face and look at things optimistically, but I am really wondering if eighteen years ago I made a mistake coming to Ford instead of finishing a four-year degree. I'm just really scared." By the deadline, approximately 1,600 out of 1,725 workers at the Twin Cities plant accepted buyout offers—so many that Ford had to hire temporary workers to keep the St. Paul plant operating until it closed. The temporary workers were paid nineteen dollars an hour, well below the twenty-six dollars an hour earned by the departing "legacy" workers. Employees who took the buyout offer could also return as temporary workers at the lower pay, at Ford's discretion, and three hundred chose that option. Separations were slated to start in January 2007, and workers could decide up until their final days.

The Dislocated Worker Program mobilized quickly. Approximately $4.4 million was allocated for career counseling, support services, and retraining, and about one thousand workers received services. More than three hundred people completed the formal program, with almost half earning a diploma or professional certificate. Of those who finished, 297 returned to full-time employment elsewhere, with an average hourly wage of twenty dollars, and were still employed six months later. Because of a continued decline in sales of Rangers, the plant was shut down the last two weeks of December 2006, accelerating the first wave of discharged workers who left on December 14. When the plant reopened on January 1, the night shift was eliminated, even as Ford needed to continue hiring and training temporary workers.

Hopes for New Environmental Manufacturers

As hopes dimmed that Ford would keep the plant open, the UAW organized a community effort to find another manufacturing option. John Van Hecke, a policy analyst, captured the shift in focus: "The Ford plant is not a huge building complex next to the Mississippi River. It is rather a very sophisticated manufacturing workforce. Ford's St. Paul facility employees are not a bunch of grease monkeys spinning wing nuts in place. They are a group of workers with deep, complex assembly systems skills." Environmental groups, labor unions, and elected officials formed a "Blue/Green Coalition" in late 2006 to look for companies that could produce environment-friendly products locally, preferably at the Ford plant. A nonprofit company, the Autoworkers of Minnesota, Inc., emerged in

2007 with a proposal to convert the Ranger trucks built at the plant to an electric vehicle. It received a state grant of $150,000 to develop a prototype, which was displayed at the state fair the following year. With a price tag of twenty-two thousand dollars, it proved to be not economically viable. Several years later, another group, the Alliance to Re-Industrialize for a Sustainable Economy (ARISE), proposed a "community-based green manufacturing plant" that would make renewable energy components, such as wafers for solar panels and wind turbine parts.

The "final decision" to close the plant in 2008 was long, protracted, and filled with anxiety—but it was not final. In the UAW contract negotiations in November 2007, an agreement was reached with Ford to delay the closing of the plant until 2009. Sales of the Ranger had picked up somewhat, particularly in Canada, because of the falling value of the dollar. In addition, the costs of making the Rangers were reduced because of the less expensive temporary workers brought in after the buyouts. There was also a surprising increase in productivity as the production totals did not substantially drop with the loss of the night shift. In 2006, the plant made 115,000 Rangers with two shifts, and the following year made 106,000 units with one shift. About two-thirds of the 925 workers at the plant were temporary. The new four-year national contract formally accepted the two-tier wage system. In a significant concession by the union, new hires would be paid about $14.20 an hour, roughly half the pay of current workers, and, even more surprisingly, less than the pay of temporary workers who had just recently been hired in St. Paul. A new temporary worker said, "It's more demanding than any other job I've had. You're on your feet for 9 hours and 10 minutes a day. But it's also the best pay I've ever had."

The new starting pay, when adjusted for inflation, was only a modest amount more than the five dollars a day Henry Ford paid in 1914. The Ford Motor Company had pushed for a two-tier wage system many times, including in 1961 when Walter Reuther rejected it because it undermined the important principle of worker solidarity. One retired worker who was distressed about the decline in wages pointed out that he was making more money in retirement than the new hires. The new UAW contract not only reduced pay, it also shortened break time from thirty to twenty minutes, and included other concessions. It had become clear that with the new contracts, wage and benefit gains of the past century were being reversed. For the UAW, the fight was no longer about another nickel or another benefit—it was only about trying to ward off more "givebacks." The brutal reality was that the options for autoworkers narrowed considerably—a job with reduced pay and benefits, or a closed plant and no job and no union. Having given up the strike option and other tools, the International UAW was virtually impotent, and with the decline of worker solidarity there was less willingness to wage the fight on the shop floor. Political pressure added to the problems, as right-to-work laws continued to be enacted at the state level—including in Michigan, the birthplace of the UAW. Workers at union plants now had the option to stop paying dues. The UAW was trapped in an increasingly untenable position. Union workers were now competing not only with foreign workers, but also with American workers at nonunion transplant companies. A UAW official said, "We can't put the [union] companies at a disadvantage by asking for more than the transplants are paying." Gregg Shotwell, a retired dissident, spelled out the inherent folly of that position: "You don't pay dues to make less or the same as somebody who isn't paying those dues."

As Ford prepared to close the plant, a spike in gas prices to four dollars a gallon caused a surprising uptick in sales of the more fuel-efficient Ranger, and the company pushed back the plant closing until 2011. Workers applauded the second extension, but some who had taken buyouts after the initial announcement in 2006 expressed regrets, and others were unhappy because they lost their right to transfer. In 2009, Ford sought additional concessions from its workers to match the labor agreements with GM and Chrysler, which had fallen into bankruptcy and had been bailed out a second time by taxpayers. The federal government now owned the companies and placed a higher premium on saving the business (and the investment of taxpayers) than meeting the demands of the workers. The UAW workers at GM and Chrysler had little choice, but frustrated Ford workers pushed back for the first time in years. Rank-and-file members on the local level refused to match concessions made at bankrupt companies. To send a message, Ford canceled the planned production of an SUV at its Louisville plant and opted to keep it at a plant in Germany. An analyst observed, "Ford is showing that with its global production footprint, it can build wherever it wants." Ford also announced plans in 2010 to build plants in India, and to make a major investment in Thailand with its partner Mazda for production of a compact pickup truck.

State and city leaders continued to work on a package of incentives for Ford. Republican governor Tim Pawlenty was now running for president, and Democratic mayor Chris Coleman of St. Paul was contemplating a run for governor. Pawlenty, who had vowed he would not throw money at Ford several years earlier, proposed a tax-free "CARZ" program, a $90 million incentive package modeled on his rural initiative JOBZ plan. The city of St. Paul proposed a sale–lease-back plan through its Port Authority that would provide funds to Ford for capital improvements at the plant. The governor and the mayor met with Mark Fields, Ford's vice president for the Americas division, on August 24, 2010, to present a package of incentives reportedly worth almost a half a billion dollars. The *Pioneer Press* described the lead-up to the meeting: "They already said please. Then pretty please. Now this, they hope, is the cherry on top." The Minnesota delegation to Detroit did not include representatives from Local 879, prompting its chairman, Jim Eagle, to

Dan Huseby *(bottom row left)* was a professional photographer who also worked at the Ford plant. Courtesy of Dan Huseby.

complain: "Somehow we're going to attend that meeting, and we're going to find out what's going on." He did fly to Detroit but was not permitted to attend the meeting. Eagle said, "The last word we got was the governor was upset and didn't want us." At the meeting, Fields reportedly said that the St. Paul plant did not have the flexibility to quickly convert to different models, and that it was located outside the supply-chain corridor.

Most people appreciated the continued efforts of the governor and the mayor, but some thought they were being too generous. One blogger wrote: "We tried to throw taxpayer money at the problem, and when that didn't work, we tried to throw taxpayer money at the problem, and when that failed, we tried out last ditch resort of throwing money at the problem. Frankly, we're out of ideas at this point." After Ford's rejection, the commissioner of the Department of Employment and Economic Development, Dan McElroy, made it clear that the state would continue to look for other uses for the site, and that the incentives were available to other companies. He revealed that Governor Pawlenty sent a letter to Toyota in 2006 and to the Tata Group of India in 2008. Given that Ford owned the site, it was unclear whether it would approve a sale of the property to a foreign competitor.

As workers' pay was reduced to be more "competitive," executive pay kept increasing. Reuther always fought hard for the principle of "equality of sacrifice." During World War II he suggested a compensation formula by which a company CEO would make no more than eight times that of a line worker. In 1984, the Ford CEO Phillip Caldwell made $7.3 million while he was pushing workers to accept concessions. This was perceived to be so exorbitant that management consultant Peter Drucker wrote an Op-Ed piece for the *Wall Street Journal* calling for a cap on executive compensation. He said that the Japanese paid their auto executives far less and got far more. Even the U.S. trade representative, William Brock, said that the executive bonuses led to higher prices, making it more difficult to compete with foreign companies and to justify additional tariff protection. By 2012, the gap had grown to the point where the Ford CEO, Alan Mulally, had a compensation package of $29.5 million—one thousand times more than that of a line worker. He earned more in 2010, 2011, and 2013 than the company paid in federal taxes.

When Ford announced the plant closing in 2006, one irate autoworker suggested to others on the line that they "run crappy units." A fellow worker disapproved of his colleague's sentiment and said that Ford had the decency to give advanced notice allowing

Workers cleared out lockers in the final days of the Twin Cities plant. Courtesy of Dan Huseby.

for transfer opportunities, buyout options, and training. "If you listen to this cowhand over here," he said, "you won't have to worry for two years [about closing] because they'll shutter before that . . . Build good products up until the very last day and you walk out tall and you walk out proud." Rangers were made right up to the last day on December 22, 2011. The generous termination benefits helped ensure that even during its last months the plant operated in a normal, businesslike fashion.

The company and the union worked together on several events to honor the legacy of one of Ford's oldest plants and recognize the contributions of its many retired workers. However, one routine was pointedly dropped in the final months. Ford typically held quarterly town-hall meetings that Jim Eagle described as being "about how well Ford Motor

As an employee, Dan Huseby was able to wander around the Ford plant during its final weeks, taking hundreds of photographs documenting its closing. These remarkable images capture the last day of the Twin Cities Assembly Plant. Dallas Theis, who worked at the plant for fifty-three years, was given the honor of driving the last Ranger pickup out the door. He is pictured on the opposite page. Courtesy of Dan Huseby.

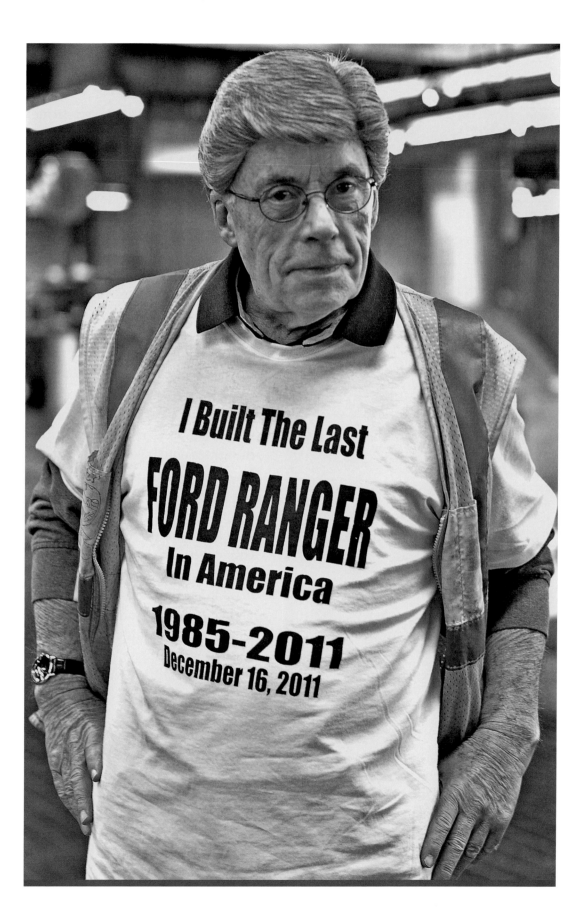

Company is doing while not including us in their plans." That was "like rubbing our pending closure in our faces." He requested that the company not hold these meetings anymore at the Twin Cities Assembly Plant. Union activists from New Directions, who had opposed Employee Involvement and other collaborative programs for more than thirty years, may have had reason to feel vindicated. In the end, cooperation and high-quality workmanship didn't matter much.

Ford's plant closings and massive layoffs helped turn the company around. It reported a profit of $2.6 billion in the second quarter of 2010, its fifth straight quarterly profit. More impressively, it had gone from losing the most money in its history to earning solid profits and increasing its market share—with half as many employees. The company also significantly reduced the time it took to develop a new model. The compressed period gave Ford more time to decide where models would be built, which further strengthened its negotiating position with labor. It could also weigh other factors such as currency exchange rates.

The closing of the Twin Cities plant ended the twenty-nine-year run of the Ranger compact truck. More than 6.6 million Rangers were sold, and an estimated eight hundred thousand were still on the road. The Ranger led the compact truck segment for eighteen years but was eclipsed by the Toyota Tacoma in 2005. Ford had made relatively few improvements to the Ranger over the years, opting instead to invest in its larger cousin, the F-150 pickup. One analyst said, "This is not the case of Toyota stealing Ranger's sales.

This is really a case of Ford not keeping the Ranger up-to-date enough to maintain sales levels." The price gap between the two models had narrowed to the point where an F-105 truck could be bought for only six hundred dollars more than a top-of-the line Ranger. Ford was, in effect, competing with itself. Domestic production of the Ranger ended, but Ford continued to make a revamped model in Thailand, South Africa, and Argentina for the foreign market.

The Twin Cities Assembly Plant opened in 1926 with the obsolete Model T, which had a nineteen-year run, and closed eighty-five years later with the obsolete Ranger pickup truck, which had a twenty-nine-year run. The last pickup to roll off the line was reserved for its largest customer, the Orkin Exterminating Company, which owned a fleet of five

thousand Ranger trucks. Photographers were generally not permitted in the Ford plant, except under very tight controls, and none were allowed access during the final weeks of operation. Dan Huseby, a professional photographer who also worked at the plant, managed to take hundreds of extraordinary pictures in the final months. Some from the last day are seen here.

When the plant finally closed, workers were not only upset about losing their jobs but also that the buildings would be torn down. "I'll tell you when it will really sadden you is when you drive by and there is no building, no nothing," said Terry Dinderman, a retired manager. "The difficult part for them is the fact that they can't drive by the buildings and say 'Well, here's where your Mom used to work,' or your grandma. It's no longer an institution."

Epilogue

Moving On

The city of St. Paul lost little time in planning for the future use of the assembly plant site. The first meeting of the Ford Site Planning Task Force was held in early February 2007, shortly after Ford announced its intention to close the plant. The Ford Motor Company participated in the community process but a representative made it clear that it was not obligated to accept its recommendations. The city and the St. Paul Port Authority retained a team of prominent planning and real-estate development experts to help guide the advisory group. By October, the consultants had completed a report showing five different development scenarios ranging from light-industrial to high-density, mixed-use development. The pace of the planning efforts slowed after Ford announced that it would delay the plant closing.

By the time the last Ranger rode off the assembly line on December 22, 2011, Ford was well under way with the complicated process of "decommissioning" the plant. More than two million square feet of industrial buildings had to be demolished. Environmental testing had to be done on the 125-acre site, and a remediation plan had to be developed before the property could be put up for sale. Given the number of plant closings around the country, Ford already had a team of experts who were brought in to oversee the process. All equipment and tools from the buildings that could be reused were carefully removed. Some items were sent to other Ford plants, including many of the 176 robots. Robots that could not be used by Ford were sold to other industrial companies or donated to a local skilled-trades training facility. Mike Hogan, the Ford site manager, invited community groups to tour the plant to select unwanted surplus items. The Highland Park District Council and the Hillcrest Recreation Center received tables, chairs, and other office equipment. Light fixtures and training equipment were donated to St. Paul College.

In anticipation of the demolition, Ford commissioned a historic structures report that concluded that the remaining section of the original 1924 assembly plant had lost

Prior to demolition, the robots, automated power tools, computer monitors, and electronic tracking equipment were moved to other Ford plants, sold off, or donated to educational institutions. Courtesy of Dan Huseby.

much of its integrity because of later alterations to the complex. A twenty-two-acre parcel on the river, which included the steam plant, was not part of the study or included in the planned redevelopment site. Much of the equipment in the steam plant had already been removed, and Ford had previously done a study of possible reuse options. It appeared that Ford was considering redeveloping the steam plant or selling it separately.

In early February 2012, Ford brought in its team of corporate historians, led by Robert Kreipke, to search the plant for potential important records or artifacts. Kreipke met with local historians, who were disappointed that they would not have an opportunity to review the materials before they were packed up and shipped to company headquarters in Dearborn. Among the three truckloads of items removed were records dating back to the original Minneapolis plant. Kreipke said that it would probably take a while to make the records available to scholars, noting that boxes of materials retrieved from an Ohio plant twenty years earlier were still sitting in shipping containers, unopened and uncataloged.

Local historians and preservationists (including the author) mounted a campaign to save the original historic showroom and entrance on the northwest corner of the complex, which were relatively intact. There were also efforts to save the adjoining Training

The Ford Motor Company held off demolition of the historic showroom until the very end, awaiting any last-minute viable proposals for preservation. Author's collection.

Elements of the original exterior limestone facade were carefully dismantled and placed in cargo containers on the site of the plant, in hopes that the historic showroom could be reassembled and possibly incorporated into new development. Author's collection.

Center, which had been built with $5 million in state funds. The Ford decommissioning team agreed to hold off on the demolition of those sections until the very end, giving preservationists an opportunity to come up with a buyer or a viable reuse plan, which they were unable to do. Several historic architectural elements from the original 1924 building were donated to the Minnesota Historical Society. Ford also donated two original exterior light fixtures to the Model A Museum in Hickory Corners, Michigan, which are now displayed in the museum's thirteen thousand-square-foot facility. At the last minute, Ford agreed to carefully dismantle architectural elements of the historic facade and store them in metal cargo containers on-site. The hope was that these sections could be incorporated into a new development or be part of a future legacy monument.

Demolition of the plant started on June 9, 2013. Mayor Chris Coleman was on hand for the countdown ceremony and remarked, "Today is a day that the landscape of St. Paul fundamentally changes . . . but it is a day that marks a giant step forward for the Highland community, for the city of St. Paul and for the region." Several retirees were also there to bid farewell to the plant that produced more than six million vehicles. Some who had worked at the plant for forty years had tears in their eyes.

Unlike all other plants that Ford closed, the St. Paul facility was located in an upscale, tight-knit residential community, one that was unafraid to challenge the company over the years for environmental or other reasons. The decommissioning team went to great lengths to share information at community meetings explaining the demolition process and reassuring residents on environmental safeguards. It reported that scrap materials would be hauled away by railroad and truck and gave a detailed estimate of the number of trucks, their routes, and hours of operation. It was anticipated that there would be twenty truck trips daily, compared to the 250 a day when the plant was operating. Demolition took approximately two years, and its cost was largely offset by the scrap value of the salvaged materials.

Environmental assessment of the site could not proceed in earnest until after the demolition of the buildings and removal of the underlying slabs. It was assumed there would be need for remediation but the amount and cost were unknown. In September 2014, an environmental group, Friends of the Mississippi River, raised concerns that Ford and the Minnesota environmental protection agencies were not properly examining the landfill mound that Ford had created along the river. Area C, as it was known, was sixty-five feet high and covered an area of approximately four acres. Ford acknowledged that it had routinely disposed of paint, solvents, and construction rubble in the mound from approximately 1945 to 1966. Retirees reported that glass chunks from the furnace were routinely dumped there, as well as elements of the original front facade that were removed in 1968. Ford covered the mound with a concrete slab and used it as a parking lot for trailers. However, some barrels and construction debris remained clearly visible. Environmentalists claimed that hazardous materials were likely being washed away during spring floods as the river rose almost halfway up the mound. Whitney Clark, from Friends of the Mississippi River, pressed to have the entire mound removed and the site brought back to its original condition. Ford may have excluded the twenty-two-acre riverfront parcel from the site being studied for redevelopment because of environmental concerns.

By the end of 2015, Ford's environmental engineers had taken more than one thousand ground samples, which are now being analyzed. The results will determine the scope of cleanup and the amount of remediation needed. Ford is responsible to clean the site to industrial standards before selling the property, but has not yet agreed to comply with the more rigid residential standards that would be required for more intensive redevelopment.

While the demolition and environmental testing were proceeding, a high-stakes trial was taking place in the Minnesota tax court over the amount of property tax owed by the Ford Motor Company. Ford sued for a refund of $10.6 million—all the property taxes it paid during the years 2007 to 2011. Ford's position was that the property was worth zero dollars, mainly because of the environmental contamination (which it had caused), and it argued that Ramsey County assessors grossly inflated its valuation. At the same time, many real-estate analysts, and even the real-estate brokers retained by Ford to market the property, described the site as one of the prime development parcels in the region. After five years of legal skirmishing, the trial finally started in early 2014. Marc Manderscheid, an attorney representing Ramsey County, described to a *Star Tribune* reporter the challenge Ford faced. The question is "whether Ford is going to pan the property at trial when they're going to try to sell it for the highest possible use."

In August 2014, the tax court ruled that Ramsey County did inflate the valuation of the 122-acre assembly property and that Ford was entitled to a refund of approximately $4 million. The ruling did not apply to Ford's twenty-two-acre parcel along the river, or include taxes the company paid after 2011. Ford and Ramsey County later negotiated a settlement for ten years of property taxes at values approximating those referenced in the judge's ruling. It was likely the largest tax refund in the history of Ramsey County.

With the closing of the Ford plant, UAW Local 879 started to plan for the future. Several local members hoped to keep the union operating with volunteers to service the needs of retirees. There were some assets remaining, including the union hall on Ford Parkway, but there would be little ongoing income available for staff, as the dues for retirees were only one dollar a month. The International UAW requested a concrete proposal that could demonstrate the long-term viability of the local chapter. When none appeared, it decided to close the Local and transfer remaining responsibilities to UAW Local 125, also in St. Paul. The UAW representative handling the closing was Rob McKenzie, the former president of Local 879 who had worked at the plant for twenty-eight years. In 2006, McKenzie was appointed to the position of servicing representative for UAW Region 4, which handled thirty-five sites in the Upper Midwest. During his tenure as president of Local 879, McKenzie spent most of his time trying to save the plant, so it was an especially difficult task for him to be responsible for closing it down.

When the St. Paul assembly plant closed, some workers transferred to the Ford Parts Depot in Menomonie, Wisconsin, which was also represented by Local 879. This small unit of about eighteen workers hoped to continue being represented by UAW Local 879, but the International UAW decided to consolidate them with another UAW local operating in Hudson, Wisconsin. Disgruntled workers appealed to overturn the decision to close Local 879, but that appeal was denied.

Local 879 had little choice but to end its operations. Records, memorabilia, and equipment were distributed to members and other union locals, and management responsibilities for its retirees were transferred to the UAW Local 125 in St. Paul. The union hall on Ford Parkway was sold to Erik's Bikes in March 2013. Owner Erik Saltvold believed the location was ideal because of the future development of the Ford site and proximity to the Mississippi River trails. The five hundred thousand–dollar proceeds from the sale went to the International UAW in Dearborn.

The ten-story Minneapolis plant Ford vacated in 1924 sat empty for thirty years until it was acquired by the Honeywell Corporation, which manufactured thermostats. In 2007, the building was purchased by United Properties, an affiliate of the Pohlad Companies, which owned the Minnesota Twins, located in a new stadium across the street. United Properties spent $50 million renovating the building to meet the historic guidelines of the National Register. In late 2011, HGA Architects, designers for the project, became the first tenants in the building, which is now completely leased.

The former Ford assembly plant on University Avenue in St. Paul is in a state of limbo. It has been owned by the state for sixty years but has been empty for the past decade. The state had hoped to demolish it to make way for parking, but these plans were thwarted by an aggressive preservation campaign. No funds have been allocated for renovating the structure, and the state refuses to sell the property. Preservationists worry that it might succumb to "demolition by neglect."

In 2015, the Ford Motor Company had record pretax profits in North America of $7.4 billion. Profit-sharing checks of about $9,300 were distributed but did little to satisfy those workers who were forced to accept decades of concessions, nor did they address the frustrations of younger workers who were subjected to the two-tier system. Given the record profits, the UAW was under considerable pressure to deliver a new contract that would make up for lost ground. The first contract proposal negotiated by UAW leaders was roundly rejected by the rank and file in a ratification vote. *Forbes Magazine* in its November 19, 2015, article "When a Union Isn't a Union: A Weakened and Divided UAW Struggles to Get Workers to March in Step," attributed the rebellion to simmering resentment over the UAW's acceptance of the two-tier system in 2007, and the fact that union leaders had abandoned the policy of pattern bargaining.

A revised contract proposal included a onetime ratification bonus of $8,500 and a commitment to eliminate the hated two-tier system. However, the long-sought parity

The original Minneapolis assembly plant was converted to offices and is now fully occupied. Photograph copyright Paul Crosby.

would be phased in over eight years and it would be moved toward the lower pay level. Ford was content to wait for the legacy workers to retire. After considerable rancor, this contract was adopted. Ford's response to the more expensive contract was to announce in early 2016 that it would build a $1.5 billion plant in Mexico, doubling capacity in that country. Even though Ford was making record profits and the labor costs per unit had dropped significantly in the United States, the company made it clear that UAW workers would have to compete directly with their counterparts in Mexico who were earning one-fifth as much. The UAW president Dennis Williams protested, saying that "they're making profits right here in the United States." In March 2015 Ford displayed a new Ranger pickup truck at the Bangkok Auto Show that would be sold in 180 markets worldwide, but not in the United States, according to the company.

Ford's decision to move production out of the country impacted its network of suppliers. Johnson Controls, which was one of the main suppliers to the Twin Cities Assembly Plant, announced in January 2016 that it was spinning off its automotive business and moving its corporate headquarters to Ireland, where it would face considerably lower tax bills. Politicians roundly denounced the move as unpatriotic. An editorial in the *New York Times* referred to the company as "quite possibly the most brazen tax dodger," noting that its president "personally begged Congress" in 2008 for part of the auto bailout proceeds that it received.

The Ford Site Community Task Force continues to meet, and the property is expected to be available for redevelopment by 2018. One of the highest priorities of the community is the preservation of the Little League ball fields. The St. Paul Department of Planning posts minutes and reports of the planning Task Force at its city Web site.

A number of Ford retirees and community activists are continuing with efforts to create a lasting tribute to the legacy of the Ford Motor Company, its workers, dealers, and suppliers. One goal is to reconstruct the salvaged architectural elements of the original building on the site of the former Twin Cities Assembly Plant. There is an ongoing effort to place a considerable amount of historic memorabilia and artifacts into a museum where the materials could be properly catalogued, conserved, and preserved for future generations. Information on these efforts can be found at www.FordLegacyMN.com.

Retirees, both "hourlies" and management, still gather at annual social events. Keeping with tradition, these events are held in separate venues.

Acknowledgments

Retired autoworkers used to give tours of the now demolished Twin Cities Assembly Plant that were very popular with school groups and others curious about how cars were made. I took the tour in 1998 and was extremely impressed with our knowledgeable guide, and of course I was amazed at seeing a jumble of parts turn into a finished vehicle right before my eyes. This experience ultimately set me on a path to writing this book.

I had been interested in industrial architecture for some time, and I pursued research projects with grants from the Minnesota Humanities Commission and the Minnesota Historical Society. After the tour at the Ford plant, my focus narrowed considerably to automobile manufacturing and the Ford Motor Company. Russell Fridley, director of the Minnesota Labor Interpretive Center, provided funding for me to interview retired Ford autoworkers for an oral history project. He recognized the importance of documenting this important American industry that was in serious decline, seemingly unable to compete in the new global economy. These interviews provide firsthand accounts and remarkable insights into what can now be seen as "the end of an era."

With Russ Fridley's strong support and encouragement, I traveled to Detroit to research the archives at the Henry Ford Museum, the Walter P. Reuther Library at Wayne State University, and the National Automotive History Collection at the Detroit Public Library, where I was helped by dedicated staff. I also visited the office of Albert Kahn Associates, the architectural firm responsible for the design of the Twin Cities Assembly Plant, where librarian Sylvia Sanders provided access to their wonderful collection of old drawings. Grant Hildebrand, who had worked at the Kahn office and later wrote several important architectural histories, generously shared information and analysis about the firm. More recently, Donald Bauman at the Kahn office located photographs and described his experiences working on designs for later additions to the St. Paul plant.

Ford had earlier built plants in Minneapolis and St. Paul that were designed by architect John Graham of Seattle. I traveled to that city to visit DLR Architects, the successor firm to Graham. Shannon Soady facilitated my search of its archives and generously provided copies of original Graham drawings. Leonard Garfield and Caroline Marr of the Museum of History and Industry in Seattle shared materials on the Seattle Ford plant, which became the model for dozens of branch assembly plants around the country. I learned more about these dispersed factories from local correspondents, including Nuala King of Atlanta, Dennis E. Horvath of Indianapolis, Donald Doherty of Pittsburgh, Barbara A. Carpenter at the architectural firm Tsoi/Kobus & Associates in Cambridge, Massachusetts, Kristenna P. Chace, from the city of Somerville, Massachusetts, and Christopher Grey, of the Office for Metropolitan History in New York City. The architectural firm Mutchler–Bartram provided drawings and considerable information about the branch plant in Fargo, North Dakota, as did the Institute for Regional Studies, North Dakota State University, Fargo.

Hoff Heiberg at Hillcrest Development, the firm that once owned the former Minneapolis Ford Assembly Plant, enthusiastically shared his personal research into this building, as did its next owner, Kit Richardson of Schafer Richardson. The Minneapolis plant was recently renovated, and Nick Koch of HGA Architects was kind enough to give me a special tour and background materials about the project. Additional information on the building was provided by the staff at the Minneapolis Heritage Preservation Commission and by Charlene Roise of the research firm Hess Roise & Company, who also sent me information on the Twin Cities Assembly Plant in St. Paul. Thanks to John Wickre, who sent me materials on the construction of the rail line that entered the Minneapolis plant, and to attorney Stuart Alger, who provided legal information on the infamous "Ford alley" lawsuit that dragged on for decades.

I am especially indebted to the staff at the many outstanding historical societies in Minnesota. Deborah Miller, Adam Scher, and Ann Regan at the Minnesota Historical Society are among those who were particularly helpful, along with John Lindley and Mollie Spillman at the Ramsey County Historical Society. I relied heavily on county historical societies to learn more about local Ford dealerships. Georgia Rosendahl spent weeks searching the collections of the Houston County Historical Society to find an important photograph she had remembered seeing. Thomas Carlson, a professional genealogist, sorted out the odd coincidence of having two Ford dealers named Onsgard within ten miles of each other in Houston County—who were unrelated. Lynda Hall and Sue Duda of the St. Louis County Historical Society provided information on the Woodhead dealership in Brainerd and helped me locate the original buildings. I received considerable help from families who owned, or previously owned, Ford dealerships: thanks to Brien Slawik, John Tichenor, Thomas Owens, Kari Rihm, Deb Tenvoorde, John Woodhead, and

Pete Onsgard for assistance. One of the early dealers in St. Paul, W. H. Schmelzel, sued Henry Ford, and I gained insights about dealership practices by studying the court filings. Thanks to Maggie Heisterkamp, who brought this case to my attention, and shared her deep knowledge of Ford history and insights gleaned from working for many years at the Twin Cities Assembly Plant. She had responsibility for maintaining and updating the numerous architectural and engineering drawings of the plant and generously shared information about the changes that took place over time. Patricia Maus, curator of the Kathryn A. Martin Library, University of Minnesota Duluth, went to considerable effort to find information on the coal dock that Ford rented in Duluth Harbor and located pictures of the large barges that shipped cars across Lake Superior. The Army Corps of Engineers in St. Paul has a wonderful collection of historic materials on the design and construction of the High Dam on the Mississippi River, which it readily shared with me. I thank present and former staff, including John Anfinson, Kevin P. Bokay, and Vanessa Hamer.

Over the past eighteen years I have come to know and admire many people who worked at the Ford plant. Even children of workers came forward, recalling stories of their fathers. Sadly, a number of people I interviewed have since passed away. I am truly indebted to everyone who has been so generous in sharing their stories and information: this book could not have been written without their help. I have been honored to be entrusted with their stories, which I hope will be preserved through their oral histories and this book. In 1999, the History Theatre of St. Paul performed several professionally staged, dramatic readings of excerpts from these interviews. Thanks to director Ron Peluso, who brought these stories to life in a production enjoyed by many retirees and their families.

I owe special thanks to the late Bob Killeen and to Al Hendricks, whose work at the plant and later careers with the United Auto Workers union spanned a half century. Tom Laney, who was president of UAW Local 879 during the turbulent 1980s, shared an enormous amount of materials, including photographs, and provided valuable analysis. His passionate commitment to the cause of working people has not diminished with the passing of time and has given me a much better understanding of the crucial labor-relations battles that took place on his watch. Rob McKenzie, who led the union during the late 1990s, has been a keen observer of the larger economic and political forces that threatened the Twin Cities Assembly Plant and its workers. He generously shared photographs and a number of other materials. Lynn Hinkle, a union committeeman, has a marvelous appreciation for the texture of everyday life on the assembly line for the workers putting in ten-hour days. Rick Magnuson, who served as unofficial custodian and conservator of the historic photographs and materials at the plant, shared many pictures and materials with me and was helpful in restoring several images included in the book. Special thanks to Peter Rachleff, a historian and labor activist, who provided context on how the political and cultural conflicts spawned by the Vietnam War led to a radicalization of the workforce. Organizers from communist and socialist organizations specifically targeted the Twin Cities Assembly Plant as part of a national "turn to industry" campaign.

Management retirees also described their experiences at the plant, covering all phases of the production process. R. W. (Bob) Johnson, who rose to the top engineering position at the plant, spent many hours sharing his encyclopedic knowledge. He also provided me with many photographs. Engineer Robert Hansen had information and materials going back to the Minneapolis plant, where his father worked, and also had firsthand accounts of his experiences at the Twin Cities Assembly Plant during the Great Depression and World War II. Del Peterson, a process engineer, described improvising ad hoc solutions to all manner of problems and the difficulty of maintaining quality control. He generously shared his collection of historic materials and photographs. Engineer Ralph Cook recounted various feasibility studies for expansion of the plant. He was also an airplane pilot who operated an aerial photography business with his wife, Yvonne; their aerial images of the plant were very helpful to understanding the sprawling complex. Mike Hogan, the last plant manager in St. Paul, has been extremely accommodating in answering inquiries relating to the "decommissioning" and demolition process.

When I needed to learn more about a particular car model or to identify a vehicle in a historic photograph, I invariably turned to Bruce Nelson and Tom Murray. These two experts are active in local automobile clubs and have owned and restored many Fords. I thank them not only for sharing their expertise but also for rekindling that sense of joy that comes from experiencing a well-made car—and even appreciating those cars that were not. Thanks to Jim Spawn of the Ford Model A Museum in Hickory Corners, Michigan, who has been helpful in answering specific car questions.

The last significant construction project at the plant was the 1998 Training Center designed by TKDA Architects in St. Paul. Thanks to this firm for sharing images and information about the building. I greatly appreciate Dale Mischke of the *Highland Villager* for providing photographs from that newspaper's in-depth coverage of the Ford plant over many years.

Over the past several years I had the pleasure of working with various history consulting firms that were researching some part of the Ford story. Thanks to Andrew J. Schmidt and Marjorie Pierson of Summit Envirosolutions, and to Meghan Elliott, Marisa Koivisto, and Greg Donofrio of Preservation Design Works for sharing information. I am grateful to Ramsey County assessor Stephen L. Baker, who provided background information on a property tax lawsuit filed by the Ford Motor Company, and to Marc Manderscheid, the attorney representing the county. Both have become quite conversant with the history of the Twin Cities Assembly Plant, which was an important part of the litigation. Marc has recently completed a study of the zoning conflicts between residential and industrial development that shaped the Highland Park neighborhood.

The contributions of many other people made this book far richer. My deepest thanks go to Linda James, Lisa Heinrich, Don Empson, Peter Myers, Greg Brick, Christine Podas-Larson, Barb Kucera, Steve Trimble, Wayne Wittman, Bob Killeen Jr., Dee Velline, John Shardlow, Bill Casey, Marsha Anderson-Shearen, David Lanegran, Anton Gerve, Hank Kushima, Andrew Hine, Joseph Szczesny, and Richard Kramer, among others.

A special thanks goes to Pieter Martin, my editor at the University of Minnesota Press, who embraced the challenge of working with a novice book author and did so with great skill, patience, and humor. It was also a pleasure to work with Kristian Tvedten at the University of Minnesota Press and copy editor David Thorstad and all the members of the Press's production department, who turned a manuscript and stack of pictures into an attractive book. I am very grateful to historian Larry Haeg, whose keen observations helped sharpen my narrative and improve my writing.

This book is dedicated with love to my wife Teresa, who provided enormous support throughout this project—as she has with all our endeavors. I thank our four children, Katarzyna, Tadeusz, Mariah, and Colm, for putting up with way too many Ford stories, trips, and distractions. Their futures were very much on my mind as I pondered how the Ford Century has impacted us all.

Notes on Sources

Hundreds of books and thousands of articles have been written about Henry Ford and his automobile company. Allan Nevins, in collaboration with Frank Ernest Hill, wrote an authoritative, three-volume account that was published from 1954 to 1962. The Ford Motor Company funded this project through Columbia University and provided the authors access to the corporate archives, which had just been opened to the public. This 1,900-page trilogy, and other books by Robert Lacey and Douglas Brinkley, effectively establish the larger national context but do not offer much information about events in Minnesota or other branch assembly plants.

Many publications on Ford the company or Henry Ford are narrower in scope, with a surprising number of books on the same topic including, among others, works about the Model T, the Peace Ship, anti-Semitism, factory design, environmental policies, by-product industries, public relations, Ford's friendship with Thomas Edison, and labor practices. Prominent literary figures wrote about Henry Ford, including novelists Upton Sinclair and Aldous Huxley and nonfiction writers John Reed, Alfred D. Chandler, and David Halberstam, whose modern classic *The Reckoning* carries the Ford story deep into the twentieth century.

Keith Sward's 1948 book casts Ford in an unsympathetic light over his harsh treatment of workers and dealers. A new field of study emerged to take critical aim at "Fordism," as his labor practices were widely dubbed. Feeling the need to present his own story, Henry Ford published a number of books and articles, with considerable editorial assistance from aides Samuel Crowther, Ernest Liebold, and William J. Cameron. Although these may not be entirely authentic in their expression, they do provide insights into Ford's philosophy and motivations. Members of Ford's key staff also wrote autobiographies, including Charles Sorensen, Samuel S. Marquis, Harry Bennett, and William Bushnell Stout. Two Ford CEOs, Lee Iacocca and Donald Petersen, later wrote about their time with the company, and several other Ford employees, including Ford R. Bryan, David L. Lewis, Timothy J. O'Callaghan, Clair J. Snider and Michael W. R. Davis, wrote about different aspects of the corporate history. This abundance of accounts by company insiders is fairly unprecedented.

Research for this book took me to several archives around the country, including the William Benson Library at the Ford Museum, the Walter P. Reuther Library at Wayne State University, the office of architect Albert Kahn (still in operation), and the National Automotive History Collection at the Detroit Public Library, all in or near Detroit. I visited the archives of architect John Graham in Seattle and the National Archives in Washington, D.C. I researched numerous history collections in Minnesota, including those at the Minnesota Historical Society, Ramsey County Historical Society, and the Hennepin History Museum library. The historical societies at Stearns County, Crow Wing County, Houston County, and St. Louis County provided important information about local Ford dealerships. The special history collections at the St. Paul Public Library and the Minneapolis Public Library were very helpful, as were the libraries at the University of Minnesota, including their institutional Archives and the Northwest Architectural Archives.

Henry Ford's accomplishments and outsize personality attracted widespread media attention throughout his life. I made extensive use of these contemporaneous accounts from magazines and national newspapers, notably the *New York Times*. Several weekly papers, including the *Union Advocate* and the *Minneapolis Spokesman*, also provided important insights, particularly about the concerns of workers and minorities. The *Highland Villager* newspaper, based in Highland Park, St. Paul, has published two times a month since 1953, giving considerable coverage to the Ford plant; staff of this paper generously shared many of its photographs.

Local newspapers, including the *Minneapolis Star Tribune* and the *St. Paul Pioneer Press* and their predecessor newspapers, covered the Ford story closely for more than a century. This coverage established the "first draft of history" for understanding Ford's local impact, which is particularly important because national histories have little information about branch assembly plants. Local media coverage intensified after 1970, as the Twin Cities Assembly Plant was buffeted by the forces of globalization, foreign competition, outsourcing, and corporate retrenchment. The character and style of the writing changed as well. The decline of the American auto industry was no longer a national abstract story, but one that impacted our community and our neighbors in a very real way. Local reporters may have shown their hometown loyalties by bringing a sharper edge to the story that looked deeper than the corporate press releases. Workers at the Twin Cities Assembly Plant, including managers, were quoted extensively, putting a human face on labor issues and the impending plant closure. These provided important context to my narrative.

I am very appreciative of the Internet as a basic tool for research, as this remarkable tool did not exist when I started this project more than fifteen years ago. Innumerable obscure magazines, journals, catalogs, and trade publications covering every aspect of automobile manufacturing are now instantly accessible, thanks to Google, Wikipedia, and other sites. I even had considerable luck finding people whose relatives had some connection to Ford history. I made extensive use of commercial sites on the Internet to acquire books, magazines, artifacts, photographs, postcards, memorabilia, and other ephemera about Ford. Fascination with Ford continues unabated, as evidenced by the unending stream of books and documentaries, the emergence of dedicated Internet chat rooms and forums, and the establishment of Ford clubs and museums.

I conducted more than forty in-depth interviews with autoworkers, car dealers, and others with a Ford connection, and had conversations with many others. This process started in 1998 with a small oral history grant from the Minnesota Labor Interpretive Center, and continued right up to publication. More than a thousand pages of conversations have been transcribed, which has proven invaluable in understanding Ford's last seventy years in Minnesota.

The UAW Local 879 has been particularly helpful in connecting me with retirees and allowing me to search its archives. The union had published a newsletter regularly since 1941, most recently called *The Autoworker*. The Ford Motor Company also published a plant newsletter intermittently for workers at the Twin Cities Assembly Plant. These newsletters give a good perspective on important events from the company perspective, as they were unfolding. The Ford Motor Company in Detroit published many books, pamphlets, brochures, and promotional materials over the years, and many of these included information on branch plants.

1. Model T for the Northwest Territories

The Stearns County Historical Society's (SCHS) vertical file on the history of Tenvoorde Ford includes a number of clippings from St. Cloud newspapers and provided important information. Additional news articles are available on microfilm at SCHS and at the Minnesota Historical Society (MHS). The Tenvoorde family has posted historical information on the dealership Web site www.TenvoordeFord.com. Books by Allan Nevins and Frank Ernest Hill, Robert Lacy, and Douglas Brinkley thoroughly documented Henry Ford's participation in the early bicycle and automobile shows and racing activities, as well as early corporate history. Contemporary trade publications also provided good information. Lindy Biggs, in her book *The Rational Factory*, writes of the Highland Park plant and the impact that Henry Ford and his architect Albert Kahn had on the development of the modern industrial factory. In their remarkable book *Ford Methods and the Ford Shops*, Horace Lucien Arnold and Fay Leone Faurote documented the manufacturing process in 1914 at Highland Park with numerous pictures from the time the assembly line was being developed. Henry Ford, in *My Life and Work*, gives his account of the development of the assembly line.

Several books on the history of the Model T informed this chapter, the most notable being Robert Casey's *The Model T: A Centennial History*. Keith Sward gives an early critical look at Ford's labor policies, which are also well documented in *The Five Dollar Day: Labor Management and Social Control in the Ford Motor Company, 1908–1921* by Stephen Meyer III. Samuel S. Marquis, who led Ford's sociological department, provided insights into Ford's corporate welfare programs.

Many advertisements and occasional articles on the Northwestern Automobile Agency were published in the Minneapolis newspapers, and additional information on this early distributor can be found in press releases of the Ford Motor Company. Stephen L. McIntyre offers groundbreaking insights into the service and repair business in "The Failure of Fordism Reform of the Automobile Repair Industry, 1913–1940."

Gordon Schindler's extensive writings informed the section on the aftermarket industry spawned by the Model T. One of the most important accessory manufacturers, Edwin Gustave Staude of St. Paul, published an autobiography. John Wickre from the Minnesota Historical Society has compiled a vertical file with significant information on tractor companies in Minnesota, including the Ford Tractor Company in Minneapolis. Several local collections offer material on dealerships, including privately owned papers on W. H. Schmelzel, and corporate documents and records on the Woodhead Motor Company made available by John Woodhead. Anne Jardim's book *The First Henry Ford: A Study in Personality and Business Leadership* is a fascinating blend of historical research and psychoanalysis that makes a convincing explanation for Ford's obsession with "The Farmer." Friedrich Kessler wrote an article in 1957 for the *Yale Law Journal*, "Automobile Dealer Franchises: Vertical Integration by Contract." Law professor M. Todd Henderson analyzed Ford's partnership conflicts in his "Everything Old Is New Again: Lessons from *Dodge v. Ford Motor Company*."

Articles in local newspapers and trade publications informed the section on the dealer Merritt B. Osborn. A corporate history published by Ecolab in 1998, *Celebrating Seventy-five Years of History*, describes Osborn's transition from car dealer to founder of the hugely successful company.

2. Drawn to the River

Ford's anti-Semitic views were published in his nationally distributed newspaper, the *Dearborn Independent*, and were widely reported in the media. Many books cover this issue, including full-length works by Neil Baldwin and Max Wallace. Law professor Victoria Saker Woeste's 2012 book describes the lawsuit brought by Aaron Sapiro against Ford as the first "hate speech case." Howard P. Segal has written a definitive study on Ford's Village Industries program. Reynold M. Wik, in his book *Henry Ford and Grass-roots America*, writes of Ford's connection to farmers, his tractor, Muscle Shoals, and anti-Semitism. Clair J. Snider and Michael W. R. Davis partnered on a book about the Ford Fleet. A companion work is Lawrence A. Brough's *Autos on the Water: A History of the Great Lakes Automobile Carriers*. Many books have been published about the Mississippi River and its use for navigation and waterpower. Lucile Kane's writings on the Falls of St. Anthony provided early history of the High Dam site, and John Anfinson and Biloine Whiting Young provide a broader context for understanding the conflicts that arose regarding use of the river. Several promotional booklets and numerous photographs at the Minnesota Historical Society provided information about the Northwestern Terminals. The dam and hydro power station at Keokuk, Iowa, built by Stone and Webster, is well covered in Philip V. Scarpino's *Great River: An Environmental History of the Upper Mississippi, 1890–1950*. Brian McMahon wrote an article for *Ramsey County History* in summer 2007, "Minneapolis and St. Paul Stumble: Henry Ford Wins the Power Struggle for the High Dam," which was the basis for this section of the book. Ford's pursuit of the Muscle Shoals project was prominently covered in national media and the subject of several books, including Preston J. Hubbard's *Origins of the TVA: The Muscle Shoals Controversy, 1920–1932*. The papers of Lewis H. Brittin and Mayor George E. Leach are at the Minnesota Historical Society, as well as the St. Paul application for the hydroelectric permit. Thomas Van Lear was the subject of an article by David Paul Nord in *Minnesota History*.

3. "The Finest Plant in the World"

The first St. Paul Zoning Code adopted in 1922 is available at the Minnesota Historical Society. David Lanegran provided the author with a copy of the original zoning map, which is surprisingly rare. George Herrold, the St. Paul city planner, was a prolific writer and published many articles in national and local journals. Many of these, and his unpublished manuscript on the history of planning in St. Paul, are available at the Minnesota Historical Society. Thanks to St. Paul planner Anton Gerve for helping me locate these materials. The history of Mississippi River Boulevard is the subject of an article by Donald L Empson in *Ramsey County History* in summer 2014. In his book *The Street Where You Live: A Guide to the Place Names of St. Paul*, Empson presents good information on the development of Highland Park and the real-estate developer Den E. Lane. A number of books have been written about Albert Kahn by, among others, Federico Bucci, Hawkins W. Ferry, and Grant Hildebrand. Brian McMahon wrote about Kahn's work in Minnesota in *Architecture Minnesota*. The papers of contractor H. C. Struchen are available at the Minnesota Historical Society. Information on the tunnels beneath the Ford plant is included in Greg Brick's book *Subterranean Twin Cities*. The University of Minnesota Engineering Department published several articles in *Minnesota Techno-log* describing the construction of the Twin Cities Assembly Plant. Benjamin M. Cowan wrote an article on the Twin Cities plant for the *Stone and Webster Journal*; thanks to Charlene Roise for sharing this. Her firm, Hess Roise, also completed several studies for the Ford Motor Company on the historical significance of the Twin Cities assembly plant. Clair J. Snider and Michael W. R. Davis have written the history of Ford navigation in *The Ford Fleet (1923–1989)*. Denis Gardner included information on the Ford Bridge in his book on Minnesota's historic bridges. A well-illustrated article on the Ford "Tent City" appeared in the *St. Paul Daily News* on July 15, 1925; thanks to Steve and Nancy Bailey for bringing this to my attention. Information on the Winter Built Demonstration House is included in Jeffrey A. Hess and Paul Clifford Larson's book *St. Paul's Architecture: A History*. An article in *Minnesota History*, "Minnesota in the World of Aviation," discusses the founding of Northwest Airlines. William Bushnell Stout, who was most responsible for engaging Edsel and Henry Ford in aviation and Northwest Airlines, wrote a fascinating autobiography, *So Away I Went*. Timothy J. O'Callahan has written about Ford and aviation, and others have written on the development of the trimotor airplane. There are also several other books about the history of Northwest Airlines and Northern States Power.

4. From Model A to M-8

Alfred D. Chandler, in *Giant Enterprise: Ford, General Motors, and the Automobile Industry,* published in 1964, documents how the new automobile industry transformed the economy and then describes its transition from a growth phase to a more competitive phase as the industry matured. Arthur J. Kuhn argues that Ford did not fare well in its competition with GM, which had created a new management system to meet evolving challenges. The new marketing approach utilized by Ford for the Model A car is the subject of a book by Jim Schild. For information on auto, truck, and bus bodybuilding companies, see www.CoachBuilt.com, a remarkable site that describes more than 1,500 companies. The quotations from workers throughout this chapter are from oral history interviews conducted by Brian McMahon. The information on John Banks came from an oral history interview by David V. Taylor, available at the Minnesota Historical Society. Information on African American employment at the Ford plant was greatly facilitated by Brendan Henehan's research published as *Minnesota Black Newspaper Index*, 2012, available on the Web site of the Minnesota Historical Society.

Eldorous L. Dayton's 1958 book *Walter Reuther: The Autocrat of the Bargaining Table* offers a contemporary look at Walter Reuther; Nelson Lichtenstein provides a later account in his 1995 book *The Most Dangerous Man in Detroit: Walter Reuther and the Fate of American Labor.*

An extensive collection relating to the rise of the United Auto Workers can be found at the Walter Reuther Library at Wayne State University.

Charles K. Hyde's book *Arsenal of Democracy: The American Automobile Industry in World War II* is a comprehensive account. The family of John Rouen provided information about his experiences at the plant during World War II.

5. Ascent of the Autoworkers

David Halberstam's book *The Fifties* provides context for understanding the cultural and economic significance of the automobile during the postwar period. His book *The Reckoning* is an extraordinary history of the events leading to the collapse of the American automobile industry. Much of the material in this section comes from interviews with the author. Information on major floods of the Mississippi River is from several internal Ford memorandums and a report titled *Twenty Days of Crisis*, prepared by plant manager F. O. Fason in 1965. Thanks to Milton Bloom for sharing this report.

Lee Iacocca was fired from Ford Motor Company and later went on to head the Chrysler Corporation. His autobiography is a candid insider's look at the auto industry. Many reports by the United Auto Workers, including convention proceedings and labor contracts, are available on their website and others.

Craig Zapala's article on worker sabotage can be found in *Autowork*, edited by Robert Asher and Ronald Edsforth. Ford published several booklets on the Henry Ford School, as well as customized textbooks for its students. Brian McMahon wrote an overview of industrial training, focusing on the Ford Motor Company, in a report he edited, *Minnesota Works.*

6. An Uncertain Industry

The University of Minnesota Archives has papers and materials of engineering professor James "Crash" Ryan. David Halberstam writes in *The Fifties* of the disdain Ford executives had for the Volkswagen, and in *The Reckoning* he recounts the collapse of the American auto industry and the rise of Japanese imports. Numerous books have been written about Quality Circles and Employee Involvement. The most comprehensive rebuttal from labor's perspective is *Choosing Sides: Unions and the Team Concept* by Mike Parker and Jane Slaughter. A *New York Times* special report by Keith Bradsher, "License to Pollute," describes the origins of the Chicken Tax and details the web of regulatory exemptions granted to manufacturers of light trucks.

Jack Barnes, a student at Carleton College in Northfield, Minnesota, in the 1960s and later a Trotskyist and leader of the Socialist Workers Party, helped launch the "turn to industry" movement in the late 1970s. Labor historian Peter Rachleff was extremely helpful in providing context for the infiltration of industry by radical groups. His book on the Hormel strike documents the considerable support UAW Local 879 provided to the striking meatpackers in Austin, Minnesota. His article "From Racism to International Solidarity: The Journey of UAW Local 879, 1980–1995" describes the evolving activism within the St. Paul local. Numerous interviews shed light on the dissident organizing activities at the plant with, among others, Rob McKenzie, Tom Laney, Bert Rubash, Rick Macpherson, Donna Lapinski, Lynn Hinkle, and Bill McGaughey, a labor economist from Minneapolis who published one of the first anti-NAFTA studies in 1992, *A U.S.–Canada– Mexico Free-Trade Agreement: Do We Just Say No?*. McGaughey worked closely with Local 879 and other progressives in creating the Minnesota Fair Trade Coalition.

Dan La Botz's book *The Crisis of Mexican Labor* details the murder of Cleto Nigmo at the Mexican Ford plant, and later correspondence with this author gave updates on the unresolved criminal investigation. After Bob Killeen's death in 2002, Bob Killeen Jr. and Wayne Wittman of the Veterans for Peace in Minnesota explained his interest in Latin American human rights. Several recent books describe the broader history of political activists from the 1970s and 1980s who tried to organize industrial plants and change the American political and economic system, including works by Todd Gitlin, Bryan Burrough, and Aaron J. Leonard and Conor A. Gallagher.

Robert Shook describes how the Taurus was developed and how it saved the Ford Motor Company. Donald Petersen, former CEO of Ford, explained in his autobiography how Ford moved away from an autocratic management style to embrace Employee Involvement and other Japanese practices and gives specific examples of how the new approach improved the company. The Department of Transportation report "The U.S.

Automobile Industry, 1980," is available at http://catalog.hathitrust.org/Record/011353430. Robert Perrucci describes the impact Japanese transplant companies had on American manufacturers and workers.

James M. Rubenstein explains how American auto companies tended to follow the lead of Japanese transplant companies in locating in clusters along "Auto Alley." Additional information on the clustering effect can be found in "Study of US 43 and US 80 Corridor Potential to Attract New Automotive Suppliers Based on Highway Improvements, November 2003," produced by AECOM for the U.S. Department of Transportation Federal Highway Administration.

Roger Smith's quotation on the girl with the lemonade stand can be found in Maryanne Keller's book *Rude Awakening: The Rise, Fall, and Struggle for Recovery of General Motors*. Information on Ford's recalls exceeding the number of cars made is included in Alton F. Doody and Ron Bingaman's book *Reinventing the Wheels: Ford's Spectacular Comeback*. The *Minnesota Daily*, as well as other daily Twin Cities newspapers, wrote of Governor Rudy Perpich's package of economic incentives for the Saturn plant.

The UAW published a report in 2001, *Sixty Years of Progress, 1941–2001*, which listed gains made by workers through the efforts of the union. Many UAW reports, convention proceedings, and work agreements can be found online. Quotations from Jim Buckman, Tom Schneider, Rod Haworth, Tom Laney, Peter Rachleff, and Ted LaValley from the labor conference in St. Paul were from the *Minneapolis Star Tribune*.

7. The End of the Line

Theresa Lippert shared the story of Governor Wendell Anderson's conversation with Henry Ford II regarding the state limousine. Jack Uldrich and Rolf Nordstrom's article "Fuel-Cell Vehicle Plant Could Help State, Ford," appeared in the *Minneapolis Star Tribune* on October 4, 2001. David Morris's article "An Electrifying Thought for Ford's St. Paul Plant" was published in the *Star Tribune* on November 24, 2007. Quotations from dissident autoworker Gregg Shotwell are from his book and blog at http://autoworkersunderthegun.blogspot.com/.

This chapter relies heavily on direct quotations from many newspaper articles and blogs about the plant closing. Articles in the *Star Tribune* provided quotations from Mark Fields, the transferee from Newark, Mike Franchino, Rob McKenzie, Fred Zimmerman, Governor Tim Pawlenty, Marvalene Johnson, the Ford spokesperson, Commissioner Matt Kramer, Wayne Cascio, Sunil Ramlall, State Representative Matt Entenza, Jim Eagle, Denny Dickhausen, John Killeen, Doug Toenjes, Commissioner Dan McElroy, State

Representative Frank Hornstein, Kari Altema, Mayor Chris Coleman, and Tracy Ausen. *Pioneer Press* articles quoted Curtis Lee, Sheator Robinson, Lynn Hinkle, and Jim Eagle. Quotations from John Van Hecke and Conrad deFiebre are from the Minnesota 2020 blog. Terry Dinderman's comment about the demolition of the plant appeared in *Maplewood Review*.

Bibliography

Interviews

Wendell Anderson
Carl Boye
Bill Brengman
Chet Brokl
Ralph Cook
Greg Davis
Jim Eagle
Robert Hanson
Maggie Heisterkamp
Al Hendricks
Lynn Hinkle
Vera Hoffmayer
Mike Hogan
Dan Huseby
Loretta Jackson
Robert (Cubby) Johnson
Robert (R.W.) Johnson

Bob Killeen
Bob Killeen, Jr.
Pete Koegel
Joe Kucera
Tom Laney
Don Larson
Donna (Donusia) Lapinski
Seth Lindsey
Rick Macpherson
Richard Magnuson
Marc Manderscheid
Roland Matson
Bill McGaughey
Al McGregor
Rob McKenzie
Ivor Mitchell
Ken Muxlow

Jack Neitz
Rodney Niven
Enon Olson
Tom Owens
Eric Pearson
Del Peterson
Peter Rachleff
Eugene Roedl
John Rouen (family)
Burt Rubash
Marv Saline
Gene Schiff
Cheryl Schmidt
Brien Slawik
Verna Welsch
Dick Williams
John Woodhead

Aguayo, Rafael. *Dr. Deming: The American Who Taught the Japanese about Quality*. New York: A Fireside Book Published by Simon & Schuster, 1991.

Alanen, Arnold R. *Morgan Park: Duluth, U.S. Steel, and the Forging of a Company Town*. Minneapolis: University of Minnesota Press, 2007.

Allard, Noel E., and Gerald N. Sandvick. *Minnesota Aviation History, 1857–1945*. Chaska, Minn.: MAHB Publishing, 1993.

Anfinson, John O. *The River We Have Wrought: A History of the Upper Mississippi*. Minneapolis: University of Minnesota Press, 2003.

Armstrong, Ellis. L., ed. *History of Public Works in the United States, 1776–1976*. Chicago: American Public Works Association, 1976.

Arnold, Horace Lucien, and Fay Leone Faurote. *Ford Methods and the Ford Shops*. New York: The Engineering Magazine Company, 1915.

Asher, Robert, and Ronald Edsforth, eds. *Autowork*. Albany: State University of New York Press, 1995.

Auto Editors Consumer Guide. *The Complete History of Ford Motor Company*. New York: Beekman House, 1987.

Automobile Manufacturers Association. *A Chronicle of the Automotive Industry in America, 1893–1949*. Detroit: Eaton Manufacturing Company, circa 1950.

Backman, Jules, ed. *Labor, Technology, and Productivity*. New York: New York University Press, 1974.

Baime, A. J. *The Arsenal of Democracy: FDR, Detroit, and an Epic Quest to Arm America at War*. Boston: Houghton Mifflin Harcourt, 2014.

Bak, Richard. *Henry and Edsel: The Creation of the Ford Empire*. New York: John Wiley & Sons, 1903.

Baldwin, Neil. 2001. *Henry Ford and the Jews: The Mass Production of Hate*. New York: Public Affairs, 2001.

Banham, Russ. *The Ford Century: Ford Motor Company and the Innovations That Shaped the World*. New York: Artisan Books, 2002.

Barclay, Hartly, W. *Ford Production Methods*. New York: Harper and Brothers Publishers, 1936.

Barnes, Ralph M. *Motion and Time Study*. New York: John Wiley & Sons, 1937.

Baruth-Walsh, Mary, and Mark G. Walsh. *Strike! 99 Days on the Line: The Workers' Own Story of the 1945 Windsor Ford Strike*. Ottawa: Penumbra Press, 1995.

Batchelor, Ray. *Henry Ford: Mass Production, Modernism and Design*. Manchester, England, and New York: Manchester University Press, 1994.

Bennett, Harry. *Ford: We Never Called Him Henry*. New York: Tom Doherty Associates, 1951.

Beynon, Huw. *Working for Ford*. Harmondsworth, England: Penguin Books, 1973.

Biggs, Lindy. *The Rational Factory: Architecture, Technology, and Work in America's Age of Mass Production*. Baltimore: Johns Hopkins University Press, 1996.

Bluestone, Barry, and Harrison Bennett. *The Deindustrialization of America: Plant Closings,*

Community Abandonment, and the Dismantling of Basic Industry. New York: Basic Books, 1982.

Boyer, Richard O., and Herbert M. Morais. *Labor's Untold Story.* New York: Cameron & Kahn, 1955.

Bradsher, Keith. "License to Pollute." *New York Times,* November 30, 1997.

Breer, Carl. *The Birth of Chrysler Corporation and Its Engineering Legacy.* Warrendale, Pa: Society of Automotive Engineers, 1995.

Brick, Greg A. *Subterranean Twin Cities.* Minneapolis: University of Minnesota Press, 2009.

Brinkley, Douglas. *Wheels for the World.* London: Penguin Books, 2003.

Brough, Lawrence A. *Autos on the Water: A History of the Great Lakes Automobile Carriers.* Columbus, Ohio: Chatham Communicators, 1987.

Bryan, Ford R. *Beyond the Model T: The Other Ventures of Henry Ford.* Detroit: Wayne State University Press, 1990.

———. *Henry's Attic: Some Fascinating Gifts to Henry Ford and His Museum.* Dearborn, Mich.: Ford Books, 1995.

———. *Henry's Lieutenants.* Detroit: Wayne State University Press, 1993.

———. *Rouge: Pictured in Its Prime Covering the Years 1917–1940.* Dearborn, Mich.: Ford Books, 2003.

Bucci, Federico. *Albert Kahn: Architect of Ford.* New York: Princeton Architectural Press, 1993.

Burlingame, Roger. *Henry Ford: The Greatest Success Story in the History of the Industry.* New York: Signet Key Book, 1954.

Burrough, Bryan. *Days of Rage: America's Radical Underground, the FBI, and the Forgotten Age of Revolutionary Violence.* New York: Penguin Books, 2015.

Cabadas, Joseph P. *River Rouge: Ford's Industrial Colossus.* St. Paul: Motorbooks International, 2004.

Caldwell, Cy. *Henry Ford.* New York: Julian Messner, 1947.

Cameron, W. J. *A Series of Talks Given on the Ford Sunday Evening Hour.* Dearborn, Mich.: Ford Motor Company, 1937.

Carson, Richard Burns. *The Olympian Cars of the Twenties and Thirties.* 2d ed. Minneapolis: Beavers Pond Press, 1998.

Casey, Robert. *The Model T: A Centennial History.* Baltimore: Johns Hopkins University Press, 2008.

Chandler, Alfred D. *Giant Enterprise: Ford, General Motors, and the Automobile Industry.* New York: Harcourt, Brace & World, 1964.

Chinoy, Ely. *Automobile Workers and the American Dream.* Boston: Beacon Press, 1955.

Clary, Martin. *The Facts About Muscle Shoals.* New York: Little and Ives Company, 1924.

Clymer, Floyd. *Henry's Wonderful Model T, 1908—1927.* New York: Bonanza Books, 1955.

Coffey, Frank, and Joseph Layden. *America on Wheels: The First 100 Years: 1896–1996.* Los Angeles: General Publishing Group, 1966.

Cohn, David, L. *Combustion on Wheels: An Informal History of the Automobile Age.* Cambridge: Houghton Mifflin Company, 1944.

Collier, Peter, and David Horowitz. *The Fords: An American Epic.* New York: Summit Books, 1987.

Cowan, Benjamin M. "The Twin Cities Plant of the Ford Motor Company." *Stone and Webster Journal* 37 (July 1925): 60–72.

Daggett, Stuart. *Principles of Inland Transportation.* 3d ed. New York: Harper Brothers, 1941.

Darley, Gillian. *Factory.* London: Reaktion Books, 2003.

Davis, L. J. *Fleet Fire: Thomas Edison and the Pioneers of the Electric Revolution.* New York: Arcade Publishing, 2003.

Dayton, Eldorous L. *Walter Reuther: The Autocrat of the Bargaining Table.* New York: Devin-Adair Company, 1958.

Dewar, Donald. *The Quality Circle Guide to Participation Management.* Englewood Cliffs, N.J.: Quality Circle Institute, 1980.

Donovan, Frank. *Wheels for a Nation.* New York: Thomas Y. Crowell Company, 1965.

Doody, Alton F., and Ron Bingaman. *Reinventing the Wheels: Ford's Spectacular Comeback.* Cambridge, Mass.: Ballinger Publishing Company, 1988.

Douglas County Publishing. *Henry Ford's Railroad: The Story of Henry Ford's Excursion into Railroading.* Waterloo, Ontario: Douglas Country Publishing, n.d.

Dubofsky, Melvin. *The State and Labor in Modern America.* Chapel Hill and London: University of North Carolina Press, 1994.

Duerksen, Menno. *History of the Great American Classics.* Sidney, Ohio: Amos Press, 1987.

Ecolab. *Celebrating 75 Years of History.* St. Paul: Ecolab, 1998.

Edison Institute. *Greenfield Village.* New York: Crown Publishers, 1972.

Eisinger, Peter K. *The Rise of the Entrepreneurial State: State and Local Economic Development Policy in the United States.* Madison: University of Wisconsin Press, 1988.

El-Hai, Jack. *Non-Stop: A Turbulent History of Northwest Airlines.* Minneapolis: University of Minnesota Press, 2013.

Empson, Donald L. "A Grand Topographical Feature: The History of the Mississippi River Boulevard." *Ramsey County History* 49:2 (summer 2014): 13–21.

———. *The Street Where You Live: A Guide to the Place Names of St. Paul.* Minneapolis: University of Minnesota Press, 2006.

Epstein, Edward Jay. *Dossier: The Secret History of Armand Hammer.* New York: Random House, 1996.

Epstein, Ralph C. *The Automobile Industry: Its Economic and Commercial Development.* Chicago and New York: A. W. Shaw Company, 1928.

Ernst & Young Quality Improvement Consulting Group. *Total Quality: An Executive's Guide for the 1990s.* Homewood, Ill.: Business One Irwin, 1990.

Factory Magazine. *Practical Ways to Cut Costs.* Chicago: A. W. Shaw Company, 1922.

Fason. F. O. *Twenty Days of Crisis.* St. Paul: Ford Motor Company. 1965.

Feldman, Richard, and Michael Betzold. *End of the Line: Autoworkers and the American Dream.* New York: Weidenfeld & Nicholson, 1988.

Ferry, W. Hawkins. *The Legacy of Albert Kahn.* Detroit: Wayne State University Press, 1970.

Fisher, Peter S., and Alan H. Peters. *Industrial Incentives: Competition among American States and Cities.* Kalamazoo, Mich.: W. E. Upjohn Institute for Employment Research, 1998.

Flammang, James M., and David L. Lewis. *Ford Chronicle: A Pictorial History from 1893.* Lincolnwood, Ill.: Publications International, 1997.

Foner, Phillip S. *Labor and World War I, 1914–1918.* Vol. 7. New York: International Publishers, 1987.

Forbes, B. C., and O. D. Foster. *Automotive Giants of America: Men Who Are Making Our Motor Industry.* New York: B. C. Forbes Publishing Co., 1924.

Ford, Henry. *Ford Ideals: Being a Selection from "Mr. Ford's Page" in the* Dearborn Independent. Dearborn, Mich.: Dearborn Publishing Company, 1922.

———. *Moving Forward.* Garden City, N.Y.: Doubleday, Doran & Co., 1931.

———. *My Friend Mr. Edison.* London: Ernest Benn, 1930.

———. *My Life and Work.* Garden City, N.Y.: Doubleday, Page & Co., 1922.

———. *Today and Tomorrow.* Cambridge, Mass.: Productivity Press, 1926.

Ford Motor Company. *The Best of the Times.* Dearborn, Mich.: Ford Motor Company, 1977.

———. *A Car Is Born: The Exciting Story of the Manufacture of a Modern Automobile from Planning to Production.* Dearborn, Mich.: 1955.

———. *Does Ford Pay Good Wages?* Dearborn, Mich.: Ford Motor Company, 1941.

———. *The Evolution of Mass Production.* Dearborn, Mich.: Ford Motor Company, 1956.

———. *Factory Facts from Ford.* Detroit: Ford Motor Company, 1912, 1915, 1917.

———. *Facts from Ford.* Detroit: Ford Motor Company, 1920.

———. *Ford Ammonium Sulphate Nitrogen for the Soil.* Dearborn, Mich.: Ford Motor Company, n.d.

———. *Ford at Fifty: 1903–1953: An American Story.* New York: Simon and Schuster, 1953.

———. *Ford Automotive Highlights, 1896–1971*. Dearborn, Mich.: Ford Motor Company, 1971.

———. *Ford Coal: From Mines to Market*. Detroit: Ford Motor Company, n.d.

———. *The Ford Industries*. Detroit: Ford Motor Company, 1926, 1927, 1929.

———. *The Ford Industries: Facts about the Ford Company and Its Subsidiaries*. Detroit: Ford Motor Company, 1924.

———. *The Ford Man 4:3*. Highland Park, Mich.: Ford Motor Company, 1920.

———. *Ford Motor Cars 1911*. Detroit: Ford Motor Company, 1911.

———. *Ford News 10:21*. Dearborn, Mich.: Ford Motor Company, 1930.

———. *Ford News 16:3*. Dearborn, Mich.: Ford Motor Company, 1936.

———. *Ford News 21:9*. Dearborn, Mich.: Ford Motor Company, 1941.

———. *Ford Pictorial*. Detroit: Ford Motor Company, 1926.

———. *The Ford Rubber Plantations*. Detroit: Ford Motor Company, n.d.

———. *Ford Times*. Dearborn, Mich.: Ford Motor Company, 1965.

———. *Ford the Universal Car*. Detroit: Ford Motor Company, 1912.

———. *Ford, the Universal Car: A Business Utility*. Detroit: Ford Motor Company, n.d.

———. *For You: Rules and Instructions for New Employees*. Detroit: Ford Motor Company, 1919.

———. *Gardening for Security*. Dearborn, Mich.: Ford Motor Company, 1945.

———. *Henry Ford Trade School*. Dearborn, Mich.: Ford Motor Company, 1951.

———. *Henry Ford Trade School*. Dearborn, Mich.: Ford Motor Company, n.d.

———. *Home Almanac*. Dearborn, Mich.: Ford Motor Company, 1937, 1938, 1939.

———. *The Human Bridge*. Dearborn, Mich.: Ford Motor Company, n.d.

———. *Industries within an Industry: Ford By-Products*. Dearborn, Mich.: Ford Motor Company, n.d.

———. *In the Service of America*. Dearborn, Mich.: Ford Motor Company, n.d.

———. *Motion Pictures*. Detroit: Ford Motor Company, n.d.

———. *Nitrogen Plant Food*. Dearborn, Mich.: Ford Motor Company, n.d.

———. *Twin Cities Ford News*. St. Paul: Ford Motor Company, 1967.

———. *What's This about "Labor Trouble" in Ford Plants?* Dearborn, Mich.: Ford Motor Company, 1941.

Freeman, Richard D., and James L. Medoff. *What Unions Do*. New York: Basic Books, 1984.

Friedlander, Peter. *The Emergence of a UAW Local, 1936–1939*. Pittsburgh: University of Pittsburgh Press, 1975.

Gardner, Denis P. *Wood, Concrete, Stone, and Steel: Minnesota's Historic Bridges*. Minneapolis: University of Minnesota Press, 2008.

Gelderman, Carol. *Henry Ford: The Wayward Capitalist*. New York: St. Martin's Press, 1981.

Gelernter, David. *1939: The Lost World of the Fair*. New York: Avon Books, 1996.

Genat, Robert. *The American Car Dealership*. St. Paul: Motorbooks International, 2006.

General Motors Institute Industrial Engineering Department. *Standards and Plant Engineering*. Detroit: General Motors Institute, 1953.

Gitlin, Todd. *The Sixties: Years of Hope, Days of Rage*. New York: Bantam Press, 1987.

Goodwin, Doris Kearns. *No Ordinary Time: Franklin and Eleanor Roosevelt: The Home Front in World War II*. New York: Simon & Schuster, 1994.

Gordon, Robert B., and Patrick B. Malone. *The Texture of Industry: An Archeological View of the Industrialization of North America*. New York: Oxford University Press, 1994.

Grandin, Gregg. *Fordlandia: The Rise and Fall of Henry Ford's Forgotten Jungle City*. New York: Metropolitan Books, 2009.

Graves, Ralph H. *The Triumph of an Idea: The Story of Henry Ford*. Garden City, N.Y.: Doubleday, Doran & Company, 1934.

Green, Hardy. *The Company Town: The Industrial Edens and Satanic Mills That Shaped the American Economy*. New York: Basic Books, 2010.

Grenier, Guillermo J. *Inhuman Relations: Quality Circles and Anti-Unionism in American Industry*. Philadelphia: Temple University Press, 1988.

Halberstam, David. *The Fifties*. New York: Villard Books 1993.

———. *The Reckoning*. New York: William Morrow and Company, 1986.

Hammer, Armand. *Hammer*. New York: Putnam, 1987.

Hamper, Ben. *Rivethead Tales: From the Assembly Line*. New York: Warner Books, 1986.

Handlin, Oscar, and Mary Handlin. *Commonwealth: A Study of the Role of Government in the American Economy: Massachusetts, 1774–1861*. Cambridge: Harvard University Press, 1969.

Hartsough, Mildred L. *From Canoe to Steel Barge on the Upper Mississippi*. Minneapolis: University of Minnesota Press, 1934.

Heckscher, Charles C. *The New Unionism: Employee Involvement in the Changing Corporation*. New York: Basic Books, 1988.

Henderson, M. Todd. "Everything Old Is New Again: Lessons from *Dodge v. Ford Motor Company*." Chicago: University of Chicago, issue 373 of John M. Olin Program in Law & Economics working paper, 2007.

Henry Ford Trade School. *Shop Theory*. New York: McGraw-Hill, 1942.

Hershey, Burnet. *The Odyssey of Henry Ford and the Great Peace Ship*. New York: Taplinger Publishing Company, 1967.

Hess, Jeffrey A., and Paul Clifford Larson. *St. Paul's Architecture: A History*. Minneapolis: University of Minnesota Press, 2008.

Hess, Roise and Company. "Ford Motor Company Twin Cities Assembly Plant: An Assessment of Significance and Eligibility." Minneapolis, November 2007.

Hildebrand, Grant. *Designing for Industry: Architecture of Albert Kahn.* Cambridge: MIT Press, 1974.

Holden, Henry M. *The Fabulous Ford Tri-Motor: The Saga of the Tin Goose.* New York: TAB Books, Division McGraw-Hill, 1992.

Hoxie, Robert Franklin. *Scientific Management and Labor.* New York: Augustus M. Kelley Publishers. 1915. Reprints of Economic Classics, 1966.

Hubbard, Preston J. *Origins of the TVA: The Muscle Shoals Controversy, 1920–1932.* New York: W. W. Norton, 1961.

Huxley, Aldous. *Brave New World.* New York: Bantam Classic, 1936.

Hyde, Charles K. *Arsenal of Democracy: The American Automobile Industry in World War II.* Detroit: Wayne State University Press, 2013.

Iacocca, Lee. *Iacocca: An Autobiography.* New York: Bantam Books, 1984.

Ingells, Douglas J. *Tin Goose: The Fabulous Ford Trimotor.* Fallbrook, Calif.: Aero Publishers, 1968.

Jardim, Anne. *The First Henry Ford: A Study in Personality and Business Leadership.* Cambridge: MIT Press, 1970.

Kane, Lucile M. *The Falls of St. Anthony: The Waterfall That Built Minneapolis.* St. Paul: Minnesota Historical Society Press, 1987.

Kassalow, Everett M. *Trade Unions and Industrial Relations: An International Comparison.* New York: Random House, 1969.

Keller, Maryanne. *Rude Awakening: The Rise, Fall, and Struggle for Recovery of General Motors.* New York: HarperPerennial, 1989.

Kenny, Dave. *Minnesota Goes to War: The Home Front during World War II.* St. Paul: Minnesota Historical Society Press, 2005.

Kessler, Friedrich. "Automobile Dealer Franchises: Vertical Integration by Contract." Faculty Scholarship Series. Paper 2727, 66:8 (July 1957): 1135–90. http://digitalcom mons.law.yale.edu/fss_papers/2727.

Kraft, Barbara S. *The Peace Ship: Henry Ford's Pacifist Adventure in the First World War.* New York: Macmillan, 1987.

Krugman, Paul. *Geography and Trade.* Cambridge: MIT Press, 1991.

Kucera, Barb. "End of an Era: Local 879 Was a Leader for Labor." *Workday Minnesota,* December 16, 2011.

Kuhn, Arthur, J. *GM Passes Ford, 1918–1938.* University Park: Pennsylvania State University Press, 1986.

La Botz, Dan. *The Crisis of Mexican Labor.* New York: Praeger, 1988.

Lacey, Robert. *Ford: The Men and the Machine.* Boston: Little, Brown and Company, 1986.

Langworth, Richard M. *The Complete History of Ford Motor Company.* Skokie, Ill.: Publications International, 1987.

Leonard, Aaron J., and Conor A. Gallagher. *Heavy Radicals: The FBI's Secret War on American Maoists.* Blue Ridge Summit, Pa.: Zero Books, 2015.

Levinson, William A. *Henry Ford's Lean Vision: Enduring Principles from the First Ford Motor Plant.* New York: Productivity Press, 2002.

Lewis, David L. *Ford Country: The Family; the Company; the Cars 1.* Sidney, Ohio: Amos Press, 1987.

———. *Ford Country: The Family; the Company; the Cars 2.* Sidney, Ohio: Amos Press, 1999.

———. *The Public Image of Henry Ford: An American Folk Hero and His Company.* Detroit: Wayne State University Press, 2002.

LeRoy, Greg. *The Great American Jobs Scam: Corporate Tax Dodging and the Myth of Job Creation.* San Francisco: Berrett-Koehler Publishers, 2005.

Levin, Doran P. *Behind the Wheel at Chrysler: The Iacocca Legacy.* New York: Harcourt Brace & Company, 1995.

Lichtenstein, Nelson. *The Most Dangerous Man in Detroit: Walter Reuther and the Fate of American Labor.* New York: Basic Books, 1995.

Lloyd, Lewis E. *The Case for Protection.* New York: Devin-Adair Company, 1955.

Mandell, Nikki. *The Corporation as Family: The Gendering of Corporate Welfare, 1890–1930.* Chapel Hill: University of North Carolina Press, 2002.

Manderscheid, Marc. "Homes vs. Factories: The 95 Year Battle for the Future of South Highland Park." Forthcoming in *Ramsey County History.*

Marquis, Samuel S. *Henry Ford: An Interpretation.* Boston: Little, Brown and Company, 1923.

Marx, Leo, *The Machine in the Garden: Technology and the Pastoral Ideal.* London: Oxford University Press, 1964.

Mathes, R. E. "Ford Gets Busy at the High Dam." *Minnesota Techno-log* 4:8 (June 1924).

Mavencamp, Rebecca A. "'Sewed, Baked Bread, and Did a Little Housework Beside': The Stork Family in St. Paul, 1914–1916." *Ramsey County History* 49:2 (summer 2014): 3–12.

McConnell, Curt. *Great Cars of the Great Plains.* Lincoln: University of Nebraska Press, 1995.

McGaughey, Bill. *A U.S.–Canada–Mexico Free-Trade Agreement: Do We Just Say No?* Minneapolis: Thistlerose Publications, 1992.

McGuffey, W., LL.D. *McGuffey's New Fourth Eclectic Reader.* Cincinnati: Wilson, Hinkle &. Co., 1857.

McIntyre, Stephen L. "The Failure of Fordism: Reform of the Automobile Repair Industry, 1913–1940." *Technology and Culture* 41:2 (April 2000): 269–99.

McLaughlin, Paul. G. *Ford Pickup Trucks.* Osceola, Minn.: MBI Publishers, 1999.

McMahon, Brian. "Albert Kahn in Minnesota." *Architecture Minnesota* (July/August 1999).

———. "Industrial Training: An Historical Perspective." *Minnesota Works* 1:1 (April 1999): 2–29

———. "Life after Ford." *The Autoworker.* Profiles of several retired autoworkers in UAW Local 879 magazine, 1998–99.

———. "Louis Hill to Henry Ford: 'No Deal!'" *Ramsey County History* 46:4 (winter 2012): 27–28

———. "Minneapolis and St. Paul Stumble: Henry Ford Wins the Power Struggle for the High Dam." *Ramsey County History* 42:2 (summer 2007): 4–14.

———. *A Short History of the Ford Plant: Industrial Archaeology and Economic Change in St. Paul.* St. Paul: Minnesota Historical Society Press, 2013.

McShane, Clay. *Down the Asphalt Path: The Automobile and the American City.* New York: Columbia University Press, 1994.

Meier, August, and Elliot Rudwick. *Black Detroit and the Rise of the UAW.* Oxford: Oxford University Press, 1979.

Merz, Charles. *And Then Came Ford.* New York: Doubleday, Doran & Company, 1929.

Meyer, Stephen, III. *The Five Dollar Day: Labor Management and Social Control in the Ford Motor Company, 1908–1921.* Albany: State University of New York Press, 1981.

Michigan Historical Review. *Special Issue 100th Anniversary of the Automotive Industry.* Ann Arbor: Central Michigan University (fall 1996).

Miller, James Martin. *The Amazing Story of Henry Ford.* United Kingdom of Britain and Colonies, 1922.

Millikan, William. *A Union against Unions: The Minneapolis Citizens Alliance.* St. Paul: Minnesota Historical Society Press, 2003.

Mills, Stephen E. *A Pictorial History of Northwest Airlines.* New York: Bonanza Books, 1972.

Morris, David. "An Electrifying Thought for Ford's St. Paul Plant." *Minneapolis Star Tribune* November 24, 2007.

Mullin, John R. "Henry Ford and Field and Factory: An Analysis of the Ford Sponsored Village Industries—Experiment in Michigan, 1918–1941." Landscape Architecture & Regional Planning Faculty Publication Series, Paper 41 (1982). http://scholar works.umass.edu/larp_faculty_pubs/41.

Muscle Shoals Commission. *Muscle Shoals: A Plan.* Washington, D.C.: U.S. Government Printing Office, 1931.

Nader, Ralph. *Unsafe at Any Speed: The Designed-In Dangers of the American Automobile.* New York: Grossman Publishers, 1965.

National Association of Suggestion Programs. *First Fifty Years: A Great Beginning, 1942–1992.* Chicago: National Association of Suggestion Programs, 1992.

National Automobile Chamber of Commerce. *Facts and Figures of the Automobile Industry.* New York: National Automobile Chamber of Commerce, 1924.

Nelson, George A. "The Twin Cities Ford Plant." *Minnesota Techno-log* 6:1 (October 1925): 7.

Nevins, Allan, and Frank Ernest Hill. *Ford: Decline and Rebirth, 1933–1962.* New York: Charles Scribner's Sons, 1962.

———. *Ford: Expansion and Challenge, 1915–1933.* New York: Charles Scribner's Sons, 1957.

———. *Ford: The Times, the Man, the Company.* New York: Charles Scribner's Sons, 1954.

Newton, James D. *Uncommon Friends: Life with Thomas Edison, Henry Ford, Harvey Firestone, Alexis Carrel & Charles Lindbergh.* New York: Harcourt Brace Jovanovich, 1987.

Nolan, Mary. *Visions of Modernity: American Business and the Modernization of Germany.* New York: Oxford University Press, 1994.

"Northwestern Terminal, Minneapolis Minnesota: The Ideal Manufacturing and Distributing Center of the Northwest." Minneapolis: Northwestern Terminal Company, circa 1920s.

Nord, David Paul. "Minneapolis and the Pragmatic Socialism of Thomas Van Lear." *Minnesota History* 45:1 (spring 1976): 2–10.

Norwood, Edwin P. *Ford Men and Methods.* Garden City, N.Y.: Doubleday, Doran & Company, 1931.

Nye, David E. *Consuming Power: A Social History of American Energies.* Cambridge: MIT Press, 2001.

O'Callaghan, Timothy J. *The Aviation Legacy of Henry and Edsel Ford.* Ann Arbor: Proctor Publications, 2000.

Olsen, Byron, and Joseph Cabadas. *The American Auto Factory.* St. Paul: MBI Publishing, 2002.

Olson, Sidney. *Young Henry Ford: A Picture History of the First Forty Years.* Detroit: Wayne State University Press, 1963.

Painter, Patricia Scollard. *Henry Ford Hospital: The First 75 Years.* Detroit: Henry Ford Health System, 1997.

Parker, David L. *By These Hands: Portraits from the Factory Floor.* St. Paul: Minnesota Historical Society Press, 2002.

Parker, Mike, and Jane Slaughter. *Choosing Sides: Unions and the Team Concept.* Boston: South End Press, 1988.

Perrucci, Robert. *Japanese Auto Transplants in the Heartland: Corporatism and Community.* New York: Aldine De Gruyter, 1994.

Petersen, Donald. *A Better Idea: Redefining the Way Americans Work.* Boston: Houghton Mifflin Company, 1991.

Peterson, Joyce Shaw. *American Automobile Workers, 1900–1933.* Albany: State University of New York Press, 1987.

Quandt, Val, ed. *Wisconsin Cars and Trucks: A Centenary.* Amherst, Wis.: Wisconsin Society of Automotive Historians, 1998.

Rachleff, Peter J. "From Racism to International Solidarity: The Journey of UAW Local 879, 1980–1995." Paper presented at the North American Labor Conference in 2013 and published at http://iowalabornews.com/?p=3329.

———. *Hard-Pressed in the Heartland: The Hormel Strike and the Future of the Labor Movement.* Boston: South End Press, 1993.

Rae, John B. *The American Automobile: A Brief History.* Chicago: University of Chicago Press, 1965.

Reed, John. "Industry's Miracle Maker." *Metropolitan* 44:5 (October 1916): 10–12, 64–68.

Richter, William M. *Companion to Transportation in America.* Santa Barbara, Calif.: ABC-CLIO, 1995.

Rothschild, Emma. *Paradise Lost: The Decline of the Auto-Industrial Age.* New York: Random House, 1973.

Rubenstein, James M. *The Changing US Industry: A Geographical Analysis.* London and New York: Routledge, 1992.

Scarpino, Philip V. *Great River: An Environmental History of the Upper Mississippi, 1890–1950.* Columbia: University of Missouri Press, 1985.

Schild, Jim. *Selling the New Ford, 1927–1932.* St. Louis: By the author, 1982.

Schindler, Gordon. *Ford Model T Catalog of Accessories: Guide to History, Ownership, and Accessories of the Era.* Osceola, Wis.: Motorbooks International, 1991.

Schonberger, Richard J. *World Class Manufacturing Casebook: Implementing JIT and TQC.* New York. Free Press, 1987.

Schroeder, Leslie L., Harold R. Harris, and Ralph H. Upson. "Minnesota in the World of Aviation." *Minnesota History* 33:6 (summer 1953): 236–46.

Segal, Howard P. *Recasting the Machine Age: Henry Ford's Village Industries.* Amherst: University of Massachusetts Press, 2005.

Shannon, Fred Albert. *Economic History of the People of the United States.* New York: Macmillan, 1934.

Shepardson, George D. "The Best Use of the High Dam Power." *Minnesota Techno-log* 2:5 (March 1922): 3,4,14,18

Shook, Robert L. *Turnaround: The New Ford Motor Company.* New York: Prentice Hall, 1990.

Shotwell, Gregg. *Autoworkers under the Gun.* Chicago: Haymarket Books, 2012.

Sinclair, Upton. *The Flivver King: A Story of Ford-America.* Chicago: Charles H. Kerr Publishing Company, 1937–87. Reprint.

Sloan, Alfred P. *My Years with General Motors.* New York: David McKay, 1964.

Smith, David C. *City of Parks: The Story of Minneapolis Parks.* Minneapolis: Foundation for Minneapolis Parks, 2008.

Smith, Terry. *Making the Modern: Industry, Art, and Design in America.* Chicago: University of Chicago Press, 1993.

Snider, Clair J., and Michael W. R. Davis. *The Ford Fleet (1923–1989).* Cleveland: Freshwater Press, 1994.

Snow, Richard. *I Invented the Modern Age: The Rise of Henry Ford.* New York: Scribner, 2013.

Sorensen, Charles. *Forty Years with Ford.* London: Jonathan Cape, 1957.

Sorensen, Lorin. *The Ford Factory.* Osceola, Wis.: Motorbooks International, 1990.

———. *The Ford Road: 75th Anniversary Ford Motor Company, 1903–1978.* St. Helena, Calif.: Silverado Publishing Company, 1978.

Staude, Edwin Gustave. *Condensed Life History of Edwin Gustave Staude.* Self-published, 1959.

Stein, Herbert. *The Fiscal Revolution in America.* Chicago: University of Chicago Press, 1969.

Stepan-Norris, Judith, and Maurice Zeitlin. *Talking Union.* Urbana and Chicago: University of Illinois Press, 1996.

Stidger, William L. *Henry Ford: The Man and His Motives.* New York: George H. Doran Company, 1923.

Stout, William Bushnell. *So Away I Went.* Indianapolis: Bobbs-Merrill Company, 1951.

Sward, Keith. *The Legend of Henry Ford.* New York: Rinehart & Company, 1948.

Sweinhart, James. *Ford and the Coming Agrindustrial Age.* Dearborn, Mich.: Ford Motor Company, 1940.

Tarbell, Ida M. *The Nationalizing of Business, 1878–1898.* New York: Macmillan, 1946.

Terkel, Studs. *Working: People Talk about What They Do All Day and How They Feel about What They Do.* New York: Pantheon Books, 1974.

Tolliday, Steven, and Jonathan Zeitlin. *Between Fordism and Flexibility: The Automobile Industry and Its Workers.* New York: St. Martin's Press, 1986.

Trostel, Scott D. *Henry Ford: When I Ran the Railroads: A Chronicle of Henry Ford's Operation of the Detroit, Toledo, and Ironton Railroad (1920–1929).* Fletcher, Ohio: Cam-Tech Publishing, 1989.

UAW-Ford National Program Center. *Sixty Years of Progress, 1941–2001.* Detroit: UAW-Ford

National Program Center, 2001. Posted online at http://uawford.org/wp-content/uploads/2012/05/sixtyyears.pdf.

UAW Local 1250 Cleveland. *The Cleveland Site History, 1950–1997.* Cleveland: UAW Local 1250. Brookfield, Ohio: Union News Publishing Company, 1997.

Uldrich, Jack, and Rolf Nordstrom. "Fuel-Cell Vehicle Plant Could Help State, Ford." *Minneapolis Star Tribune,* October 4, 2001.

U.S. Department of Transportation. "The U.S. Automobile Industry, 1980." Available at http://catalog.hathitrust.org/Record/011353430.

U.S. Department of Transportation Federal Highway Administration. "Study of US 43 and US 80 Corridor Potential to Attract New Automotive Suppliers Based on Highway Improvements." November 2003.

Vlasic, Bill. *Once Upon a Car: The Fall and Resurrection of America's Big Three Automakers—GM, Ford, and Chrysler.* New York: William Morrow, 2011.

Wallace, Max. *The American Axis: Henry Ford, Charles Lindbergh, and the Rise of the Third Reich.* New York: St. Martin's Griffin, 2003.

Walton, Mary. *Car: A Drama of the American Workplace.* New York: W. W. Norton, 1997.

White, Richard. *Railroaded: The Transcontinentals and the Making of America.* New York: W. W. Norton, 2011.

Wik, Reynold M. *Henry Ford and Grass-roots America.* Ann Arbor: University of Michigan Press, 1972.

Winpisinger, William W. *Let's Rebuild America.* Washington, D.C.: International Association of Machinists and Aerospace Workers, 1984.

Woeste, Victoria Saker. *Henry Ford's War on Jews and the Legal Battle against Hate.* Stanford, Calif.: Stanford University Press, 2012.

Womack, James P., Daniel T. Jones, and Daniel Roos. *The Machine That Changed the World: The Story of Lean Production.* New York: Macmillan, 1990.

Worster, Donald. *Rivers of Empire: Water, Aridity, and the Growth of the American West.* New York: Pantheon Books, 1985.

Wright, J. Patrick. *On A Clear Day You Can See General Motors: John Z. De Lorean's Look inside the Automotive Industry.* New York: Avon Books, 1979.

Yates, Brock. *The Decline and Fall of the American Automobile Industry.* New York: Vintage Books, 1983.

Young, Biloine Whiting. *River of Conflict, River of Dreams: Three Hundred Years of the Upper Mississippi.* St. Paul: Pogo Press, 2004.

Zieger, Robert H. *American Workers, American Unions.* 2d ed. Baltimore and London: Johns Hopkins University Press, 1994.

Zipf, George Kingsley. *Human Behavior and the Principle of Least Effort: An Introduction to Human Ecology.* Cambridge: Addison-Wesley, 1949.

Index